Audrey M. Yandle

Janvier 1976.
Binghamton

À ma sœur

A Study of **ARCHEOLOGY**

by Walter W. Taylor

Southern Illinois University Press   Carbondale and Edwardsville

Feffer & Simons, Inc.   London and Amsterdam

A Study of Archeology was first published in 1948
  as No. 69 of the titles in the Memoir Series
  of the American Anthropological Association. Reprinted
  1964, by Walter W. Taylor
Reprinted by special arrangement with Walter W. Taylor

Arcturus Books Edition, March 1967
Second printing, May 1968
Third printing, May 1971
Fourth printing, November 1973

This edition printed by offset lithography
  in the United States of America
International Standard Book Number 0-8093-0242-X

CONTENTS

ILLUSTRATIONS

Between Pages 158–159

Between Pages 174–175

E R R A T A

Page **5**, line 4: For **visulaized** read **visualized**

Page **9**, line 23: For **debt and** read **debt, and**

Page **15**, line 15: For **Peirisc** read **Peiresc**

Page **33**, line 17: For **used** read **uses**

Page **61**, line 27: For **(1943, 1945)** read **(1943)**

Page **86**, line 32: For **culural** read **cultural**

Page **93**, line 3: For **will** read **shall**

Page **105**, line 15: For **finished,** read **finished;**

Page **111**, line 32: For **lead** read **leads**

Page **160**, line 18: For **Coahula** read **Coahuila**

Page **167**, line 19: For **viewopint** read **viewpoint**

Page **197**, line 35: For **inches** read **cms.**

Page **240**, line 6: For **Lowie, R. L.** read **Lowie, R. H.**

FOREWORD TO THE 1968 PRINTING

THAT this fourth printing of *A Study of Archeology* is to appear full twenty years after the monograph was first published is gratifying indeed. It seems that the ideas which were presented then are still viable and possibly of even increasing interest, if the accelerating tempo of distribution is any criterion. In 1948, I said that it did not matter whether my ideas turned out to be rallying posts or targets, so long as the attention of archeologists could be brought to focus upon the nature of their objectives, their practices, and their conceptual tools. Evidently this has happened. The introspection which I explicitly hoped for has come about and produced results. Archeology in the United States today is a remarkably different discipline from what it was in 1948 and, from my viewpoint, the outlook for the future is tremendously encouraging and exciting.

It is to the new generation of archeologists that I would like to dedicate the present printing. I do not think I need point out to them that what they find here is merely a beginning, a door to the future. I know that many of them have already gone through that door and are busily tilling the greener and broader fields on the other side. In fact, many of the methods of the so-called "new archeology" implement the theoretical points and aims of what I have called the conjunctive approach: the use of computers facilitates multivariate factor analysis and the construction of contingency tables which in turn help to make multiple classification at once more feasible, more operational, and potentially more objective; emphasis is being placed upon broad culture configurations, cultural contexts, settlement patterns, and ecological relationships; conscious and intensive efforts are being made to squeeze the utmost from the empirical data and to develop ever fuller cultural inferences, especially in the realms of behavior and the non-material results of behavior. In view of these and other present practices of the younger archeologists, it seems that the tenets of the conjunctive approach, at least a goodly number of them, have been accepted at long last. A prediction made many years ago by one of my more sympathetic colleagues has certainly come true: that *A Study of Archeology* would not be widely accepted until a new generation of archeologists had developed without so much subjective and emotional involvement in the then *status quo*.

I have been asked many times whether my ideas have changed since I wrote these pages. Of course they have—not basically but certainly in many details. But that is a rather meaningless question anyway, because its answer is foreordained: whatever the truth, one is not apt to admit to an unchanging mind! I must confess that my greatest urge has been to add new ideas, to expand and follow further some of the propositions put forward in 1948, but this would

1

involve much rewriting, virtually a new book, and I have had no inclination to tackle such a project. Often I have been asked whether, in a new edition, I would delete or revise or update the chapter on the analysis of Americanist archeology. My answer has been a strong and confident "no." Contrary to what has apparently been the widespread view, that chapter is not a "polemic." I have always regarded it as an objective analysis from an explicitly stated point of view, a critique as detailed and comprehensive and fair as I could make it of archeological theory and practice, not of men. Therefore, until my opinions change in regard to archeological research—and they have not—the chapter may be allowed to stand as a series of illustrative, essentially impersonal, and thus timeless examples.

What, then, of *A Study of Archeology* and the conjunctive approach today? It is my hope that they will become more and more accepted as a source of insights and fundamental ideas for a consistent theory of archeology and an explicit point of departure for modern practice. I hope that they will continue to encourage archeologists to make every effort to orient their problems along cultural lines, to seek out available data with an ever finer perception, to combine and recombine these data in order to abstract from their intrinsic conjunctives their cultural significance, to push analysis and inference to the limits of acceptable logic and analogy, and to construct the fullest possible contexts for the cultures they investigate. If the archeologists do these things, with or without the aid of *A Study of Archeology,* I feel certain that many of them will wish to pursue their studies into the realm of culture itself with which, as Anthropology, I hope they can learn to deal—and in ways that will be applicable and profitable to that broader discipline of which Americanist archeology has so long claimed to be a part.

PART I

INTRODUCTION

WHEN responsible newspapers and intelligent laymen identify the Sunday afternoon adventures of eager schoolboys as archeology and the little curio-hunters themselves as archeologists, it may seem gratuitous to offer a full volume on a conceptual scheme for archeological research. Nevertheless, it is just this point of view, generous to a fault as it is, which prompts the present study. For even within academic and scholarly circles, what passes for archeology has a compass that is truly Jovian, and the resultant confusion of theoretical precepts is largely responsible for the false position which, in many instances, the discipline of archeology has come to assume.

The development of archeology has been due to very diverse interests on the part of those engaged in the work. History and folklore, art and architecture, geology and the study of human evolution have all had their influence, and all have brought concepts and objectives to bear upon the recovery of the remains of man's cultural past. Thus it is not strange that archeology displays a considerable divergence and even confusion in its theoretical structure, its aims, and with regard to its relationships to other disciplines. At one moment we hear that it is a branch of anthropology, at another that it aims to reconstruct the past and to write history, and at yet another that it is chiefly concerned with art and art history.

The significant point is that there has been no concerted effort on the part of the archeologists to resolve these conflicts of a theoretical order. There seems to be either an unawareness of, or an unconcern with, the present ambiguous situation. When statements of policy are made, and even these are but rare occurrences, they are all too often set forth without regard for other, equally positive but quite contradictory, pronouncements. Obviously basic concepts and relationships to other disciplines need clarification, but this should not be done, as has been the case in the past, in terms of some itself-undefined master discipline or by reference to concepts and objectives whose implications are left unexamined. Rather, the situation calls for explicit analysis and the subsequent construction of an internally consistent, externally aware, and more or less comprehensive conceptual scheme for archeological research. And above all, the theoretical framework should be related by example to the practicalities of actual research in order to clarify the whole.

Any scheme which purports to serve as the conceptual structure of a discipline should take into account the history of that discipline, should explicitly analyze and either accept or reject (in whole or in part) its present condition, and should offer some constructive plan for the future. Since it is my intention that this volume offer such a scheme, in Chapter 1, I shall give a brief outline of the development of archeology as a field of study for the purpose of providing a context and in order to bring out some of the causes contributing to what I believe to be its unhealthy state. Beginning with Chapter 2 and throughout the rest of the book, I shall reduce the scope of the analysis to archeology as it is practiced in the United States upon cultures of the Western Hemisphere. I shall be speaking exclusively of Americanist archeology in the United States, and whether what is said applies to other fields and other traditions is for the people concerned to judge: if the shoe fits, let them put it on. Chapter 2 itself consists of an analysis of what seems to me to be the major theoretical ailment: the fact that the archeologist of today is a Jekyll and Hyde, claiming to "do" history but "be" an anthropologist without attempting to determine the relationships, if any, between these two fields of study as they pertain to his own investigations. In this analysis, history and anthropology will be defined, at least for present purposes, and from this will come an explanation of the characters of Dr. Jekyll and Mr. Hyde and a resolution of the archeologist's split personality. Chapter 3 examines the condition of Americanist archeology in the United States by detailed consideration of the published works of certain men who are generally conceded to be among the leaders of that field. This will conclude Part I and the analysis of the history and present status of (Americanist) archeology.

Part II consists of the discussion of some concepts basic to archeology and the presentation of a series of practical procedures for archeological research. While Part I is to an appreciable extent destructive criticism, Part II is designed to be constructive. A more specific and detailed preamble will be given in the Introduction to the section itself.

But it must be emphatically stated and continually remembered that although there are two parts to this study there is but one conceptual whole. Both parts together express a single theory of archeology which, in addition to its own proposals for the future, takes cognizance of the past and the present. At the risk of being trite to the professional and overly abstract to others, I have made an effort to develop a full-rounded picture in the knowledge that no such treatment exists in the literature today. On the other hand, I am well aware that many of the ideas are not new. A considerable number of them lie at the base of much recent research, especially that of the younger archeologists. In fact, not a few publications which have appeared since 1942, when I first began to write this book, have made the present publication less important in one way and more important in another: less, because the trend of archeological thought seems to be going in the proposed direction and there is less need for radical change; more, because an explicit formulation of this trend is needed to bring it into full recognition and provide an opportunity for review and criticism.

To propose a rigid and universally applicable system for the gathering, analysis, and synthesis of archeological materials would be impossible as well as presumptuous. The handling of such data is too contingent a procedure to be amenable to more than a very general systematization. But for this very reason, it is all the more important that objectives be visulaized and that a firm (if flexible) conceptual structure be provided in order that the ever-changing contingencies can be met in consistent fashion and with constant purpose. Otherwise, as has happened all too often, the practical eventualities will so warp the results, not to say control them, that little consistency will be achieved and few acceptable conclusions obtained.

Therefore, the scheme should be regarded as the theoretical foundation for a viewpoint, a point of attack, or an approach rather than for a particular method. Its most vital aspect consists of a way of looking upon archeological materials and problems, not of any set of procedures for handling data. On the other hand, to convey this viewpoint entirely in abstract terms would be difficult and perhaps impossible. Therefore, I have exemplified it more or less concretely in the form of specific criticisms (Chapter 3) and a series of practical procedures (Chapter 6), both of which however stem from, and are intended to illustrate, a single point of view.

This perspective I have called the conjunctive approach. It stands in contradistinction to that which is currently popular with Americanists in the United States and which may be termed the comparative or taxonomic approach. The conjunctive approach takes as its first concern the description of the cultures of human groups. It does this by studying the data which are "Conjunctive: conjoining, connecting, connective; . . . Serving to connect the meaning as well as the construction" (Webster's *International Dictionary*). It is primarily interested in the interrelationships which existed *within* a particular cultural entity, while the comparative approach occupies itself primarily with data which have relationships *outside* the cultural unit and attempts to place the newly discovered material in taxonomic or other association with extra-local phenomena. Although in a way the two are complementary, I believe that the conjunctive approach is basic and offers by far the greatest number of possibilities, while the comparative approach is wasteful, is of very narrow applicability, and is often unreliable even for comparative purposes.

However, in the long run, it will make very little difference whether the ideas to be put forward here turn out to be rallying posts or targets. If they become either, the study will have served its purpose. The really important thing is to focus the attention of the archeologists upon the nature of their objectives, their practices, and their conceptual tools. This has been tried before, particularly in the fine article by Steward and Setzler (1938), but the effort has rolled off the archeologists like water off a petrified puddle duck. If only they can be brought to be less blissfully extroverted and more introspective about what they are actually doing, I believe that the greatest obstacle will have been overcome. The concreteness of much of their material perhaps has blinded them to the realities of less "objective" data and the essential functions of a theoretical framework for their pursuits. Nevertheless, if by chance it has been forgotten, they should be reminded that their results should depend at least as much upon the work of their minds as upon that of their spades.

THREE PREMISES

In the following pages, I shall use the concepts *theory, method,* and *technique* according to the definitions stated by Kluckhohn in his paper on *The Conceptual Structure in Middle American Studies:*

... the category theory refers to the conceptual framework of a single discipline; the category method refers to the sheer analysis and ordering of data (as opposed to the formulation of abstract concepts in terms of which such ordering is carried on); ... Technique is distinguishable from method only in so far as method involves the interrelations and consistency of a number of techniques. For example, archaeological method encompasses a number of techniques such as surveying, photographing, field cataloging and the like. (1940, pp. 43-44)

A WORD ON NOTES AND BIBLIOGRAPHY

The reader will discover that there are no footnotes. The text has been written to be read without interruption and is intended to stand on its own without recourse to supplementary evidence. What notes there are will be found in a separate section at the end of the text. They are included only for the curious and the critical and need not concern the general reader. They consist of additional quotations and references and, in one or two instances, some additional examples whose inclusion would have made the text overly encumbered. I promise the general reader that he will miss nothing if he omits them altogether and that, if he bothers himself with continual eye-shiftings and page-turnings, it will be of his own doing. I have tried to save him these customary inconveniences.

Documentation in the form of bibliography and quotation has been made extensive for two reasons. The first is that I feel there may be some argument on certain points, and I wish to give my sources now rather than in the shape of a rebuttal. The second is that I have done considerable library work in preparation for writing this book and I believe it would be a boring waste of time for others, in the future, to have to plod through as many stacks as I did in search of merely the same set of references. If others can build on the bibliographic foundations of the present study, they will be able to spend their time in more profitable and, I am sure, more enjoyable enterprises.

Citations have been arbitrarily ended with the year 1945. Coverage had to end some time if I was ever to complete the manuscript, and so when I began the final draft on January 18, 1946, I decided to include no publications issued there-after. However, I have used J. O. Brew's monograph on Alkali Ridge (1946) because it is so pertinent and so parallel in certain respects that to have omitted it would have been much to the detriment of the present study as well as cause for suspicion that I might be dodging an issue. Furthermore, I have included Thompson's paper on Maya tobacco, published in 1946, because of its unique status among the publications of the Carnegie Institution. To have overlooked it might have appeared like an unfair selection of evidence. Because of the date-line, I have been forced to slight two papers which I regard very highly and which are very much to the point of this discussion. I refer to Kroeber's article on *History and Evolution* (1946) and Lewis and Kneberg's *Hiwassee Island* (1946), possibly the best archeological report I have had the pleasure of reading.

ACKNOWLEDGMENTS

The ideas projected in the present study were given their first formal ex-pression as a doctoral dissertation presented to the Faculty of Harvard University in the winter of 1943. I wish to thank that body and especially the Faculty of the Peabody Museum of American Archaeology and Ethnology for permission to expand and publish this material.

Most of the re-working and elaboration has been done under a Post-war Fellowship in the Humanities granted by the Rockefeller Foundation. I wish to express my thanks to that organization for its generosity and understanding foresight in making available the opportunity to take up again what the war so rudely interrupted. However, my initial debt and possibly the greatest for that reason, is to the friends who proposed my name and carried through all the arrangements while I was considerably occupied and not a little incommunicado overseas. Their modest reticence and/or my stifling gratitude has prevented me from learning all their names, but to Henry Collins, Clyde Kluckhohn, Frank Setzler, and all others who had a part in handing me such a home-coming, I can only say thanks—and mean it.

So many people have read these pages, in one form or another, that it would be extravagant to name them all and thank them individually for their truly great help. However, certain ones have had such a hand in this undertaking that I would be ungrateful if they were not personally thanked here. First and foremost of these is Clyde Kluckhohn, who has battled against my foolishness on so many occasions and for my viewpoint on so many others that *A Study of Archeology* would not be in existence had it not been for him. Professor Tozzer has also taken a personal interest in its welfare and has, in more ways than a score, been a factor of en-couragement and counsel. Lyndon Hargrave probably started the whole thing by the stimulation of his free-flowing ideas on the archeology of northern Arizona; this volume would have profited if I had taken notes during some of those long winter evenings in Flagstaff. I feel, although I cannot be explicit, that Cornelius Osgood is responsible for much of the manner in which I look upon archeology; the discussions, not to say arguments, in which we engaged during the years from 1931 to 1936 keep coming back in many forms and in many contexts. I wish to thank W. H. Kelly and J. Charles Kelley for their hours of debate and pages of correspondence whereby a great number of points were clarified by being brought into the open and subjected to criticism with no holds barred .

I can do no less than to offer my sincere thanks to those who have given me detailed or written criticisms: J. O. Brew, Erik Reed, Maurice Ries, Paul Reiter, F. H. H. Roberts, Jr., F. M. Setzler, Leslie Spier, W. S. Stallings, Ruth Underhill, W. R. Wedel, Gordon Willey. I should make special mention of the kindness of Professor Crane Brinton, who read the section dealing with the analysis and definition of history.

The share which my wife has had in this undertaking is not to be measured in words. I cannot begin to tell my appreciation of her role of Devil's advocate and her long hours of tedious work. I can only hope that our joint effort is worthy of her patience and devotion.

CHAPTER 1

THE DEVELOPMENT OF ARCHEOLOGY

ONE OF the first things that strikes the observer of archeology as a discipline, whether in the United States or abroad, is the persistent and rather sharp separation between the Classical and Near Eastern fields on the one hand, and those fields which are tilled under the banner of anthropology on the other. In the United States, the two are so divorced with respect to academic and learned society affiliations, personnel, and the channels of publication that one is apt to forget the fact that they are both given the label of a single discipline.[1]

Whether this separation is a superficial, historical fact of no immediate significance or whether it is indicative of some fundamental split in the theoretical structure of archeology constitutes a problem which is of considerable consequence for the present discussion. Therefore, I propose to give a brief outline of the chronological development of archeological research, whereby both the historical and theoretical import of this intra-disciplinary distinction will be clarified. To begin our study in this fashion has the added advantage of leading easily and logically into the major topic: the theoretical framework of Americanist archeology in the United States.

The lineal and continuous development of antiquarianism, from which modern archeology has developed, began with the return of Humanism to Italy at the close of the Middle Ages. Although such men as Pausanias and the Venerable Bede, many years earlier, had studied their local antiquities, these men represent isolated instances cut off by a void of considerable time from the continuum which culminates in the discipline of archeology. But beginning with Petrarch and Poggio Bracciolini in the late 14th and early 15th centuries, that interest in the antiquities of Italy and Greece which was to lead to formal antiquarianism burgeoned into full flower.[2]

In the year 1453 the Turks captured Constantinople. Whatever had survived of the civilization of the Greeks thereupon fled toward the West and was given a refuge in the universities of Italy and France and Germany. . . . This was a tremendous boon to the study of archaeology, for now the people of the West were at last able to decipher those Greek texts that had been a closed book to them for almost two centuries. Archaeology suddenly became the favorite pastime of the rich. . . .

Indeed, it was during this age that the word "dilettanti" was coined to describe a person who "delighted" in the fine arts. All over Europe these *dilettanti* were laying the foundations for those vast and often unwieldy collections of statues and pots and pans and coins and ancient jewelry which afterwards developed into some of our best known museums. (Van Loon, 1937, pp. 19-20)

In Italy under the Popes, antiquarian research flourished. Pius II (1458-1464) was a devotee of Roman relics; Alexander VI (1492-1503) initiated

9

excavations in Rome; Raphael is said to have sought the Pope's aid to protect the ancient remains, fearing the destruction and dissipation of those that yet survived.[3]

While the initial impetus which set these men of the Italian Renaissance on such a path of investigation was their newly awakened pride in the glories that had been Rome, it seems that this soon gave way, at least in the major part, to an interest in ancient literature, art, and architecture. This emphasis upon the artistic aspect was especially marked among the French and German antiquaries, whose background provided them with little or no local or national sentiment for things Roman or Greek. Thus from the Renaissance until Schliemann demonstrated the pre-Hellenic cities of the Aegean, antiquarianism in the region of the Mediterranean, Classical and otherwise, was to a large extent dominated by the vindication of literary legends and the search for art treasure. Art and literature were prime movers in the general scramble for Greek, Roman, Egyptian, and Near Eastern loot. Wincklemann, considered by some to be the founder of archeology, made his major contribution in the field of art.[4] In addition, philology entered the field of "Mediterranean" studies toward the end of the 18th century and further divorced antiquarianism from its sentimental and humanistic attachments to local Greek and Roman history. The classification of human groups occupied much thought during the 18th and early 19th centuries and language, as Boas has said (1904, pp. 517-518), offered pertinent and obvious data that, furthermore, were easily obtained. Inscriptions were sought among the ancient ruins, and philology became an important factor in the development of antiquarianism.[5] Schliemann modified all this, but before it will be profitable to inquire into his contribution, the development of archeology in other quarters of Europe will be discussed.

It appears that formal, historical antiquarianism, as apart from dilettantism and the study of art, had its origin in England. It is not to be doubted, however, that these English beginnings were influenced, if not initiated, by the late and peripheral effects of the Continental Renaissance. Although the Irish may have created a college of antiquaries as early as 700 B.C. (American Antiquarian Society, 1820), the first society of English antiquaries was founded in 1572, only shortly after these effects can be clearly observed in English life. It seems hardly coincidental that the founders of this society were eminent historians and students of the classics, who have been claimed as the first historians of England.[6] At approximately the same time, England felt the impact of the Reformation, which involved her in civil strife and doubly affected the growing historicism. In the first place, the civil unrest caused James I to disband the nascent society of antiquaries fearing that it might be a haven of political intrigue. But in the second place, Kenneth Clark has stated that

Perhaps they [the antiquaries] owe their origin to the Reformation, for they saw monasteries destroyed and libraries dispersed, and were moved to perpetuate their vanishing glories. Though there seems little of the crash and swagger of Elizabethan patriotism in these dull volumes, yet they too were written for patriotic ends, and boasted their country's treasures as poets did her wars. . . . A small circle of antiquarians grew up, having its center in the Bodleian library, and from 1660 onwards there is a steady flow of County Histories and Local Antiquities. (1928, pp. 19-20)[7]

The Society of Antiquaries of London was re-founded in 1717, and in 1734 the Society of Dilettanti was organized by men directly influenced by travel in Italy and by Classical art.[8] Thereafter antiquarianism rose with the rising crest of the Romantic Movement characterized in England by the literary rebellion of Macpherson, Gray, and others, against the preceding austerity of the Reformation and Neo-classicism.[9] While it may be true, as Lowell has said (1870, p. 158), that the Romantic Movement started with Lessing (e.g., *Minna von Barnhelm, 1767; Wie die Alten den Tod gebildet,* 1769), nevertheless it seems that Lessing himself was influenced by British Romanticism, especially by Macpherson's Ossianic poems (1761-1765). The latter, though perhaps the first true Romanticist of the period, was in turn but one sample of a general reactionary trend against the literary figures of the days of Pope and Dryden. Thomas Gray probably best characterizes the first phase of this trend, and we see in his poems the beginnings of the typical Romantic concern with the past and ancient, the weird, and the ruinous:

> Save that from yonder ivy-mantled tower
> The moping owl does to the moon complain
> Of such as, wandering near her secret bower,
> Molest her ancient solitary reign.

> Beneath those rugged elms, that yew-tree's shade,
> Where heaves the turf in many a mouldering heap,
> Each in his narrow cell forever laid,
> The rude forefathers of the hamlet sleep.
>
> (Elegy Written in a Country Churchyard, 1751)

This concern, in its most violent form, appears as the guiding spirit of the horror-romantic novels of Walpole, Beckford, Radcliffe at the end of the 18th century. It is significant that the first of such writers was Gray's best friend, Horace Walpole, the author of *Castle of Otranto* (1764). "By now Archaeology and Romanticism walked hand in hand, familiar twin figures in the English scene." (Piggott, 1937, p. 36)

Another factor came to the aid of the developing antiquarianism. For the first time in human history, the innumerable implements of stone that had been found throughout England and elsewhere were popularly recognized for what they really were—the remains of ancient times before man knew the use of metal. As early as the time of Lucretius (*ca.* 98-55 B.C.) and later in the writings of Mercati, Dugdale, Plot, Mahudel, the true nature of stone artifacts had been surmised. But it remained for the evidence gathered by the explorers and colonists of the 17th and 18th centuries to establish in men's minds the identity of stones as human implements. This same evidence, it should be noted, constituted the foundation of much of the social and political philosophy of the Age of Enlightenment in France. The writings of Lafitau, Montesquieu, Goguet, the German Eccardus were replete with references to the savage mode of life and, with their appeal to the intelligent layman, served to disseminate a knowledge of the stone and other artifacts of "natural," "primitive" man.[10] No longer were the "thunderstones" and "elf-arrows," as celts and projectile points had been called, merely curiosities with an esoteric charm; they were the actual tools, the objects of daily use belonging to an ancient people. They were, therefore, new grist to the antiquarian's mill; they were true relics and not natural curios; they belonged to the same category of national antiquities as did the Gothic and Norman ruins and the metallic remains of bygone days, that had long been recognized and properly identified. The antiquarian field had been extended farther into the past and the "elf-arrows" tied to national history.[11]

By the end of the 18th and the beginning of the 19th century, there appeared yet a third aid to antiquarianism in Britain. The Gothic Revival, stemming as it did from the Romantic Movement and the developing interest in past times, tremendously stimulated the already blooming study of architectural and other ruins which covered the English countryside. "Above all the antiquarians made Gothic ruins their quarry; they were the chief conveyers of Gothic sentiment" (Clark, K., 1928, p. 19). The wave of medievalism which spread over the land and which was reflected in the novels of Scott and his lesser contemporaries created a setting in which the antiquary flourished.[12]

Somewhat opposed to these forces but nonetheless supporting the growth of antiquarianism, another social reaction made its appearance at this time. With the start of the 19th century, the Industrial Revolution came upon England. As Crawford has pointed out (1932, p. 170), the development of a leisure class and the formation of newly propertied families, both functions of the industrialization of England, provided the human minds and energies for the study of those mysterious non-essentials which so intrigued the age.

The 40's and 50's saw the beginnings of that most English of all institutions, the local archaeological society, which with its lectures and excursions played so important a part in the leisured life of Victorian England and which is today the backbone of our local archaeological research. (Piggott, 1937, p. 37)

But it remained for Pitt-Rivers, in the last half of the century and under the influence of another discipline, to set antiquarian pursuits in England on the road to formal archeology, meaning by the latter a recognized profession displaying a sense of problem and a definite attempt at accuracy in excavation and recording (Pitt-Rivers, 1869, 1887-1898).

From this summary treatment of the genesis of British archeology, one thing should be very obvious: British archeology grew out of a romantic interest in local and national antiquities. The ruins and the relics which occupied the people were conceived as representing the ancient mysteries and past population of their own land, of their own forebears. Their own medieval, Anglo-Saxon, Roman, and pre-Roman heritage was the vitalizing factor in their endeavors. And it is an important fact that these early antiquarians and later archeologists were fully aware that their investigations pertained to a segment of their own history which, in many cases, antedated written archives and other literary sources.[13]

In France, there is a very similar development of archeology. The first men who extensively concerned themselves with antiquarian studies, Peirisc (1580-1637), Spon (1647-1685), and Caylus (1692-1765), treated primarily of Greek and Roman materials. After this period of Classical interest, there grew up, influenced by British activities, a group of Celtophiles who were instilled with a pride of their national entity and local districts and who thus created a counter-balance to the predominantly Classical orientation of French academic antiquarianism. La Societie Royale des Antiquaries de France sprung, in 1814, from a reorganization of L'Academie Celtique which had been founded in 1804. In 1810, questionnaires had been sent from the Ministry of the Interior to the prefectures of the country requesting information on local antiquities, and in 1818 a commission was formed to investigate:

. . . all the national monuments . . . the Gallic, Greek, and Roman antiquities, the vestiges of the ancient roads, the mile stones, etc. (Reinach, 1898, p. 294)

Although this committee failed to achieve its purpose, it was indicative of a nationalistic trend that others continued.[14]

A third and similar development took place in Central Europe. Up to the middle of the 18th century, Czech antiquarianism seems to have been little more than the collection of artistic objects. But during the last half of the century, there appeared symptoms of the Romantic Movement and from that time forward publications were issued on antiquities as national, rather than purely artistic, treasure. It was not until the middle of the 19th century, however, that extensive and active work was undertaken, and it was not until 1874 that excavation with a problem, nationalistic and historical, began. This shift to archeology, as opposed to antiquarianism, was probably due to influence from outside the country, especially from Denmark.[15]

The development in Germany was slow to take on a national tone, possibly because of the lack of national unification within Germany itself or possibly because of the strong artistic tradition started by Wincklemann, but nevertheless strange in view of the flourishing Germanic Romanticism and local Nationalism. A *Gesamtverein der Deutschen Geschichte- und Altertumsverein* was organized in 1852, but as late as 1879 Kohn and Mehlis complained that too little attention was being paid to early German history. (1879, pp. 1-2)[16]

In Scandinavia, nationalistic antiquarianism evolved directly from a historical interest, with but little if any dependence upon Romanticism. In Sweden, it dates from the time of Charles Gustavus (1654-1660). In Denmark a society was founded in 1792 and a commission appointed to investigate the history, natural history, and geology of the country. The results of this commission's work led to the formation of the Royal Danish Museum of Antiquities, and from this institution, through the efforts of Thomsen, Worsaae, and Steenstrup, came the concept of archeological stratigraphy, probably the most basic concept in the theoretical structure of the discipline.[17]

Before leaving the historical and nationalistic aspects of the development of archeology, we may turn once again to the Mediterranean area. There, the Greek and Roman researches had so held the attention and overshadowed other fields that little had been accomplished along other lines of antiquarian investigation. Artistic and architectural incentives still influenced the work, and to these had been added philology and comparative religion—until 1871.

Then Heinrich Schliemann realized his lifelong ambition to test with the spade the tradition that Homer's "City of Troy" underlay the ruins of Graeco-Roman Ilium . . . this archaeological evidence [that it did in fact underlie the ruins] provided a fresh and independent background of prehistoric periods of culture. . . . (Myers, 1930, p. xxvi)

From these discoveries it became evident that just as modern European art and civilization were, in a measure, founded upon Rome and Greece, so the latter were founded upon other sources. The flowering of archeological schools at Rome and Athens in the period directly following Schliemann's excavations at Troy may be taken as an indication of the effect of his work. The Mediterranean basin and the Near East were recognized as the cradle of Western European culture. That same interest in their own past and in the origins of their own culture, which had spurred the national antiquarians, led European archeologists into the Classical and Near Eastern fields. While art and architecture were still potent inspirations, European history in the guise of culture origins and developmental sequences had been added to the incentives of exploration. "Archaeology then came to the rescue of history from the morass into which philology had dragged her" (Hall, 1915, p. 1). Classical antiquarianism, after an interim of some centuries of ministering to other disciplines, had returned as archeology to the historical fold, not as local history this time but as the background of Western European civilization.[18]

It is now time to anticipate the argument, toward the establishment of which the preceding pages and those immediately to follow are directed. It has been shown that until about 1860 the excavation of ancient remains had been pursued principally for two reasons: art treasure, and local and national history. But in the years between 1860 and 1875, what had once been rather formless dilettante antiquarianism became a formal profession and split into two segments. Classical and Near Eastern archeology continued their long-standing affiliations with philology and art, and further extended their connections into the realm of history. It was the growing discipline of cultural anthropology which absorbed the other segment of European archeology. The context and significance of these changes will be more fully elaborated following the next section of the present chapter.

There was a second line of archeological development. The establishment of pre-Neolithic archeology (hereinafter designated as "Paleolithic") can be attributed to geology and its affiliate paleontology. It was founded by a man primarily interested in paleontology; it was admitted to professional consideration on the word of geologists; and for the first few years of its formal existence it was pursued primarily by geologists and paleontologists.

Some of the reasons for this may be inferred. Paleolithic artifacts offer slight satisfaction in themselves to persons romantically or artistically inclined. Their romance lies in their age, not in their appearance. Therefore, since the great age of the Paleolithic finds had not been determined or even vaguely imagined, it is small wonder that the crude implements should have been overlooked or relegated to the status of natural or supernatural curiosities by the antiquarians of the Romantic Movement and Gothic Revival. Their interest was in the artistic, the bizarre, the historical past, not in the meaning of rough flints. Even after the stone implements of Neolithic and later times had been accepted for what they actually were, Paleolithic implements remained unidentified.[19]

A second factor in the lag of Paleolithic research was religious in nature. The Church and the Christian chronology stood directly in the path of an understanding of the meaning of deeply buried and very crude stone objects. Archbishop Ussher, a member of the first antiquarian circle in Britain, had pronounced the world to have been created in the year 4004 B.C. This date was accepted as the studied judgment of an erudite Man of God and consequently, on pain of incurring the Church's wrath, all calculation as to human antiquity had to be fitted into the time-scale thus erected. Criticism was flatly denounced or was rebutted by re-assertion, as when Lightfoot retorted that not only was the world created in 4004 B.C. but at nine o'clock on the morning of October 23 of that memorable year! Furthermore, since the patently high civilization of Egypt and the relatively sophisticated culture of Biblical Abraham filled practically the whole of this Christian chronology as stated by Ussher, there remained no frame of reference into which the idea of primeval antiquity could fit. Despite an occasional brilliant insight by such men as Vosius and Sir Walter Raleigh, it appears that there was no conception of a stage in human history at which objects of Paleolithic crudity would have been used as the only implements of mankind.[20]

The force that eventually resolved this intellectual stalemate was the English Industrial Revolution. The great churning of swamps, the building of buildings, the digging of canals, the cutting of railroad beds provided magnificent and entirely new opportunities for observation of geologic phenomena (Crawford, 1932). From the time of "Strata" Smith onward, the discipline of geology progressed by leaps and bounds. By 1830, Lyell had laid the groundwork of modern geology, and by 1834 Agassiz was on the trail of his theory of Pleistocene glaciation. Together with the growth of geology came the gradual weakening of the biological theory of Catastrophism, which had, at the end of the 18th century, partially supplanted the theory of Special Creation held by Church and layman alike since the days of Father Suarez.[21]

With the publication of *The Origin of Species* in 1859, the concept of progressive evolution within a geological time of tremendous duration replaced Catastrophism, and the stage was set for the acceptance of the antiquity of man.

It was paleontology which served as the ultimate catalyst to formulate Paleolithic archeology from antiquarianism and the discipline of geology. During the first stages of the Industrial Revolution, the same churning of the land which assisted geological studies also sectioned vast numbers of Pleistocene deposits and brought their contents to light. The earth literally opened before the eyes of the new and energetic antiquarian societies which thereupon included the bones of "antediluvian" fauna in their repertory of collected items pertaining to the mysterious past. Paleontological researches boomed and a tremendous amount of fossil bone was recovered. Activity and controversy prospered, especially in England and France as witness the writings of Lamarck, Cuvier, Geoffroy St. Hilaire, Deshayes, Brongiart, Lyell, Pengelly, Buckland, and others.

As part of this trend, Boucher de Perthes of Abbeville on the Somme was studying the alluvial gravels of his local river terraces. By 1836, his paleontological investigations had led him to wonder whether the remains of some "antediluvian" form of man-like creature, or at least his implements, might not be found together with all the other mammalian remains which themselves were not so very dissimilar from existing modern forms. In 1847, the first volume of Boucher's *Les Antiquités celtiques et antediluviennes* appeared. In this work he put forward, with his evidence, the contention that his finds represented the handicraft of "antediluvian" men. Although a few of his colleagues grad-

ually became convinced of the ·correctness of his views, the general reaction
to his publication was either indifferent or hostile. But in 1858, the British
paleontologist Falconer saw Boucher's collection of flints and was greatly
impressed. The next year Falconer prevailed upon other British geologists,
Lyell and Prestwich, to visit Abbeville and see for themselves the sites from
which the artifacts had been taken. When these eminent scientists, as the
result of their inspection, became fully convinced of the authenticity of
Boucher's finds, the future of Paleolithic archeology was secured. Lyell, the
most influential of the geologists, still held some of his views on Catastrophism,
but the evidence brought forward by Darwin in that same year of 1859 convinced him of the true meaning of the terrace gravel artifacts of Abbeville. In
1863, he published his work *The Antiquity of Man*. This was the final victory
needed to clinch the position of Paleolithic archeology. The final authority was,
then, geology. It was in this field, or related sub-field, that Boucher's ideas had
their first inception, their first trials, their first acceptance, and their first
intensification. For, following the recognition of the Abbeville finds, paleontologists and geologists in Britain and on the Continent began intensively to
search the glacial gravels and ancient caves for traces of early man.[22]

However, this geological affiliation was short lived. Just as part of historical
antiquarianism had been absorbed by cultural anthropology, so the investigation
of ancient man and his culture was also drawn toward that growing discipline.
"Prehistory," or "Prehistoric Archeology," retained strong connections with
geology and paleontology to be sure, but academically and in general viewpoint
it seems to have associated itself with the anthropological rather than the
Classical branch of what was then, and is today, called archeology.

Thus, of the two lines through which archeology had developed, the Paleolithic gravitated toward cultural anthropology, and the historical split in two.
The archeology of Classical and Near Eastern civilization was either retained
by long-standing disciplines such as Classics, Philology, and Art, or was absorbed by the discipline of History as contributing to the sources of Western
European civilization. The other part of the historical segment was absorbed
by anthropology. The explanation for this shift of disciplinary affiliations is to
be found in the growth of cultural anthropology.

From the days of the Age of Exploration, through the social and political
philosophies of the Enlightenment, men in Europe had become increasingly
aware of the customs of mankind, particularly those of non-European peoples.
By the beginning of the 19th century, the study of human customs had
become an important field of scholarly endeavor. The relationships, physical
and cultural, between the varieties of the human species constituted problems
about which speculation and armchair philosophy occupied ever more manpower and printer's ink. The masses of data collected by explorers, colonists,

and missionaries contributed greatly to the knowledge of, and interest in, the strange practices of strange peoples in strange places. Ethnological societies were founded and treatises were written upon culture and environment, culture and physical man, culture and human psychology, one culture and another, the significance of folk tales, etc.[23]

But these efforts seem to have been little organized. Other than a general interest in custom and the newly appreciated varieties of mankind, especially the bizarre and foreign, there seems to have been no central theme, no structural framework or single guiding concept around which all these scholars could rally or against which they could inveigh. It was Darwin's theory of biological evolution that changed this. It provided the required rallying point, and the result was the creation of the formal discipline of Ethnology or Cultural Anthropology with the purpose of elucidating the evolution of human custom.

Two consequences followed the acceptance of Darwin's theory as applicable to cultural phenomena: first, Western European civilization came to be viewed as the culmination or acme of an evolutionary process; and second, the contemporary but non-literate cultures came to be considered "survivals" or living fossils, representing the stages through which individual culture traits or whole cultures had passed in their evolutionary progress. From this, it followed that, to those scholars interested in culture, the modern and literate civilizations lost their attraction. The elucidation of the evolution of human custom was to be effected, not through study of its final forms, but through the study of those cultures which represented the developmental stages. Thus it came about that, rallying around the concept of evolution, those men who had already been interested in culture intensified their researches among the "primitive" and non-literate peoples, and their studies became crystallized into a formal discipline: Cultural Anthropology.

It should be emphasized at this point that the primary interest of these ethnologists had been, and still was, culture. That they believed the "primitive" to be their best source of information was due, not so much to their predilection for the savage as such, but rather to the assumptions stemming from their acceptance of the evolutionary doctrine. Their primary interest, as it had long been, was still the relations, the nature and workings, of the varieties of human custom. Their preoccupation with the "primitive" and non-literate was a means to an end, not the end itself.

Thus I would modify Kroeber's interpretation (1923, pp. 1-2) of the course of anthropological development. Rather than have cultural anthropology, as he does, slyly entering the scene and beginning to cultivate a corner or modestly turning its attention to subjects untouched by established disciplines, it would seem better to picture cultural anthropology as developing from the organization, around a single basic conception, of men already engaged in the cultivation of that corner and already interested in those subjects unappreciated by existing disciplines. In other words, when the concept of evolution struck the minds of the students of human custom and history, the ethnologists were sitting just where the lightning fell. Granting as axiomatic a cultural evolution as then envisioned, it was but a simple, logical step to the theorems that Western European civilization was the culmination, that "primitive" cultures were survivals, and that those men who knew "primitive" cultures were thus in the best position to study and define cultural evolution. Those ethnologists who accepted cultural evolution were naturals to fall into the role of students of "primitive" man, and from this point the formalization of their studies into a discipline could only be expected.

Thus the idea arose in academic and intellectual circles that cultural anthropology meant the study of undocumented cultures in contradistinction to history which studied cultures with written records. It is hardly to be wondered, therefore, that the archeology of non-literate peoples gravitated toward cultural anthropology. The archeology of literate cultures, as we have seen, suffered a dispersed fate. Some Classical and Near Eastern archeology was incorporated in historical studies and some actual excavation was carried on for that purpose; some continued to be taught and conducted in the field under the banner of Classics; some is today, academically speaking, still connected with philology and art. And the significant thing is that it is all labelled *archeology*.

Although I am not prepared to argue the actual case as applied to English and Continental archeology, we see here a potential source of theoretical confusion. In the first place, the practice of a profession which is designated by a single name is carried on under very diverse, even conflicting, auspices. In the second place, cultural anthropology, which was developed by men primarily interested in culture, has gathered to itself Paleolithic archeology, which started as paleontology or geology, and non-literate archeology including that of Neolithic, Bronze, and even Iron Age Europe, which has been shown to have stemmed from interest in local and national history. More will be said on this subject at a later time.

We may now take up the development of archeology in the United States. First, it will be possible to eliminate discussion of the Classical and Near Eastern field, since its development in the United States has, for present purposes, followed that of Europe. The genesis of Americanist archeology, however, presents its own picture.[24]

From the first European settlement in what are now the United States, there had been continuous and intense speculation about the origins of the aboriginal inhabitants. The range of assumed antecedents of the native population and of American culture extended all the way from the "Indians" of

Columbus through Persians, Basques, and Welsh, to the Ten Lost Tribes of Israel.[25] These hypotheses were the results of *a priori* reasoning and poorly grounded deductions. Very few men during the first years of colonization observed the living Indian population except over a gun barrel or through the eyes of exploitation and trade. With the exception of a few missionaries and evangelists, those men that went most frequently among the natives were not the ones from whom books upon the subject derived. Still fewer sought to study pre-Columbian America by means of the spade. Thomas Jefferson's excavation, carried out in 1784, is generally considered to have been the first "dirt archeology" accomplished in the Western Hemisphere. But it is an isolated instance, and a considerable number of years elapsed before any extensive, purposeful digging was done.[26]

After the first period of speculation and when, following the close of the Revolutionary War, settlers began to move across the Allegheny mountains into the Ohio Valley, antiquarian research in the United States took its first major step. The colonists and adventurers trailing westward observed the great monumental earthworks in the newly opened region and began to describe what they saw. From the end of the 18th century, there appears an ever increasing and more detailed body of information on the antiquities of "The West." It should be stated, however, that these reports were primarily descriptive, and descriptive of only the more obvious features. They attempted little more than plans and surveys of mounds and earthworks. What few artifactual details made their way into print did so purely incidentally and secondary to the prevailing concern with monumental and "architectural" features. Speculations as to the authors of these structures continued, if anything, more intense than before. The flood of new data provided just that much more material from which to erect hypotheses. Rafinesque carries his views on the trans-Pacific and Atlantis-derived peopling of America to extreme limits. Somewhat later, William Henry Harrison notes the abandonment of the Ohio Valley and argues that the Aztecs had once occupied this region whence they had set out for Mexico. Bradford maintained that the nomadic Indians had degenerated from a former uniform, agricultural level in America, and he traces the origin of the "Red Race" from Europe, Egypt, Mesopotamia, and other parts of Asia. An interest in the culture history of the Indians and the peopling of America was the generating and guiding force in most, if not all, antiquarian thought and effort during the first part of the 19th century.[27]

As exploration and settlement pushed farther and farther west and especially when the Mexican War gave access to vast new territories, fresh and more extensive fields were offered the antiquarian. The first period of expansion into the Far West brought the same sort of men and resulted in the same sort of survey and reconnaissance that had characterized the beginnings of antiquarian observation in the Ohio Valley. Nevertheless, the striking and entirely different aspects of the ruins provided new material for speculation and further fanned the interest in the history and origins of the Indian.[28]

About the year 1870, the second major step in Americanist archeological development was taken. Up to this time, investigation of American antiquities had been characterized by a rambling and coincidental curiosity as to the identity of the builders of the remains.[29] The history and derivation of the "Red Man" had fired the inquiry which, except for such men as Atwater, Lapham, Squier and Davis, and Henry Schoolcraft, had been carried out with little if any program. Around 1870, researches began to take on an intense and diligent character. The Governmental geographical and geological surveys brought trained observers and inquisitive men into the field, and these men developed their own interest and that of others in the living Indian and the vestiges of past life in the areas explored. Having time and the means for observation and recording, they produced invaluable data and stimulated study in other quarters.[30] Archeological surveys and excavations were initiated with a definite purpose in mind and were no longer merely for the sake of discovering what lay beneath a particular mound of earth or heap of rubble. That this purpose had largely to do with excavations to obtain museum collections is beside the point. The important thing to realize is that the digging of sites for specimens and other information had become an end in itself (Mitra, 1933, Sec. IX).

At least some of this new spirit may be attributed to the energies and manpower released by the close of the Civil War. Wissler has called this period the Museum Period (1942, p. 190), but it is probable that the growth of museums and other institutions was alike in its debt to the release following the war and to an increase of European influence upon the United States after 1865. It is hardly a coincidence that this period also marks the appearance in the United States of formal anthropology. At this time, Brinton, Mason, Morgan, Powell, and Putnam entered upon their careers as anthropologists.[31] The founding of the Bureau of American Ethnology, the International Congress of Americanists, and the Archaeological Institute of America, the organization of the Subsection and shortly thereafter of the Section of Anthropology within the American Association for the Advancement of Science, the formation of the Anthropological Society of Washington (later to become the American Anthropological Association), all reflect the new and anthropological spirit that impinged upon the study of American Indians and American antiquities.[32] From this date onward, Americanists in the United States have pursued their research under the banner of the discipline of Anthropology whether they have been working in ethnological or archeological materials, whether upon the living or the dead Indians.

Here again we see antiquarianism, starting with interest in history and ending by absorption into the discipline of cultural anthropology. In the case of the United States, the reasons are even clearer than they were abroad. Americanists had not even the slight cause for hesitancy which might have assailed British or Continental archeologists: culture sequences in the Americas did not end in archives full of written documents which were the recognized field of the discipline of history. Nor did Americanist archeology deal with the culture history and ancestors of those who were engaged in its pursuit. It dealt with culture history, but of the American Indian, of "primitives." It did not merge into the history of self-documented societies; its subject matter was "primitive" from beginning to end. It was therefore and patently anthropological since, by the time formal archeology had been established in the United States, the discipline of cultural anthropology had already been recognized as that which treated of the non-literate and "primitive."

Thus we have seen, both in the United States and abroad, that within the ranks of those who call themselves archeologists there has been a separation: on the one hand a drift toward cultural anthropology, on the other a persistence in history, and the latter current has continued to carry eddies of art, the classics, and philology, fading somewhat in the present day but still persisting as active elements. The point upon which the archeological stream is observed to split is the literacy, the "primitiveness," and perhaps the artistic quality of the subject cultures.

To men immersed in European art traditions, Greece undoubtedly offers more inducements than do the mounds of Minnesota. That men excavating in Egypt should have more of common interest with men excavating in Palestine than with those digging in Arizona is understandable. That men working in the Long Barrows of England should separate themselves from those working in the Roman Forum might be expected. But if, to continue our figure of speech, the splitting of the current has muddied the intellectual waters of the archeological stream, then we have cause for concern rather than complacency. Whether or not this has happened will occupy us next.

CHAPTER 2

ARCHEOLOGY: HISTORY OR ANTHROPOLOGY?

A DISCIPLINE may be defined in two ways: first by a statement of its subject matter, and second by a statement of its aims and objectives with regard to that subject matter. There are, of course, other criteria that may be used, but for the designation of scholarly and scientific fields these seem to be the ones most commonly employed and most satisfying of the usual requirements. Thus, for example, geology may be defined as the science having the earth's form and composition as its subject matter and aiming to explain the history, the nature, and the dynamic characters of this subject matter.

When, however, we come to define the more particular and specific disciplines which are subsumed under the heads of the broader fields of study, we find that each of these two major categories of definition may in their turn be approached in two ways. The first is direct and explicit: "The subject matter of physiography is such and such; its aims and objectives are thus and so; and it strives to derive the following results from the study of its subject matter." This, of course, is the clearest and best way. The second method is by implication, is less clear, and usually begs the question. By this method, a discipline is stated or implied to be a branch, a sub-field, a part of some other discipline. The implication is that it has the same subject matter and objectives as the master discipline to which it pertains, but with some modification or variation that may or may not be designated. Thus physiography may be stated to be a branch of geology, and its subject matter and aims are thus implied to be somehow related to those of geology. Or physiography may be implicated as a branch of geology by being included in a geological curriculum, a geological textbook, or a geological periodical. Physiographers are implicated as geologists when they belong to geological societies and associate predominantly and professionally with geologists.

For the purposes of the remainder of this discussion, I shall arbitrarily narrow the scope of inquiry to Americanist archeology as conducted in the United States. Thus the subject matter of archeology, as that concept will be used hereinafter, will consist of American Indians and Eskimos. About this subject matter there would seem to be little cause for controversy.

The case is otherwise with respect to the aims of Americanist archeology. They have been stated in both the ways mentioned above, i.e., explicitly and by subsumption. But the point of importance is that there is disagreement in the aims stated according to the two methods.

When Americanist archeology has been subsumed under another discipline, it has been overwhelmingly designated as a branch of cultural anthropology. From the time of Brinton, Powell, and Putnam this has been true.[33] With respect to the academic system, Brand (1937) and more recently Chamberlain and Hoebel (1942) have shown archeology to be consistently included under this discipline. The contents of the *American Anthropologist* and the *Southwestern Journal of Anthropology,* from the first to the current issues, reveal in the regular inclusion of archeological articles the incorporated status of archeology. The membership of practicing archeologists within anthropological societies and the topics on the agenda of anthropological meetings are further demonstration of this inclusion. In order not to beat too much upon this rather obvious point, the words of two Americanists may serve as illustrations:

The two other subsciences in the field of cultural anthropology, namely archaeology and ethnology. . . . (Linton, 1945c, p. 8)

The term anthropology now stands for the specific science of man. Ethnology, archaeology, and somatology are merely divisions, or convenient groups of problems within the scope of this science. (Wissler, 1938, p. xv)[34]

It would seem, then, that the aims of archeology, by implication at least, are related to those of cultural anthropology.

On the other hand, when the objectives of Americanist archeology are explicitly stated, it is found that they are consistently said to be historical, specifically the "reconstruction of history." There have been other opinions expressed, to be sure, but these have been significantly few; they have had no apparent effect upon the writings of the vast majority of archeologists; and they may be regarded merely as the exceptions which prove the rule.[35] The archeologists, as a group, appear to be consciously driving toward history, toward the re-creation of the aboriginal past of the Americas. For example:

McKern seems to be in complete agreement that to reconstruct histories is archaeology's main job. (Steward, 1944, p. 99)

Since archaeology is a historical discipline which aims to reconstruct the past. . . . (Griffin, 1943, p. 11)

Archaeology has two chief aims, the reconstruction of the life of the people in the past and the arrangement of this life into an historical development. (Vaillant, 1930, p. 9)

Archaeology, by etymology the study of beginnings, has historical reconstruction for its objective. (Kroeber, 1937, p. 163)[36]

Here then, we have Americanist archeology included within the discipline of cultural anthropology, yet having the explicitly stated objective of reconstructing history. What are we to infer from this? Are the aims of sub-discipline and discipline the same; is the aim of cultural anthropology to reconstruct history?

What is the aim of the discipline of history; is it also to reconstruct history? And are these disciplines, then, the same thing with regard to objectives? Or is cultural anthropology more than a reconstruction of history? Is the archeologist's concern with history merely indicative of his particular contribution to the broader aims of cultural anthropology? If so, what is the relation of this contribution to the whole of which it is a part? What is the use to which anthropology as cultural anthropology can put the findings of archeology as history?

Such questions and a multitude of others are raised by the position of Americanist archeology in the United States. Aside from this cultural anthropology-history ambivalence itself, the really significant fact is that there has been no attempt to resolve the discrepancies if they are real, or to discount them if they are only apparent. Whether this is because of a failure to realize the condition, or because of a conscious refusal to deal with theoretical aspects of archeology, or for whatever reason, the situation remains and is indicative of a positive weakness in the disciplinary structure. With the exception of Kidder, whose work will be treated in detail in the next chapter, there seems to have been no archeologist in the United States who has even approached treatment of this problem. The archeologists state they have been doing history and that they are anthropologists without an effort to discover the relationships, if any, between these two fields.[37]

Of course, the crucial question is: What has history to do with cultural anthropology? If archeology is a branch of the latter and yet is doing history, there must be some connection or else the archeologists are off on a completely wrong track. Assuming that they are not, and in order to answer the crucial question, it will be necessary to define history and cultural anthropology. Once these disciplines have been defined to our present satisfaction, the answer to the problem of their relationship will probably be found to have been established in the process or, at very least, to have become clearly apparent. It may be expected also that concurrently with the clarification of these problems, the relationships of archeology to these and other disciplines will be clarified. The next section, then, will be concerned with answering the crucial questions: What is history, what is cultural anthropology, what is the relationship between the two, and finally what light do these findings throw on the nature of archeology?

As a first step, one claim which has been advanced by each of the separate disciplines may be eliminated. Neither history nor cultural anthropology, even when the latter is taken together with the coordinate and conjoint data of physical anthropology, should consider itself to be *the* study of man. Neither is justified in visualizing itself as the particular discipline which is destined to pull all the innumerable threads of human experience into a single tapestry with the meaning of every fiber and stitch explained. To weave this fabric, to be the Study of Man, to "reconstruct" the History of Man, Universal History as it is sometimes called, will require the services not only of historians *and* anthropologists, but also of psychologists, biologists, meteorologists, geologists, chemists, and a host of other specialists in more or less autonomous disciplines. Man in his entirety cannot, and will not, be understood as a phenomenon isolated from the physical and psychological worlds any more than as a phenomenon isolated from the social or cultural worlds. The organic foundations upon which human culture has been developed and the influence of the natural environment are factors that cannot be ignored when the Universal History of Man is written.

Thus it is impossible to accept some of the definitions of history and anthropology (as a whole, combining both cultural and physical aspects) that have been proposed by their advocates. For example:

History tends to embrace life in the entirety of its aspects and thus to unite all the special disciplines and all the so-called historical sciences which have sprung from analysis. . . . (Berr and Febvre, 1937, p. 360)

In its amplest meaning History includes every trace and vestige of everything that man has done or thought since first he appeared on earth. . . . It is the vague and comprehensive science of past human affairs. (Robinson, 1912, p. 1)

The science of history is that science which investigates and presents, in causal context, the facts of the evolution of men in their individual as well as typical and collective activity as social beings. (Bernheim, 1903, p. 6)

The anthropologists strike the same note:

. . . the time would seem to be ripe for a new synthesis of science, especially of those sciences which deal with human beings and their problems.

By its very definition, the science of anthropology makes a bid for this position. In all English-speaking countries the term is taken to mean "the science of man and his works." In Europe the term has been given a somewhat different meaning, being limited to the study of man's physical characteristics, but we will adhere to the broader definition. (Linton, 1945c, p. 3)

The ideal of anthropology is to coordinate all the data concerning man's culture, language and anatomy, past and present, with a view to solving the problems of his origin and the interpretation of his culture. (Wissler, 1938, p. xv)

Anthropology is the science of Man, a master-science. . . . (Penniman, 1935, *Preface*)[38]

The above quotations, in so far as they are definitions, are identical and for this reason alone cannot be accepted at their face-value as distinguishing two disciplines which in actual practice are, and which themselves claim to be, distinct. These statements do not merely outline the subject-matter of their respective disciplines, giving later and appropriate qualifications as to the segment which their particular aims and objectives delimit. These statements make the bald claim that each discipline is in fact or potentially *the* Science, *the* Master-science, *the* comprehensive and synthetic Study of Man. While it may be too much to impugn the breadth of vision of the men quoted above,[39] it is not too much to contend that these quotations, unqualified as they are, point to a looseness of thinking which is characteristic and indicative. Neither history nor anthropology can ever be capable, by itself alone, of synthesizing and understanding the totality of human experience or of being, in a word, *the* Science of Man.

The task of investigating, understanding, and projecting the totality of human experience is, at very least, a cooperative undertaking. Such a venture requires information which is to be obtained only from the particular disciplines which have made specialized studies—physics, chemistry, geology, biology, psychology, economics, political science, sociology, etc., in addition to, and together with anthropology and history. To assemble and assimilate such a mass of material is distinctly outside the scope of any one discipline which, at the same time, is actively engaged in empirical research within its own special field of human or non-human phenomena. Each discipline may provide its own information toward the common project, but by this very token it is effectively prevented from assuming control over the mass of information gathered by the others. The value of the separate contributions will depend not only upon their applicability to human problems but also, and as vitally, upon their own logical and empirical validity. In short, since it is of primary importance for each contributing discipline to order its own house and to establish the validity of its own findings, it is not likely, in fact it is impossible, that any empirically oriented discipline, at the present stage of scientific and intellectual development, will have the time or the extra energy, even granting the vision and depth of knowledge, to perform the far more stupenduous task of ordering the house of total human experience and writing the Universal History of Man.[40]

It seems that such a task, by its very nature, constitutes the realm of philosophy. It is for philosophy, and not the specialized and fact-finding disciplines, to assemble and synthesize and interpret the vast body of relevant data provided to the cooperative project by those disciplines. In the words of Flint:

Thus, when a department of knowledge is very comprehensive; when it manifestly cannot be properly cultivated otherwise than in relation to the whole of knowledge; when it implies, includes, and utilizes a number of special studies or disciplines, themselves entitled to be called sciences, the name of philosophy may well be preferred to that of science as the generic part of its designation. (1893, p. 20)[41]

Kroeber has stated, and very rightly, that history cannot possibly tell what really happened in the totality of past time, because to do so would take as long as the happenings themselves (1935a, pp. 547-548). It is obvious, then, that for any Universal History or Study of Man a selection must be made, an essence distilled, which will give an accurate picture of past human experience in the absence of the details of every thought and deed. Since random sampling cannot, with any assurance, be expected to provide the necessary material for the desired "accurate picture," a conscious selection must be made. Reasoning further, it is apparent that any conscious selection with a view to accuracy and relevance must be made in terms of what the selector considers to be accurate and relevant, i.e., in terms of a conceptual scheme.[42] Now conceptual schemes which attempt to order the mass of data pertaining to an accurate picture of the totality of human existence have long been designated as philosophical and the men who develop them as philosophers. According to Znaniecki,

Every thinking man wishes to obtain some understanding of the totality of the civilization to which he belongs, compare it with other civilizations, interpret their history, discover if possible some guiding lines in the apparent chaos of the whole historical evolution of mankind. These interests are as undying and as justifiable in their way as the old metaphysical interest in interpreting the whole world of nature as some kind of ordered and rational whole. And there is an old and well established discipline which satisfies them: it is the *philosophy of history.* (1934, p. 100)[43]

It seems better, therefore, that anthropology and history should provide their own material toward the cooperative project of the Study of Man, than that both or one should claim to be *the* Master-science which is to synthesize the totality of human experience. Just to the extent that the historians and anthropologists are practicing historians and anthropologists, to that extent are they not philosophers and should not aspire to write Universal History or alone to pursue the Study of Man.

Having indicated what history is *not,* I shall proceed now to take up the problem of what history is, of what constitutes a definition of history. Two premises may be made explicit immediately: first, the term *history* "as normally understood, means human history" (Steefel, 1937, p. 307); second, *history* will be used, as is commonly the practice, to denote the history of man as a cultural, rather than a biological, being. Therefore in the succeeding exposition, *history* will refer only to the history of cultural man.[44]

The term *history* has come to have four different denotations which may be grouped into two divisions: (a) actuality and (b) abstraction. It is absolutely necessary to make, and to keep, these distinctions clear before treating of the concept and comparing it with other concepts.

1. The first meaning falls within the division of actuality and denotes the totality of "past actuality," as Beard calls it (1934, p. 219), without chronological or sequential implications. Thus it is possible to say: "One of the most interesting periods of history was—" and mean "One of the most interesting periods of the past was—," without commitments as to particular time or

order of time. Historians, writing about their subject, usually do not recognize this first, broad meaning. While it is, perhaps, of minor usage, it is different from the other meanings, is quite frequently used especially by the lay public, and therefore I believe should be included for clarity and completeness.

2. The second denotation, also within the division of actuality, is differentiated from the first by a definite consideration of chronological sequence of past actuality from the oldest to the more recent. Thus one may speak of *the history of England* and mean "the coming of things and phenomena into being or into successive stages and states of being, the flow of occurrences in time." (Flint, 1893, p. 7)

3. The third meaning of the word *history* falls within the second or abstract division and denotes the exposition, written or verbal, of "what actually happened." It is, as Croce maintains (1921), "contemporary thought" about past actuality and particularly this thought set down in writing or somehow projected in words. It denotes an abstraction or a set of abstractions from actuality, not that actuality itself.

The word *contemporary* is used advisedly and with certain connotations which will be of importance at a later point in this study. Any segment of past actuality which is verbalized, in writing or orally, is not that segment itself but merely an abstraction filtered through the mind of the verbalizer. As Cohen and Nagel say (1934, p. 324): "History as the knowledge of the past, and indeed all knowledge, can be achieved only through inference." Now it is impossible "to infer" or "to filter something in the mind" in the past—or in the future for that matter. Thought is synchronous and contemporary with the thinker, i.e., with the verbalizer, with the historian. The written or spoken record of past actuality is, then, "contemporary thought" about actuality.

History in this third sense has sometimes been given the name of *historiography,* literally "the writing of history." Although there seems to be some ambiguity in the use of this term today among historians, it will nevertheless be used in the course of this study to denote the third meaning of the word *history,* to designate the projection, written or spoken, of contemporary thought about past actuality in terms of cultural man and time sequences. There seems to be no other word or phrase which is applicable, distinctive, and concise.[45] Thus one may speak of Buckle's *History of Civilization in England* and mean Buckle's historiography, the account which projects his thought about that segment of total past actuality which embraces the civilization of the people of England in its chronological order.

4. The fourth meaning of *history* also lies within the division of abstraction and identifies the discipline or formal branch of knowledge which is occupied in the practice, the teaching, and the study of historiography. Thus one may say: "History employs such and such methods" and mean that a certain discipline

which has to do with historiography employs such and such methods.[46]

It is obvious that "history is both a descriptive record of human events and an existential series of events" (Meadows, 1944, p. 53). Meanings (1) and (2) denote the "events themselves" according to Shotwell (1922, p. 2). They imply the actual happenings about which the abstractions, inferences, and other thoughts denoted by meanings (3) and (4) are made. Since the comparisons to be effected in this study are between the discipline of cultural anthropology and the discipline of history and since the latter has been defined in terms of the concept of historiography, it will be possible hereafter to deal only with historiography and anthropology. The other meanings of the word *history*, except in so far as they are pertinent to a specific argument and are explicitly indicated may be eliminated from consideration.

The so-called historical, non-experimental disciplines which deal with actual, non-repeating, unique, rather than "laboratory" events and which include historiography, are characterized by four steps or levels in the procedure by which they seek to attain their objectives. These steps are roughly, although by no means consistently, sequential. They are: *first*, the definition of problem in terms of a conceptual scheme; *second*, a gathering, analysis, and criticism of empirical data; *third*, the ordering of these data in chronological sequence; and *fourth*, the search for and, to the extent that it is possible, the establishment of "the reciprocal relationships within this series: the continual actions and reactions—the interaction" (Berr and Febvre, 1937, p. 363). This is the level of integration and synthesis, of context and so-called historical reconstruction, toward which all the historical disciplines are directed, whether one is speaking of geology, astronomy, historiography, or cultural anthropology.

The essential characteristic of the historical approach is the endeavor to achieve a conceptual integration of individual phenomena ("facts" or "events") in terms of specified time and space. (Forde, 1939, p. 224)

The ideal of the social historian is to trace the evolution of a people with reference to all the conditions and influences that helped to shape its aspirations and its way of life. In other words, the social historian seeks to depict the human past at a given period in its totality, with the various forces and factors duly interrelated and appraised. (Schlesinger, 1937, p. 60)[47]

That historiography has aspired to this goal is most evident from the facts of its development as a discipline. Since the day that Herodotus, "the father of history," stated his intent of leaving to posterity the details and the cause of the Persian War, through Thucydides, Polybius, Augustine, Machiavelli, Gibbon, Macaulay, Carlyle, von Ranke, Prescott, Freeman, etc., the grand topic and the grand manner typified historiography.

Its point of view was primarily political. It concerned itself largely with the activities and interests of government, political parties, diplomacy, and war. . . . The eyes of European historians had always been dazzled by the pageantry of kings and armies, the pomp and circumstance of dramatic occasions. (Schlesinger, 1937, p. 57)

This traditional or "academic" type treated, to the virtual exclusion of all else, of great events and "grand character" (Stubbs, 1877, p. 98), of topics believed to represent the most worthy achievements of mankind: the Church, the State, and the Military.[48]

Until the end of the 19th century, perhaps even until the first decades of the 20th, this brand of historiography prevailed. However, around the turn of the century, there appeared a feeling for broader subjects, a sensing of the inadequacies of past politics as present history, to paraphrase Freeman (1886, p. 44).

The exclusive idea of political history, *Staatengeschichte*, to which Ranke held so firmly, has been gradually yielding to a more comprehensive definition which embraces as its material all records, whatever their nature may be, of the material and spiritual development, of the culture and the works, of man in society, from the stone age onward. . . . (Bury, 1903, p. 19)

This new type may be identified as "social" or "cultural" historiography. It rejects the dogma of former days, that concern should be confined to princes and politics, the military and the mighty, and recognizes the importance of the masses of common people, of everyday life, and of the normal happenings of the past. Man's past in all its aspects is the subject matter of this later historiography, limited only by the interest, capabilities, and capacities of the individual student.

Of course in actual practice labour is divided; political history and the histories of the various parts of civilization can and must be separately treated; but it makes a vital difference that we should be alive to the interconnection. . . . (Bury, 1903; p. 19-20)

Adumbrations of the "social" historiography had been present since the very first: Herodotus wrote of Scythian and Aethiopian customs, Tacitus of those of the Germans, Montesquieu and Voltaire of customs and arts. But it remained for the growth of science and Nationalism in the early and middle 19th century to point up the importance of the masses and their culture. From this influence, first *Kulturgeschichte* arose and then the New History of Jameson and Robinson which attained prominence before World War I and flowered thereafter in the twenties. Of recent date, the so-called "cultural approach to history" is reacting against certain tenets and practices of the New History.[49]

In their work, historians have certainly attained the third level of historical procedure as outlined above. They have been guided into realms of the past by specific problems and interests; they have gathered and criticized their data; and they have either worked out their chronology or had it given them by the nature of their material. Furthermore, the attainment of the fourth level, that of context and interrelation, has consistently been the goal of historians since they first began to work. Even in the days when only the grand events and high personages were treated, there was a conscious attempt to synthesize the pertinent facts into an integrated picture. From Herodotus and Livy to Gibbon and Carlyle, this "picture of the past" was the thing sought after in historiography. In fact, it was a reaction against the painting of too highly integrated pictures on too little evidence, against the philosophically subjective narratives of historians, which brought about the "scientific" and "unbiased" historiography of von Ranke. Whatever the technical failings of the earlier historians might have been with respect to the first three levels of procedure, it is clearly apparent that they were primarily bent upon the attainment of the fourth level, upon writing literary narratives which, *ipso facto,* called for synthesis, interrelation of facts, and the development of context and a cultural picture. The school of von Ranke and the succeeding *Kulturgeschichte* were no less interested in synthesis and narrative; their difference lay in more rigorous attention to procedure as such and, in the latter school, a broader viewpoint. That the resultant syntheses were not objective, as the historians so wishfully thought, is beside the point. The important thing to note is that they, as those who preceded them, thought of their goal as "literary re-creation" of past actuality. It is superfluous to stress the fact that modern historiography also is primarily interested in context. Full and inclusive context, within the chosen frame of reference, is the very canon of its work. Even though, as Shotwell says, "each historian now specializes [and] great enterprises of the totality of history are cooperative and even then cover only a fraction" (1929, p. 597), the pertinent contexts of these chosen segments are recognized to be the bases for valid criticism and valid "reconstruction" of past actuality.[50]

One more line of evidence may be adduced to the proof of the contention that historiography's interest lies at the level of integration, of synthesis, and context. The commonly accepted distinction between annals and chronicles on the one hand and historiography on the other is this very concept of contextual synthesis. The former terms are usually defined as temporally sequential records of events, while the latter term implies that the data are handled with regard for their relationships and mutual meaning. Thought about past actuality becomes historiography only when facts are related to one another and a picture is created from them by the efforts of the historian. The hallmark of historiography is its concern for the picture of past actuality.[51]

Since this is so and since this is what the historians have been doing all along, it constitutes the definition for which search has been made. Historiography is the discipline characterized by the construction of cultural contexts abstracted from the totality of past actuality. More specifically, it is *projected contemporary thought about past actuality, integrated and synthesized into contexts in terms of cultural man and sequential time.*[52]

Before leaving the subject of historiography, two corollaries may be derived from this definition. First, being "historical" does not mean having a concern merely with time; to have that is being "chronological." Second, being "historical" does not mean having a concern merely with the past; to have that is being "antiquarian."

Because an event belongs to the past it is not necessarily historical. Indeed, in so far as the antiquarian isolates his material for our inspection, interested in it for its own sake, laying it out like a curator of a museum, he robs it of its historical character. For the facts of history do not exist by themselves any more than the lives of historical personages. They are part of a process and acquire meaning only when seen in action. The antiquarian preserves the fragments of the great machinery of events, but the historian sets it to work again, however faintly the sound of its motion comes to him across the distant centuries. (Shotwell, 1922, p. 6)

Finally, before proceeding to the subject of anthropology, it will be well to comment on the fallacy and mental hazard engendered by the used of the term *historical reconstruction.* The words *reconstruction* and *resynthesis* are fundamentally erroneous and have been responsible for much loss of confidence, particularly among the anthropologists. To quote Pirenne:

All historical narrative is at once a synthesis and a hypothesis. It is a synthesis insomuch as it combines the mass of known facts in an account of the whole; it is a hypothesis insomuch as the relations it establishes between these facts are neither evident nor verifiable by themselves. (1931, p. 441)

If, then, only the facts and not their original relationships and interactions are subject to verification, it certainly follows that the historical contexts themselves are not verifiable. If this is the case and it cannot be told for sure whether past actuality has, or has not, been recreated in detail or in essence, it cannot be claimed that these contexts are, or are not, *re*syntheses or *re*constructions. These terms imply a re-building to exact former specifications which, from the above, are not verifiable and, hence, not knowable. The unknowable cannot be taken as a standard of value. Therefore, the arguments both for and against historical reconstruction in anthropology or in any other particular discipline are irrelevant, and it becomes apparent that the work of all historical disciplines really leads to construction and synthesis, not reconstruction and resynthesis. From this, it is further apparent that the real task of the students in historical disciplines settles down to seeing how sound, how plausible, and how acceptable their constructions can be made. Neither the anthropologist nor the historian should use the term *reconstruction* and thus make himself feel inadequate because he knows that his research will never permit him actually to reconstruct the life of past times with certainty and completeness. Rather, he should realize that even the contexts written from the best and fullest archives are constructions and that the differences lie in the nature of the respective data, not in the procedures or basic theoretical factors.

With regard to a definition of anthropology, it may be stated explicity at the start that *cultural anthropology* will be the concept defined. It is outside the scope and requirements of the present study to inquire into the objectives of anthropology as a whole, meaning both the cultural and physical branches and their interrelation. Whether anthropology as a whole has for its objective "the interpretation of those phenomena into which both organic and social causes enter" (Kroeber, 1923, p. 3) or whether it "aims at understanding the workings of human culture, the relations between individual mental processes and human institutions, and the biological foundations of human custom" (Malinowski, 1934, p. xvii) or whether "it is the ultimate aim of anthropology to discover the limits within which men can be conditioned, and what patterns of social life seem to impose fewest strains upon the individual" (Linton, 1936b, p. 5), these are questions whose answers lie beyond the range of present needs. Our problem here was stated above and is simply: What is *cultural* anthropology, what is history, what is the relationship between them, and finally what is the position of archeology in the light of the conclusions thus arrived at?

When we come to examine the concept of cultural anthropology, we find that it too, as was the case with historiography, denotes the projection, written or verbal, of contemporary thought about past actuality in terms of cultural man and time sequences. To pronounce so bluntly that it deals with the past may be a point of issue to some anthropologists, especially the "functionalists." But Lesser has pointed out (1935, pp. 390ff) that anthropology *should* deal with the past to be sound, and I wish to point out now that it *does* deal with the past whether this is recognized by the functionalists or not. Becker has given us the concept of the "spurious present" (1932, p. 226) to designate the fact that any study of events or actual happenings must, by the nature of things, deal with the past, whether that past be distant by a second, an hour, or a century. Once an event has happened, i.e., once it is an event, it is already past. Neither functionalists nor other students can study an event until it is an event, until it is past.[53] Thus, the difference between what the functionalists identify as the present and what they designate as the past is merely a matter of degree. Even if it is claimed by the functionalists that anthropology should deal with the "spurious present" while historiography is said to deal with the "considerable past," the difference is relative and the dividing line so subjective that these concepts cannot be used to differentiate distinct disciplines. That cultural anthropology considers its data in terms of cultural man and time sequences is taken as axiomatic, requiring no exposition. Time is neither reversible nor able to be discounted when dealing with cultural man or any segment of actuality whose interrelations it is desired to understand.

Up to this point, cultural anthropology and historiography denote the same thing. How then can there be a difference between the two concepts? The answer is, of course, that the definition of anthropology is not complete enough and that the differences, assuming them to exist, must lie elsewhere than in the realms of past actuality, sequential time, or the cultural character of man. The investigation will have to be pressed further if differences are to be found.

Cultural anthropology, like historiography, is one of the so-called historical disciplines, being non-experimental and dependent on phenomena which are not contingent upon "laboratory" manipulation or the activities of the observer. It is, therefore, characterized by the same four levels of procedure by which all such disciplines seek to attain their objectives. Ideally, it approaches its material with a particular interest or a definite sense of problem; it collects, analyzes, criticizes its data; it sets them in chronological order; and synthesizes them into a context.

The hallmark of the proper anthropologist, at the present date, is the realization of the vital importance of context and of the fact that cultural data, torn from their setting or without the weighting and balance which context gives them, are of little or no significance. To this level of procedure, then, both cultural anthropology and historiography (as well as geology, sociology, and all historical disciplines) profess to aspire. And while it is a fact that they do not always attain their goal in this respect and that, actually, they sometimes do not even attempt to attain it, nevertheless, this realization, this immediate objective, is the recognized canon of the two disciplines. Once more it has been shown that there is no difference between historiography and cultural anthropology. How, then, do they differ?

Since procedure is intimately connected with objectives by being specifically oriented toward their attainment, it is expected that similar procedure indicates similar objectives. Are the objectives of the two disciplines, then, the same? They are—up to the fourth level of procedure, the level of cultural integration and synthesis. Beyond this they are not. Here, finally, they diverge. Here lies the difference between them. The manner in which they diverge will be elaborated below, and by this means it will be possible first to define cultural anthropology and then to show the interrelation between cultural anthropology and historiography.

The concept of culture has been the greatest contribution which the discipline of cultural anthropology has made to the cooperative project of the Study of Man.[54] Ever since the time when cultural anthropology was first formalized into a discipline around the concept of evolution, its major interest has been the elucidation of the nature, the processes, and the development of culture. In fact, Teggart has very rightly pointed out in his provocative discussion of the theory of historiography (1925, p. 122) that the early, evolutionist anthropologists continuing the line of comparative method stemming from Descartes through Comte and Spencer to Tylor, turned to the new concept of culture so wholeheartedly as to neglect, by failing to reach, the vitally important level of context. Their belief in parallelism led them, in their fashion, through the first three levels of procedure: problem, data, and chronology. But it also induced them to stop there in order to investigate individual elements of culture in so far as these reflected the current evolutionary ideas.[55]

From its preoccupation with elements of culture and deductive "evolutionary" chronology, anthropology was rescued by Franz Boas. Lowie has described Boas's contribution in the following manner:

Boas, with a keen sense for differences and for the complexity of social life, was able to distinguish like and unlike features. He insisted that before equating phenomena we must first be sure of their comparability, which could be determined only from their context. (1937, p. 144)

In other words, he demonstrated the necessity of the fourth level of procedure. But it is also apparent that he advocated this extension of procedure for the purpose of getting a better perspective and a better understanding of culture itself. In short, the level of synthesis was sought and demanded by Boas as a means to an end; and, just as with the evolutionists, that end was an understanding of the nature, the processes, and the development of culture. Thus, after establishing the need for a fourth level of procedure, Boas went on to use this as a stepping stone to a fifth level, one of the study of the nature of culture, of cultural constants, of processes, of regularities, and of chronological development.

The immediate results of the historical method are, therefore, histories of the cultures of diverse tribes which have been the subject of study. I fully agree with those anthropologists who claim that this is not the ultimate aim of our science, because the general laws, although implied in such a description, cannot be clearly formulated nor their relative value appreciated without a thorough comparison of the manner in which they become manifest in different cultures. But I insist that the application of this method is the indispensable condition of sound progress. The psychological problem is contained in the results of the historical inquiry. When we have cleared up the history of a single culture and understand the effects of environment and the psychological conditions that are reflected in it we have made a step forward, as we can then investigate in how far the same causes or other causes were at work in the development of other cultures. Thus by comparing histories of growth general laws may be found. (Boas, 1896, ed. 1940, pp. 278-279)

Although Boas later qualified his views on "laws," his interest in process and culture itself appears to have remained undimmed.[56] Once more culture as such was the ultimate in anthropological procedure, but this time on a sound rather than on an insecure basis.

But the purpose of Boas's insistence upon the fourth level, i.e., as a means to the attainment of the fifth and important level, was evidently misunderstood by not a few anthropologists. His strictures on the necessity of cultural contexts and against schematic and tenuous "reconstructions" and "laws" seemed to divert attention from culture *per se* and to concentrate anthropological energy upon collecting data, interrelating them, and synthesizing them into accounts of particular cultural entities. This and the need to gather the "primitive" rosebuds while they might, developed among the anthropologists a certain disregard for the problems of culture and of cultural processes toward which cultural anthropology had been oriented from Tylor to Boas. More recently, due to the influence of such men as Sapir, Malinowski, Radcliffe-Brown, and to what might be called an active resurgence of the original Boasian interest in culture itself, the study of the nature, the processes, and the development of culture has resumed its primacy in much of anthropological thinking. The analysis and synthesis of particular entities has become, as Boas apparently intended it to become, a means to the end of a better understanding of culture, its statics and dynamics, its form and functioning, and its "history."[57]

If the above abbreviated account of the growth and concerns of cultural anthropology is correct, it will now be possible to define that discipline in terms of its accomplishments and interests. In brief, cultural anthropology is the *comparative study of the statics and dynamics of culture, its formal, functional, and developmental aspects.* In contradistinction to sociology, economics, political science, art, etc., which also study culture, but specific segments of culture, and which have limited themselves, with few exceptions, to the modern period and to Western European civilization,[58] cultural anthropology studies culture wherever and whenever found, restricting itself to no special segment but considering the totality as its potential field of research.

It is often alleged that there is a difference between cultural anthropology and historiography on the basis of the literacy and cultural "primitiveness" of their respective subject matter. Hulme, a historian, says:

Anthropology, then, deals with the life of man before history takes up the subject. . . . [history] begins at the point where the individual can be clearly seen and his doings recorded. . . . (1942, p. 147)

Anthropologists also follow this line:

The so called "primitive" societies which Anthropologists have made their special field of investigation. . . . (Linton, 1945a, p. xvi)

Anthropology is, literally, the science of man. . . . its distinctive field, which is entered only incidentally by other disciplines, is the realm of preliterate cultures. (Wallis, 1937, p. 92)

And finally Robinson, the champion of the New History, speaks of

. . . those investigators—namely, the anthropologists—who deal with the habits, customs, institutions, languages, and beliefs of primitive man. . . . (1912, p. 89)[59]

It is a fact that cultural anthropologists have in practice confined themselves pretty well to the study of such peoples. And therefore, it may be perfectly true that its "special field of investigation" is the so-called primitive. But it would appear that this preoccupation is the result of historical accident and does not comprise the fundamental interest of the discipline. As Leslie Spier has often said: "Anthropology doesn't mean Indians," and it doesn't merely mean "primitives" of any sort. It was mentioned in the first chapter above that the concern of the cultural anthropologists with the "primitive" is traceable to the presuppositions of the early evolutionists. This trend was further strengthened through the influence from the comparative sociology of Comte and Spencer: Western European culture was taken to be uniform to all intents and purposes, and anthropology, therefore, in its trend toward comparative study, turned to non-European cultures, which, to Europeans, were "primitive." In recent years, other reasons have been offered for the study of "primitives": their culture is simpler and thus more understandable; ideally it is free of European influence and hence represents the independent diversity necessary for proper comparison; more objectivity is possible when dealing with cultures other than one's own, etc.[60] Whatever the reasons and whatever their validity, it remained that the cultural anthropologists have stuck pretty close to "primitive" man.

But when clear thinking has been done on this topic, this preoccupation has been viewed purely as a means to an end. One can hardly overlook the fact that the early evolutionists were interested primarily in culture. As long ago as 1896, Brinton disavowed the narrow scope of ethnology (1896a, p. 7) and in 1917 Lowie said:

For purely practical reasons, connected with the minute subdivision of labor which has become imperative with modern specialization, ethnology has in practice concerned itself with the cultures of the cruder peoples without a knowledge of writing. But this division is an illogical and artificial one. As the biologist can study life as manifested in the human organism as well as in the amoeba, so the ethnologist might examine and describe the usages of modern America as well as those of the Hopi Indians. (p. 6)

His later reiteration of this point (1936a, p. 301) and Kroeber's blunt statement that "anthropology has never accepted the adjudication sometimes tacitly rendered that its proper field is the primitive" (1923, p. 6) are evidence enough that it was not "primitives" themselves that interested the anthropologists.

Furthermore, neither cultural anthropology nor historiography has preserved inviolate this alleged boundary between them. Literate cultures, such as the Maya priesthood, Arab, and West African, have been reported upon in anthropological journals by avowed anthropologists; while illiterate and non-literate cultures, such as the Kentucky mountaineers and the African Zulu, have been the subject matter for much writing by avowed historians. And today in the United States, the foundation of a Society for Applied Anthropology, the use of cultural anthropologists by the United State Government in its resettlement and food programs and its Japanese relocation program during the late war, the strong influence of the Lynds and Lloyd Warner, are but examples of the vigorous trend toward the study of our own, hardly "primitive," and quite literate culture by avowed anthropologists using anthropological methods.[61]

Thus for a long time on inherent grounds, and more recently and growing in practice, there has been a feeling that it is a false dichotomy that separates cultural anthropology from historiography on the basis of non-literacy and so-called primitiveness of subject matter. It seems, therefore, that there is nothing inherent in either discipline to prevent it from dealing with the totality of past actuality, literate or not, "primitive" or otherwise. This does not mean, however, that either can compass this totality or that either one or the other, or both, can claim to be *the* discipline which alone is operating in this field. Rather it should be understood that there is a common pool of source material from which they both may draw, with which they both have the potentiality of dealing, from which both may abstract any material which suits their special purposes. It is, therefore, in these special purposes that the differences between the two disciplines lie. The purpose of historiography has been shown to be the construction of cultural contexts, while that of cultural anthropology is the comparative study of the nature and workings of culture.

In conclusion, it may be of advantage to point out specifically the manner in which these definitions interpret the activities of cultural anthropologists and historians. It is apparent that historiography is basic to cultural anthropology.[62] In order to "do" the latter, it is necessary to have done, or to have available, the former. The contexts have to be constructed before a comparative study of culture and the history of culture may be begun. Following this reasoning, it develops that the operation which is called ethnography is really a branch of historiography and not of anthropology. The confusion that has arisen from anthropology's preoccupation with "primitives" has resulted in an erroneous separation of what really are two phases of a single operation: non-literate and "primitive" historiography on the one hand, and literate and "advanced" historiography on the other. It has obscured the real difference, the one between a major concern for the construction of cultural contexts and a major concern with culture itself. Only so far as the student makes use of his cultural context for the purpose of deriving and comparing cultural abstractions, does he "do" anthropology in the present sense. If he stops his investigations at the fourth level of procedure with his context, he is not doing anthropology but historiography—whether his subject matter is 18th century England, Blackfoot Indians, or an industrial community in Indiana.

This implies another point which should be cleared up here. It can be shown that historians have, of recent years, attempted to derive cultural regularities or so-called laws from their data.[63] Men who call themselves historians have as good a prerogative to make such derivations as any other men calling themselves what they will. This fact, however, does not negate the contention that in doing so these historians are not "doing" historiography. When historians utilize their material to study culture itself, they are "doing" cultural anthropology or sociology or economics, or philosophy of history if their schemes embrace large enough segments. Or rather, they are doing what the anthropologists, the sociologists, the economic theorists, or the philosophers have been doing since they crystallized their activities into disciplines.[64]

The relations between historiography and cultural anthropology are complementary: each uses the findings and methods of the other, but to attain each their special objective. Mandelbaum has expressed this idea:

However, the formulation of such principles [historical principles corresponding to scientific laws] is not the goal toward which the historian, as historian, strives; on the contrary, these principles serve merely as working hypotheses in concrete descriptive analysis. It is here that the difference between history and theoretical social science emerges. . . . History, as we have shown, depends for the furtherance of its analysis upon principles which only sociology and other theoretical social sciences can disclose; sociology depends upon historical investigation for the material upon which it works, examining and comparing historical instances in order to disclose the laws which may be implicit within them. (1938, pp. 264-265)[65]

If the definitions of the present study are accepted, the term *cultural anthropology* may be substituted for sociology in the quoted passage without loss of meaning. In short, it seems that the historian studies the nature and workings of culture itself as a means to the end of better understanding his unique events and thus of better constructing his contexts or cultural pictures. The anthropologist constructs historical contexts as the means to the end of deriving sound cultural abstractions which will further his study of culture itself.

Having come to some conclusions with regard to cultural anthropology and historiography, we may now turn back to the original problem: what is the position of archeology in relation to these two concepts? How is archeology related to anthropology and history thus defined?

To start with, it seems justifiable to state as axiomatic, (1) that archeology deals with past actuality and sequential time; (2) that although it may produce data on human biology, its interests lie in man as a cultural being; and (3) that it is one of the nonexperimental, so-called historical disciplines. From this last axiom it follows that archeology also employs the same procedure which, it has been stated, is typical of all such disciplines. Thus, ideally at least, it proceeds from problem, to data, to chronology, to the integration and synthesis of these data into a context, in this instance a cultural context.

Here, then, is the relation of archeology to historiography: to the extent that archeological research attains the fourth level of procedure it is to be considered historiography. The fact that the archeologist works, for the most part, in what Holmes called the "nonintentional or fortuituous records" rather than in the "intentional or purposeful records" (1919, p. 1) is no grounds for altering the designation of his results. At most, there is a difference in the method and techniques required to handle the "unintentional records." Both historiography and archeology have the same procedure, and at the fourth level, both have reached the same end point. Both may be called "antiquarian" so long as they do no more than secure isolated and unrelated information. Both may be termed "chronicle" so long as they merely obtain cultural data in chronological sequence. Both become historiography, no more and no less, when they interrelate and integrate their cultural information into cultural pictures or contexts. One may "do" historiography by interpreting the written record (archives, letters, cuneiform tablets, Maya hieroglyphs, inscriptions on seals and coins and monuments), by interpreting the oral record (informants of non-literate or illiterate peoples, oral tradition of literate peoples), or by interpreting "non-verbal documents" (stone axes, Greek temples, Toltec pyramids, Hohokam pottery, Magdalenian cave art). The important fact is that the moment cultural data are synthesized into a context representing past actuality, the result is historiography.

Archeology's relation to anthropology may be understood after the same fashion. When the archeologist collects his data, constructs his cultural contexts, and on the basis of these contexts proceeds to make a comparative study of the nature and workings of culture in its formal, functional, and/or developmental aspects, then he is "doing" cultural anthropology and can be considered an anthropologist who works in archeological materials. The fact that his subject matter is American Indians or non-literate Britons does not, of itself, make his work anthropological. Nor does the fact that he uncovers and studies written inscriptions make his work non-anthropological. The critical test is what the archeologist does with his discoveries, not his subject matter.

Archeology *per se* is no more than a method and a set of specialized techniques for the gathering of cultural information. The archeologist, as archeologist, is really nothing but a technician. When he uses his findings to study architecture, he must employ the concepts developed in that field, and when he studies culture, he must use the theoretical structure erected by those who have made it their business to study culture, namely, the anthropologists. Therefore, archeology is not to be equated either with ethnography which is the writing of cultural contexts, or with ethnology which is the comparative study of cultural phenomena. It is on a lower level of procedure and ceases to be merely archeology when it utilizes the concepts of other disciplines such as ethnology, art, mythology, ceramics, architecture.

There are archeologists whose training and interests lie in the classics, in Semitic philology, in Oriental history, in ethnology, and in potentially an innumerable number of subjects. There are also competent archeologists who have had no specialized academic training, even no "higher" education at all. And these are often among the most capable. While it is probably true that the man with the broadest background of specialized training will obtain the better information, yet it is often the case that the non-academic "field man" with broad practical experience and less formal training will produce the better data. In either instance, it is the gathering of the cultural materials that is the touchstone by which the archeologist, as archeologist, stands or falls. How he handles the information after its collection is impertinent to him as an archeologist, although it is very pertinent to him as anthropologist, art historian, philologist, or whatever.

Here, then, is the answer to the query which titles this chapter: archeology is neither history nor anthropology. As an autonomous discipline, it consists of a method and a set of specialized techniques for the gathering or "production" of cultural information.

CHAPTER 3

AN ANALYSIS OF AMERICANIST ARCHEOLOGY IN THE
UNITED STATES

HAVING established a critical standard, it will now be possible to examine critically the character of Americanist archeology in the United States. In a later chapter, this will be done by implication through the advocacy of a particular and somewhat different approach to archeological problems and materials. Here, however, the task will be to analyze what the archeologists say they have been doing and what they have actually done, and then to see how these two bodies of fact compare. This will be accomplished explicitly, by reference to the published writings of particular archeologists and in terms of the definitions arrived at in the preceding chapter.

It is not to be thought that, in the following pages, the men selected for analysis are being criticized on a personal basis. Both the analysis and criticism will be of published results. It is realized that many times the archeologist may wish to include in his reports certain data or certain treatment of data but is prevented from doing so because of publication or other restrictions. In such cases, the vision and intentions of the archeologist may not be criticized, or perhaps may not even be known. The only fair criterion for judging Americanist archeology is, therefore, the extent to which the final results of empirical research measure up, or do not measure up, to the aims stated or implied by the various researchers themselves. If the results do measure up, it is probably safe to give the archeologist credit. On the other hand, if they do not measure up, the placing of blame is an unimportant detail for the present study. It will be sufficient to have shown that the archeological reports do not come up to the expectations claimed for them.

Thus, the men will be examined and criticized as representatives of the traditions, the aims, and the methods which have been recognized as the best in Americanist archeology in the United States. The choice of those who are to be analyzed will in no way be a measure of central tendency. It will be consciously weighted toward men whose influence in academic and professional circles has been of the highest. Furthermore, selection will lean toward men whose direct and most intensive influence is contemporary rather than of an earlier time. But even within these limits, it will be impossible to include all the influential archeologists of what might be considered the contemporary period. Some influential men, J. A. Ford, for example, have not published enough to provide a fair basis for analysis; others, such as H. B. Collins, Jr., while authorities in their fields, have been omitted because their influence is restricted. But complete coverage is hardly necessary for the present study. After the writings of certain men have

been examined, the critical findings will be found to fit, with but minor accommo-
dations, the work of the majority of Americanists, most of whom employ more
or less patterned variants of a single approach and are concerned with more or
less the same range of data.

The influence of A. V. Kidder upon archeological research in the Americas has
been, and is now, of the greatest proportions. It is not too much to suggest that
he is the most influential exponent of the discipline active in the Western
Hemisphere today. It was his vigorous and enlightened prosecution of the trend
initiated by himself, Nelson, and Spier,[66] which brought Southwestern archeology
out of its Cushing-Fewkes stage and to the lines of investigation which have
been but broadened and intensified in the succeeding years. It was his re-orienta-
tion of the Carnegie Institution's Maya program that has set those researches
upon their way toward a sound chronology and a knowledge of cultural relations throughout much of Middle America. It has been his influence upon both
these fields of archeology which has developed the broad foundation of their
research programs and served as a guide for most of the subsequent investigations in the regions.

While specifically an archeologist, Kidder has maintained his broader affiliations predominantly with the discipline of cultural anthropology. Although his
Chairmanship of the Division of Historical Research of the Carnegie Institution
might seem to controvert the last statement, it can be demonstrated that over
the years he has been associated overwhelmingly with cultural anthropology,
both academically, professionally, and with respect to learned societies.[67]
From this it would seem legitimate to impute anthropological aims, or at least
some variation thereof, to his researches. In his own words, Kidder has proclaimed archeology to be "that branch of anthropology which deals with prehistoric peoples" (Kidder and Thompson, 1938, p. 494) and has called the
archeologist "the mouldier variety of anthropologist" (1940a, p. 527). He has
also identified the aims of the two disciplines:

Together with and closely allied to acceptance of dogma comes failure to grasp the
bearings of our researches upon those broader problems of anthropology whose solution
should be the final aim of all our studies. (1937b, p. viii)

At the same time, in his writings upon general and theoretical archeological
topics, he has consistently held to the point of view that archeology is "doing"
history:

We must not, of course, lose sight of our ultimate historical goal. . . . And this we can
most effectively accomplish by grasping the fact that archaeology, because of the nature
of the materials spared to us by the hand of time, must, in the first instance, be a study,
not of history in the commonly accepted sense of that word but of the history of
material culture. There we can be on solid ground. (1942, p. iii)

Archaeology, rightly conceived, is a historical discipline. Its primary task is to re-construct man's career through the uncounted centuries of his preliterate, undocumented past. (1937c, p. 160)

In designating the group engaged in studies of the pre-Columbian career of the American Indians, the term history has been used as symbolic of a desire to do away with the somewhat rigid distinction which has generally been drawn between archaeology and history. The work of the Section [of Early American History, Division of Historical Research, Carnegie Institution] is, of course, archaeological in that it deals with material remains rather than with written records. But archaeologists seek to gather from ruined buildings and potsherds the same sort of knowledge that historians derive from books and manuscripts, and while the subject matter and, therefore, the primary methods of the two disciplines are naturally unlike, their ultimate aims are identical, for both archeology and history strive to recover and to interpret the story of man's past. (1930a, p. 91)[68]

Kidder, however, unlike most other Americanists, has provided a resolution for this anthropology-history ambivalence. This way out is neither clearly marked nor a point of frequent reference in his writings; in fact, its only explicit statement is pretty well hidden from the general archeological public, being found in an obscure typewritten progress-report filed in the library of the Peabody Museum of Harvard:

It should be emphasized, I think, that the sort of [archeological] work the Museum is doing on the Mimbres is not merely the accumulation of curious information about an extinct tribe, nor solely the collection of handsome exhibits for the Museum's cases. It is much more than these, for it constitutes a definite contribution to one of the most important problems of anthropology. . . . Anthropology seeks to reconstruct the history of man, of his works, of his bodily structure, and of his mind, in order that there may be deduced from a study of that history, the basic laws which have governed in the past, and which therefore may be expected to control in the future, the destinies of the human race. (1926, pp. 1, 2)

While there are no other such direct statements, Kidder has implied what is virtually the same thing in several other papers.[69] In the light of the definitions arrived at in the preceding chapter of this study, these views expressed by Kidder are some of the most pertinent and significant comments that have appeared in the literature of Americanist archeology. Here, both archeology and anthropology are said to be doing historiography for the purpose of aiding further, more specialized research. But the next question which arises is: How do these statements conform to the actual contributions which Kidder has made through his field work and through the field work of those under his direction?

The answer is that there is little or no conformity. To date, no cultural synthesis, no picture of the life of any site or any group of sites, has come from his pen. Nor has he used his empirical data to analyze or discuss specifically and in detail any cultural process, regularity, "law," or so-called non-material aspect. He has "done" neither historiography nor cultural anthropology.

His nearest approach to these accomplishments has been his discussion of the pottery of Pecos in the light of Shepard's findings (Kidder, 1936b). But even here the tone is not so much one of analyzing and presenting the nature and the changes of the ceramic complex of a people, as it is one of investigating the significance of certain ceramic evidence for the relationship of Pecos as a site to other particular sites in the vicinity, chronologically and in respect to culture-influences. The discussion seems primarily comparative rather than an exposition of the ceramic complex, its position and significance within the total culture of Pecos pueblo. Not that Kidder is unaware of the latter possibilities, for he asks some very pointed questions as to the nature of the ceramic complex: for example, the question of the relations between pictography, ceramic decoration, and the ornamentation of ceremonial objects (p. 626). But these problems are merely stated, and the failure to pursue them is credited to lack of time. If such problems had been attacked with regard to the nature and interrelations of pottery within Pecos itself, Kidder would have been "doing" historiography, at least of the ceramic complex. If he had then proceeded to compare his findings with similar findings from other sites or areas with the intent of abstracting the regularities between the two sets of (ceramic) data, he would have been "doing" cultural anthropology. As the matter now stands, he has done neither.

Other than this, Kidder has not even approached the construction of a cultural synthesis of Pecos pueblo. He has not brought his raw data together in any cultural sense, much less painted a cultural picture. We know roughly the broad outlines of the growth of the pueblo, but for all the superposition and sequent construction mentioned in his reports (Kidder, 1924, pp. 16-32) there is no analysis or presentation of the details of that growth or of the cultural objects found associated with its various phases. For all the descriptive detail in *The Artifacts of Pecos* (1932a) and despite the establishment of several periods of ceramic art (1936b), *there is neither any provenience given for the vast majority of artifacts nor any consistent correlation of these specimens with the ceramic periods.* The description of the artifacts seems to be for its own sake and for the sake of comparative study on a purely descriptive level with similar artifacts from other sites. It may well be asked whether the meaning of the artifacts for the culture of Pecos is thought to lie in their form and classification of form, or whether it lies in their relations to one another and to the broad cultural and natural environment of Pecos.[70] If it is true, as Kidder says (1932a, p. 12), that provenience "would be of interest to a very limited number of persons," then this is the most damning criticism of Americanist archeology that has appeared in print to date!

The influence of Kidder and Guernsey's *Archaeological Explorations in Northeastern Arizona* (1919) has, I believe, been second to none in the development of Southwestern archeology. For this reason and because there is a rather widely held idea that Basket-Maker II "is certainly well understood" (McGregor, 1941, p. 207), this and his other Marsh Pass report (Guernsey and Kidder, 1921) must be considered here, although they were written many years ago upon work done at an even earlier time. An additional reason for consideration is that, other than these and his Pecos publications, Kidder has nowhere to date published a detailed site-report.

The Marsh Pass reports make two vitally important contributions to the field of Southwestern archeology: they once and for all established the chronological priority of the Basket-Maker over the Cliff-Dweller materials, and they provided a body of clear and pioneering descriptive data. Beyond this, however, they do not go. Even taking into account the work of Nusbaum, Prudden, and Pepper, it is impossible to agree that Basket-Maker II is "well-understood." Except for detailed descriptive knowledge of a range of artifact types and some apparently correct and very sagacious interpretation of use, we know very little about Basket-Maker II from the papers of Kidder and Guernsey, or from any source.

For example, on the one hand we have Guernsey and Kidder's word that the Marsh Pass caves were occupied sporadically if at all and were probably used more for storage and burial than as dwellings (1921, p. 110). On the other hand, there is considerable evidence, in the reports themselves, of habitation features such as thick ash beds, floors, layers of grass, smoked roofs, and other cultural refuse (1921, pp. 30-31; 1919, pp. 27, 31, 75-77, 86). Whatever may be the actual case, it is impossible to reconcile these apparent contradictions by appeal to the publications, since excavation procedure and the details of the deposits have not been reported. At the present time, we do not know, and cannot know without further excavation, even such an important cultural fact as whether the Basket-Maker people used the Marsh Pass caves as habitation sites or not.

Nor do we know much of the cultural objects beyond descriptions of certain selected artifacts. We know that the Basket-Makers made twined woven bags, and we know the weaves of some of the individual bags. But we do not know the weaves of all bags, nor which weave was the most common, nor the quantity of twined bags in relation to, say, coiled basketry, other textiles, or other containers. This is because no account was taken of fragmentary specimens or "rags," and there is no quantitative summary of bags, textiles, or containers. Nor is it possible for the reader to make such an enumeration from the data given in the reports. No information is given on the proportions within the several descriptive categories that do show variation: for instance, on the ratio of the several sandal types, or of the different kinds of sandal ties, or of the number of decorated sandals in relation to the number of decorated baskets. Above all there is little information on the provenience of the majority of objects, except as to the cave from which they came. Even this site-provenience, in a great many cases, must be extracted from the tables explaining the illustrations and cannot be obtained from the text.

There is no analysis of the association of object with object; contents of cists are listed, but it is often impossible to identify the finds of a particular cist with the descriptions of specimens given later in the report. There is no analysis of cultural categories, such as the textile industry: its materials, its methods, its products, and its quantitative and aesthetic position within the cultural whole of the site or area. In other words, there is no summation, no bringing together, no synthesis, of the wealth of descriptive material. As at Pecos, description seems to have been an end in itself and has been used almost wholly for the purposes of comparison with other descriptive material. No picture of the culture has been constructed from even those data that are at hand.

It is apparent, therefore, that these reports have attained, but not fully, the level of data; have attained the level of chronicle with respect to the separation of Basket-Maker from Cliff-Dweller data; but have attained neither the level of historiography nor that of cultural anthropology. Once more, however, I would like to point out that this is not a criticism of the authors of the reports, to whom allowances can be made for a pioneer effort. It is, rather, to point out that these reports do not constitute, at the present date, an acceptable basis for constructing a picture of Basket-Maker culture.

The archeological work of the Carnegie Institution of Washington, which has been under Kidder's direction since 1927, is seen to fall into the same pattern. Although in his capacity as Chairman of the Division of Historical Research he has many times proclaimed that archeology, especially Maya archeology, aims at "reconstructing" history, it is a fact that no history, at least in the sense defined above as *historiography,* has come from Carnegie's work in the Maya field, either under Kidder's direction or before. This work has been recently and, in my opinion, justly criticized from the standpoint of theory (Kluckhohn, 1940). In the present study, however, the task will be to inquire into the field work and publications accomplished under Kidder's direction and to see how these results compare with Kidder's stated aims.

Individual reports of the members of the staff will be dealt with only by way of example. It is the over-all program and its results, together with his own publications, that will best and most fairly reflect Kidder's influence upon Carnegie's archeological research. The papers dealing with the Temple of the Warriors and with Cobá will not be included because, although they appeared during Kidder's Chairmanship, they had been started and nearly completed before he came into full charge.

In the following crude, but nevertheless adequate, classification of Carnegie publications, only those works are included which deal with Maya archeology.[71]

DESCRIPTIVE	MAJOR WORKS	MINOR WORKS	TOTALS
Reconnaissance and brief excavation	7	5	12
Site reports	3	0	3
Ceramics	1	7	8
Artifacts	5	14	19
Buildings	7	0	7
Topical synthesis	1	0	1
			—
			50
EPIGRAPHY, CALENDAR, AND CHRONOLOGY	5	16	21
			—
			21
INTERPRETIVE			
Religion	1	2	3
Cultural inferences	4	0	4
Topical synthesis	0	1	1
			—
			8
			—
			79

It is immediately apparent from the table that Carnegie's publications under Kidder have been overwhelmingly descriptive. Even within the category of *Epigraphy,* there are a great number of papers which are primarily, if not wholly descriptive. Out of a total of seventy-nine papers, there are only eight which are specifically designed to interpret, in a cultural sense, the mass of descriptive data collected by the Institution's field workers. Seven of these eight papers are by Thompson; and of these, six deal with religion and associated epigraphy (1934a and b, 1939b, 1942b and c, 1943) and one deals with tobacco (1946). In other words, we have Roy's paper on *The Engineering Knowledge of the Maya* (1934) and Thompson's paper on tobacco, as the only contributions of the Carnegie Institution toward an interpretation of the non-hierarchal culture of the ancient Maya, and even here it is probable that engineering, if not tobacco, was characteristic of the hierarchal rather than the common Maya.

Apart from these few papers, we have descriptions, with now and then a sentence or paragraph interpreting the use of individual artifacts or buildings or assigning some class of objects to some cultural category, again mostly religious or at least calendrical. Pollock's publication on the round structures (1936b) is not primarily an interpretive, but rather a descriptive synthesis, and will be discussed later. We have descriptions of Maya artifacts, of Maya buildings, of Maya epigraphy together with comparative data designed to determine their derivation or inspiration and their chronological position relative to other material from other parts of middle America. But we have no discussions of the place of all these objects within Maya culture, or even within the culture of any one site or part of one site. For example, we have many detailed descriptions of hierarchal buildings and many maps of Maya cities. But except for Ricketson's work in the plaza of Group E at Uaxactun (1937), we have no detailed studies of the growth and integration of Maya cities or their constituent parts. Reports on the sites intensively excavated, such as Chichen Itza and Uaxactun and Copan, do not give the details of interrelationship between plaza floors, separate buildings, stelae, or other objects. In the sites visited during reconnaissance little excavation seems to have been done, the major interest apparently lying in epigraphy, mapping of the city plan, hierarchal architecture, and in collection of potsherds by occasional test-trenching. Obviously, it is not the cultural pictures of the various sites, but their comparative materials, which have been sought, and if it were not for the writings of Bishop Landa and other documentary sources our knowledge of pre-Columbian Maya culture would be meager indeed, despite over thirty years of work.

For example, what do we know of the houses of the ancient Maya? Of the hierarchal buildings we have many descriptions, but these have so far produced little insight into the lives even of the Maya hierarchy and none into the lives of the presumed majority of Maya population. Many Carnegie archeologists have becried the lack of excavation in house or domiciliary mounds which Ricketson has said "occur in every part of the [Yucatan] peninsula which has been investigated" (1937, p. 15). But their literary tears remind us of those shed by the Walrus and the Carpenter: most copious but accomplishing little to remedy the situation. As early as 1934, Kidder said:

For example, we know next to nothing as to what Maya "cities" really were. . . . Excavations are needed in the inconspicuous little mounds so abundant at Chichen Itza, which presumably cover whatever is left of the domestic structure. (p. 93)

But as the matter stands today, we have a single report on four house mounds and part of a fifth excavated in 1932 by Wauchope at Uaxactun (Wauchope, 1934). This work occupied seven weeks and constitutes our only Carnegie publication on ancient Maya dwelling houses, despite the fact that Ricketson found no less than seventy-eight in 0.3 square miles of habitable land near Uaxactun (1937, p. 16). Wauchope makes a very urgent plea for more such work and gives the names of other archeologists who at earlier times had pointed to the same need (1934, p. 113). Yet four years later, he still finds it necessary to give considerable space to the same plea (1938, pp. 146-153). At Benque Viejo, Thompson chose to excavate in an area thought to contain residential mounds. But his purpose, as stated (1942a, p. 2), was to obtain sherds which he reasoned would be more abundant in such an area. Although he gives some details of "constructional activities," he fails to give an analysis of whether the mounds actually were residential or not. It is quite obvious from the report that his interest in the Benque Viejo mounds was in their production of pottery which could be used for comparative purposes. The mounds as vestiges of former Maya dwellings and as sources of cultural information of a domestic and plebian sort appear to have intrigued him little, if at all.

What do we know of the food habits of the ancient Maya? Gleanings from the Carnegie Institution Year Book tell us of excavations in refuse deposits conducted by Roberts, Brainerd, and before Kidder's time by Vaillant at Chichen.[72] But we have no published results of these operations. Trik found 50-60 centimeters of black refuse at one place in Temple XXII at Copan (1939, p. 103). This deposit contained many sherds, animal bones, obsidian flakes. In another place in this same ruin, an entire floor was covered with a thin layer of ash refuse with sherds, several bone tools, burned stones. But Trik grants only two short paragraphs to these finds and fails to list, quantify, describe, or identify any of the contained materials. He says that the ruin was selected for excavation because it contains "one of the finest compositions of architectural sculpture known in the Maya area" (p. 87). He is apparently not interested in the associated cultural material of a less artistic type. In Ricketson's report on Group E at Uaxactun (1937, pp. 204-205), there is mention made of refuse and a list of the animal species found. But the implications of these finds for the subsistence of the Maya are not developed. There are no quantitative data given; nor is anything said as to signs of fracture, cutting, cooking, or general use; nor is the age or edibility of the individuals or species discussed. What we have in this instance is mere biological identification and no cultural information. Such data may be of use to a biologist but are hardly usable by one who would wish to approach cultural problems. Smith and Kidder have said that

. . . even in the refuse deposits and domiciliary mounds that have been dug, surprisingly few implements and weapons have come to light. (1943, p. 162)

But what is even more surprising in view of Kidder's contention that he is attempting to "reconstruct" Maya culture history is the scarcity of reports upon even those deposits which have been dug. Since the nature of the information which has appeared in print about excavated refuse is such as to be virtually useless for attack on cultural problems, we are left to assume that other aspects of the research program are more important and more rewarding of publication, so that as a result they have been published instead of data on food refuse and other cultural detritus.

What do we know of the costumes of Maya ceremonial personages? There is a chapter on *Representations of Dress, Ornaments and Accoutrements* in

Ricketson's report on Group E at Uaxactun (1937, Chap. V). But the description is typological, i.e., examples of feathered and other types of headdresses are described, as well as examples of robes and sandals, etc. But quantitative data are given only incidentally, and we are not able to know which type is most prevalent. Nor are we able to know which type of sandal, for instance, is found with which type of headdress or what type of accoutrement is found in what sort of depiction upon what sort of monument. In other words, the descriptions given by Ricketson, being atomized and not synthesized, cannot be used to "reconstruct" the habiliments of Maya personages or used to make inferences as to the role or cultural significance of the figures that wear them. The descriptions can be used only for comparing the representations of headdress and sandals at Uaxactun with similar representations at other sites.

What do we know of the pottery of the ancient Maya? Here again the Carnegie archeologists have becried the inadequacy of investigation but have done little publication to remedy the situation. In 1932, A. L. Smith said that ceramic studies in the Maya area were handicapped by a paucity of specimens and the rarity of any specimens whose exact provenience and stratigraphic relations were known (p. 3). In 1935, Kidder said that "our present knowledge of Maya ceramics is almost exclusively based on fine mortuary vessels" (1935a, p. 119). In 1939, Thompson speaks of the "abysmal ignorance of ceramic history throughout almost the entire area" (1939a, p. 7). And in 1943, Andrews said:

Perhaps one of the greatest barriers in the way of an understanding of the general perspectives of Maya history has been a really blissful ignorance of the ceramics of the Yucatan Peninsula. (p. 62)

Thus, from some of the earliest to some of the latest of Carnegie's publications under Kidder's direction, we hear the same cry. And when we remember the major role which ceramic studies have played in the development of archeology in other areas of the Americas and abroad, and particularly when we recognize the growth and value of ceramic knowledge in such regions as the American Southwest and the Mississippi Valley within the same period from 1927 to the present, any comparison with Carnegie's work in the Maya area is prejudicial to the latter institution's program.

It has long since been recognized in areas where pottery has helped in developing a chronology and a series of cultural relationships, that descriptions must be detailed and standardized in order to be usable. Yet Carnegie's descriptions of pottery are meager, superficial, and far from consistent in the aspects covered or in amount of detail. In fact we find Thompson as late as 1942, writing for a professional audience and saying:

Maya pottery reveals such diversity of form, and so few descriptions of material other than the more grandiose mortuary types exist, that the task of combining an adequate enumeration of types with a due regard to cost of publication and *the necessity of not burdening the reader with too many pages of description* presents a serious problem. (1942a, p. 4, italics mine)

To anyone fully aware of the value of ceramic studies and equally aware of the requirements of comparative study, the real need would seem to call for a fuller and more regularized description rather than an apologetic effort to produce the reverse.

But if the descriptions are inadequate for satisfactory comparative studies, it still remains that the Carnegie archeologists are primarily interested in this very comparative study and not in the ceramic complex *per se*. They apparently are intent upon using pottery to establish cultural and temporal relations between sites. They are not intent upon developing and analyzing the pottery complex at a given site or in deriving, from a study of such pottery, any inferences as to the nature of the particular cultural expression or of Maya culture as a whole. There are many examples to support this contention.

One of Kidder's first acts on becoming Chairman of the Division was to inaugurate a combined pottery-architecture study (Kidder, 1939, p. 238). This was for the express purpose of placing the respective types in proper chronological sequence and of supplementing the epigraphic chronology (Kidder, 1930a, p. 101). A. L. Smith seems to be offering a vindication of Carnegie's concern with the fine, mortuary ceramics when he observes that the utility wares are conservative and show local and temporal variations only in subtle technological differences, while the fine wares, on the other hand, reflect the individual maker, vary more, and hence are more reliable criteria for "regional and chronological" classification (1932, p. 3). At a later date, we have the statement of Kidder and Shepard:

We have described these specimens in detail because, as has been said, they exhibit the earliest known examples of the decorative use of stucco; also because preliminary study of stuccoed vessels from subsequent horizons at Kaminaljuyu and elsewhere in Mesoamerica indicates that various materials and techniques were employed and that these may prove to have *regional and chronological* significance. (1944, pp. 28-29, italics mine)

In his report on Structure A-1 at Uaxactun, Robert Smith says that the six complete mounds of the structure constitute the most perfect single medium yet discovered in the Maya area for the correlation of architecture, ceramics, and burial customs (1937, p. 226). But in the succeeding pages he fails to go into this correlation or to give information on the burials found, and he leaves the pottery to be treated in another, to date unpublished volume (p. 230). His conclusions are occupied with inferences as to chronology.

Thompson's use of pottery is likewise dominated by chronological and comparative considerations. His very approach to Benque Viejo was instigated by such concerns and his use of the pottery of San José was wholly "to fit San José into Maya history by comparisons with ceramic types already placed in sequence at other sites" (1939a, p. 7). How else can one explain the fact that at both the sites he worked only with rim and "significant" base sherds or kept only rim, bottom, and shoulder sherds unless some other fragment revealed "significant" form or decoration (1939a, p. 65; 1942a, p. 4)? Furthermore, other sherds apparently were not even counted, at least at San José. One may legitimately ask: what made those certain sherds "significant" and why, in the Maya area, is shape "of more importance than ware in classifying the common monochrome forms" (1942a, p. 4)? A glance at the reports themselves will return the answer: not for an understanding of the ceramic complex of the sites or of Maya ceramics as a whole, but for comparative studies on a regional and chronological basis with a view to establishing the relation of one site to another.

In Carnegie's publications on excavation or reconnaissance, rarely if ever are we provided with sherd percentages, the ratio of decorated to undecorated pottery, the relative amounts of the several pottery types within or around the several types of buildings, an analysis of the types and quantities of ceramic objects found with burials of varying categories such as age, sex, location, etc. As quoted above, Kidder and others have noted the incompleteness of our knowledge of Maya ceramics other than the mortuary wares. Yet despite this awareness, there has been no increase of publications covering the domestic wares, and this in the face of much field work and much publication in the architectural, religious, artifactual, and epigraphic realms. I am aware, of course, that Roberts and Brainerd have worked a great deal on ceramics and that Shepard has been doing ceramic technology; but I am equally aware that published results have been indicatively few and that other Carnegie archeologists have neglected ceramics, at least in publication if not in the field. Whatever the reasons behind this situation may be, the results are clear. Carnegie's publication list and the contents of its various papers indicate much less intensity of stimulation along ceramic lines than along other lines. If Kidder's direction had been vigorously oriented toward comprehensive and detailed ceramic studies, it seems highly probable that more published results would have appeared, and the ratio of ceramic to, say, architectural or epigraphic studies might have been more on a par. Our knowledge might now encompass more than merely mortuary ware, and we might know more about ceramics as a cultural complex. And all this would be in addition to comparative and chronological information which would hardly have been impaired by such further data.

Before taking up the final point in the analysis, I would like to mention four papers which go beyond mere description and contribute most substantially to our knowledge of Maya culture. I refer to Roys's *The Engineering Knowledge of the Maya* (1934) and three papers by Thompson, *Maya Chronology: the*

Fifteen Tun Glyph (1934a), *The Moon Goddess in Middle America* (1939b), and *Maya Arithmetic* (1942b). In his monograph, Roys says that he is writing

... to present facts which will allow us to picture the mental traits and trends which were responsible for the spectacular results which the student and the traveler now see in Yucatan and Guatemala. (p. 35)

And Thompson projects an idea along a similar vein when he says that "if we are ever to achieve a comprehensive reconstruction of Maya culture, we must have some insight into Maya mental processes" (1942b, p. 41). Earlier he had said that the bridge between our mentality and that of the Maya should be strengthened by making our translations of the glyphs follow as closely as possible those distinctions which were made by the Maya themselves (1934a, p. 253). Other than these few papers, it has remained for non-Carnegie archeologists to give us even our topical syntheses, for example Butler's work on dress and ornament (1931). Although Morris as early as 1931 said that "it would be of marked interest to know what units of measurement were employed" by the Maya in their architecture (p. 210), it remained for a non-Carnegie student actually to make a study of this problem (Cramer, 1938; *see also,* Blom, 1935). Tschopik analyzed and synthesized the weaves of textiles and textile patterns painted on Uloa Valley pottery (Ms., 1937), and Cresson attacked the problem of whether the Maya used sweat houses (1938). Such problems and approaches to problems have been left strictly alone by Carnegie, except for Thompson's brief note on *Some Uses of Tobacco among the Maya* (1946). Pollock's monograph on the *Round Structures of Middle America* (1936b) is descriptive, classificatory, and distributional. As a topical review, it is descriptive rather than interpretive or integrative. There is little which helps to fit these structures into the culture of their respective sites or into Maya culture as a whole. They are without cultural contexts, except certain Quetzalcoatl and Mexican connections.

And so it goes. Carnegie has sought and found the hierarchal, the grandiose. It has neglected the common, the everyday. And even within its chosen segment of Maya culture, it has produced data for the most part in a narrowly descriptive range. Kidder himself has several times alluded to this one-sided predilection for the grandiose and the "fancy" in archeology:

Non-ceramic specimens have proved to be relatively rare at all Middle American sites so far investigated. This is partly to be accounted for by the fact that excavators have confined themselves largely, as did we at Guaytan, to work in ruined ceremonial structures in which, of course, little was left at abandonment and into whose massive rubble construction went clean, new material, unlikely to contain artifacts of any sort. (Smith and Kidder, 1943, p. 162)

Thus, archaeologists are often only allowed to excavate when spectacular discoveries may be expected and are turned aside from their proper business, which is the study of the long, slow growth of human culture and the formulation of those problems of the development of society whose solution is, in the last analysis, the common aim of both anthropology and history. (Kidder, 1937c, p. 160)

But this realization seems to have produced little or nothing in the way of action in the field or results in print. A most illuminating case in point is the excavation at Kaminaljuyu (Kidder, 1945a).

At this locality, the original intention had been to conduct stratigraphic tests in a midden which had already produced a large amount of material and which is evidently of considerable extent. Gamio had previously worked there in what appeared to be early deposits, and Lothrop had discovered sculptures which seemed late. The site presented, therefore, "a likely place for finding deposits representative of at least two phases of Guatemala Highland culture" (p. 65). In the face of the scarcity of stratigraphic excavations in the Maya area as a whole, this would seem to have been a very worthy project and one which might give promise of some well-grounded conclusions upon cultural manifestations, their modifications, and their sequence. But the road to Hell and the field of Maya archeology are paved with good intentions. The project was abandoned for an attack on a mound which they "figured could be cleared in three weeks or so at the cost of about a hundred dollars." (p. 66)

The readiness with which stratigraphic excavation was abandoned for a mound which promised no more than three weeks' work is the point that I wish to emphasize here. Expediency and a need to preserve the mound from destruction cannot be considered to have been of vital importance in making the choice between midden and mound. Five meters had been cut off the mound to enlarge a football field, but the bounce of an Association football would hardly endanger the structure, and there were some 198 other mounds in the site. Perhaps Dr. Villacorta was importunate in asking "if the Carnegie Institution would care to make further investigations" (p. 66). But it is very questionable that the strongest urging would, of itself, have made Kidder abandon excavations that he considered more important or induced him to attack a project that did not hold equal or more promise from his own point of view. This promise could not have been stratigraphy or impressive finds, because these were not in evidence in the mound. Nor could it have been the promise of shedding light on Gamio's or Lothrop's finds, because material of such types had not been encountered in the mound. Nor could it have been a promise of clarifying the culture of the site as a whole, because the mound was obviously hierarchal on the evidence of a substructure already exposed. Kidder says that the offer to excavate the mound was accepted because

. . . the potsherds found [in the mound] were not of Miraflores types. Furthermore, aside from the "brick-kiln" stairway, no remains of buildings had appeared at any of the Kaminaljuyu mounds and we were keen to learn something of the site's architecture. (p. 66)[73]

That this reason is based purely upon an interest in comparative studies outside the site can easily be demonstrated. For even if the dig were successful in uncovering a quantity of those as-yet-unknown potsherds and a specific example of Kaminaljuyu architecture, if these discoveries could not be associated with the trash accumulations and other cultural aspects of the site, what value had they? The answer is that they had value as data to be compared with other potsherds and other architecture from other sites for the purpose of showing regional and chronological relations. Excavations in the hierarchal mound alone would leave their connection with the life of the ancient inhabitants of Kaminaljuyu an almost unknown factor.

And this is exactly what happened. The archeologists found a great deal of entirely new material, but Kidder says that the epoch represented, the so-called Esperanza phase, is "the only period in the life of that site with which we are even reasonably familiar" (p. 74) and that even about this phase, the only information concerns the ceremonial set-up:

. . . as to the people who labored under so heavy a weight of service to their rulers and their rulers' gods, we know very little. Some day we shall get around to excavating the village sites and the little unspectacular house mounds. [Cf. what he said in 1934 about Chichen Itza, quoted p. 52 above.] These will give us an insight into the domestic arrangements of the commoners: their houses, their implements, their methods of cooking. Their graves may teach us, perhaps, something of humble folk cults. Such work will also be of the greatest archaeological significance, for the small amount of digging we did outside of the mounds showed that temple furniture and the mortuary equipment of the overlords was in a class by itself. It no more represented the general contemporary culture of Esperanza Kaminaljuyu than the contents of a Park Avenue drawing room does that of the United States. (p. 75)

The cultural objects from the Esperanza phase are merely ceremonial specimens usable for comparative purposes. At the site itself, they are descriptions floating unattached between the Miraflores and the late prehistoric phases. They cannot be fitted into a cultural picture of Kaminaljuyu because they represent at best only the hierarchal segments of their own phase, because they have few, and only the vaguest, ties with the other local cultural phenomena, and because these other phenomena are themselves virtually unknown. Once more we have heard about what needs to be done, while observing the results of the very opposite procedure.

From the facts cited above, it may be concluded that both the field work and the publications of the Carnegie are weighted overwhelmingly toward the hierarchal. They have hardly touched, and then only incidentally, the cultural remains of the common Maya. But even within the hierarchal culture, the emphasis has not been to construct a picture of how the Maya hierarchy lived: what they did and where, when, how, and with what. Such intensive excavations as have been made have not been directed toward the clarification of these problems, but rather toward the finding of material for comparative and chronological studies or, many times, just to excavate a structure which appeared to be of rare or unknown type or was prominent or artistically beautiful.[74] Architecture, sculpture, epigraphy, and ceramics to a lesser extent have occupied the efforts of Kidder and his archeologists, and these categories have been treated for their comparative value with regard to origins, influences, and chronology. It is a further fact that, when comparisons have been made, they have been of physical descriptions of phenomena rather than of the relationships of these phenomena within one site compared with the relationships of similar phenomena at another site. In other words, comparisons have been based, not upon similar cultural contexts, but upon similar physical appearance. Description and not culture has been compared.[75]

On the assumptions that such physical similarities indicate cultural connections and hence a rough contemporaneity under normal circumstances, comparisons of this sort are valuable for the establishment of chronological relationships between sites and areas. But the nature of the cultural connection, whether trade or stimulus diffusion or migration or whatever, and the significance of the connection for the cultures themselves, cannot be told from descriptive similarities alone. Inferences as to such factors, if they can be made at all, have to be made with the added evidence of their contexts at the two sites or areas in question; and in addition much information, both cultural and natural, about the intervening area will have to be known. In short, a comparison of artifact descriptions may indicate chronology and the fact of cultural connections, but what those connections were and how exact the chronological indications may be, can be learned, if at all, only from the relationships of the compared artifacts to their own and to each other's cultural and natural contexts.

This point will be treated at some length later in the present study. It is mentioned here only to emphasize the fact that Carnegie's work does not picture or compare the culture of Maya sites nor provide the information for others to do so. Relationships *outside,* rather than *within,* the site seem to be the results consistently attained and thus, presumably, those that have been sought. There is little or no attempt to use comparative methods for the purpose of making inferences as to the significance of the material for the culture of the individual sites or for the Maya culture as a whole. Some of Thompson's papers are exceptions to this generalization, and from time to time others have hazarded a word or two of comparative interpretation and synthesis. But it is quite apparent that Kidder has not set his staff especially to work on such problems; and they have not done so themselves, of their own accord. Supporting this view is Kidder's own emphasis on reconnaissance and spot excavation:

During that period [the nineteen thirties] the Division's archaeological activities have to a certain extent been reorientated, in that emphasis has shifted from large-scale excavations at single sites to surveys designated to extend knowledge of the development and distribution of various elements of Maya culture. . . . In archaeology, for example, we must still further decentralize, devoting less of our resources to large excavations and more to small reconnaissance digs which will aid in delimiting the range of Maya culture and determining its chronological and cultural relations with other Middle American civilizations. These minor excavations should be supplemented by comparative studies of certain categories of evidence which earlier work has shown to be of outstanding significance: pottery, architecture, sculpture, the hieroglyphic record. (1939, p. 238)[76]

Why, we may ask, are these categories of evidence of such outstanding significance? Is it not because they have provided "regional and chronological" comparisons with other sites on a hierarchal level? Surely it is not because they are especially significant for Maya culture as a whole, including the way of life of both the common Maya and the hierarchy. It cannot be because these categories provide the only or yet the best means of constructing a picture of the life of any particular site, even of the hierarchy.

Information on such cultural topics would be better obtained from researches of a different nature. For example, we might have papers on such topics as: Food and its preparation among the Uaxactun Maya during Tepeu times; The costumes of Maya religious personages connected with the quetzal bird; A quantitative study of pottery in domestic and hierarchal structures at Benque Viejo; The social organization of the Uaxactun Maya as seen from their domestic architecture; A comparative study of the making and use of pottery at three Maya sites; The effects of environment and cultural diffusion upon sandal types as seen from the art of Peten and Yucatan; The relations of Maya mathematics to Maya architecture, city planning, and graphic art; The ball court as a functional part of Maya city planning; Evidence on the domestic and civil religion at San José at two different periods; A comparison of the relative importance of religious and lay culture in early and late Maya sites. If papers, or pages, had been written on such problems by Carnegie archeologists, or if the excavations had been conducted to produce the data on which they could be written, our knowledge of Maya culture as opposed to Maya chronology and extra-territorial relationships would probably be much advanced over its present state. In addition, it is safe to say that our "regional and chronological" studies would be set upon a much firmer foundation due to the weighting and balance given by a fuller cultural context.

In the light of this analysis, it is quite apparent that Kidder, despite his stated aims, has neither "done" nor provided the data for "doing" anthropology or historiography, at least in the sense in which these two terms have been defined in the present study. Certainly there is more to historiography than merely making physical descriptions of architecture, ceramics, and cities and placing them in chronological order. This is chronicle. What Carnegie has been doing is really chronicle of a restricted range of Maya culture: the artistic, religious, and epigraphic remains of the hierarchy.

It is my opinion that three factors are responsible for the character of Kidder's archeological work, both in the Maya area and in the Southwest. It is possible that these factors are, in turn, due to confusions arising from a failure to analyze thoroughly and explicitly his own conceptual scheme. But before proceeding to discuss these particular points, a possibly significant example will be given by way of introduction.

In 1940, speaking in general of Middle American studies and specifically of the Carnegie Institution, Kluckhohn noted the tendency to ignore the concept *theory* or to use it in a derogatory sense as a synonym for *speculation*. He forcefully and most convincingly pointed to the need for an explicit awareness of theory and its place in scholarly and intellectual pursuits, not as hypothesis and speculation but as "the conceptual framework of a single discipline." The very next year a new series of publications was inaugurated by Carnegie entitled *Theoretical Approaches to Problems*. In the second issue, Thompson says:

The fact that the paper is published in the present series is sufficient indication that the case is not considered to have been completely proved. (1944, p. 23)

From this statement and the tone of the papers themselves, it is plain that Carnegie still subscribes to the view that *theoretical* means *speculative* or *hypothetical*. One may wonder whether Kidder, in starting this new series, was trying to answer Kluckhohn's criticisms and was confused, whether he was implicitly denying Kluckhohn's definition of *theory*, whether it was an oversight, or just what.

The first of the factors held to be responsible for the character of Kidder's work is the need to develop a chronology as the first step in archeological research. To this may be attributed the high development of epigraphic, architectural, and art studies in his Maya program. These remains of hierarchal culture are relatively easily observed, of considerable aesthetic and esoteric interest in themselves, and therefore are represented by a considerable body of literature from the time of the earliest explorers to that of the present archeologists, and extending over the length of Middle America. They thus provide a wealth of comparative data which are more voluminous and ready-to-hand than those derived from the so-called minor antiquities such as ceramics, domestic architecture, and other everyday artifacts. Chronology is chronology, and one built purely from a small range of hierarchal material is perfectly satisfactory—provided either of two premises: first, that one is interested only in the chronology of hierarchal material; or second, that other cultural materials can be tied into the hierarchal chronology by association. Chronology is admittedly an important factor in any archeological research, and the earliest and surest method of establishing it is to be commended. But after a sequence of periods has been established, if then the very culture of those periods is unknown, we may justifiably ask "so what?" If we claim that chronology is a means to the end of understanding culture and if we erect our chronology but produce no cultural information, we delude ourselves, for we are no further along in our study of culture than before. This seems to be what has happened in the case of Carnegie's work in the Maya area. A series of time periods have been set up on the basis of epigraphy, architecture, art, and ceramics; but outside of this restricted range of subjects, little or nothing is known about the life of the Maya during those time periods. Food, shelter, clothing, implements, social groupings, domestic religion, methods of manufacture, motor habits, the nature of trade, these subjects and many more are to all intents and purposes as unknown today, after nearly twenty years of research under Kidder's direction, as they were when Maudslay and Maler worked the Maya area. Chronology is vitally important for cultural studies, *if culture is also studied.*

Possibly connected with the first is the second factor of Kidder's work. He has seemed to favor a wait-until-all-the-evidence-is-in policy with regard to any broad-scale treatment of Maya history. It may be that controversies in the chronological research and the failure to build an absolutely sure sequence, especially in Yucatan, has led him to this position. But whatever the cause, his words indicate that the policy is in effect. In 1939, he said that a history of the Maya should be synthesized at the end of the 1940's to be based on all the various branches of investigation which the Carnegie Institution has pursued in that area (p. 239). In 1935, he had said: "Many data have to be accumulated before synthesis can become worthwhile" (1935b, p. 115). To this policy may be attributed the scarcity of topical syntheses and the failure of the Carnegie archeologists, with the exception of Thompson (1943, 1945), even to essay chronological syntheses of hierarchal events from the mass of collected data.

While it is true that many data are needed for any history and that an extensive and detailed history requires much information from many sources, it is also true that waiting for over twenty years to begin assembling the cultural data necessary for writing history is a dubious procedure. It would seem better to have written certain sections of the proposed historiography as the data came in or as research projects on certain topics were completed. As the situation now stands and as it has been demonstrated in the preceding pages, Carnegie's publications contain little information which can be used to construct a picture of ancient Maya culture, its character and its development. If Kidder's history, which he has proposed to write at the end of the 1940's, is to come from those publications, it certainly will not be historiography as that term was defined in the preceding chapter of the present study. Nor is it at all probable that unpublished field notes or uncompleted research projects, aimed, as they quite certainly have been, at chronological and comparative conclusions, will be able to provide the details which are necessary for abstracting other cultural information out of the archeological materials. Even were this possible on the basis of Carnegie's unpublished information, such a procedure would demand a complete and intensive reworking of the data already worked. This would be a thankless, expensive, repetitive, and thus wasteful task and one which therefore has small likelihood of receiving attention. It does not seem likely that Kidder intends completely to re-orient the Carnegie's approach to archeological materials, to wash out and wring dry once again the same data in order to abstract a completely different set of inferences. It is much more likely that when he finally accomplishes the synthesis and interpretation which he has several times mentioned (1935b, p. 114; 1933, p. 83), he means to bring together and interpret, on a foundation of more data, the same "regional and chronological" aspects of the same range of (hierarchal) materials. He probably does not mean a cultural interpretation and a synthesis into a cultural picture of Maya culture as a whole.

Perhaps the writing of Maya history does not mean to Kidder the description of their cultural life and its concomitant events moving and changing in time and space. Perhaps when he claims that Carnegie's program of Maya research is dealing with the history of the Maya (1932b, 1933), he does not mean that it is attempting to write history in the sense of *historiography* as defined in the present study. Perhaps Kidder has a different idea of what constitutes the writing of history. This, I believe, is the crux of the matter.

It is concerning his conception of the writing of history, the third factor of his work, that Kidder shows most clearly those contradictions which confuse and make difficult any analysis of his writings. In some of his publications and in his own field work together with that of the men under his direction, he seems to hold the opinion that the writing of history concerns itself with the grandiose, with the rise and the flowering and the fall of civilizations. This tendency has already been demonstrated explicitly and by implication in the preceding pages: a tendency which appears to go beyond the requirements of expediency in establishing a chronology. One of Kidder's own statements may be used to lend support to this analysis:

Likewise, though the career of the Maya has even less bearing upon the problems of the moment, it gives opportunity for study of the rise and spread of a culture, the dominance of absolute rulers, political rivalries and civil wars, the decline and eventual fall of a virile civilization, submission to foreign military conquest, adjustments between a dense native population and a small class of alien overlords. Such events and such situations have shaped the course of history at all times and throughout the world. (1940b, p. 261)

This reads like a prospectus of one of Gibbon's or von Ranke's *Staatsgeschichte* historiographies. With the exception of the phrase about adjustments between a native population and their overlords, there is nothing that might be called culture-history, and it is a far cry from the tenets of the New History and other recent historiographic trends. The "pomp and circumstance" of the Maya past are what seem to impress Kidder here. The rise, flourishing (or spread and flowering), the fall of the Maya civilization is a theme which runs through a significant number of Carnegie publications.[77] To attain such Gibbonesque results, it is obvious that events and not cultural conditions must be given first place in research. Or at best, what cultural context is provided will be of the hierarchy and not of the Maya as a whole.

It is confusing to find that Kidder has several times made statements which can only be interpreted as direct contradictions of this point of view, as when he says:

Only when we have much fuller knowledge of everyday household utensils, corn-grinders, common stone and bone tools, objects which were not subject to shifting whims of fashion or influenced by new and perhaps quickly and widely spreading cults, shall we be able to discern the basic relations of cultures. (1945a, p. 75)

Only by constant repression of the desire, ingrained in human beings as well as in magpies, to collect for collecting's sake, can the archaeologist force himself to eschew the sensational, to search for in the field, and to study in the laboratory, the common everyday objects which alone can tell him the true story of cultural development. (1937a, p. 218)[78]

To such preaching we can but say *amen*—and continue to search in Carnegie's record for the practice.

A second aspect of this third factor is that Kidder appears to regard events, rather than "descriptions of cultural life and its concomitant events" as the hall-mark of history-writing.

The first step [in a historical discipline] is to make record of the chain of sequent events marking the career of the people under investigation. The second and more difficult step is to seek the causes and to explain the inter-relations of those events. And, finally, attempt must be made to extract, by study of the above two classes of information, materials for use in formulating those fundamental laws which have governed in the past and which therefore may reasonably be expected to shape, in the future, the course of human affairs. (1937a, pp. 218-219)[79]

Here the laws are to be derived from a study of events and the explanation of events. Perhaps what Kidder means by an event is something on the order of a change in pottery style, the diffusion or development of a religious idea, the modification of dress design, and so forth. But it is impossible to believe that this is a true representation of his viewpoint when his own and Carnegie's publications are taken into consideration. Events to him seem incontrovertibly to consist of such phenomena as the abandonment of the Peten, the return of the Itzas to Chichen Itza, the arrival of basal-flange bowls in Yucatan, the date of the appearance of slab-legged vases at Uaxactun. For example, such topics as the impact of the arrival of those vases upon the ceramic complex of Uaxactun and the significance of such an event for the culture of that site seem not to have been investigated by Kidder or the Carnegie archeologists at all. Their interests appear to have lain in the time-at-which and the direction-from-whence. Beyond that, they have not been inclined to go. Such "surveys" as those of Thompson (1943, 1945), while they contain remarks and even sentences on the results of such impacts upon the recipient cultures, are primarily and predominantly taken up with "episodic" events à la Kidder and with compara-tive studies to determine the chronology and derivation of the hierarchal ma-terials from which these events have been inferred.[80]

When Kidder refers to Carnegie's "pan-scientific" program, whereby arche-ology, documentary history, biology, and other disciplines are being employed in the study of Maya history, it is the light which these studies throw on the *events* that he constantly stresses:

As I have said, the Carnegie Institution's work in the Maya field was originally epigraphic, then more broadly archaeological. At the conclusion of the first decade of the investigation we were in possession of a large body of facts, and many concrete problems had been formulated whose solution could be counted on to throw additional light on the nature of the Maya culture and upon events in the Maya area. But other questions had arisen which could not be answered by the purely archaeological methods we had, until then, been using. Furthermore, early attempts at interpretation of our archaeological findings in terms of history found us without adequate information in many fields which the archaeologist has neither the ability nor the time to till. So there has gradually been organized what might be called a panscientific attack. . . . (1937c, pp. 162-163)

It is difficult to escape the conviction that only by coordinated research, involving the cooperation of all the disciplines devoted to the study of man, and the collateral support of many biological and physical sciences, can we attain understanding of any given episode [read "event"] in human history. (1932b, p. 91)[81]

If one could believe that Kidder meant "events against their cultural back-ground" or events in the sense of "every and all cultural change," one could gladly accept these statements. But on his record, Kidder cannot be thought to mean these things. By "event," he quite apparently means a *mutation* in the life of the Maya hierarchy, not the cultural *variations,* both magnificent and minute, which occurred throughout the entire Maya culture and which in the aggregate comprise the stuff of which Maya history was made and of which Maya history should be written.

To Kidder, history seems to be a series of episodic events and their dates of relative chronology. When he mentions a historical development he most often means a chronological development; and he has actually identified a historical viewpoint in the broadest sense as "a consciousness of the implications of the time element in the recording and interpretation of phenomena" (1930c, p. 391). When he mentions a historical problem, he seems to mean a problem of chronology, or more specifically the chronology of large events.[82]

But once more we are faced with contradictions. For in other places he seems to hold for a writing of history more in keeping with the definition of historiography as proposed in the present study, for example, in his *The Development of Maya Research* (1937a, p. 221). But despite Kidder's occasional bows to a different and broader conception of history writing, it is impossible to understand how he expects, given his more usual viewpoint, ever to derive laws of cultural evolution or

... to reach understanding of the all-important whys and wherefores of Maya history and by so doing contribute toward comprehension of the infinitely complex interaction of those biological, environmental and social factors which govern the evolution of man? (1935b, p. 114)[83]

The attempt upon such goals he envisions for archeology, but it is difficult to see how he will be furthering these ends while actively engaged in such restricted researches as those of the Carnegie Institution's program.

I believe that enough has been said to bring out the points I have wished to make concerning Kidder's archeological work. It is obvious that his results have led to the clarification of three aspects of the sites and areas which he has investigated: their more episodic events and their chronological and cultural relationships relative to other sites and areas. But it is also obvious that his efforts have not placed these findings within a context of culture, which would be historiography. They have placed them chronologically and demonstrated by comparative methods the fact of their cultural derivations; this is chronicle, or perhaps better, comparative and derivational chronicle.

Kidder has provided us with some of our finest statements as to the obligations, aims, and potentialities of archeology. But he has been saying one thing, while his results have added up to quite another. When Kidder writes theory he often talks historiography and anthropology. When he directs field work and publishes reports, he talks comparative chronicle.

Kidder's tremendous influence upon the development of archeological research in the United States is nowhere more apparent than in that region known as the Southwest. Although both Nelson and Spier shared with him the revolution against the archeological approach characterized by Cushing and Fewkes, it was Kidder who remained in the field. It was he who became the guide and champion of the new approach: the search for cultural and chronological relationships over the length and breadth of the Southwest by the use of comparative studies and extensive as well as intensive field work. His *An Introduction to the Study of Southwestern Archaeology* (1924) sketched the major outlines of those relationships, and the work of the archeologists who have followed has but filled out, and in some spots corrected or sharpened, those outlines which he drew with such remarkable insight. The aims and objectives, however, have remained as they were established by Kidder, Nelson, and Spier: to ascertain the coordinates of time and space for the cultural manifestations in the Southwest.

In the intervening years, two men have been especially outstanding in the furtherance of those aims: F. H. H. Roberts, Jr., and E. W. Haury. In the case of these men, as it will be found to be in the case of those to be discussed later, definite statements of aims, by which results may be judged, are virtually absent from their writings. Unlike Kidder, the majority of archeologists have not been articulate as to what they are doing or intend to do. They seem to assume that their proper aims are not only well known but also much alike, so that there is no need to make themselves explicit on these points. One thing is certain, however: both Roberts and Haury, for one reason or another, consider anthropology to be their field. Both have taken their higher degrees in departments of anthropology; Haury is head of a Department of Anthropology, and Roberts is connected with an organization which may justifiably be considered anthropological (the Bureau of American Ethnology), and from time to time, largely by implication, each has indicated that he believes himself to be conducting anthropological research.[84] In view of this, in analyzing their work, we may look for anthropological results, or at least we may expect to find cultural contexts from which anthropological results might be derived.

We may expect to find these things, but we do not. Both Roberts and Haury have been responsible for great and valuable increases in our knowledge of what the people of certain localities and certain times had or did not have in the way of cultural objects. They have defined and set upon a sound basis the objects characteristic of the so-called cultures and culture-periods of the Southwest. But their recordings have been almost entirely in the way of presence and absence, and they have offered little or nothing to explain the relative importance, the associations, the "depth" as it might be called, of all these objects. They have neither provided us with a picture of the life of those "culture-periods" by synthesizing their discrete facts nor given us the data with which we might construct such a picture ourselves. They have been signally successful in erecting the coordinates of time and space, but they have failed to superimpose the graphic diagram of life and culture upon the axes thus delineated.

For example, in his Canyon Creek paper (1934), Haury has provided really fine descriptive detail and even used synthesizing categories such as *Food, Dress, Cradles* and *Household Articles*. On the other hand, neither provenience, association, nor quantitive information is given except very rarely and incidentally. Specimens have been described, but their relationships to the site and to other specimens within the cultural whole have not been analyzed and cannot be derived from the data published. There is no cultural synthesis of the mass of descriptive data, and the *Conclusions* are concerned with chronology, episodic events, and comparative studies to determine the time and space relations of the site with respect to other sites and areas. And these comparative studies are not of cultural categories such as *textiles, food, dress,* etc., but of specimens and specimen types on a descriptive level.

In his Mogollon report (1936b), quantitative data on specimen types have been provided, but in this case description is the stepchild. It is very meager and not oriented toward the range of variation. Classificatory tags on a descriptive level are offered instead of detailed information designed to indicate the significance of the specimen for the cultural picture of the site. No provenience or association is given. The *Discussion* is purely chronological and comparative with an outward rather than an inward view.

It is difficult to evaluate Haury's part in the account of the Snaketown excavations (Gladwin *et al.*, 1937). But those sections that carry his by-line will be analyzed as indicators of the direction which his contributions, if not his original and personal intention, have taken in this particular case. The whole tenor of his sections and the implications of his approach to them indicate that his interest lay in demonstrating the horizon-markers for the various "culture-periods" represented at the site. These time criteria and their relations with similar materials from other areas are very important aspects of the Snaketown, or any, archeological problem. But they are only aspects among others, and it seems that Haury has dealt with them to the exclusion of the others. This is most apparent from the fact that quantification, provenience, and association, except rarely, are given by Period and Phase and not by actual association or position in the ground. The dangers of this procedure are obvious when we consider what would happen to these vital associational data if ever the present classification should be changed or modified. Nothing would remain to which to tie the finds. Here, the point to be raised is that an interest in the life of the Hohokam people as they lived in those bygone days would have dictated a different policy, one which would have assembled and analyzed as a unit all the evidence which could be associated together, say, in particular houses or single rubbish pits. Of course, the publication of house data did not fall to Haury, and pits seem not to have been individually treated at all, but his treatment of *Figurines* shows the same disregard for any but the horizon-marking potentials of the material. He says:

As in Mexico, where figurines have been used so successfully as indicators of horizon, so here, they have definitely shown their value in this respect and have added one more significant element in rounding out our conception of the phases. (Gladwin *et al.*, 1937, p. 233)

Surely this "conception of the phases" cannot mean a conception of the *life* of those phases. For, time and time again, he notes the presence of "head-dresses" (p. 234), "articles of clothing and leg and ankle bands" (p. 235), "ornaments" and "tattooing" (p. 236), yet nowhere is there an attempt to describe, interpret, or synthesize these items to derive a picture of the costume and ornamentation of the ancient Hohokam. We read of several types of figurines which are rare and not to the usual fashion; it might be of interest to know the provenience and associations of these specimens so as to attempt some interpretation or abstract some inference as to their cultural implications within the site. But they are mentioned and then ignored. Could this be because, as freaks and non-representative types, they are of little importance as horizon-markers? Animal figurines are not common and "most" of them were found in the rubbish (p. 238; Plate CCVIII). If some of the remainder were found in other, possibly more significant, associations, is it not important from a cultural standpoint to know in what association they were found? How may we interpret them, if we are ever going to do so, unless we know what other material they were found with, in what surroundings, in what possibly significant position, etc.? If I should dig tomorrow in a Hohokam site and find animal figurines in two different associations, how am I to make use of the Snaketown data? I can say that at Snaketown they "probably do not antedate the Santa Cruz Phase" (p. 238) and that, therefore, my finds indicate such a date for my site. But if my examples were found in a house entrance and also in child cremations, how may I make comparative studies with Snaketown to help me interpret the cultural significance of my figurines? Thorough comparisons might indicate that such objects began in Santa Cruz times as house offerings and then were transferred to child-burial offerings. This in turn might corroborate other evidences pointing to an association of children with houses or with certain animals. This in turn might lead to comparative data between the Hohokam and those groups that customarily buried the children in their dwelling rooms and interred the adult dead in refuse mounds or other locations away from the living quarters (Roberts, 1931, p. 170). More evidence and more inferences along these lines might lead to a hypothesis that in those ancient times there was an idea that child spirits were harmless while adult spirits were to be feared.

Such chains of interpretation and inference, if made explicitly and with an awareness of their contingent nature, may potentially lead to results which will be accepted, at least tentatively, by the majority of archeologists and which will help to fill out our sequent pictures of the life of the past and the cultural dynamics thus implied. If such results are accepted as working hypotheses, they will not only point the way to new problems but also by their very weight, when a body of them has been assembled, serve to set our comparisons of a temporal and spatial nature upon much sounder bases. A further discussion and empirical examples of this point will be taken up in the final chapter of the present study.

Although in general the information provided by Haury in his Forestdale report (1940) is of a much higher order than in his earlier works, he still does not present his data in such a way as to enable the reader to conduct his own research upon the material. One example will suffice. The Bear Ruin contains a cultural manifestation which is a blend of Mogollon and Anasazi features of a most interesting and significant sort. This fact was one of the major reasons for its excavation. An examination of the burial-data table (p. 65) produces the fact that of forty burials only five were without pottery offerings and that, of these five, four lacked all offerings and one had a "bone" at its shoulder. Of the graves with pottery, however, those with, and those without, other grave goods were about equally divided, there being sixteen with and nineteen without. This would seem to suggest a correlation between no pottery and no other grave offering. Turning to the appendix on skeletal remains, we discover (p. 132ff) that the majority of crania seem to be brachycephalic, but two are dolichocephals of a Basket-Maker-like type. We further discover that these two atypically long-headed burials are two of the five which had no pottery and that one of them is the one which had no pottery and the "bone" offering at the shoulder.

In view of the intermediate cultural and geographic position of the Bear Ruin, the suggestions of correlation in the above-cited facts might seem to warrant further investigation. But we have gone as far as the report will take us. Was the "bone" really an offering or was it a point which might represent a wound? In what locations and with what associations were the pottery-less burials found? The one very Anasazi-like house contained a "great number of specimens (fifty-eight)": could one of these have been of the same type as the "bone" grave offering? We learn that the pottery type *Forestdale Plain* shows much Anasazi influence, but we do not know from what parts of the site these sherds came or whether some, many, or none were found near the long-headed burials or the Anasazi-like house. These are just a few of the things we do not know and cannot find out from the report.

Although F. H. H. Roberts, Jr., has given us what are undoubtedly our best and most thorough descriptions of the architecture at Southwestern sites, the over-all impression to be gathered from his work is much the same as from Haury's: the seeking for temporal and cultural relationships with other sites on a descriptive level. Like Kidder and Haury, he has been "doing" comparative or derivational chronicle, not historiography or anthropology. The houses and their individual features have been treated at great length, but there has been no assembling, no synthesis of those "lesser," "minor" objects of "material culture" which have been found in those dwellings. The houses and their features are descriptive units; the smaller artifacts are also descriptive units; and both are discussed for the purpose of comparisons with other such phenomena at other sites, not as the material environment of human activity. The data are not brought together into an assemblage for the purpose of making inferences as to the life and customs of the people who lived in those rooms or those house blocks. And the information is not provided whereby such assemblages, as they were excavated in the field, can be regrouped. Provenience and association, except rarely, are given only for those specimens which are illustrated, and even these locations are noted only within the range of a room or pithouse, with some burial, or merely from "trench south of house E" (1929b, p. 151) or "E refuse" (1931, p. 180).

For example, although five bone awls are said to come from a single burial (1931, p. 152), the only means of identifying that burial is to find the illustration and check its number in the Appendix where the provenience of illustrated specimens is given. We find that they come from Burial E-5, but I have been unable to locate any other reference to Burial E-5 in the volume. What sort of person was buried in Burial E-5, where was it, what other material was with it, what context or significant association went with it? These data are not provided. The section on Human Burials (p. 168f) is taken up with generalized, typological, and narrative account of this cultural aspect. There is neither detailed nor specific reference made to individual burials, except the single rare finding of a skeleton in a ventilator, and here one short sentence is given merely stating the fact (p. 169).[85] For the rest, the generalizations are compared with generalizations from other regions, and a cursory attempt is made to make inferences, or rather to refute possible inferences, as to the meaning of certain practices. There are also statements as to the differences between the pit-house and the pueblo interments for the purpose of differentiating them chronologically and typologically.[86]

At two sites, Kiatuthlanna (1931) and the Village of the Great Kivas (1932), Roberts was able to demonstrate and delineate exactly several sequent phases of building activity within pueblo structures. It seems that to anyone interested in the cultures of those sites, in how the people lived and changed over the years, this would have presented an unrivalled opportunity to develop room by room, section by section, artifact by artifact, feature by feature the nature and changes of the cultural picture. From such data, for one interested in the problem, it would be possible to make inferences and even to come to some conclusions as to the nature and workings of culture itself as represented at those sites. Since Roberts has attempted neither to construct a cultural context nor to study culture in the abstract, it is permissible to assume that such investigations were not his intention.[87] What he has done is to provide the time and space coordinates for his finds as discrete entities. As in his other reports, he has not put back in place, by writing, those data which his excavations tore from their setting and his laboratory study teased apart for typological and comparative analysis. The vestiges of cultural integration which had endured in the ground for centuries have generally been ignored. The weighting that quantification might give has been neglected. The natural environment, in which the cultures were set and from which they satisfied their needs, has itself been treated as a separate unit, and relationships that might be inferred between it and the cultural environment have not been pursued with consistent and vigorous purpose.

To perform the tasks and develop the information which I have implied in the above analysis of Roberts' reports would involve making many inferences and proceeding upon the basis of many assumptions. But it has been shown in the preceding chapter of the present study (pp. 31 and 35) that any picturization of past actuality requires more or less inferences and assumptions; direct and empirical proof is an impossibility when one is dealing with the unique happenings of the past. These tools of method are the very foundation of a historical, nonempirical discipline such as archeology. And Roberts has made them himself, and along lines which, if followed out, would have led him to the construction of much fuller and more significant cultural contexts for the sites of his investigations.

For example, in his Piedra District report (1930), using environmental and cultural factors connected with an underground structure presumably ceremonial, he has made some inferences as to winter and summer ceremonies of the former inhabitants. If all the other data from the site had been combed, with imagination and persistence, for evidence bearing upon this topic, or if it had been explicitly stated that such a study had been made with negative results, he would have been demonstrating his concern with the life of those ancient people. As it is, his remarks on the ceremonies seem incidental and rather by-the-way. It is difficult to agree with him when he says:

The writer believes that the data from the Piedra investigations give a clear and distinct picture of the life of the people of the Pueblo I period in that portion of the San Juan archeological area. (1930, p. 168)

From time to time, he has in fact made remarks upon the life of the people, as when he discusses the question of family privacy and suggested "several sidelights on the character of the builders" of a certain house (1931, p. 35). From time to time he has quantified his data, rarely if ever a full quantification (except on individual or rare specimen types), but sometimes a series of percentage figures based on total counts (e.g., 1940, pp. 10-11).

It is only in his latest paper on the Southwestern field that he has taken account of the stratified fill of abandoned pit-houses and pueblo rooms (1939), and even in this report, as in his others, refuse mounds, although they were trenched, have not been dealt with stratigraphically or in detail. However, the use of the stratigraphic data from dwelling-fill is very disappointing. For example, in calculating his percentages for the different ceramic wares, he has lumped those from the Developmental with those from the Great Pueblo period to arrive at the relative amounts of gray utility, black-on-white, smudged, black-on-red, and fugitive red wares for the site as a whole irrespective of period or provenience (1940, pp. 10ff). The value of these findings for cultural, or even comparative, purposes seems doubtful, although he notes correspondence with like figures from Pueblo Bonito. No other percentages and absolutely no raw figures are given for ceramics. The stratigraphic sherd counts for dwelling-fills or refuse-mound trenches are not given, and very little use of these data seems to have been made at all. He says:

Some of the more significant features emphasized by the material from the stratigraphic tests are those pertaining to the Modified Basket Maker wares, progress in the development of the culinary or gray wares, the sequence in which some of the early Developmental period black-on-white types made their appearance, and changes in the burnished-black group. (1940, p. 11)

There is even less stratigraphic, quantitative data given for other categories of material objects. He says:

There is little in the way of period or horizon differences in the bonework. Except for the fact that the short, stubby cannon-bone awl was more numerous in the early part of the Developmental Pueblo stage than later and the long awls made from the same bone predominated at the end, the bone tools were the same throughout the occupation. From first to last the tubes, whistles and gaming dies exhibit the same forms. The rings presumably were restricted to the Great Pueblo horizon. (1940, pp. 116-117)

Bone awls might have exhibited the same forms from first to last, but there might also have been a significant difference in their numbers relative to other bone artifacts or to some other significant control factor. In other words, there are other ways of looking at the data than the mere presence or absence on the basis of form or type. But if the reader of the monograph wishes to view the finds from some angle other than that of Roberts, he is prevented from making these regroupings by the lack of raw figures, provenience, association, and other details of the material as it lay in the ground before excavation. As they now stand, the data can be used only for those ends for which Roberts used them: comparisons on the basis of form for the purpose of extracting temporal and spatial relationships.[88]

Archeological practice and publication in the Mississippi Valley and eastern field reflect the same time-and-space approach, the same development of comparative chronicle, that characterize the Southwest and Maya areas. Whether this is due, directly or indirectly, to Kidder's influence or that of the Southwest as a whole, is interesting as a subject for thought but irrelevant for the present discussion. What is important to note here is the dominating role taken by the Midwestern or McKern classification. The need for some ordering of archeological materials, already felt for a considerable time (McKern, 1937), was greatly increased by the accelerated program of research carried on under the auspices of the various Federal relief agencies during the 1930's and early 1940's (Setzler, 1942). With a vast body of data being produced by these excavations, there was urgent call for some method whereby the information could be ordered quickly and clearly and thus become usable rather than a mere jumble of extraneous detail. The answer was a so-called culture classification which is primarily of a time-and-space nature, which deals with descriptive types of cultural manifestations for the purpose of comparing them with other descriptive types from other sites, and which has colored the archeological program and performance throughout the entire area since its inception. As is to be expected, however, its impress upon the several archeologists conducting researches in the eastern field has not been identical. In the following discussions of W. S. Webb, W. A. Ritchie, and J. B. Griffin, it will become quite apparent the extent to which the ideas and requirements of this classification have impinged upon their work.

As in the case of Roberts and Haury above, these men have written very few statements as to their aims or disciplinary affiliations. But it may be noted that the latter two have taken their higher degrees in departments of anthropology and are affiliated with the anthropology sections of their respective museums; the former is Chairman of a Department of Anthropology and Archaeology. From this and their common membership in the American Anthropological Association, one may legitimately infer a connection between their work and the discipline of anthropology.

The researches and publications of W. S. Webb have been among the most important and extensive in this eastern area. He has given us some of our clearest and fullest reports and has developed for his readers cultural pictures and cultural interpretations more consistently, I believe, than any of his colleagues. From his earlier works (e.g., Webb and Funkhouser, 1928, pp. 55-62, 180) to his latest contributions (e.g., Webb and Snow, 1945, pp. 313ff), Webb has continually demonstrated his interest in how his archeological subjects actually lived (e.g., Webb and Haag, 1940, pp. 106ff), how and for what purposes they used the material objects which he has found in the ground (e.g., Webb and Haag, 1939, pp. 50ff; Webb and Elliott, 1942, pp. 394ff), and how these same objects reflect ancient customs which themselves have left no material embodiment (e.g., Webb, 1942, pp. 362ff).[89] Although his cultural syntheses are brief, nevertheless it remains that he has made them, and in this he is practically unique among the recent Americanist archeologists in the United States.

But Webb presents a paradox. In the face of this very obvious interest in cultural contexts, we find that his cultural syntheses fail to take into account many facets which might have been included on the basis of his excavated data. For example, his summary in *The Adena People* (Webb and Snow, 1945, pp. 310ff) fails to treat in detail of houses and house life, foods other than vegetal, textiles and clothing, the manufacture and use of pottery, weapons and implements, and many other categories of cultural phenomena, the evidence for which had been given in his previous publications on Adena sites. In his report on the Pickwick Basin sites he has attempted in two places to give a picture of the life of the people who made the great shell-heaps along the Tennessee River (Webb and DeJarnette, 1942, pp. 307ff, 317ff). But he has done so only in generalities. He has failed to make use of all the published data in constructing these contexts. Instead he has given a list of traits "which seem to present the outstanding customs, as revealed by excavations" (p. 311). This is a purely presence-and-absence listing and gives no quantification or association of traits within the occupational levels. That this procedure may obscure some valid and significant cultural groupings is evident from the obvious breaks which occur in the stratigraphic columns, for example the break in stone and bone-work at the 5-foot level or Zone A at site Lu[o67] (pp. 180, 190ff). Nor does this trait list help us to visualize or assay the importance of the not inconsiderable evidence for a sporadic or even seasonal occupation of some of these river-side shell-heaps.[90] Neither is the list applicable to studies of burial customs: for one thing, there is no way to identify the sex of burials except rarely and incidentally, and thus to learn what materials were buried with adults of what sex. There is some indication that children and infants were accompanied more often than adults with cultural objects (Webb and Haag, 1939, p. 13; Webb and DeJarnette, 1942, e.g., sites Lu[o67], pp. 186ff, site Ct[o27], pp. 239ff), but this investigation has not been pursued, apparently because Webb is more interested in the typology of adult burial and its stratigraphic and comparative significance than in the totality of the burial customs of the shell-mound people. This is explicitly stated when he says:

It is believed that in the case of infants the type of burial was not significant, hence they are not considered in the study of depth distribution. (Webb and DeJarnette, 1942, p. 240)

If a guess may be hazarded as to the reasons behind this evident paradox in Webb's work, the suggestion is made that it is due to the particular trend taken in his development as an archeologist and to the influence, upon this development, of the Midwestern classification. By training a physicist, he seems originally to have approached archeology as an avocation out of an interest in local antiquities and the ancient life of the local Indians. This is very evident from his book *Ancient Life in Kentucky,* stated to be written for the layman (Webb and Funkhouser, 1928). From such beginnings, Webb has developed into one of our most accomplished field technicians and a comparison of his later reports with those of earlier date will indicate the extent of his advance toward controlled, pertinent, "scientific" excavation and publication. But this progressive "scientification" has not followed his original and obvious interest in how the Indians lived. He has not refined and elaborated his techniques for cultural interpretation. He has not extended his range of materials for constructing cultural contexts. Nor has he sought, by the use of assumptions which he so admirably defends (Webb and Snow, 1945, pp. 200ff), to delve ever deeper into the culture of the people whose remains he has been digging from the ground. Or perhaps it might better be said that he has not advanced along these lines to the extent that he has advanced in field technique and—and this is the important point—along the lines of comparative study and a grasp of the classificatory picture as it is now envisioned in eastern archeology. Since his interest in cultural pictures has endured, however curtailed, a paradox has arisen from his definite and, of late, dominant leanings toward a concern with taxonomy as exemplified in the Midwestern system. His original interest in Indian life has been allowed to languish, and he has followed current custom and developed his work in comparative and classificatory directions.

It seems hardly coincidental that his first trait list appears in a report (Funkhouser and Webb, 1937) which is probably the first to be written and published, in its entirety, after the Indianapolis Conference which inaugurated the Midwestern classification and which Webb attended. This innovation was undoubtedly to be expected since the eastern archeologists turned as a body at this point to fit their data into the classification, and trait lists are the basis of the classification. But the point to be raised here is that from this time onward Webb has bent his major efforts to elaborating trait lists and their comparative implications and has made a stepchild of his former interest in more detailed cultural pictures of life as it was led. For example, while in two of his earlier reports he gave much study to the weaves of textiles as seen from impressions upon pottery (Webb and Funkhouser, 1929b, pp. 14-17; Webb and Funkhouser, 1931, pp. 375-388), in his post-Midwestern-Classification reports no such detailed examinations have been effected, and he has not anywhere dealt with these fabric impressions except in connection with pottery typology. In other words, he has not attempted to get at the textile complex of the people through analysis of fabric-impressed potsherds. Similarly, in an early publication he analyzed the cordage (Funkhouser and Webb, 1929, pp. 86-87), but in later works he merely mentions cordage and knots and passes on (Webb, 1938, p. 48; Webb, 1939, pp. 50, 56). It seems that those objects which are thought to have no importance for comparative and classificatory studies have been relegated to passing references and omitted from consideration in final syntheses.

This preoccupation with trait lists may be responsible for certain other aspects of Webb's publications. There is a tendency to slight description of artifacts and to give instead a typological tag: a bone awl is a bone awl, a hoe is a hoe, with often not so much as a word about shape, size, material, details of use, wear, or such matters (Webb and De Jarnette, 1942, pp. 116ff, 224ff). Often potsherds or vessels found in graves are left unidentified (Webb, 1939, pp. 76-77; Webb and De Jarnette, 1942, pp. 117, 188). There is a tendency to neglect associations such as inclusions in midden pits (Webb and Haag, 1940, pp. 72, 107) and to fail to give provenience from which associations could be worked out (Webb and Haag, 1939, pp. 17ff). There is a tendency to omit quantifications as a regular adjunct to typology and instead to give illustrations of types or "the best" examples without giving the quantities within the various categories (Webb, 1938, pp. 110, 130; Webb and De Jarnette, 1942, pp. 40, 42). It should not be understood from these remarks that there is no description, quantification, association, or provenience given. Actually, there is a great deal of quantification and somewhat less description, association, and provenience, and in this respect his University of Kentucky reports surpass those issued as *Bulletins* of the Bureau of American Ethnology. But the effort to provide such data seems largely incidental and not consciously consistent. Lapses are too frequent for there to have been a rigorous prosecution of these points of detail in assembling his material for publication. His failure to utilize fully the special geographical and biological studies included in two of his more recent works (Webb, 1939, pp. 9ff; Webb and De Jarnette, 1942, pp. 337ff) may be another sign of his unconcern with factors not readily applicable to trait-list comparisons and classifications.

From the above, it should be very apparent that Webb has not constructed cultural contexts as fully as the data to hand must have warranted. It is also clear that, from his published data, it is impossible for the reader himself to construct a cultural synthesis, weighing and balancing the quantity and quality of the various traits and complexes, searching associations for constant features, noting breakage and wear to arrive at an idea of use, investigating the sources of raw materials in the hopes of defining trade routes and possible extra-regional connections, and probing other lines of evidence to extract the cultural significance and "depth" of the finds. This is so because the necessary details are not given.

Perhaps Webb considers that he has given a cultural synthesis by compiling those trait lists. His own words might lead one to this belief:

In order to understand the life of the shell-mound dwellers and to characterize their culture prior to the use of pottery, a list of traits has been prepared. Table 43 is a list of traits which seem to present the outstanding customs, as revealed by excavations. . . . (Webb and De Jarnette, 1942, p. 311)

The following list of traits describes the cultural manifestation at this site as accurately as present knowledge permits. (Funkhouser and Webb, 1937, p. 200)[91]

If this is the case, as it seems to be, here is one more proof of a fundamental assumption underlying his field work and publications: namely, that the important factor about a cultural manifestation in archeology is its presence or absence within a given site. This assumption is accompanied by a corollary: that the manifestation's location, association, quantitative and qualitative relation to its cultural and natural environment seem to be of secondary importance. These two assumptions are basic to the current comparative approach, and Webb is not alone in his acceptance of them. They lie at the bottom of the so-called McKern or Midwestern system of classification. This point will be dealt with at some length at a later time in the present study. Here it is only necessary to state that culture, and thus a cultural context, does not consist of artifacts or other material manifestations alone. It is impossible to get at the cultural significance of any artifact merely by classifying it with certain more or less similar artifacts and noting its presence within an archeological site. There is, I believe, more to the study of culture than this.

Before leaving this analysis of Webb's contributions, I wish to state once again that I believe he has given us some of our best archeological reports. Although it is true that he has failed to make the most of his opportunities, it is possible to abstract more out of his publications than from those of the majority of his colleagues. There seems to be no doubt that he has been influenced toward a purely time-and-space, comparative approach by the need to go along with his fellow archeologists and find a place for his discoveries within the Midwestern system. Perhaps this need has changed the course of a development that would have led to more detailed and refined cultural pictures and thus eventually to more detailed comparative studies. Perhaps if he had managed to carry on according to his own inclinations, he would not have become so concerned with presence-and-absence trait lists and comparative studies. As the matter now stands, Webb's contributions are considerable and he presents an enlightening paradox.

The publications of W. A. Ritchie present in general the same character as those of Webb. While his pictures of ancient life have not been even as full as

Webb's and whereas he has gone over to the Midwestern classification with an even greater wholeheartedness, nevertheless his development has been essentially parallel. He demonstrates an incidental, unformulated, but quite definite interest in how the Indians lived, especially in his early reports but also appearing in some of his later papers. However, this incipient inclination has been almost completely overwhelmed by his enthusiastic embracing of the classificatory system, and his latest works are occupied exclusively, to all intents and purposes, in the effort to place his archeological material in some taxonomic pigeon-hole. His interpretations as to the contextual significance of his data have become fewer and fewer and more incidental, while the elaboration of trait lists and his cross-cultural comparisons have proportionately increased.

His association with Parker's already-established "culture sequences" in New York State, based as they were on comparative studies of artifact types (Parker, 1922), might have made him an easier mark for a system such as the Midwestern. But his publications up to the Castle Creek report (1934), which is the one immediately preceding his first mention of the classificatory system, show an increasing number of inferences and interpretations and a growing concern with filling out the bare bones of excavation and artifact description. Although ro effort was made to make full and elaborate syntheses of the data retrieved, a considerable amount of the means by which this can be done is present in the reports. For example, he gave a detailed interpretation of local events involving a violent fire at the Alhart site (1930, p. 72); and in the same report he discussed the method of manufacture of a bark barrel (p. 67) and later included the use of bark buckets to round out an inferential picture of the Mason site (p. 75). In his monograph on the Lamoka site (1932), he gives an ecological setting for the site (p. 83), infers the importance of fishing from the artifact roster (p. 104), interprets methods of manufacture (p. 108f), infers a feast from artifacts associated with masses of mammal bone in the refuse pits (p. 115), gives a somatological picture of the ancient inhabitants (p. 131), and gives a brief picture of the life of the people at this particular site (pp. 131-132). In the Castle Creek report (1934), he has gone into great detail on the structure and contents of some of the pits encountered (pp. 10-29). Interpretations of pit groupings are given (p. 10), even seasonal use of some is envisioned (p. 11), events in one special pit are recounted (p. 29), and throughout the discussion many data are given which, if assembled and studied in a body, would produce a very adequate picture of their nature, use, contents, and position within the cultural whole of that site.

Of those reports issued after he explicitly recognized the Midwestern system, only the first two, *New Evidence Relating to the Archaic Occupation of New York* (1936a) and the Canandaigua paper (1936b), contain interpretations such as are found in his earlier works. In the first of these volumes, the artifacts are described under what might be termed cultural headings, i.e., vegetal food, game-getting, fishing, cooking (pp. 4-8). In the latter (1936b), the categories "hunting as well as fishing paraphernalia" and "domestic industries" are mentioned, followed by the listing of a few artifact types (p. 70), but there is no further discussion of such cultural aspects. His interesting analysis of the meaning of multiple burials showing signs of violent death (pp. 79ff) is the only other instance of such interpretation in this report. In his monograph on the Frontenac Island site (1945a), he gives two short paragraphs on the mode of life reflected in the finds (p. 26), but the major part of the volume consists of trait lists and cross-cultural comparisons. However, there is one sentence which, had it been developed, would have added a most interesting and valuable cultural insight:

When interpreted in terms of existing knowledge of Lamoka and Brewerton burial customs, the Frontenac data appear to afford a case of cultural inertia, reflecting the persistence of diverse traits already known from each. (1945a, p. 18)

However, these occasional bits of cultural context, synthesis, and interpretation appear to be an incidental rather than a consciously integral part of Ritchie's reports. This is nowhere more clearly seen than in the case of his recording of the quantities, provenience, and association of his artifacts and other finds. In general, he has divided his accounts into two sections, one dealing with the excavations and "occupational" features and another dealing with the artifacts found. In the excavation sections he gives both provenience and association for the various artifacts but he distinguishes these objects only by a typological tag such as *arrow point, potsherd, bone awl,* etc. In the second section, he describes the artifacts, sometimes individually and sometimes generally, but he does not give their provenience or association and fails, except in two reports (1934, 1940b), to cross-reference the specimens. Thus, there is no way to tell which bone awl was found in which pit or which burial. In the case of awls this might or might not be of importance, but in the case of potsherds it would surely seem of great importance to know what type of pottery was found with what other cultural material. But even in those reports (1934 and 1940b) which do cross-reference their descriptions and provenience by giving the field catalogue numbers (and for this Ritchie is to be loudly praised), this system is not followed consistently, there being many instances of specimens described or located without an identifying catalogue number (e.g., 1934, the sherds, sinkers, awl, and celt, p. 23; 1940b, the scraper, p. 12; the chopper, p. 15).

The extent to which Ritchie has quantified his data is to his great credit. But here again the procedure is not consistent. In the Lamoka report (1932) for example, while many classes of artifacts are given exact quantification, there are not a few which are designated with such terms as "several," "a number," "not infrequently . . . among these" (p. 105). Two facts seem to point to the probability that from Ritchie's viewpoint quantification is primarily for the purpose of cross-cultural comparisons and not for the purpose of assessing the various complexes at the sites themselves. First, the consistent quantification is found only in those reports (1936 *et seq.*) published after Ritchie began to be influenced by the Midwestern system. If one wished to be generous, this might be attributed to his developing realization of the importance of such information. But when, even in these later reports, he fails to quantify fragmentary artifacts of *uncertain type* (1940b, p. 64), we may be permitted the suspicion that it is really the comparative approach which motivated him: for comparative purposes within the Midwestern system, typology is required, and typology as it is practiced requires virtually complete specimens. However, at least for some aspects of the assessment of cultural complexes within a given site, a point is a point and a drill a drill whatever the type may be or whatever the condition of a specimen may be. Therefore, for one really interested in the culture of a site, fragmentary points and drills may be as important as whole specimens—and as deserving of quantification. A failure to realize this fact may be an indication of the comparative, cross-cultural trend of one's archeological thinking.

With regard to Ritchie's *magnum opus, The Pre-Iroquoian Occupations of New York State* (1944), Johnson has already said what I should wish to say, namely that Ritchie has excluded any feeling for his material as the product of human behavior (Johnson, 1944, p. 535) and that method, by which both Johnson and I mean the Midwestern system, has been favored over considerations of culture and human life (p. 533). This monograph, just because it is such a broad and inclusive compilation, is the final step in Ritchie's march toward submersion in the taxonomic system.

Although J. B. Griffin is not a field archeologist and although he has specifically implied that he considers himself to be a "laboratory student" (e.g., 1939, p. 128), his works will be included in this series of analyses for a number of reasons. Griffin's knowledge of eastern ceramics and his taxonomic studies have given him an influence in eastern archeological circles that is of very considerable proportions. A look into the bibliographies of publications covering work in that region will be sufficient demonstration of the extent to which his influence goes: Griffin's publications are rarely absent. In the second place, marking an exception to the common practice, he has given us statements that generalize upon methods and theoretical topics, and these may be used as touchstones against which to compare his empirical research. Finally, since his monograph on *The Fort Ancient Aspect* (1943) has been acclaimed as "the most comprehensive treatment of a single major North American archaeological cultural manifestation" (Ritchie, 1945b, p. 398) and as "the most exhaustive study of an archeological 'culture' in the history of eastern United States archeology" (Collier and Quimby, 1945, p. 143), it will be of interest to examine the volume to see just what sort of information has been provided by this "most exhaustive and comprehensive" study. It will be interesting to note the extent to which it exhibits correspondence with Griffin's own statements of theory and method and the extent to which it attains the levels of historiography and anthropology as defined in the present study. In the succeeding pages, therefore, particular cognizance should be taken of reference to (1943) which is the bibliographic designation of *The Fort Ancient Aspect.*

Pertinent to these interests, Griffin's publications show several important contradictions between statements of theory and method on the one hand and the results of empirical research on the other. In the first place, on a number of occasions he has either stated or implied that the ultimate aim of archeological investigation is to reconstruct the life of the past.[92] But it is difficult to credit him with anything more than lip service to these ideals. Time and time again he has failed to make use of the data at hand, to synthesize into any sort of picture the information gathered from a site or area, to abstract from the material objects their meaning for the life of their former possessors, to interpret in terms of broad categories such as subsistence and social groupings the information from archeological materials. He has consistently failed to follow up leads which might have led him to some significant information concerning the life of the people and has been content merely to investigate factors of taxonomic, i.e., comparative, significance. For example, in several sites which are classified as within the Fort Ancient Aspect a net-impressed pottery has been found (1943, pp. 85ff, 141, 177f), but nowhere is this netting analyzed or described. Surely the netting thus indicated was a factor in the life of those ancient people just as was pottery—possibly not as important a factor, but the making of netting and the making of pottery were both characteristics of the culture of those sites and both are intrinsic to a proper picture of the life of the people who lived at those locations. And again, it may be satisfactory for comparative purposes to say, as he does (1943, p. 168), that "on hardly a single sherd from any of the Fort Ancient sites are there the fabric impressions" which prevail on salt-pan-type vessels in other regions. But for a student who is interested in the life of those people, the implication contained in this remark, namely that there were *some* sherds that *did* carry fabric impressions, is but a tantalizing indication that if all the data had been given, the nature of the Fort Ancient textile industry, at least in part, might be added to our information. That Griffin has neglected to go into this matter is hardly to be reconciled with his profession of interest in reconstructing the life of the past.[93]

Similarly, it may be adequate for comparative purposes, i.e., for the differentiation of one site or series of sites from other such units, to note that "little use was made of shell for such implements as hoes or spoons, in marked contrast to its frequent use as such at Fort Ancient sites" (1943, p. 236). But this information is hardly significant in any cultural sense, until the environmental aspects are checked. That is to say: if the shell which was used for hoes and spoons had been equally available to both types of sites, then it might be proper to infer some culturally significant difference between them. If, however, within the environment of one type of site the proper shells were not present or equally available, one could hardly draw the same cultural inferences, although for the purely comparative purposes of distinguishing the two types of sites the situation would not be altered in the least.[94] In his publications, Griffin is satisfied to note presence and absence, or sometimes the relative frequency of such objects without relating these data to environmental factors. Once again, this is hardly the procedure one would expect of a student bent upon recreating the life of the past.

A second contradiction is to be found in the fact that he demands the full culture-roster, or the "total complex" as he calls it, in order properly to compare two groups, yet he consistently fails to synthesize and compare full subdivisions of that roster, full subcomplexes of that total. He says:

In my own opinion such [diagnostic] traits, though interesting and valuable, are in some ways rather a side issue in archaeological research, for our proper aim is the recovery of the total complex of the group to be studied, and this total complex must be compared with other artifact assemblages equally complete in order to determine the true connection between groups. (1944b, p. 366)[95]

If this is true with regard to the "total complex" of a group, why is it not also true of, say, the total complex of their bone work, their hunting equipment, their utilization of the environment, their seasonal activities, their patterns of design, etc.? Griffin gives the impression that such groupings of data would be too subjective, when he says:

In the discussion of the artifacts from each site, arbitrary divisions based upon the type of material used in their construction have been made, in order to simplify treatment and comparison and to eliminate the use of *subjective groupings* based upon such terms as "art" and "ceremonial." (1943, p. 3, italics mine)

When he says "total complex," he apparently means the total number of those particular discrete entities which he has seen fit to isolate and describe.

To group these entities under headings which state or imply their position within the cultural whole seems to be too subjective a procedure for him. Yet, to me at least, it appears to be assuming a false position to call an artifact a fishhook and then refuse to postulate a fishing complex, or to identify an object as a gorget and then refuse to admit a complex of personal ornamentation, or to note a "musical rasp" and not associate it with "rattles" in a music complex (1943, trait list following p. 376). In other words, despite Griffin's implied contention that the entities in his comparisons are non-subjective, he himself actually begs many questions, and at the same time he does not permit himself the freedom of following out his implicit hypotheses to see where they lead. When he labels an illustration (shell) "spoons" (1943, plate XLVIII), but nowhere gives his reasons for thus identifying the shells, he begs the question of their identity by the use of a descriptive or classificatory "tag." When, therefore, he refuses, on the grounds of subjectivity, to list some object as "ceremonial" or to group certain designs, shapes, or decorative elaborations under a heading of "art," he is only misleading himself. It is no more subjective to include the designs found on pottery and gorgets and incised beads under "art" than it is to identify, *with no supporting evidence,* a particular shell as a spoon or some bone object as a hair-spreader or some rock as a whetstone.[96]

Nor is objectivity being served by a refusal to group objects already identified as fishhooks, net-sinkers, gorges, and the like, into a fishing complex and to compare it with the fishing complex at another site. Let us suppose, for instance, that at two sites the typological range of fishing gear is identical but that at one site the harpoon heads greatly outnumber fishhooks, while at the other harpoons and fishhooks are approximately equal and net-sinkers are vastly more common; or that at one site the fishing gear is quantitatively much less than the hunting gear while at the other the reverse is true; or that at one site fishing gear is found with many burials, while at the other it is never so found; or that at one site, which lies five miles from the nearest fishable water there are many harpoons and many large fish bones, while at the other, which lies on the shore of a large lake containing today many large fish, there are very few harpoons but a multitude of fishhooks, gorges, and bones of small fish. Are not these findings valuable for comparative purposes, and are they not valuable for developing inferences as to the mode of life characteristic of each site? Might we not demand comparisons of such separable segments of the "total complex" as well as comparison of the total number of discrete, descriptive entities? When Griffin demands the latter and fails to consider the former, is there not an inconsistency, even a contradiction, between his theory and practice as well as a loss to his archeological information?

Connected with the above is the third contradiction: although Griffin states that quantification of the data and the giving of relative amounts of various categories is of great importance, he has failed to follow this precept in his own publications. In 1935, he said:

Another objection was that the relative amount of materials was of as much significance as their occurrence at all. I tried to show this difference in the percentage of the material, which was difficult to obtain and to present. (1937c, p. 54)

Later he said:

One of the most important factors by which cultural connections may be ascertained is the relative abundance of an individual trait, of a group of traits, or of all the traits. In many instances the text description of the cultural elements at each site contains a record as to whether a trait is common or rare. It will be noted that the prevalence of a trait is not indicated on the nonpottery trait lists. To make an accurate quantitative trait comparison it would be necessary to have data which were not available. (1943, p. 3)

But he gives the show away when in the next sentence he says:

Moreover, to express trait quantities in the comparative lists would confuse rather than clarify the record for the reader. (1943, p. 3)

Ritchie's use of quantities in trait lists (e.g., 1940b, 1944, 1945a) has shown that this practice is not necessarily confusing. But even if this were the case and if Griffin were thoroughly convinced of the importance of quantitative evidence, it seems unlikely that he would delete it so completely from his published data. Griffin has actually given some relative quantitative information throughout *The Fort Ancient Aspect* (1943), by recording "rare," "abundant," etc., for many categories; but no raw figures or percentages have been given. Now it is true that some of these designations (rare, abundant, scarce) must have been taken directly, as the only data, from the original sources. But also it is apparently true that many of these designations were made by Griffin himself on the bases of original figures which, perhaps, seemed more or less inconclusive to him and which, therefore, he changed into approximations rather than to reproduce in cold, rigid numbers what he considered to be incomplete or doubtful data. Nevertheless, if this is a true representation of the case, it must be pointed out that Griffin has merely compounded the approximation. He has imposed approximations of a second order upon approximations of a first order. If the original sources were inconclusive, they still constitute the basic data upon which all judgments must be made, and approximations of a second order merely make the results more inconclusive. That Griffin has offered the reader only his own judgments rather than the original figures removes the reader's control over the data just one step further.

Two other contradictions will be no more than mentioned here. First, at certain times, Griffin asserts that the Midwestern taxonomic system is an objective means of arriving at an idea of cultural relations.[97] Yet at other times, both by word and deed, he contradicts this viewpoint and gives definite evidence that the system is not objective but highly subjective.[98] Second, he has maintained that the higher units of the Midwestern system, such as the *aspect* and *pattern,* do not represent a "historical entity" or a cultural actuality, but rather are merely classificatory abstractions assembled from a synthesis of focus "traits." For example:

When foci are combined into the more generalized unit called an aspect a personal conception of the important features is introduced and individual elements are selected and recombined in a pattern which, in a sense, never actually existed. Abstracting the pottery elements common to the pottery of the four foci of Fort Ancient does not reproduce a type that was ever made by any Fort Ancient artisan. The resultant list of traits does have, however, an individuality which, presumably, would not be exactly matched by any similar list made up for another cultural division. (1943, p. 205)

If by the word *cultural,* used in the last sentence, Griffin meant "pertaining to a (particular) culture," he is both misleading himself and contradicting himself. If the pattern "never actually existed" it can hardly have belonged to "a culture." *Cultural,* therefore, can only mean that the division was made up of descriptive units which themselves pertain to culture as a whole, not to one particular culture. This difference, which is so neglected or unrecognized by many archeologists, will be discussed below when it comes time to go into the matter of the concept *culture.*[99] Yet in many places in his writings, we find that he has used interchangeably the terms *aspect* and *culture* (meaning a discrete cultural entity)[100] and that he has identified in at least one instance an aspect with a linguistic unit.[101] However, since both these contradictions deal with the Midwestern taxonomic system, they will be passed over here to await further treatment later when the problems of archeological classification and typology are discussed (see Chapter 5). It is sufficient to note that these ambivalences are quite typical of those who employ the classificatory systems, and this seems to point to some basic confusion between descriptive and cultural categories. This in turn may be the result of a failure to come to some conclusion as to a definition of culture and to decide what has significance for the study of culture and for the construction of a particular cultural context.

With the above, and additional, data it will now be possible to hazard some judgments as to Griffin's theoretical beliefs on archeological topics. In the first place, it seems evident that he believes presence-and-absence trait lists satisfactorily represent, and may be used to define, human cultures. Trait lists are the only assemblages or syntheses which he derives from his discrete archeological data. When, therefore, he refers to these lists, these "total complexes" from his various sites, as "cultures," the implication is obvious. For example, his work entitled *An Analysis of the Fort Ancient Culture* (1935) consists of an analysis of his Fort Ancient trait lists. Later he says:

This analysis [of Baum Focus trait lists] represents what might be called the more objective statement of the characteristics of the *cultural content* of the Baum Focus and of its interrelationships with other groups. (1943, p. 69, italics mine)

One of the primary obligations of an archaeologist in preparing a report is to furnish an accurate inventory of the cultural content of the units he is describing. . . . In this paper it has been done by analyzing the material available into traits. (1943, p. 335)

If records of a reasonable number of communities having a high degree of correlation are obtained, a complete trait list will represent, to some extent at least, the material remains of a human group or groups who were united by identical or nearly identical cultural habits. In a comparison of this order one is dealing with concrete data that have the most intimate connection with ethnography and that come closest to a part of the culture of a pre-existing human group. (1943, pp. 335-336)[102]

In the second place, Griffin seems to believe that the importance of the cultural data lies in their value for comparative purposes. This is taken to be the case since nowhere has he attempted to construct a cultural context, to paint a picture of the life as it was lived at any site. In one report, he (among others) says that no comparative study was done but that an effort was made to place the data on record in such a fashion that they could be used for future comparative studies (Griffin and others, 1941, p. 47). Nothing was said about leaving the material in shape for other purposes. In another paper, he says:

There is no record of the [particular] mound from which the various specimens came, but, since the entire group is undoubtedly of Hopewellian character, this lack of information is not of great importance. (1941, p. 184)

It is true that this lack is not of importance *for certain purposes*. But the purposes for which this lack is unimportant are obviously comparative on a purely presence-and-absence basis. The lack of provenience is most certainly an important, and a very important, omission if one is interested in looking at the culture in a more-than-two-dimensional perspective.

In the focus summaries the specific groups were linked with each other and with surrounding cultures and areas. This was done primarily on the basis of traits which were not characteristic of the unit as a whole, but which, nevertheless, belong to various facets of the Fort Ancient Aspect and are, therefore, of considerable importance in interpreting this cultural group. (1943, p. 195)

In this quotation, there can be only one construction put upon the claim that these traits are important "in interpreting the culural group." It is not the group's cultural life that is to be interpreted. It is the group's "cultural and chronological position" (1943, subtitle) that is to be understood, not the details of its culture-structure but the details of its comparative relationships with surrounding groups. The delineation of the time-and-space coordinates and not the development of a more-than-two-dimensional, more-than-time-space, picture was the factor which gave these traits their importance for Griffin.

This leads us to the third belief which seems to be a part of Griffin's theoretical premises. It appears that to him *culture history* signifies this very "cultural and chronological position" relative to other sites or areas, with the added feature of a temporal continuity. For example, after going most extensively into the possible relationships, both cultural and chronological, of the Fort Ancient Aspect, he says:

An attempt has been made in this study to gather all the available evidence bearing upon the cultural history and position of the Fort Ancient cultural division in the archaeology of the Ohio and Mississippi valleys. (1943, p. 208)[103]

Griffin is not thinking of a culture history consisting of events against their background of local human culture and local natural environment. He is thinking of a purely time-space, two-dimensional chronicle. He is not concerned with the acquiring and development of cultural complexes among the individual peoples of the Ohio and Mississippi valleys, and not with the implications of such cultural dynamics for an understanding of culture itself as an abstraction.

There are three things that interest Griffin in his archeological work: the cultural and chronological positions of sites and groups of sites relative to other sites; and the connections of the archeological manifestations with documented, i.e., "historic" tribes. These goals are plainly indicated by the nature of his work, and he has several times stated them explicitly in print.[104] I am aware of only one place where there is a hint that he might have other ideas with regard to his archeological material:

It [Ritchie's *Pre-Iroquoian Occupations of New York State*] can be viewed as almost a "necessary" step in providing the skeletal outline upon which future interpretations will lean for the data to substantiate theories regarding local cultural evolution and for *"ethnological"* reconstructions of the life of the people. (1945b, p. 407, italics mine)

As was mentioned in the case of the Maya archeology of the Carnegie Institution, information for archeological "reconstructions" of an "ethnological" nature is not to be found in most publications written with a purely taxonomic, comparative approach. The "ethnological" goal must be visualized at the inception of archeological work, not at the end.

From the above discussion of Griffin's work, it is quite apparent that he is not concerned with culture, its nature and dynamics. Nor is he concerned with the construction of cultural contexts for the purpose of picturing the mode of life of bygone peoples. Ritchie has already pointed out (1945b, p. 399) that Griffin's "running description" of the non-pottery data from the Fort Ancient Aspect leaves much to be desired as to completeness and detail. To this may be added the notation that Griffin has entirely neglected to summarize Fort Ancient physical type, house type, cache pits, burials, implements, etc., etc. His summaries of the various foci are occupied with comparative studies of individual artifact types for the purpose of discovering "cultural and chronologi-cal" relationships between the various taxonomic units. Furthermore, Griffin has seemed to overlook the fact that the more detailed and successful the cultural picture of a site, the more sound and the better grounded will be the cultural comparisons drawn therefrom. Like other American archeologists, he proceeds on the basis of comparing descriptive types, claiming to be objective because there is a certain mathematical element in his comparisons, and failing to abstract, or at least to provide, many of the culturally significant factors from his data. Griffin is using his great and valuable knowledge for building a two-dimensional structure, for "doing" comparative chronicle. He is not attempt-ing to construct a more-than-two-dimensional picture, to "do" either historiog-raphy or anthropology as defined in the present study.

Before closing this analytical and critical discussion, it might serve to clarify the points I wish to make if I were to name some of the publications which, in my opinion, follow lines other than the purely comparative or taxono-mic and which seem to indicate some feeling on the part of their respective authors for the broader potentialities and cultural character of the archeological data. In thus identifying these publications, it is beside the present point to argue whether or not the factual details or the derived inferences presented therein can be accepted as established by the evidence adduced. Here it will be sufficient to state that, whether evidence and conclusions are valid or not, the authors seem to have felt, or envisioned consciously, the fact that the potentials of archeological data go beyond mere time-space correlates. It will be enough to show that they have attempted to make their facts tell a broader, deeper story than usually is derived from excavated material by Americanists. It will be enough to show that they have tried to study the nature and workings of culture as an abstraction or have tried to substantiate particular facts which would be of help in constructing fuller cultural contexts. When archeologists, reporting in detail upon site excavation, include as a regular part of their monographs discussions and analyses such as are contained in the following cited publications, then Americanist archeology will be on its way toward fulfilling its implied obligations of writing American Indian history and making a study of human culture.

W. R. Wedel's paper on the *Environment and Native Subsistence Economies in the Central Great Plains* (1941b) provides an analysis of the culture-environment relationship which is an imperative requirement for every archeo-logical report or every report which deals with a region for the first time. Wedel had the vision to see that there might have been other factors than historical accident which had reacted with local cultural manifestations to produce the stratigraphic and areal picture uncovered by archeological excavation. Until these environmental factors could be assessed, it would have been futile to make specific statements as to the role played by interacting cultures within the area. Without some knowledge of the environmental aspects, it would be foolhardy to evaluate the relative importance of cultural and environmental influences in the ebb and flow of life in the Central Plains—or anywhere for that matter. When this paper of Wedel's is taken in conjunction with certain passages (e.g., 1941a, pp. 153-156; 1943, pp. 185-191) in others of his publications, there is evidence of a feeling for the picture of life as it was led and for the development of a fuller cultural context. Despite the fact that he is keenly and, it must be said, predominantly aware of the taxonomic aspects, Wedel seems to sense the fact that taxonomy is not the only product that may be forthcoming from the manipulation of archeological materials.

Several papers by J. W. Bennett make it very evident that he also is concerned with going beyond mere taxonomy and chronology. Although most of his publications follow the taxonomic line, he has shown another and most significant side to his archeological interests. In fact, his article *Recent Developments in the Functional Interpretation of Archaeological Data* (1943b) says, if in slightly different words, many of the things that have been, and will be, said in the present study. In that publication he cites other archeologists who have viewed their data from what he calls a "functional" point of view, naming, among others, P. S. Martin (1938, pp. 295ff; 1939, pp. 467ff), P. Holder and A. J. Waring, Jr. (1945), and J. Adams. These particular citations most assuredly indicate a trend among certain archeologists to include in their interpretations more than the usual Americanist range. And Bennett himself has given us two of our most ambitious and provocative papers: his study of the interaction of culture and environment among Indian and White settlers in southern Illinois (1944a) and his discussion of *Middle American Influences on Cultures of the Southeastern United States* (1944b) in which he notes the "organizational-structural" accretions. In my opinion, Bennett's three papers cited here comprise the most significant group of contributions, by a single author, from the standpoint of promise for archeological historiography and cultural anthropology, that have appeared to date. Once again, however, I wish to say that I am not prepared to argue the facts of these papers, merely that they represent an idea and an approach which I believe to be very much to the present point.

In the field of Middle American studies, G. C. Vaillant has written an account of the so-called Middle Cultures of the Valley of Mexico which is historiographic in the sense defined in the present study. It is to be found in his *Aztecs of Mexico* (1941, pp. 28-47) and provides a very fine and much-needed cultural background for the later developments of civilizations in that area. His accounts of the Toltec and Chichimec occupations contain less interpretation and picturization, are more purely descriptive of objects, and are more concerned with episodic events such as the succession of rulers and peoples. The sources for his detailed, cultural, and most excellent picture of Aztec culture are mostly documentary and therefore remove that section of the volume from consideration here. It is this last circumstance which also prevents crediting archeology with the accounts of Maya culture which Thompson and Gann have written (Gann and Thompson, 1931; Thompson, 1927). In a short paper in the *Gazette des Beaux-Arts,* G. Kubler (1943) has made some very interesting and suggestive inferences, based on sculpture, as to certain mental characteristics of the Aztecs. His remarks are definitely in a category which transcends the purely comparative and chronological and might, if corroborated by further testing of his hypothesis, lead to a better understanding of aspects of Aztec culture or of Aztec culture as a whole. In the Maya field, several papers on astronomy, mathematics, and measurement have already been cited as going beyond the usual time-space limits of Americanist archeology (Cramer, 1938; Roys, 1934; Thompson, 1934, 1939a, 1942a).

Tucked away in the midst of an archeological bibliography that otherwise consists entirely of descriptive and comparative studies lies W. C. Bennett's short article entitled *Interpretations of Andean Archeology* (1945). Here he has pointed to cultural situations which, if their implications are developed and their details elaborated by further work with a view to testing and broadening the inferences, will instigate in that area some of the most valuable investigations upon archeological historiography and cultural anthropology that will have been conducted in the Americanist field. In what can only be called a complete reversal of form, Bennett has demonstrated that he too, when given the opportunity and when expressing himself before an audience other than the usual professional archeological one, is thinking along the lines of fuller cultural pictures and the meaning of his data for problems of culture dynamics. This paper of only four and one-half pages is a remarkably stimulating document—if one is interested in more than the chronology and classification of cultural manifestations.

For all the years that archeologists from the United States have been engaged in Peruvian archeology, it remained for one who is not an archeologist to attempt to derive more than the obvious technical and comparative information from the vast and varied textile industry preserved in the arid coastal region. In her monograph on *Paracas Embroideries* (1941), Stafford says:

To show some of the thought-processes underlying the repeating patterns of Paracas embroideries is the major purpose of this study. (p. 13)

She then proceeds to write one of the most pertinent, important, and interesting accounts of an archeological cultural feature that has been published. If we had many such intensive studies and if at least some analysis of this type were done during the writing of all archeological site-reports, we would have a body of data which would indeed be cultural. It will not be until other researches have been done in similar channels that we will really have knowledge of the peoples and the cultures which we are so diligently arranging in chronological order and setting within a web of cultural interrelationships.

Before closing this section, mention should be made of some other archeologists who have in one way or another treated their material from a more cultural and less purely taxonomic viewpoint than is the usual case. As long ago as 1899, Harlan I. Smith wrote a paper suggesting the advantages of *The Ethnological Arrangement of Archaeological Material*, describing how he had made museum displays of the material from a site in Kentucky in order to show the tribal life and ethnology "of those ancient villagers" (p. 1). His words have taken a long time to reach his public, but of recent years several eastern archeologists have heeded his words and employed cultural categories and/or complexes in the presentation of their data. I refer to Cole and Deuel (1937), Fairbanks (1941, 1942), and Setzler and Jennings (1941). Problems of a cultural nature are also to be found discussed in Colton's *Reconstruction of Anasazi History* (1943b) and in the pages on painted pottery designs in *Archaeological Studies in Northeast Arizona* (Beals, Brainerd, and Smith, 1945). Finally, Osgood has drawn a cultural picture of the life around Lake Valencia, Venezuela, by the use of archeological evidence excavated from the ground (1943).

We may now return to the dichotomy which at the beginning of the second chapter was noted to occur within the conceptual structure of Americanist archeology in the United States. That the discipline as a whole should claim affiliations with cultural anthropology while maintaining that its objective is the reconstruction of history is a confusion which, unanalyzed and unresolved as it is, points to a significant disinterest in the fundamental structure of the discipline itself. It is quite apparent that the archeologists have accepted the admonition to do and die without the incumbrance of reasoning why!

The origin of this confusion may be attributed in part, if not entirely, to an uncritical appropriation of theoretical principles which impinged upon the discipline during its development. Contrary to the origin of cultural anthropology which evolved from an intensification along a single line of interest, namely culture, the present status of archeology (and this is as true of European as of Americanist) is the result of a break in tradition. In the first chapter of the present study it was shown that archeology, as it developed both abroad and in the United States, had for its major interest the past, the "history," of the people whose cultural remains were being investigated. "Historical reconstruction," then, became its purpose.

However, when the growing discipline of cultural anthropology began to take over the study of "primitives" and non-literate peoples, that part of archeology which dealt with such subjects was duly and promptly absorbed. The important factor is, however, that although incorporated within anthropology, archeology retained its major interest in "historical reconstruction" and made no effort to reconcile this purpose with the aims and objectives of the larger discipline of which it claimed to be a part. It seems that Americanist archeologists thought that, just because they were working on the culture of American Indians, i.e., "primitives," they were *ipso facto* anthropologists. They have not bothered to analyze their own activities or to inquire into exactly what, if anything, "historical reconstruction" has to do with anthropology. Furthermore, and for reasons which are not at all clear, they have come to look upon "historical reconstruction" as mere chronicle, the ordering of cultural materials in temporal sequence together with an attempt to demonstrate their derivations and cross-cultural relationships. They have failed to see, as Kroeber has stated it so well, that:

All history—whatever the field—which is worth its salt does deal with relations, with functions, with meanings. It certainly is not a tracing of the wanderings of detached and unrelated items through time and space, nor a precise but arid roster of names, dates, and places. (1946, p. 2)

They have categorized events and items, tagged them, but not investigated them in their contexts or in their dynamic aspects. As a result of these conditions, Americanist archeology is not in a healthy state. Its metabolism has gone awry. It is wasting and not assimilating its foodstuffs.

PART II

INTRODUCTION

DESPITE the claims of Americanist archeologists that their discipline belongs within the range of anthropological studies and that they themselves are anthropologists, and despite the espousal of "historical reconstruction" as their major objective, it is the blunt fact that archeology, as it is currently practiced by the majority of Americanists, is neither historiography nor anthropology. These levels of procedure have not been reached.

Of recent years, fellow students have more or less openly subscribed to the popular conception of the archeologist as a lover-of-the-great-out-of-doors or a dirt-scratching mental codger who interests himself prodigiously in the paste of Patameragouche pottery but not at all in Man as a biologically and socially functioning organism. They have accused the archeologist of tatting endless taxonomic rosettes out of the same old ball of "material culture" and maintained that his findings are next to useless for the purposes of history and culture study. It seems that the archeologists are becoming, as Tolstoy once said of modern historians, like deaf men answering questions which no one has asked them.

In their broader implications, these accusations are all too true. Today more than ever archeologists have become engrossed, to the virtual exclusion of all else, in the building of chronological sequences and so-called culture classifications with purely taxonomic inherencies. Their outlook has turned, in full face, toward temporal and spatial comparisons with the explicit or implicit purpose of writing cultural chronicles. The apparent be-all and end-all of archeological excavation appears to be the placing of the resultant finds in one or another of the taxonomic pigeonholes, and a glance at the *Conclusions* of most monographs will show them to be chiefly concerned with comparative studies and seldom with the cultural integration or implications of the data themselves.

This approach to archeological research has been called the comparative or taxonomic approach. It is primarily an attempt to determine the significance of specific cultural items with regard to relationships *outside* the cultural unit being investigated. Instead of seeking to construct as full a cultural picture as possible for the particular manifestation, this approach applies itself mainly, if not wholly, to those phenomena which have comparative significance *outside* of the site or component. It neglects much of the local cultural "corpus." It is narrow and therefore wasteful of the potentialities of the archeological data.

The conjunctive approach, on the other hand, has as its primary goal the elucidation of cultural conjunctives, the associations and relationships, the "affinities," *within* the manifestation under investigation. It aims at drawing the completest possible picture of past human life in terms of its human and geographic environment. It is chiefly interested in the relation of item to item, trait to trait, complex to complex (to use Linton's concepts) *within* the culture-unit represented and only subsequently in the taxonomic relation of these phenomena to similar ones outside of it.

It is an integral part of this major aim to make every effort to interpret the concrete, empirical findings of archeology in terms of culture itself, of cultural behavior, and of the non-material results of cultural behavior whereby the materialistic and "lifeless" data may be given life and depth. Such objectives should help not only to bring about the construction of fuller cultural contexts but also to provide material for the study of culture itself, i.e., for anthropology on a fifth level of procedure. It is one of the premises of the conjunctive approach that, when the archeological data have been gathered in satisfactory fashion and subjected to an intensive analysis, they may be expected to provide adequate bases for deriving information on the so-called non-material aspects of culture and cultural behavior.

While it is perfectly true that all the evidence for a complete cultural context cannot be obtained by archeologists from archeological sites, it is equally true that all the evidence cannot be obtained by historians or ethnographers from their sources either. Since, as Pirenne has pointed out, only the events and not their inferred relationships are empirically demonstrable in any study dealing with man's past, the difference between the archeological, documentary, and ethnographic records is merely one of degree, not of kind, and the archeologists should not consider that the limitations of their finds impose interpretive strictures upon them any more than upon other students dealing with past actuality. Up to the limits of their evidence, theirs are the same privileges and the same obligations that impinge upon ethnologists and historians.

Furthermore, it is probable that much more of the archeological evidence than has been obtained in the past can be obtained in the future merely by approaching the material with a different attitude. This attitude, the conjunctive approach, considers a site to be a discrete entity with career and cultural expression(s) of its own. It is no longer just one more unit in a spatial and temporal range of comparable units. With a vigorous effort to reveal and interpret the minute associations and relationships within the site, much more information of a cultural, as well as of a purely comparative nature may be expected. When such studies have been made for many localities and upon many time-planes, archeology will have a body of data from which the social sciences may draw with profit. It is hoped that archeology may thus progress beyond mere description and chronicle to attain, within the limits of its empirical data, the level of historiography.

CHAPTER 4

A CONCEPT OF CULTURE FOR ARCHEOLOGY

ALTHOUGH much was said in the pages of Part I about "cultural contexts" and although the terms *culture* and *cultural* were freely used, these concepts were not defined. But some agreement as to a concept of culture is absolutely vital to a conceptual scheme for any discipline, such as archeology, which identifies its subject matter as cultural. Thus it is a necessary and integral first step in the conjunctive approach to establish a concept of culture. In the present study, the definition of this concept will be specifically oriented toward archeological materials and serviceability to archeologists. Although I believe that the concept will be found useful for other disciplines dealing with cultural studies, it is not to the present point to argue this belief. If the concept proves of value for archeology, that will be justification enough, and the course of the conjunctive approach can be charted forward from there.

There have been many definitions of the concept *culture*. Some of them have been complex and a few have been overly simple. My only excuse for offering another, somewhat modified version is that none of the current examples appears to fulfill the needs of archeological study, and some of them seem to be actually misconceived. But above all, there is one point, consistently encountered in statements about culture, with which I find I must take particular issue. To anticipate briefly: the word *culture* denotes not one concept, but two. This fact is regularly overlooked by the culture-definers. The two concepts are related, but they are distinct and on two different levels of abstraction. This ambivalence is the source of basic misconceptions and will be the first point taken up in developing a concept of culture for archeology.

In the following discussion, I have made an especial attempt to keep down the number of quotations and references in the text. For those who might be interested in pursuing the topic, a bibliography is included in the *Notes*. But it has seemed conducive to a clearer presentation of my own point of view not to interrupt the train of argument too often with corroborative or antithetical documentation. I wish to thank the authors in the cited bibliography for their stimulating ideas and to draw attention to the obvious fact that, without their thoughts acting as a back-board against which to bat my own, it would have been impossible to develop the concept offered here. I admit to having made extensive use of their ideas and do not mean in any way to slight or plagiarize those who have fed my mental processes. Nevertheless, in these days of expediency, I hope my manifestly great debt will be forgiven without more specific credit for the sake of easier reading and more concise argumentation.[105]

The development of a concept of culture for archeology may be inaugurated by making three fundamental points. First and most basic is that, as it is now commonly used, the word *culture* designates two concepts: (1) a concept which is holistic and used to distinguish phenomena that are "cultural" from those that are "natural," i.e., organic and inorganic: biological, geological, chemical, etc.; and (2) a concept which is on a secondary level of abstraction, which is partitive, which denotes a segment of the holistic concept, i.e., *a* culture. The second point is that culture is a mental phenomenon, consisting of the contents of minds, not of material objects or observable behavior. And the third point is that a "trait" or unit of culture can be either shared or idiosyncratic, i.e., it can be common to many individual minds or to the mind of a single individual. These three points will be taken up in order, and their substantiation will constitute a reasoned development of a concept of culture.

The archeologist who finds an oddly shaped stone during the progress of his excavations will ask himself whether that stone is "natural" or "cultural." By this question, he means to inquire whether it is a product of human activity or merely a peculiar formation caused by some geologic or meteorologic force. A recent article in *American Antiquity* (Goldsmith, 1945) is at great pains to distinguish between skulls exhibiting a pathologic anomaly called the "Catlin Mark" and skulls which have been modified through the act of trephining. In other words, the article desires to distinguish between the "cultural" and the "biological." Lowie has said that "ethnology is simply science grappling with the phenomena segregated from the remainder of the universe as 'cultural' " (1936a, p. 320). In effect, this is saying that there must be categorization on the basis of cultural as opposed to non-cultural phenomena before ethnological study can begin. Strong said that the major aim of anthropology is to elucidate the relationship between "man and culture" (1936, p. 364), and Kroeber said the aim is to interpret those phenomena into which both "organic and social causes enter" (1923, p. 3). For problems involving two factors, the primary procedure must be to differentiate between those factors. Thus both Kroeber and Strong imply that the prerequisite for anthropological study is to distinguish the cultural or the social from the organic and then to examine their interrelationships and mutual products.

If, as seems to be the case, the cultural is to be segregated from other categories in the problems set for themselves by the archeologists, ethnologists, and other students of the so-called social sciences, then it is an absolute necessity that the primary breakdown of their data be made upon exactly that basis: the cultural and the non-cultural. The fact that non-cultural factors often impinge upon and influence phenomena which are considered cultural does not alter this requirement. The fact that culture is not literally "super-organic" means only that there actually is a relationship between what can be defined as cultural and what can be defined as organic. But the crucial point is that the two sets of phenomena have to be defined, if only for the sake of study. If two factors are so hopelessly mixed that they cannot be separated, there are no means of studying their interrelationships or their individual effects upon tertiary phenomena into which they both enter as factors or "causes."

Thus it is that for all the so-called social sciences the primary breakdown of data, the first level of abstraction, hinges upon a concept of culture set against concepts of the same level, such as the organic, the inorganic, the geologic, the chemical, etc. Culture must first be defined so as to discriminate between it and those other concepts which are on the same level of abstraction.

The second concept of culture is on a secondary level of abstraction and serves to denote *a* culture. Whereas the first was holistic, the second is partitive. It designates a more or less cohesive and separable segment of that whole which was denoted by *culture* in the first sense. The first concept serves to designate what is cultural from what is not; the second serves to distinguish between the unitary segments of the whole that is culture. For example, we identify Western European culture, Eskimo culture, or the culture of second generation Swedes in Minnesota. But we would be unable to partition the whole into segments unless we had already determined what made up that whole, i.e., what was cultural and what was not. The logical order of procedure is first to determine what is cultural and then to determine whether certain of these cultural phenomena are such that they can acceptably be grouped into *a* culture.

It may appear that discriminating between these two meanings of the word *culture* is splitting hairs, that actually we are faced with a single concept and its constituent parts rather than two concepts. This would be a justifiable criticism if all those particular individual cultures denoted by concept No. 2 added up to the whole denoted by concept No. 1. But this is not the case. The holistic concept is in a manner of speaking an emergent. It includes more than the sum of those separable segments denoted by concept No. 2. The whole that is *culture* is greater than the sum of all the particular cultures which are part of it. This assertion will not be defended at this time because the entire third section of this chapter, i.e., the one devoted to the point that culture "traits" can be either shared or idiosyncratic, is nothing more than such a defense. Here, only two aspects of a corroborative nature will be presented.

In the first place, as far as the need to distinguish between the two concepts is concerned, it makes little difference whether the whole is, or is not, greater than the sum of its parts. The need is still present. It has been shown that we are dealing with two levels of abstraction when we talk of *culture* and *a* culture. This fact alone is sufficient to make a separation worth while. This is distinctly so, if only in order to avoid theoretical confusion and guard against falling into the Fallacy of Misplaced Concreteness (Whitehead, 1927, pp. 73-86). In the second place, this *quasi* emergent quality of culture should not be difficult to visualize, for the case here is no different from that in, say, zoology. For example, a sport or drastic mutation in an ornithological species may be unassignable to any one particular species. It may be taxonomically isolated and unclassifiable on a specific level, but it nevertheless must still be regarded as a bird. Thus the Class *Aves* is greater than the sum of all the members of all the identifiable avian species. For another example, let us imagine the offspring of a mating between an Eskimo and a Hottentot. This "Hotteneskimo" could not be pigeon-holed with either of these "pure" biological categories. As the only one of his kind, he would not fall into any "racial" group. Yet, our Hotteneskimo would surely have to be classified as *Homo sapiens,* and thus he would increase by one the number of the whole, i.e., Mankind, while altering the statistics for the "races" not a whit. That this same set of circumstances is operative in the realm of the cultural will be shown later in this chapter.

It should be most clearly stated that, in the following discussion, I shall be defining culture only as a holistic concept. The relation of the partitive to the holistic concept will perforce have to follow the establishment of the latter.

The second point in this definition of the concept *culture* is that culture is a mental construct, having to do with the contents of minds and not with material objects or observable behavior. This contention is based on deductions from two premises which have assumed axiomatic character in the literature of cultural studies. The first is that "the prolonged infancy of man is regarded universally as one of the necessary conditions of culture" (Powdermaker, 1945, p. 310). As Linton has said (1936b, p. 72), the importance of this long period of parental dependency is that it permits and insures learning on the part of the infant. That is to say, it facilitates the acquisition of mental constructs. Its value for culture most certainly does not lie in the acquisition of material objects or the accumulation of behavioral acts divorced from their mental residue. The advantages of a lengthy infancy are not in the collection of innumerable old shoes, building blocks, parts of internal combustion engines, and radio tubes. Nor is it of any advantage to the child to perform whole constellations of behavior without retaining in his mind a residue of ideas pertaining thereto. By themselves, neither objects nor behavior will be of value to the infant or to culture. The important factor is obviously the one which remains in the mind to be carried on, modified, transmitted. The premise that prolonged infancy is important for culture implies and is based on the fact that culture is a mental phenomenon.

The second premise is "the fact that the cultural content is a heritage of the past and that it is cumulative" (Goldenweiser, 1929, p. 566 fn.). The culture-whole existing today owes its form and at least the majority of its content to what is called the cultural heritage. Students of culture seem to be agreed on this point. The reason we are able to progress the way we do (they say) is because we are able to build on pre-existing culture foundations. The reason that certain civilizations have flourished more than some others (they say) is because they have received more, or more elaborate, "culture streams." The deductions from this premise are the same as from the first: culture is a mental construct and does not consist of material objects or observable behavior.

The test of this contention is in an examination of the transmission of culture. The reason that the culture corpus is more elaborate today than formerly is not because of the transmission down through the ages of a lot of old Roman chariots or Chinese firecrackers, or because the *actual acts* of early Teutonic, Slavic, or Arabic behavior have survived, or because the *actual sounds* produced by bygone Africans have been preserved to the expansion of modern music. These objects and acts of the empirical world have long since passed away and become as nothing. What has remained to fertilize present-day culture are the mental components of these phenomena. The modern steamboat is based on Fulton's ideas, not on physical additions to the structure of the original *Clermont*. Once a dance pattern has been stepped out upon the ground of some tribal plaza, it has gone. What remains to be passed on as a culture heritage, to be added to and taken from, are the mental constructs pertinent to that pattern and from which that pattern was derived.

Malinowski has several times made this point (e.g., 1931). Mere physical form is extraneous as far as culture is concerned, being a property of the world of physics and not of culture. But in one place Malinowski has also maintained that culture "is nothing but the organized behavior of man" (1936, p. 440) and in another that culture is "the integral whole consisting of implements and consumers' goods, of constitutional charters for the various social groupings, of human ideas and crafts, beliefs and customs" (1944, p. 36). These statements seem to encompass a large range and to controvert the limited view expressed in the present study. There arises the question, therefore, of the relations between behavior, implements, and the concept of culture as a mental phenomenon.

According to the concept of culture being developed here, culture is a mental construct consisting of ideas. Under the term *idea,* for present purposes, are subsumed such categories as attitudes, meanings, sentiments, feelings, values, goals, purposes, interests, knowledge, beliefs, relationships, associations. These ideas are not themselves observable. They are objectified and made observable through the action-systems of the body, being activated in the form of behavior that is observable both visually and audibly. In turn, this behavior results in material objects such as axes and automobiles, and non-material manifestations such as dance patterns, musical tones and rhythms, styles of graphic and fictile representation, etc. For example, there is present in an Indian's mind the idea of a dance. This is the trait of culture. This idea influences his body so that he behaves in a certain way. The result of this behavioral activity is the pattern of the dance, the sequence of body motions, etc. Both the behavior itself and the resulting patterns are observable, but for this very reason they are fleeting. The culture idea is not observable but endures in the Indian's mind to be repeated again.

Both behavior and the results of behavior, if they stem from ideas, pertain to culture. They are not culture, but they are "cultural." Thus we are dealing with three orders of phenomena, two of which pertain to culture and are thus cultural, but only one of which *is* culture. A stone axe, a song, a dance performance are not culture traits. They are objectifications of culture traits. The elements or traits of culture are unobservable and must be inferred from their objectifications, from behavior or the results of behavior. This is true whether we are dealing with data that are ethnographical, archeological, archival, verbal, observational, or whatever.

It also follows from this that the concept of "material culture" is fallacious. Culture is unobservable and non-material. Even behavior, although observable, is non-material. It is only when we come down to the third order, the results of behavior, that there is a problem of material and non-material categories. But this order consists only of objectifications of culture and does not constitute culture itself. Therefore, the term *material culture* is a misnomer and the dichotomy between material and non-material relates only to observable results of cultural behavior, not to culture itself.

Thus it is that culture itself is completely inferential and non-experiential from the observer's or objective point of view. The primary data of all culture studies, therefore, are found in categories of the second and third orders, in cultural behavior and the material and non-material results of cultural behavior. The implications of this fact for archeology are easily envisioned. A detailed discussion of this point, however, will be postponed until the next chapter.

The third point in this definition of the concept of culture is that culture traits may be either shared or idiosyncratic, belonging either to one mind or to several individual minds. It follows that an object or a bit of behavior may be cultural even if it is the only example of its kind in existence or ever to have been in existence. These assertions are in contrast to the stated or implied beliefs of the majority of those who have written on the subject of culture. Variously, it has been said that culture is "social behavior" (Sapir, 1927, p. 117; 1938, p. 9), "social heredity" (Linton, 1936b, p. 80), or that one indispensable factor of a trait of culture is its quality of being shared (Kluckhohn and Kelly, 1944, pp. 4-6, 32). These views, I believe, are the result of shifting between culture concepts No. 1 and No. 2 without making due allowance for the change in level of abstraction. They are the result of starting to talk about *culture* and ending by talking of *a* culture, or *vice versa*. For example, Linton says:

Any item of behavior, and so on, which is peculiar to a single individual in *a* society is not to be considered as a part of *the society's* culture. . . . Thus a new technique for weaving baskets would not be classed as a part of *culture* as long as it was known only to one person. (1945a, p. 35, italics mine)

I would be in agreement with his first sentence: an individual peculiarity is not part of *a* society's culture, part of *a particular* culture. But on the holistic level, where the anthropologist must distinguish between what pertains to culture and what pertains to the organic and inorganic realms, just how is this weaving technique to be classified? It seems to make more sense to categorize it as cultural than to say that it is biological or chemical. Whatever the decision, it is very apparent that Linton has slipped from talking about the culture of *a* society, or *a* culture, to talking about what is part of *culture*. Perhaps this is a literary slip, but that fact in itself might be significant. It becomes more so, and one begins to wonder if after all it was purely literary, when one finds him virtually repeating himself by saying that *"culture as a whole* consists of the sum total of *a* society's patterned responses to its needs" (1936b, p. 411, italics mine). The case begins to look even more conceptual when we find Kluckhohn and Kelly saying:

But *culture* is like a map. Just as the map isn't the territory but an abstract representation of the territory so also *a* culture is an abstract description of trends toward uniformity in the words, acts, and artifacts of human *groups*. (1944, p. 26, italics mine)

For another, Murdock lists the seven basic assumptions of culture by starting with "culture is learned," "culture is inculcated," and then for his third assumption saying:

Habits of *the cultural order* are not only inculcated and then transmitted over time; they are also social, that is, shared by human beings living in organized aggregates or societies and kept relatively uniform by social pressure. They are, in short, *group habits*. (1940, p. 365, italics mine)

And again, Dollard says that " *'culture'* is the name given to these abstracted (from men) intercorrelated customs of *a* social group." (1939, p. 50, italics mine)

I believe that there is shifting from one level of abstraction to another in these examples, and I also have two other beliefs concerning the statements themselves: first, that demanding the shared or "social" criterion before archeological data can be considered cultural is an unworkable and impractical requirement; and second, that when the ethnologists and sociologists demand it for their own data, they are confused between the discrimination of one culture from another and the discrimination of what is cultural from what is non-cultural. I believe that, if they were taxed with this conceptual ambivalence, they themselves would deny the criterion of sharing as a requisite for the holistic concept. As I will attempt to show somewhat later, it is a logically untenable position and is not held even in their own writings. First, however, I shall argue a more immediate claim: that the requirement is unworkable and impractical for archeology.

Let us return to the archeologist who dug up the oddly shaped stone and wished to know whether that object pertained to his research as a student of cultural phenomena or whether it belonged to the investigations of his colleagues the geologists, the students of "natural" rock formations. Let us suppose that the archeologist found (as we did in Coahuila, Mexico) the surface of the stone to be covered with tool marks, its present shape obviously the result of carving, and its color due to an application of red paint. And let us suppose that only one specimen was found at the site and that no other examples were known in archeological literature. In what category would the archeologist be justified in classifying this specimen? According to those who would restrict the terms *culture* and *cultural* to shared or "social" ideas and objectifications, this single specimen could not be classified as cultural and therefore would fall outside of the range of cultural studies. It would be foreign to the investigations of the archeologist as a student of culture. Is this what the culture-definers have intended? Is this stone to be rejected from consideration by "social scientists" and turned over to . . . but to whom? Does it fit more readily into the researches of the physicists? Or is it more significant to geological studies or chemical studies?

Perhaps we should demand that the archeologist find another similar stone before we permit either example to be the subject of study by students of culture. Here the problem arises as to just how exact the likeness must be before the two stones can be adjudged the results of a shared idea and thus attain the status of cultural objects. Let us suppose that the archeologist does find another similar stone. How is it to be told whether the second is the work of the same or a different artisan? If both stones were the product of one man, they represent but a single, unshared idea and would consequently fall into a non-cultural category. On what grounds is the archeologist to tell whether two worked stones were made by two individuals? Does the closeness of similarity indicate a single artisan or a single idea shared by two craftsmen? Does a difference indicate a change in one man's idea or skill, or does it signify a single idea in the minds of two men but subject to variations in skill? These questions must receive an answer if we are to determine whether an idea is shared and whether material objects are indicative of a shared idea. It is rare or impossible that the inferences necessary to such answers can be made from archeological materials without an unconditional surrender to purely subjective, unsupported, and non-testable hypotheses. In ethnology, sociology, and other disciplines working on living societies and with living informants, such hypotheses can be checked and validated, but with archeological materials this is out of the question.

In other words, whatever the case may be for living societies, the requirement that an idea must be shared to be cultural is not a practical criterion for archeology. It serves no purpose for the ethnologists to insist that archeologists cry for the moon or that the archeologists themselves should seek it. Archeological materials at best are meager and, having run an almost mortal gauntlet between the ranks of preservation and excavation techniques, they are in no condition to be attacked from what should be a friendly flank. If the archeologist is prevented from treating as cultural all those finds of which he has been unfortunate —or fortunate—enough to discover only one example, he is being further and probably disastrously handicapped. If, beyond this, he must disregard, as noncultural, even those multiple specimens for which a shared idea cannot acceptably be inferred from the archeological data, the archeologist might as well shut up shop. He will better employ his efforts merely collecting pots and other *objets d'art*. As a discipline dealing with cultural phenomena, archeology is finished, in fact it never started!

Some may argue that this is exactly the present status of archeology. Perhaps many would say that archeology can serve the "social sciences" by developing the time and space coordinates of the past irrespective of cultural content, but that as a student of culture the archeologist is out of the running. I believe that this would be an unfair judgment. I believe that archeology can provide some very important data for the study of culture. If it can be demonstrated to the general satisfaction that this criterion of sharing is an unwarranted restriction, even in non-archeological researches such as ethnology and sociology, then much of the foundation for this derogation of archeology will be shorn away. If the demand that a culture trait be a shared trait can be assigned to a confusion between concepts of culture No. 1 and No. 2, between concepts of *culture as a whole* and *a* culture, then the argument will fail, and the archeologist may proceed with his work as a student of culture and things cultural.

In not a few anthropological and sociological monographs, we find statements which, in effect, say that "culture always, and necessarily, satisfies basic biological needs and secondary needs derived therefrom" (Murdock, 1940, p. 366). This same thesis has been expounded many times by Malinowski (e.g., 1931; 1944, Chaps. 9-13). If culture is in any way responsive to biological needs and if we must accept the "social" or sharing criterion, how is it that an idea which is common to, and caters to the biological needs of, several individuals *is* culture, while an idea which caters to the needs of one individual *is not?* Are we to imagine a Group Biology which creates culture and an Individual Biology which creates something else? Is this not perilously near to the repudiated "Group Mind" type of thinking? I do not think that the culture-definers intend this conclusion to be drawn from their work. There is some misunderstanding here, and I suggest that it lies in a failure to recognize a holistic concept of culture.

To take another example, we note that La Barre (1938, pp. 111ff) says that the Kiowa appear to have obtained the peyote cult from the Mescalero Apache, that in 1868 or 1870 Big Horse was the only Kiowa using the narcotic, and that by 1886 Mooney found the Kiowa as a group embracing the cult. How do these facts throw light on the present discussion? Taking the sharing criterion as our standard for the moment, we find that peyotism was shared by the Mescalero as a group and was, therefore, a "trait of culture." By 1886, it was also shared among the Kiowa and was thus a "trait of culture." But what was the situation between those dates? To an investigator of the Kiowa in 1868, there was but a single individual using peyote. Peyote represented an unshared, idiosyncratic idea. If that investigator did not happen to have the Mescalero data at hand, he would have been forced into the position of saying: "Peyotism belongs only to Big Horse; it is idiosyncratic and therefore non-cultural; I am a student of culture and should investigate only what pertains to culture; therefore, this peyote business is no concern of mine; I will forget about it."

I believe that there would be general agreement that when Big Horse alone practiced it, peyotism was not a part of *Kiowa culture*. But was peyotism, therefore, noncultural? Was the ethnologist justified in rejecting the evidence of peyotism as impertinent to his studies? If he had rejected it, would he not have been losing important evidence which did, in fact, pertain to cultural studies, even if at that time, and to him, it did not show signs of being shared? Can a single idea be alternately cultural and non-cultural in a holistic sense? If so, what does it become when it is no longer cultural?

Suppose for a moment that by 1868 the peyote cult had disappeared from Mescalero life and that Big Horse was the only living practitioner. Would it then have no importance or significance to ethnologists? Can an idea, whose antecedents and whose descendants both are admitted to be traits of culture, suddenly change and require classification in some other category *on the same level of abstraction?* While Big Horse's idea cannot be considered a part of Kiowa culture in 1868, I maintain that his idea was even at that time a trait of culture in the holistic sense. Yet the culture-definers say that "to be cultural, it must be shared." What they really mean is: "to be part of *a* culture, it must be shared." They fail to recognize that some phenomena, which may be cultural in the sense that they are not organic or geological or some such, at the same time may not be a part of some particular, separable *segment* of the whole that is culture.

All individual instances of a shared trait are usually not experienced by the investigator simultaneously. The normative or shared character of these instances must be pieced together from many multiple observations over what is possibly a long period of time or a considerable range of space. The individual cases, therefore, although they may appear idiosyncratic for the time being, must be recorded in order even to ascertain any shared or normative characteristics. The ethnologists do this very thing and thus admit, if only tacitly, that individual cases are grist to their mill. By doing this, they further admit that single instances are cultural in the holistic sense, whether or not they are eventually found to be cultural with respect to the particular segment of the culture-whole that is being investigated.

In short, it does not seem that the idiosyncratic can be overlooked in studies of culture. It is the basis for the development of the normative or shared. Linton, it seems to me, assumes an untenable position when he says:

Individual Peculiarities cannot be classed as a part of *culture,* in the sense in which the term is ordinarily used, since they are not shared by any of *a society's* members. At the same time they are of extreme importance in cultural dynamics since they are the starting point of everything which later becomes incorporated into culture. (1936b, p. 274, italics mine)

His shifting from one level of abstraction to another is very clear in this statement. It is also apparent that what he means by culture "in the sense in which the term is ordinarily used" is *a* culture, not culture as opposed to the "natural," the "biological," etc. How something which is "the starting point of everything which later becomes incorporated into culture" is not to be considered as cultural, pertaining to culture, is difficult to understand. What is it then? If it is not pertinent, if it is not cultural in some sense or other, may we be permitted to disregard it in our cultural studies? For one who has written that:

Except in the most superficial terms, the workings of society and culture cannot be understood without constant reference to the needs and capacities of the individual. (1945d, p. v)

this refusal to admit that Individual Peculiarities constitute culture, at least in some sense, is indeed a paradox. Further, Linton says:

Individual Peculiarities occupy somewhat the same position with regard to culture that individual mutations occupy with regard to a biological species. (1936b, p. 274)

In the first place, he equates *culture as a whole* with *a* species, whereas the equation should have been between *a* culture and *a* species. Furthermore, while mutations may have little importance as far as species or other *particular* taxonomic categories are concerned, they are still classifiable and of importance to more generalized taxonomic groupings. To cite but one simple example, a mutation produced by parents of the species *Falco sparverius sparverius* (the Sparrowhawk) might not be assignable on a rigid taxonomic basis to that species. But it might very well be assignable to the genus *Falco* or to the family FALCONIDAE, and the very fact that a species of *Falco* had a tendency to produce mutations might be of considerable interest and significance to ornithologists studying the genus or the family. The range and number of mutations within the species of the genus, the direction of the variation, the geographic and ecological relationships and signficance, all are factors of importance to a student of the genus *Falco*—whether or not the individual bird can be assigned to the species *sparverius* or not.

Similarly, just because some idea or man-made object is not shared and cannot, therefore, be assigned to a particular culture, we are not justified in saying that it has no significance for the study of culture, in short, that it is not cultural. Are we to believe that the range of individual variation from a shared or normative trait is of no significance in cultural studies? And if it is of significance in actual fact, then is not the individual variation cultural? Logically, for one phenomenon to have significance for another within a particular field of study, both phenomena must lie within a single frame of reference, at least for the purpose of that study. Some common denominator is required before comparisons and relationships can have significance. When a mouse is compared with the Empire State building, some common ground for pertinence must be established, weight, cubic content, location, etc. It would be useless to compare them on the basis of whiskers or eye color. Thus, if idiosyncratic ideas or objects have significance for other ideas or objects within the framework of culture studies, it must be assumed that both the idiosyncratic and the normative are within the realm of culture. Therefore, traits of culture and objectifications of culture traits may be either idiosyncratic or shared.

In point of actual fact, as it is used today by the ethnologists, this criterion of sharing is based on the implicit premise that the sharing be within *a* culture, *a* society. Although they do not specifically make the point, they obviously do not mean that any idea which is the possession of more than a single mind is "social" and to be designated as a culture trait in their terms. It is assumed that the sharing will be within the confines of one of those separable segments which they have identified as societies or cultures. This was the conclusion reached by the analysis of Kiowa peyotism above (p. 106). I will give another, brief example, part fictional and part factual.

During the recent war I had occasion to teach the disassembly and assembly of the Colt .45 caliber pistol. During the course of this teaching I worked out two minor short-cuts in the operation. Among my students were a Gurkha from India, a Frenchman from Marseilles, a Navaho from New Mexico. Let us suppose either that these men were the only ones to whom I taught the short-cuts or that they were the only survivors of those who received this special instruction. When they returned home and once more took up the life and culture of their own people, what would be the status of the idea concerning the two short-cuts? It would be a shared idea. But would this fact of itself be enough to make the idea "social"? Would similar handling of the Colt .45 by single individuals in France, India, and the United States be enough to satisfy the criterion of "social behavior" or shared behavior? I believe not. If, on the other hand, once the Gurkha got home he taught the tricks to his fellows, and the short-cuts spread to many thousands of Gurkha soldiers, what then would be the status? I believe that then the idea would be considered to be part of Gurkha (military) culture, a socially shared idea and thus a part of culture according to the culture-definers. But this example has shown that a critical factor is not sharing *per se*, but rather the sharing by *a* culture, *a* society. In other words, the criterion of sharing is itself premised on sharing within a separable, unitary segment of culture. The criterion of sharing operates on a lower, partitive level of abstraction. It pertains to culture concept No. 2.

If the anthropologists, sociologists, and other culture-definers insist that the term *culture* be reserved for those phenomena which are shared and "social," they will have to do one of two things. They will either have to recognize the difference between the holistic and partitive usages of the term and make the distinction clear in their thinking and writing, or they will have to find another name by which to refer to the holistic concept. The property of being shared must not implicitly and erroneously be demanded of phenomena which are cultural in the holistic sense. If it is realized, as Bidney has done, that

. . . a particular cultural trait may be either individual or social; . . . [and that] cultural behavior may be socially acquired by man as a member of society without being social or common to all members of his group. (1944, p. 35)

there will probably be no need to burden the literature with another term. Nevertheless, it is of the utmost importance for archeology and other disciplines dealing with cultural matters to make, and keep clear, the distinction in levels of thinking between the holistic and the partitive concepts of culture.

The three points have now been made: (1) the term *culture* stands for two concepts, one holistic and the other partitive; (2) a trait of culture in the holistic sense may be either shared or idiosyncratic, but in the partitive sense it must be shared; (3) the concept of culture designates a mental construct consisting of ideas. These are but three factors in the definition I propose to develop for archeology.

From this juncture onward, however, I shall be following, with merely minor modifications, the arguments brought forward by Kluckhohn and Kelly (1944). I shall, in part, use their terminology and shall imply by this procedure that their arguments express my views and may be used to justify the present definition. And as I have already said, the concept defined will be the holistic one unless otherwise stated.

A "descriptive" concept of x tells what x "consists of." *By culture as a descriptive concept, I mean all those mental constructs or ideas which have been learned or created after birth by an individual.* As I said above, for the present purposes the term *idea* includes such categories as attitudes, meanings, sentiments, feelings, values, goals, purposes, interests, knowledge, beliefs, relationships, associations. I have not used Kluckhohn's and Kelly's factor of "designs" because, whether they meant it so or not, the word has overtones of the sharing criterion which has been repudiated as a factor in the holistic concept of culture.

An "explanatory" concept of *x* tells what *x* "does." *By culture as an explanatory concept, I mean all those mental constructs which are used to understand, and to react to, the experiential world of internal and external stimuli.* In this, I have rejected Kluckhohn's and Kelly's use of the word *men* because it begs the question, not yet settled to the general satisfaction, of whether non-human animals can be said to have culture. Also I have not used their factor of "processes" since I believe that processes such as diffusion, culture contact, and acculturation (which they name) do not constitute culture. They are sometimes cultural in that they pertain to culture, but they are by no means confined only to that category. Diffusion, for example, is a concept which denotes either a dynamic force or the state resulting from a dynamic force. It may mean the act of diffusing or the results of having diffused, and the concept may refer to culture, to plants, to animals, or even to such objects as glacial erratics. The concept of diffusion is merely the designation for a set of relationships existing between certain phenomena which may be ideas, objectifications of ideas, rocks, elephants, or whatever. Culture itself consists of ideas, not processes. In the same way, an engine consists of pistons and spark plugs, not of combustion or electrical energy.

By a culture, i.e., by culture as a partitive concept, I mean a historically derived system of culture traits which is a more or less separable and cohesive segment of the-whole-that-is-culture and whose separate traits tend to be shared by all or by specially designated individuals of a group or "society." This concept must be distinguished from the holistic concepts which were defined in the first two definitions above. Except for word changes which I believe to be minor, there is no difference between this and the definition given by Kluckhohn and Kelly.

To summarize: culture consists of the increments which have accrued to individual minds after birth—when the increments of a sufficient number of minds are enough alike, we say we are dealing with *a* culture. Culture traits are manifested by cultural agents through the medium of vehicles, to borrow Sorokin's terms (1943, pp. 4ff). In the case of human culture, these agents are human beings; the cultural vehicles are the objectifications of culture, i.e., the observable behavior and the results of behavior. Cultural processes are the dynamic factors involving culture traits; they do not constitute culture but comprise the relationships between culture traits.

Culture, consisting as it does of mental constructs, is not directly observable. It cannot, therefore, constitute the empirical data of any discipline. Culture can be studied only through the instrumentality of observable phenomena, through what have been called the objectifications of culture: cultural behavior and the material and non-material results of such behavior. A tribal dance, the avoidance of a woman by her son-in-law, the identical appellation used between a small child and an old man, the designs of a Navaho sandpainting, a stone axe, all these are observable phenomena. The culture ideas behind them can only be inferred. Even the statements of a living informant do not empirically demonstrate and establish the ideas they allege to reproduce. Checking and cross-checking of informants is a common practice and a vital requirement. Its purpose is to attain by progressive stages an ever closer approximation to the actual idea held in the informant's mind. But whether or not the idea is ever exactly reproduced cannot be a matter of certain demonstration. It remains always in the realm of plausible inference. If the inference explains other phenomena satisfactorily and if it serves as a practical and trustworthy premise for logical reasoning and the explanation of observable fact, then it may be accepted as an approximation of a culture idea. It is only to this extent that any culture trait may be ascertained.

The method is one of successively nearer approximations. Conclusive assurance or exact knowledge is forever out of reach. It develops into a question of continued testing and modification in order to reduce error and attain a closer correspondence between inference and actual idea. It is for this reason, if for no other, that context is of such tremendous importance in all culture studies. If it were possible empirically to test inferences about culture ideas merely by some laboratory experiment which would produce a definitive answer, context would be of much less value. For example, the mineral cobalt, when subjected to blow-pipe analysis involving borax and sodium metaphosphate beads, invariably gives a blue flame in either oxidizing or reducing atmosphere. This is a very delicate and sure test. If by some such empirical procedure we could obtain as conclusive knowledge about the ideas which gave rise to a certain Navaho sandpainting, the constant checking and modification, the continual recourse to cultural context would be eliminated or, at least, much curtailed. But we have no such open-and-shut tests for mental constructs. We must turn to other procedures. In effect, we must say: "A set of observed facts lead us to make a given inference. How does this inference fit and explain other related observations: not at all, exactly, or askew? If askew, in what direction and what modification can be made to bring it more in line? How does the modified inference fit yet other empirical data impinging upon the current frame of reference? If exactly or not at all, is this coincidental or can we assume actual correspondence? We shall need to check other aspects of the context." And so it goes. The testing and alterations require an ever increasing circle of context.

This context consists of two sets of data: first, the objectifications of culture (behavior and results of behavior); second, those culture traits which have been accepted as plausible or which are assumed as plausible for the sake of the immediate investigation. In addition, the relationships between objectifications and traits, between objectifications themselves, and between traits themselves are of intrinsic concern in the development of a cultural context. By the term *relationships* is meant, for example, such factors as the connection between ideas of economic value and the behavior of parents in giving and receiving wedding exchanges, the relation of designs on Pueblo pottery to Pueblo kiva paintings, the concordance between concepts of the supernatural and empirical knowledge of the natural environment, the relative quantitative utilization of stone and bone or of animal and vegetal foods, the relative care displayed in the manufacture of ceremonial and utilitarian goods, etc. In other words, in addition to the description of cultural behavior and its results, a cultural context consists of the associations and relations of these elements, of the balance between them, of their relative quantitative and qualitative positions within the whole.

It is not being too pedantic to point out that there is a difference, in the conceptual scheme proposed here, between a cultural context and a culture context. The former has just been described. The latter consists of a context of inferred ideas, of configurations of mental constructs. Historiographies, whether derived from documentary, ethnographic, or archeological materials, when they attain the level of context, are *cultural,* and not *culture,* contexts. To be sure, ideas and their relationships are often part of such writings. They serve many times to tie together and give integration and balance to the recorded acts of behavior and results of behavior. But they are secondary to the primary purpose of a historiography, which is to elucidate, not the ideas which structure the particular culture, but rather the observable and recorded phenomena, to offer some explanation for their actuality, to integrate the cultural picture which the investigator wishes to paint. The difference between historiographies and culture studies is one of the degree to which emphasis is placed on objectifications of culture traits or on the traits themselves. The difference lies in the purposes and end-results of research. Here, we come back once more to the points raised in Chapter 2 above. Many historians use culture traits, i.e., inferred mental constructs, to help them interpret and fill out their cultural picture of past actuality. Likewise cultural anthropologists use cultural contexts, and they develop their inferences about the culture of the particular people and about culture in general therefrom. The two disciplines use the same range of materials but have different emphases and aims.

CHAPTER 5

THE NATURE OF ARCHEOLOGICAL DATA: TYPOLOGY AND CLASSIFICATION

THE materials upon which the archeologist must work are restricted. Nevertheless, while the cultural contexts of ethnography, sociology, and historiography may thus be fuller and broader, it should be pointed out that they are not to be considered *culture*-contexts any more than those of archeology. Students of written documents and of the living, as well as the archeologists, must rely on inferences from *cultural* contexts to construct a culture-context or to attain understanding of culture and its workings. Therefore, the difference between archeology and the other disciplines lies in the fullness of their respective materials and in the number, and potential corroboration, of the inferences derived therefrom, not in the inability of archeology and the ability of the others to obtain immediate knowledge of culture itself. The difference is thus one of degree and not of kind.[106]

The archeological materials are restricted both as to quantity and range of representation. In the first place, as in all cultural studies, the archeologist can empirically deal only with objectifications of culture. But his data are further reduced because behavior is transitory and does not "fossilize." Therefore the archeologist is dependent upon the results of behavior. Even here there is restriction. The non-material results of behavior, i.e., the forms of dances, the cadences and rhythms of song, the patterns of religious ritual do not endure. There remain for the archeologist's study only the material results of behavior, and only such of these as have withstood the inroads of man and the elements.

However, there is one source of archeological data, not mentioned above and, oddly enough, rarely mentioned or fully utilized in archeological literature. I refer to what may be called the *affinities* existing between the material remains: between individual cultural objects, between groups of objects, between objects and the natural environment. These affinities are as much facts and as much integral parts of the archeological data as are the material objects themselves. For example, the fact that a particular bone tool has been found within a certain coiled basket is to be dealt with in a manner exactly comparable to the fact that there existed at the site a bone tool and a basket. That there is a three-to-one ratio between axes and celts in a site or region is just as much a bit of archeological data as that axes and celts were present. The circumstance that a shell came from the Pacific Ocean is to be reckoned with just as much as that the shell formed part of a necklace. If the archeologist does not specifically search for, and consciously make use of, these affinities, he is overlooking a great proportion of his already meager data. Often they lie hidden to the casual eye within the cultural and natural contents of an archeological site. But without them there is possible only description and superficial quantification of material objects; interpretations must depend on only a fraction of the potential evidence; and the result is a flat and shallow picture which foreswears even those few integrating factors which have survived the swath of time. The general neglect of these affinities seems to be the greatest failing of Americanist archeology in the United States. Evidence for this viewpoint has been presented in Chapter 3 of the present study.

Archeological data, then, consist of the material results of cultural behavior, and the affinities—quantitative, qualitative, spatial, etc.—which can be found to exist among them, and between them and the natural environment. But mere description of these phenomena cannot satisfy the requirements of archeological study—if the archeologist is bent upon writing history or studying culture. Description must be made, to be sure; but there is also the need for interpretation and synthesis. The empirical facts which have been produced by the archeologist's spade and the affinities between them must be interpreted in a "cultural sense" and combined into a cultural context. The significance of the observational facts for the life and custom of the site must be drawn by inference. This is the work of construction which falls to the archeologist.

An archeological cultural context, therefore, *is based* upon material results of cultural behavior and their affinities. On the other hand, it *consists* of a presentation, in narrative or synoptic form, of the life-ways characteristic of the former occupants of the site, component, area under investigation. It should be most emphatically stated that it does not consist of a series of descriptions and quantifications under what may be termed *empirical categories*.

There is a most definite and important distinction to be made between empirical and cultural categories. The former include such rubrics as *Stone, Bone, Objects of Copper, Environment*. The latter include *Food, Dress, Hunting, Textile Industry, Utilization of Environment, Containers, Transportation*. In fact, one may make a very trenchant comparison between the empirical categories of almost any standard archeological monograph and the cultural headings found in such a work as the *Outline of Cultural Materials* (Murdock *et al.*, 1945). "Cultural headings" may, in some ways, be equated with the "trait complexes" or "activities" as described by Linton (1936b, p. 397ff).

Empirical categories have their very specific place in archeological studies and reports, but they do not comprise, either singly or in the aggregate, what may properly be called a cultural context. This point will be treated at some length later in this chapter. Here it is sufficient to indicate that an archeological cultural context, by the very nature of the basic materials, is constructed by inference to a greater extent, perhaps, than contexts based on written or living sources. But there is no other means to construct them, and without contexts there is no way either to write history or to study culture. Therefore it behooves the archeologist not to maintain the untenable position of "sticking to the facts," meaning the renunciation of inference, hypothesis, and testing. It rather is incumbent upon him to derive his observational data as objectively as possible, to differentiate between observed fact and derived inference, to make explicitly labeled interpretations of as detailed and full a nature as possible, and then to look, either in the ground or among the data at hand, for evidence by which his hypotheses may be tested. Thus, more interpretation is called for, not less! If his readers find fault with his conclusions, they have but to examine the observational data and make their own inferences or set about producing, from the ground or elsewhere, more empirical evidence upon which to base alternative interpretations.

The question of the difference between empirical and cultural categories brings us face to face with the problems of archeological typology, classification, and so-called culture classification. But before it will be possible to enter upon a discussion of these problems, it will first be necessary to make a somewhat arbitrary distinction between the concept of type and the concept of class, between typology and classification. The purpose of this discrimination is, once more, to offer a conceptual scheme whereby the processing of archeological data will be clarified. Once the steps of procedure are known for what they are, their validity and pertinence can more easily be tested. By establishing concepts and showing their mutual relationships, even if the concepts are thought to be overly precise, the muddied waters of archeological theory will be settled, and the light, whatever it is, will have more chance of penetrating. "Hair-splitting" seems to be anathema to some archeologists but, even more, an implicit and confused conceptual scheme is anathema to straight thinking and acceptable results.

As used in the present conceptual scheme, *type* and *class* are concepts of different orders, and each may be empirical or cultural depending on the nature of the criteria used. The accompanying tabular presentation will serve to make this clear and also to bring out graphically the other points which will be discussed below. (See Table 1)

In this table, the borrowing of concepts from Linton (form, item, use, function, meaning), Kluckhohn (configuration), and Rouse (designs, techniques, specifications, group and modal types, mode) has been adaptive in nature and not precisely exact. Therefore considerable explanation is called for in order to justify their use in the present scheme.

Linton's concepts of form, use, function, and meaning (1936b, pp. 402ff) were originally developed with specific regard to trait complexes and not to

TABLE 1

	EMPIRICAL CATEGORIES (Observational)	CULTURAL CATEGORIES (Inferential)	CULTURE CATEGORIES (Inferential)
FORM	Individual manifestations, their empirical affinities and their constituent parts, "elements," "attributes," "designs," "specifications," "units," "items," etc.	The "use" and "function" and/or the technique of manufacture of an individual manifestation (or part thereof) as inferred from the empirical data.	The culture-idea, the culture-trait, objectified in the individual manifestation; also the "meaning" manifest in it. A "mode."
TYPE	A group of manifestations which possess certain specified similarities in their affinities and/or constituent parts, or an ideal abstracted therefrom, either mean, modal, or median.	A group of manifestations that possess certain specified similarities in their inferred "use," "function," and/or technique of manufacture.	The culture-idea objectified, and/or the "meaning" manifest, in a single type, either empirical or cultural. An "archetype."
CLASS	A group of empirical types (or types and forms) that possess certain specified similarities in their affinities and/or diagnostic criteria, i.e., a grouping of groups.	A group of types (or types and forms) either empirical or cultural, that possess certain specified similarities in their inferred "use," "function," and/or technique of manufacture.	The culture-idea objectified, and/or the "meaning" manifest in a class, either empirical or cultural. An "archeclass." When the classes under this heading are broad enough, it is probably best to designate the structuring idea as a "configuration."

individual manifestations. Nevertheless, there seems to be no reason why they cannot be applied to single objectifications. Linton was concerned with "functional studies" of whole cultures and was speaking from the viewpoint of the society itself and not of the ethnographer. But the definitions he has given may be paraphrased, with equally applicable results, into an archeological frame of reference. For example, he says:

The *form* of a trait complex will be taken to mean the sum and arrangement of its component behavior patterns; in other words that aspect of the complex whose expressions can be observed directly and which can, therefore be transmitted from one society to another. (1936b, p. 403)

Converting this concept into one serviceable for archeology, we find the definition to read something as follows: *The empirical form of an archeological manifestation will be taken to mean the sum and arrangement of its component chemico-physical parts taken together with its empirical affinities; in other words that aspect of the phenomenon, whose expression can be observed directly and which, therefore, can be utilized as empirical data by the archeologist.* Thus the form of any archeological representation includes not only its "design," "technique," and "specifications" as Rouse has indicated (1939, p. 11) but also its associations and position relative to other cultural and natural phenomena, i.e., its affinities.

When the concept *form* is understood as a cultural rather than an empirical category, the following definition may be used: *The cultural form of an archeological phenomenon will be taken to mean its technique of manufacture and its use and function within the body of cultural activities of the particular human group under investigation, as inferred from its empirical form.* The employment of Linton's concepts *use* and *function* is more exact than in the case of *form*. He says:

The use of any culture element is an expression of its relation to things external to the social-cultural configuration; its function is an expression of its relation to things within that configuration. Thus an axe has a use or uses with respect to the natural environment of the group, i.e., to chop wood. It has functions with respect both to the needs of the group and the operation of other elements within the culture configuration. It helps to satisfy the need for wood and makes possible a whole series of woodworking patterns. (1936b, p. 404)

Other than changing the word *culture* to *cultural* and making a reservation as to his use of the term *configuration*, we may apply Linton's concepts to archeological data without modification. The use and function of any empirical form as well as the technique by which it was made must depend upon inference. Therefore, cultural forms are inferential in archeological studies. The same is not true in ethnographical investigations, for in these the investigator may directly observe the use, function, and making of at least a good number of the empirical forms.

Rouse's concept *mode* has been adapted to the present scheme and denotes "form" as a culture-category or a mental construct. Rouse himself appears to use the term to denote both the actual attributes observed by the archeologist (1939, p. 11) as well as "conceptual patterns set up by the archeologist to represent *ideas* possibly held by the artisan" (1939, p. 15, italics mine). I have chosen to have the term *mode* stand for ideas rather than for physical attributes or both, because I believe that in this way an important point is clarified and emphasized, namely, the mental nature of culture itself as opposed to the chemico-physical and behavioral nature of the objectifications of culture. Also by this means, the chances of falling into the fallacy of misplaced concreteness, of confusing between two levels of abstraction, are reduced.

The concept *meaning* was also defined by Linton in connection with his trait complexes. He said:

The *meaning* of a trait complex consists of the associations which any society attaches to it. Such associations are subjective and frequently unconscious. They find only indirect expression in behavior and therefore cannot be established by purely objective methods. (1936b, pp. 403-404)

It is, perhaps, a debatable question whether or not archeologists can derive "meanings" from their data. Although, in the final chapter of the present study, I shall attempt to demonstrate that this is indeed possible, here the question is not of immediate concern. It is enough to say that, if the derivations *are* possible, then Linton's concept is usable for archeology. It need only be pointed out that "expression in behavior" in archeological terms means "expression in results of behavior." These results are themselves empirical, but inferences are required to derive meanings. Hence Linton's last statement is perfectly applicable.

The concept *type* as defined in the above table represents very closely the concept which A. D. Krieger advocated in his paper *The Typological Concept*. He says:

Any group which may be labeled a "type" must embrace material which can be shown to consist of individual variations in the execution of a definite constructional idea; likewise, the dividing lines between a series of types must be based upon demonstrable historical factors, not, as is often the case, upon the inclinations of the analyst or the niceties of descriptive orderliness. (1944, p. 272)

When he argues the importance of "demonstrable historical factors" he is advocating, in the terms of the present conceptual scheme, the study of those affinities which were said above to comprise archeological data equal in importance with purely chemico-physical characteristics. In other words, Krieger has obviously felt the need both to regard archeological specimens as objectifications of ideas and to demand that their associations and relationships be included in any typological treatment.

The distinction between an ideal or modal type and one which is composed of the actual objects has been made by Rouse. It seems a valid and important one and is, therefore, included in the present scheme. He says:

In current anthropological literature, the term "type" seems to have been applied to at least two different concepts, a group of artifacts or an abstract kind of artifact which symbolizes the group. . . . [The latter concept] refers to the attributes which artifacts of a given kind have in common, not to the artifacts themselves. (1939, p. 11)

A type which is, in effect, the abstract least-common-denominator, median, mode, or mean of a series of empirically similar and associated artifacts has much value in the course of archeological study (see Osgood, 1942, p. 24, fn. 8). For example, it is only through the medium of such abstractions that we can hope to infer the ideas which lay in the minds of the former artisans and thus attain an insight into their culture. It is those attributes which a group of specimens have in common that provide data for an interpretation of the maker's ideas and conceptualizations. A single specimen or a group of specimens, however well described in their heterogeneity and variability, cannot provide these data. Even the use and function, i.e., the basis for the cultural type, often cannot be interpreted without the abstraction of an ideal type. By an analysis of the central tendency within a series of artifacts, it is frequently possible to obtain an insight into their basic and requisite features and thus to make a hypothesis as to the ideas, the purposes, aims, beliefs, etc., which influenced the original makers.

Also it is possible from such ideal types to note the range of variation and the dispersal around the central concept. From this it may be possible to make some inferences as to the integration of the particular type within the culture. For example, the hypothesis may be made that a type which shows great homogeneity in all its elements and associations is better integrated into the culture than one which shows considerable variation and dispersal. Such a hypothesis will call for testing, and this in turn will lead to ramifying investigations which carry the expectation of further understanding of the culture and of culture in general: are there any inferable reasons why this particular type should vary so; are there outside sources which could account for it, or are local origins to be hypothesized; does this type vary more than others, and if so in what ways and why; is the range of variation equal on both sides of the central tendency or is there skewing; is similar variation found in other types, and if so, in what types and what might be the relation between them; is the degree of homogeneity, i.e., integration, due to the length of its existence within the culture, to its intrinsic nature which permits or demands that particular degree, or to what? These and other questions can be profitably investigated, but only after an ideal or abstract type has been established.

On the other hand, the concept of type as a group of actual objects also has its uses. In not a few instances it will be impossible to establish any ideal abstraction: the variability of the phenomena may be too great and too general to permit of being represented by a single set of elements and associations. This in itself might be culturally significant, and the only way of making use of the data is to describe the artifacts themselves. The success of Southwestern pottery study, is ample proof of the practicality and applicability of such types, based as the study is upon the concept of type as a group of objects.

The concept *archetype* has been evolved in order to provide a convenient term for the handling of inferences as to culture ideas. The term *pattern* has not been used because, in the first place, it is too useful a word to be restricted and, in the second, the limitation of its meaning to mental constructs would require tedious and rather unconvincing argument in the face of other more inclusive definitions such as Kluckhohn's (1941). In the present conceptual scheme, observable patterns, as for example the patterns stepped out by the feet of dancing men, the patterns of painted design found on pottery vessels, the regularities of city plan, the consistent avoidance of a mother-in-law, are considered to be results of behavior and therefore the empirical data of culture studies. Patterns in this sense are not behavior, nor are they culture traits. They are the results of behavior which has been performed by human agents under the influence of ideas (culture traits). Thus they are overt, behavioral, action patterns. The covert, ideal, and idea patterns of which Kluckhohn wrote (1941, pp. 114ff) are not included. It seems best, therefore, not to make further modifications of the concept of pattern but to offer another term which will cover the so-called covert segment of the broader concept. Webster's dictionary defines *archetype* as

The original pattern or model of a work, or the model from which a thing is made or formed. . . . *Metaph.* In Platonism, one of the pure ideas or realities of which existent things are imitations.

Under the heading of *prototype*, the dictionary further defines *archetype* as ". . . an original, often ideal, pattern or model." The word has been chosen in preference to *prototype* because the latter is the more common word and is already in general use for a number of valuable concepts, and because in *archetype* there is conveyed an implication of mental constructs, which is congenial to its use in the present conceptual scheme.

The concept *configuration*, used in connection with the archeclass compartment, has been adapted from Kluckhohn (1941, pp. 114, 124). Here there is no need for modification, as in the case of archetype, because Kluckhohn's concept is stated to be concerned with so-called covert or mental constructs and to have no overt segment. He says:

Configuration looks to an *inner* coherence in terms of the large structuralizing principles which prevail in the *covert* culture. Patterns are forms; configurations are, so to speak, interrelationships between forms. (1941, p. 126)

Thus if an idea, conscious or unconscious, be inferred to structure several types or classes of culture objectifications, that idea may rightly be designated as a configuration. If a single idea, simple or complex in nature, appears to be one of the principles underlying, say, the decoration of pottery, the performance of religious rites, the construction of dwelling units, it may be termed a configuration. In the final chapter of the present study, an example of just such a configuration will be given.

In summing up this explanation of Table 1, we may examine the relationships first between the vertical compartments and then between the horizontal ones. The concepts of form, type, and class may be explained by adapting an example presented by C. C. Zimmerman (1938, pp. 75-78). In describing a certain community, he says: "Littleville is parasitic, good natured, negroid, rural and urbanistic." These adjectives are the descriptive units which together comprise the "form" of Littleville in so far as Zimmerman is presently concerned. They constitute the basic, observational data from which both the type and class will eventually be derived. According to the present scheme, a type is a primary grouping which brings together certain individual forms which have specified descriptive attributes in common, exactly which depending upon the needs or whims of the investigator. Thus, Littleville might be included with other hamlets within a type whose sole criterion is a parasitic nature; or the type might include all hamlets which are parasitic and good natured; or it might include all towns that are parasitic, good natured, have a population of exactly 503 souls, and contain a water tower painted green. In other words, a type may be characterized by specific similarities of any number, degree of detail, or intrinsic character.

The concept *class* designates a secondary grouping. It consists of types which manifest specified similarities in some, but not all, of their type characteristics. Thus let us say that Littleville belongs in a type which is parasitic and good natured, that Bigville belongs in one which is parasitic and ill natured, and that Mediumville belongs in one which is good natured and has green water-towers. When it comes to classifying these types, we may class Littleville and its co-members with Bigville and its co-members on the basis of their parasitic character; or we may class the Littleville type with the Mediumville type on the basis of their good nature. In both instances, there has been a grouping of groups, a classifying or classing of types, not of individual hamlets. It is not the number, the nature, or the detail of the specified criteria that distinguishes a type from a class in the present scheme, but rather it is the difference between a primary and a secondary grouping. It is perfectly possible for identically the same criteria at one time to designate a type and at another to designate a class. *Type* and *class* are concepts of different relative, not absolute, magnitude based upon the same range of data, and this holds true whether we are dealing with empirical, cultural, or culture categories.

We may now examine the relationships between the horizontal compartments of the above tabulation, between the empirical, cultural, and culture categories. Although all three are creations of the archeologist, it is important to note that they pertain to different realms of phenomena, that they are established by different means, and that, unless the archeologist is aware of these differences, he is apt to go astray when it comes to drawing conclusions from his data. The differences to be noted are those that obtain between (a) the empirical categories and (b) the cultural and culture categories: (1) the former relate to the world of the archeologist; the latter relate to the world of bygone people; (2) the former are based on chemico-physical attributes and their affinities; the latter are based upon criteria pertaining to cultural or culture attributes, such as techniques of manufacture, use, function, meaning, and culture idea; and (3) from the archeologist's standpoint, the former are the only ones having wholly observable criteria and thus the only empirical ones; cultural and culture categories, although they may be partially or wholly based on observable data, are established by means of interpretation and hypothesis and are thus inferential. Thus when investigations lead into the latter realms, they advance by inference from the empirical, and the results are to be viewed as hypotheses to be tested. For the archeologist, the empirical or purely observational has only a mediate function, forming merely the basis, not the goal, of his studies. By definition, he is interested in cultural contexts or in culture itself, and the categories which obviously he should seek are those pertaining to those fields. Also, and for the same reasons, his interests lie, not in the phenomena of his own world, but in the world of the original makers, users, or possessors, individually or as groups. In other words, the pertinent question to be asked is, "What may be inferred today from present evidence as to those things that were relevant, significant, meaningful *to the bygone individuals and societies under investigation?*"

As long as these differences are fully realized by the archeologist, he is forewarned and forearmed and will be able to act accordingly. But if they are overlooked to the extent that he regards the empirical categories of his own making as if they were, axiomatically, the same as the cultural or culture categories of a bygone people, he is making an assumption which may lead him into serious error. From the standpoint of theory and method, it is not permissible to transmute an empirical category into a cultural or culture category except as a working hypothesis explicitly stated or as a conclusion drawn from a reasoned

argument. To do otherwise is to beg the cultural question. There is no automatic, axiomatic assurance that the forms, types, and classes established today
by the archeologist are coextensive with any separable entities that existed in
the minds or life ways of a bygone people. At best, the declaration of any such
correspondence is a matter for explicit hypothesis and testing, not implicit
assumption. It constitutes one of the archeologist's greatest problems, not one
of his self-evident truths.

This fact lies at the foundation of the theory of archeological typology proposed by the present study (in the following, only typology will be mentioned,
although the same things could be said with regard to classification). For when
an archeologist says that the presence of Type A at both Site 1 and Site 2
indicates some sort of direct cultural relationship between them, he is really
saying one or both of two things: either (1) that actual specimens of Type A
had come from one site to the other by some means, however direct or devious,
or (2) that the idea of Type A or how to make Type A had been transmitted
from one site to the other with the recipient proceeding to manufacture one or
more examples. In either case, the archeologist is forced to assume that the idea
behind Type A or the idea behind the technique which produced Type A was a
consistent factor, conscious or unconscious, in the mind(s) of a bygone individual
or group. In order to be applicable to interpretations concerning cultural relationships, the typological similarities which the archeologist recognizes must
be proved, or assumed, to be based on an actual idea and on one consistent
enough to have produced, at a minimum, two similar specimens.

Since such ideas are not among the archeologist's empirical data, it further
follows that the seeking for, and the demanding of, "objectivity" in archeological studies is only partially a valid point of issue. In fact, the concept of objectivity should be clarified before we even discuss this point at all. It is sometimes said that an individual is thinking "objectively" or that a certain group
of phenomena is an "objective" category. And it is often implied that "objective"
thinking is concerned with "objective" categories. Now this may be so, but is
not necessarily so. According to the way one uses the terms, one can do a lot of
objective thinking about highly non-objective categories, and vice versa. The
crux of the matter lies in the difference between a procedure or method and the
data to which this procedure is applied. It would perhaps be better if we reserved
the terms *objective* and *subjective* to describe the nature of thinking and used
some terms such as *empirical* and *inferential* to refer, respectively, to the
observational and non-observational nature of the phenomena thought about.
Thus it would be that one could think either subjectively or objectively about
phenomena that were either empirical or inferential. To make these distinctions
would help to keep our own thinking clear, and this is, after all, the purpose
of this or any other conceptual scheme.

Returning to the question of "objectivity" in archeological studies, it appears in most instances that when the archeologists use this term they mean what I am here calling "empirical." This can be seen from the fact that they use it in connection with the criteria basic to their typologies and hence in connection with the nature of their data and not of their thinking. This being so, it may be categorically stated that their insistence upon "objective" criteria for their so-called culture classifications reflects a misconception as to the nature of archeological analysis as applied to cultural studies. I have been at some pains to show that empirical types and classes (and this applies especially to those that are founded on chemico-physical attributes alone) are only mediary to cultural studies. This is true for the plain and simple reason that, of themselves, they have nothing to do with the cultural world of the people under investigation. It is only by inference from them that the archeologist can reach the realms of past actuality. He may transmute his empirical categories into cultural ones if he is willing to make explicit hypotheses or to present his evidence and argue his views. In fact, this is the only way which is open to him! But by this very procedure he leaves the empirical and embarks upon the tide of inference.

And so it is not for the archeologist to cry blindly for "objectivity." Rather let him realize that his empirical studies are but mediate and that, if he aspires to historiography or anthropology, he is required to deal with the inferential as much as with the empirical. But let him deal with all categories of data as explicitly (objectively) as possible, eschewing the emotional and implicit (subjective) approach. And above all, let him analyze whatever in fact he does do, so that he may bring into the open the procedures and premises upon which his results are based. Perhaps, if he accepts these admonitions, he will also come to realize that empirical typologies based on chemico-physical specifications alone are not satisfactory for cultural studies because they fail to take into account many data that are vital as foundations for the necessary inferences. And perhaps he will come also to realize that we have returned to the point which I have stressed from the start: criteria for the empirical designation of form, type, and class include provenience, association, qualitative and quantitative facts and relationships, etc., in addition to the chemico-physical specifications.

After this glimpse into the theoretical aspects of archeological typology, it might be profitable to examine hurriedly some of the typologies and classifications appearing in the literature of Americanist archeology.

W. D. Strong says of his version of Thomas Wilson's chipped-stone-point classification that

For the purpose of describing and comparing types of chipped arrowpoints, spear heads, and knives, a classification based entirely upon form [read "shape"] rather than assumed function has been employed. . . . These outlines [of shapes] are entirely irrespective of size. (1935, p. 87)

The obvious intent of this denial of "assumed function" in favor of shape is the usual one of wishing to be "objective," i.e., to deal with empirical rather than inferential attributes of the points. With this desire there can be no quarrel—as far as handling the specimens *on an empirical level* is concerned. But when later (pp. 279, 281, 282) Strong uses these types for the purpose of ascertaining cultural and temporal relationships between sites, he forfeits his purely empirical position and, albeit implicitly, assumes that his groupings are coextensive with cultural groupings developed consciously or unconsciously by the bygone people who made them.

In other words, he is taking for granted that those people saw the same shapes as he does and grouped them in the same way. Any conclusions which Strong might base upon the presence or absence of "parallel-sided stemmed" points would be vitiated if the former people were completely indifferent as to whether their points had parallel-sided or contracting stems or if it made no difference to them whether their points had stems at all. Furthermore, if the ancient people viewed "side notches" as functional equivalents of the indentations produced by an "expanding stem," and if they thus classed them together and made them interchangeably as a means of securing binding sinews, the separation of these two shapes because of "the niceties of descriptive orderliness" in a modern empirical classification would most probably warp the archeologist's conclusions. On the other hand, if the people classed together all points which were developed from a triangular-shaped blank as against those developed from an oval blank, an empirical classification which separated side-notched points from those with expanding stems might be in accord with the cultural facts. The crucial aspects of the matter, of course, lie in data over and above mere physical shape. They lie in the interpretation of associations, in making inferences and interpretations, and in following an "if-then" method until the archeologist can satisfy himself (and eventually his colleagues also) that his answer fits best with other data and has the most chance of being correct. Mere "objectivity" is of little value by itself.

As the facts actually stand, Strong himself cites documentary and archeological evidence to the effect that the significant functional difference between the various chipped points is size and not shape (pp. 260, 267). Yet in his monograph we find no following up of this lead, no analysis of the provenience and distribution of large and small points within the pre-Pawnee sites in Nebraska. In the face of an apparently significant cultural dichotomy, he has continued to manipulate a purely empirical classification as an entity discrete from other data. He has not analyzed the associations in which the points were found nor given cross-references between the descriptions of specimens and the account of their finding within the sites. In short, to summarize the issues brought up in the preceding paragraphs, a classification such as Strong's permits comparisons with specimens from other sites *only* on the basis of shape. If to the criterion of shape were added other attributes and the empirical affinities, the classification might expectably be more precise and valuable; but it would, of itself, be no more applicable to cultural comparisons. It would still remain purely empirical.

Indeed, there is other, possibly even more conclusive evidence to support this contention. How can it be maintained that Strong's classification represents the cultural categories or culture ideas of the former inhabitants of Nebraska, when the same classification has been used for central California (Gifford and Schenck, 1926; Schenck, 1926; Schenck and Dawson, 1929), and the Columbia River region of Oregon-Washington (Strong, Schenck, Steward, 1930), and southern California (Wedel, 1941a), unless it is further argued that all these groups were culturally identical with regard to chipped stone points? It is even more obvious that such classifications are purely descriptive or empirical, when a classification of stone work developed for a late pueblo in New Mexico (Kidder, 1932a) is used to group specimens at Uaxactun, Guatemala (Ricketson and Ricketson, 1937), and specimens found in the La Plata district of northern New Mexico and Colorado with dates ranging from Basket-Maker III to Pueblo III (Morris, 1939). The classification of bone work, developed for artifacts dating from around A.D. 1300 onward at Pecos (Kidder, 1932a), is likewise used irrespective of time and location: Wedel uses it for his Kern Lake, California, specimens (1941a), and Cressman finds it applicable to specimens taken from Oregon caves minimally dated at 5000 years ago. The latter even goes so far as to say that:

Kidder's system of classification of bone awls (1932) is followed as far as possible, not intimating that there is any connection between our area and Pecos, but because his system has great utility and provides a convenient frame of reference. (1942, p. 63)

It is hardly to be thought that the archeologists themselves believe that one classification of stone and one of bone reproduces the cultural groupings and ideas of American aborigines ranging from the State of Washington to Guatemala and from 3000 B.C. to around A.D. 1800. Their use of the Pecos systems is primarily for descriptive convenience and not for cultural elucidation. But they sometimes make the mistake of employing the categories as if they were actually cultural ones. Unless the archeologist is willing explicitly to assume, or to argue, that his empirical types and classes are coextensive with the categories characteristic of a bygone culture, he is wrong to use them to draw cultural conclusions.

The same can be said of typology within the field of Southwestern ceramics. In fact, if the difference between empirical types and cultural types had been clearly envisioned, the great proliferation of pottery types, which has aroused so much criticism, would have been seen in its proper light and the long-standing argument between the "splitters" and the "lumpers," recognized in print by Brew (1946, p. 55), Judd (1940, p. 430), Kidder (1936b, pp. xxv, xxvii, 626), Martin and Rinaldo (1941, p. 655), and Reiter (1938, pp. 489, 490), would not have been inflicted upon the literature and discussion of Southwestern arch-eology. Both parties to this quarrel seem to be off the mark: the "splitters," proceeding from their starting point of descriptive analysis, make the mistake of assuming without demonstration that their empirical types represent cultural types; the "lumpers," viewing pottery primarily from a cultural angle, refuse to believe that the minute differences recognized by the other faction have any real cultural significance either as indicators of relationships between sites or as separable entities within the aboriginal ceramic complexes. If it had been realized by both sides that empirical categories are one thing and cultural categories another, much needless misunderstanding would have been avoided. The "splitters" would not have attempted, without discussion or explicit assump-tion, to use their empirical types as cultural entities, and the "lumpers" would have seen that the fine discriminations made by the other faction were potentially basic to, but not identical with, the cultural discriminations in which they them-selves were particularly interested. Both would have realized that the reconcilia-tion of their differences lay, not in an agreement as to the degree of refinement acceptable in descriptive analysis, but in the correlation to be inferred between empirical and cultural types. Both would have seen that the support of either position required field and laboratory research, not polemics or *ex cathedra* pronouncements as to the number of pottery types acceptable or unacceptable for the Southwestern area and fractions thereof.

Arguments against a multiplicity of types, if by this is meant empirical or descriptive types, will not hold water. In the first place, from the viewpoint of archeological reporting, it is of the utmost importance to grant the archeologist freedom to recognize and record all those similarities and differences which, within his experience and a cultural frame of reference, seem significant to him. The publication of his empirical descriptions, named for convenience of handling and usually called *types,* serve to acquaint his colleagues of his findings, to elicit from them the antithetic or corroborative information urgently required, and to provide the general literature with comparative material with which to lend depth and significance to other finds from other sites.

For the archeologist to sit on his ceramic eggs with no attempt to bring them forth into the light of day through publication is recognized as bad practice. If this is true, then the only limits are those set by the potential cultural significance of the descriptive minutiae. But who can determine these limits? The archeolo-gist is never sure, nor will he ever be, just what detail may turn out to be of importance to his own studies or to those of his associates. If the limits are un-definable because, in all probability, there are no limits, then the archeologist himself is the only possible judge of the extent and detail to which his descriptions should break down the material. His particular judgments may be adversely criticized by specific argument, but his right and duty to make as detailed judgments as he sees fit cannot with justice be denied.

Furthermore, the often intimated criticism that such atomizing typology produces too many names and descriptions and "clogs" the literature will not hold water either. Surely the critics do not mean to imply that they are able now, and plan to be able in the future, to memorize and retain in the mind the names and descriptions of even the generally accepted types within the Southwest. If this is not implied and they will admit the necessity of recourse to published descriptions for their comparative studies, the addition of more names is of no import, providing only that the names and descriptions can be systemized for easy reference as, for instance, in a key like the one developed in the *Handbook of Northern Arizona Pottery Wares* (Colton and Hargrave, 1937). Taxonomists of other disciplines make no such effort to keep in mind their entire typology or to work from memory when comparing specimens. There is no reason for Southwesternists to restrict the scope and refinement of their descriptive typology merely for the sake of a primitively simple system which might safely be retained in the mind. To do so would be to fly in the face of scientific progress, which has consistently advanced by way of more detailed analysis as the basis for more far-reaching synthesis.

Also there have been depreciations of the practice of defining a pottery type on the basis of a single potsherd. Strictly speaking, according to the system proposed by the present study, this is indeed an impossibility because any single manifestation is by definition a "form" and cannot be a "type." However, two sherds of the same form can and do constitute a type and, although I may be mistaken here, such a two-sherd type would probably be subjected to the same criticisms as have been directed at a single-sherd category. By way of example, let us suppose that from some definitely pre-Spanish ruin in the Southwest an archeologist has excavated two small sherds which exhibit a bright orange glaze upon which flowers had been painted in blue. For the purposes of the example, let us further suppose that it could not be conclusively demonstrated one way or the other whether the two sherds originally belonged to the same or to different vessels. Such unique and unprecedented specimens would surely warrant description, and when they were discovered to be significantly alike they would be thrown together in a common account. What else would this be but an empirical type? Whether or not the description was dignified with a name for the sake of ease in reference is of no theoretical consequence. It is to be very much doubted whether any archeologist would suppress the data concerning these two sherds, and if he did so it would be a glaring example of malpractice. The description of a single sherd thus constitutes an empirical form, and the description of two or more sherds with specified similarities comprises an empirical type. If this is an acceptable procedure in the case of unique sherds, it is also possible and acceptable with sherds which display a lesser degree of unusualness. As before, the dividing line between the non-conformities which warrant type differentiation and those that do not is not "given." It is safe to say that no one is qualified to lay down the law in this regard, and so each archeologist must be his own judge, letting both his conscience and his experience be his guide. If, at some later date, other data indicate that the archeologist was in error, then let his statements be revised and corrected. This is the way of any scientific discipline, and it is perfectly properly the way of archeology. (See below, Chapter 6, pp. 157f)

Up to this point I have been talking of empirical types. The correspondence between these and cultural or culture types is an additional matter which calls for further study, assumption, and argument. Types which have been established on the basis of descriptive analysis are not, *ipso facto,* cultural types. Often they will be found to have no inferable cultural significance. Often they will have to be regrouped or subdivided in order to satisfy the cultural implications of the data. Differences which, from an empirical point of view, had been thought of no significance and which had not been used to separate types, might later be found to distinguish important cultural categories and would thus require more minute break-downs. The reverse might also be the case: several categories, which had been distinguished on empirical grounds, might be discovered to have identical cultural significance and thus to call for amalgamation into a single cultural type. These eventualities in no way adversely affect the validity of empirical types or complicate the cultural issue. All that is required is for the archeologist to be aware of the difference and use the categories with regard for their limitations and potentialities. In doing this, he should find a welcome freedom of research procedure and a considerable clarification in his archeological thinking.

This brings us to another point which has been the cause of some confusion among the archeologists. In a recent publication, J. O. Brew has made much of the fact that typologies (and classifications, to use the present terms) are arbitrary, that such systems are made by the student, and that types are not discovered but rather created and put in a system (1946, pp. 44-66). This appears to be a perfectly true statement as far as it goes. The archeologists, as well as students of other disciplines, can and do build their categories on the basis of criteria of their own choosing, depending on the requirements of their current problems. It is possible to type automobiles on the basis of the length of the scratches in their paint, to classify sand-tempered potsherds on the number of sand grains in each, or to group together all chipped stone points which have side notches. It would be possible, but the pertinent question is

"So what?" And the answer to this is, of course, "So that the results will be of help in pursuing the investigations in which I am currently engaged." Now the alleged aim of archeological research is to obtain a knowledge of the culture of the people of some presently uninhabited site. Therefore it is wrong to say, as Brew does, that "No typological system is actually inherent in the material" (1946, p. 46). In cultural material, as it is found by the archeologist, there *are* inherent systems, namely, the ones developed by the people who made, used, or possessed that material. Brew says, "Systematic classifications are simplifications of and generalizations of the natural situation" (1946, p. 46), but a cultural situation is *not* a "natural" situation! Those bygone people imposed their own particular system upon nature and their own products, they had their own way of thinking about things, and it is *their,* and not *our,* system(s) which the archeologist should attempt to discover. He should try to make his systematic creations (and his typologies are just that) conform to those of the former culture. How else can he hope to understand it? Inherent in cultural products is the systematics of the people who produced them, and Brew's biological analogy has but led him astray. (See also McKern, 1939, p. 312)

It is probably true that culture—the whole of culture, i.e., in the holistic sense defined in the preceding chapter—is a continuum and that any attempt to break it up into segments on a purely cultural basis is arbitrary. This fact accounts for some of the difficulties in applying the culture-area concept. But when the term is used in its partitive sense, meaning *a* culture or *a* socio-political grouping, where we are dealing with a well-defined segment possessing a characteristic culture, culture is not a continuum, except in time. Individual ideas, patterns, types are often adhered to consciously; and even to those that are unconscious, there is a more or less consistent adherence which produces recognizable aspects of the particular culture. Brew himself, while insisting upon the arbitrary character of typology, commends the Beals-Brainerd-Smith analysis of pottery decoration styles (1945) which is nothing more nor less than an attempt to arrive at an understanding of the decorative concepts of bygone potters. Their analysis is their own construction, but it aims to discover the ancient concepts *inherent* in the material. The extent to which they have been successful in this is the extent of their attainment, and I hasten to add that I heartily concur in Brew's enthusiasm for their results. Therefore, while the distinction between what is called Plains Culture and what is called Eastern Woodland Culture may be purely arbitrary, the distinctions *which do exist* between the designs on Hopi ceramics and those executed by Acoma potters, beween spiral-grooved Pecos axes and the three-quarter-grooved axes of Snake-town, between the moccasin patterns of various Plains tribes, are the results of ideas held by the Indians themselves and are inherent in the results of their culture-influenced behavior.

Following this line further, some light may be thrown on a problem which seems to have vexed the archeological taxonomists for a considerable time. Many of them have found difficulty in deciding just what attributes should be recognized in making their types and classes. They have been uncertain as to the degree of refinement which their analysis should encompass and have been looking for some mechanical means of determination. They have been worried about the proliferation of recognized ceramic attributes as opposed to the paucity of those within some category such as chipped stone points or bone "awls" (e.g., McKern, 1939, pp. 306f). But I believe that there would have been much less of this uncertainty if the archeologists had viewed their material in some such light as that proposed in the present study, if they had viewed culture traits as ideas and not as material objects, if they had envisioned cultural behavior as mediate between ideas and material objects, in short if they had recognized the difference between their own empirical, descriptive groupings and the cultural and culture categories pertinent to the peoples they were studying.

For example, let us take the attribute of hardness so common in the pottery typologies and classifications in both the Southwest and Midwest. Here we have a physical property, an empirical specification which is useful in describing the objects. But culturally speaking what is it? Is the archeologist willing to contend that the Indians recognized hardness or had an idea as to the appropriate hardness of their pottery in terms of the modern mineralogical scale? If he is unwilling so to argue, then hardness is an empirical specification only and does not belong in cultural and culture typologies. Even if the archeologist argues that hardness is the result of some technique of manufacture which was indeed recognized by the Indians, hardness itself is not cultural but only a sign of some cultural attribute, an indication of the existence of a certain technique. Thus, while hardness remains empirically valid, the really significant attribute from any cultural point of view is the technique of manufacture, say the firing temperature or the paste composition, which were the products of consistent ideas, i.e., culture traits.

From this, a test may be established for the inclusion or exclusion of any specified attribute. In his empirical descriptions, the archeologist is free to include any specification that he wishes. In his cultural categorizations, he may include any specification which he is willing to assume is the material embodiment of a consistent idea in the mind(s) of the former maker, user, or possessor. Such a test permits great freedom to the archeologist but, at the same time, makes him explicitly responsible for the cultural implications of the systematics which he uses. If he is willing to assume that the side notches which he has empirically described under a classification such as Strong's were also recognized by the Indians, then he is free to incorporate the attribute of side notches in any cultural classification he might create and to make use of them in cross-culture comparisons. The testing of his working hypothesis will be his responsibility or that of his critics, and it will depend upon the marshalling of evidence *pro* or *con.* In other words, so long as the archeologist is willing to make an explicit assumption and to look upon it as a working hypothesis, he is free to make his cultural and culture groupings in whatever manner he sees fit.

This brings us to the final point in this discussion. The theoretical problems of the so-called culture classifications of the Southwest and Midwest have received considerable attention. The similarity of these systems to the Linnaean classification of biology has been attacked on a number of occasions (e.g., Brew, 1946, pp. 44-66; Steward, 1941) and not without some justice, although I shall have something to say about this later. However, two of the most basic points of misconception seem to have escaped the critics, with the result that their arguments are somewhat beside the point.

The first of these is the use of presence-and-absence "trait" lists as the foundation of classification. This usage is based on the assumption that the important factor about archeological discoveries is their presence or absence within a given site. And although the fact will probably be vehemently denied by the taxonomists, this assumption is accompanied by its corollary, namely, that the location, association, quantitative and qualitative relation to the cultural and natural environment is of no, or at least of secondary, importance. But actually, and contrary to McKern's statement (1940, p. 19), a list showing the presence and absence of "traits" does *not* represent the former inhabitants of a site, at least in any cultural sense; nor do cultures, archeological or otherwise, consist of lists of typological tags as Griffin implies (1935). Surely there is more to "a culture" than this.

But the taxonomists, in their preoccupation with such lists, have gone so far as to modify an anthropological concept of long and respected standing and to involve themselves thereby in not a little confusion. I refer to their use of the term *culture complex* or, as it sometimes is written, *trait complex.* In the bulk of anthropological literature this concept is defined, as Linton put it (1936b, p. 397), as "a larger functional unit," the traits within which "are all more or less interrelated and interdependent from the point of view of both function and use." But the taxonomists applying the Midwestern system have adopted the term in the sense of a mere assemblage or congeries of "traits" or descriptive items which they have seen fit to isolate, name, and list. McKern says:

If substantially the same traits are found to occur repeatedly at site after site, one can be quite sure that this persistently grouped lot of traits is characteristic of a single culture. Such a repeatedly recurring series of traits is called a *culture complex.* (1940, p. 19)

Earlier he had said:

The more simple and direct method is that of analyzing materials from a site or community as such, comparing the *list of traits* so determined with similarly determined *trait complexes* from other sites or communities, and classifying on a basis of similarity or dissimilarity to establish foci. (1938, p. 370, italics mine)

Throughout his work he seems to use *complex* in this, rather than in the integrative, sense. Cole and Deuel, on the other hand, in their *Rediscovering Illinois* use it sometimes to signify a mere assemblage (1937, pp. 34; 207, fn 4) and sometimes as it was defined by Linton (1937, pp. 36-39, 209). Ritchie makes the same shift (1940b, p. 100; 1944, pp. 52, 325). Fairbanks (1941, p. 12) uses *complex* and *activity*, following Linton, and Griffin (1943, pp. 328, 330) follows McKern.

With regard to ethnographical data, Opler has pointed out the dangers of dependence upon trait lists. Specifically, he says:

The difficulty in placing these traits and deciding whether or not they belong on our list involves a critique of a statistical approach to anthropological data which assumes that a trait in one culture is the counterpart or equivalent of a formally similar or comparable trait in another culture. (1935, p. 705)

The same warnings apply to archeological materials and even more so, because the qualifications which Kluckhohn has apparently rightfully made pertain much less to archeology than to ethnology. He says:

. . . what he [Opler] seems to me to demonstrate is that formal similarity can sometimes mislead us. So far as I am aware no one has given an inductive demonstration that in the greater number of cases (or in any number sufficient to disturb statistical results) highly specific similarities (within a not too great geographical area) do not indicate some sort of historical connection past or present, direct or indirect. Granted freely that the same trait is by no means always the same behavior, it does not follow that detailed parallelisms are without historical significance. (1939, pp. 351-352)

In the first place, the archeological classifications which are based on "formal similarities" use, for the most part, very simple and not "highly specific" similarities. An ax is an ax, and an awl an awl. Even within the more elaborate complexes such as ceramics, the whole is broken down to such a degree that the items which are compared on a one-to-one basis are, of themselves, very simple. Secondly, at least within the Midwestern system, the comparisons are often made irrespective of time and space, so that Kluckhohn's strictures about "a not too great geographical area" do not hold. Finally, Kluckhohn is talking of the value of formal similarities for comparative purposes, for the connections and cross-culture relationships which they imply. He is not talking from the standpoint of constructing a cultural context. To be sure, a list of typological tags will give some idea as to the nature of the culture, but is "some idea" what the archeologist is looking for? Is it enough to take the place of the fuller contexts available to the ethnologist and historian? Can the archeologist depend on his comparative studies if they are based on no more than "some idea"? I think not, and an example will show why.

Let us take the textile industries as reported from two cave sites: Lovelock Cave, central Nevada (Loud and Harrington, 1929), and Frightful Cave, central Coahuila, Mexico, as excavated by the U. S. National Museum's 1940-41 Coahuila Expedition.[107] Tabulating these industries on a presence-and-absence basis, we find the following results (Table 2). Looking at the two industries as wholes, we certainly see a "highly specific" similarity. It is hardly to be doubted that any of the archeological taxonomists would hesitate to equate the textile industries of the two sites or, if other industries showed a like similarity, would fail to classify the sites together.

When quantitative information is added, the results are as shown in Table 3. The picture has changed radically. The quantitative data indicate a decided difference rather than a similarity between the sites. The frequency order of the categories is different, pointing to a different orientation of cultural needs. The frequency order within the categories (in five out of six where it exists) shows a reversal as between the two sites. The differential number of "miscellaneous artifacts," absolutely and relative to the total textile category, points to a haphazard versatility among the Coahuila cave people which was not characteristic of the inhabitants of Lovelock, and it also marks a definite cleavage between the two sites. These and many other implications can be derived even from the few data and slight manipulation presented here. For instance, it is much more significant that wicker basketry is present in Lovelock Cave *and is the dominant type* while it is absent in the Mexican site, than that it is merely present in one and absent in the other. A presence-and-absence table would tend to smooth the line of what is really a sharp peak in the graph of basketry difference. A presence-and-absence table would show absolutely no variation in the knot complex, while in actual fact the variation is noteworthy, both within the category and within the textile industry as a whole. The vast quantitative difference in the sandal category provides another lead for hypothesis and investigation. Can it be accounted for by the former presence and subsequent decay of leather footgear at Lovelock? The finding of a few leather moccasins suggest such a possibility. Does the disparity indicate considerable travel, even nomadism, over the jagged limestone rocks of Coahuila and a more or less sedentary existence near the tule marshes of the Nevada lake? What other evidence can be adduced to the support or contradiction of these hypotheses? Or assuming their correctness for the moment, what light do they shed on other facts of the respective cultures?

TABLE 2

	Lovelock	Frightful
Basketry		
wicker	x	—
coiled	x	x
split stitch	x	x
twined	x	x
plaited	—	x
Matting		
twined	x	x
plaited	—	x
Netting		
knotted	x	x
knotless	—	x
Knots		
sheetbend	x	x
overhand	x	x
granny	x	x
slip	x	x
square	x	x
Cloth		
feather	x	—
fur	x	x
twined	—	x
Braid	x	x
Sandals		
twined	x	—
plaited	—	x
Aprons	x	x

Total items from both sites	21
Items common to both sites	13 or 62%
Lovelock items common to both sites	13 out of 16 or 81%
Frightful items common to both sites	13 out of 18 or 72%

TABLE 3

	LOVELOCK	FRIGHTFUL	FREQUENCY ORDER WITHIN CATEGORY
Basketry			
wicker.............	1115	0	
coiled.............	309	112.	
split stitch.........	typical	rare	same (?)
twined.............	104	10	
plaited.............	0	6	
	1528 (1)	128 (4)	
Matting			
twined.............	1418	24	
plaited.............	0	76	reversed
	1418 (2)	100 (5)	
Netting			
knotted.............	1016	10	
knotless.............	0	70	reversed
	1016 (3)	80 (6)	
Knots			
sheetbend............	185 (1)	5 (5)	
overhand.............	83 (2)	294 (2)	
granny...............	22 (3)	17 (4)	reversed
slip.................	14 (4)	28 (3)	
square..............	4 (5)	379 (1)	
	308 (4)	723 (3)	
Cloth			
feather..............	203	0	
fur..................	40	12	reversed
twined.............	0	15	
	243 (5)	27 (7)	
Braid.................	142	26	(none)
	142 (6)	26 (8)	
Sandals			
twined.............	87	0	
plaited.............	0	912	reversed
	87 (7)	912 (2)	
Misc. artifacts (exclusive of cordage)...........	64	3540	(none)
	64 (8)	3540 (1)	
Aprons.................	9	5	(none)
	9 (9)	5 (9)	
TOTAL...........	4815	5541	

Without the weighting and balance given by, among other things, the quantitative data, the cultural context is the loser. But is not the comparative study also? It has been shown above that even the not inconsiderable presence-and-absence similarities to be found in a broad complex such as the textile industry can be very misleading as the basis for cross-culture comparisons and taxonomy.

Before proceeding, it should be emphatically stated that the example given above is not a rigged case. It was discovered in the course of routine comparative study in connection with the writing of an archeological report. The only crucial assumption that has been made is that there was not too much difference in the efficiency of the two excavations. Granting a representative sample from each cave and a conscientious effort to save and report the evidence of human handiwork, there is no bar to full and detailed comparisons. The first of these provisions is, of course, a limiting one with respect to some archeological material. Where there is no assurance that the complete site has been excavated or a representative sample secured, as for example in much of the data used by Griffin for his study of the Fort Ancient Aspect (1943), quantitative information is unreliable and would be misleading to use without qualification. But such extenuating circumstances are not the rule, fortunately, and most of the so-called culture classifications have been built on the basis of sites recently excavated where, if not the actuality, at least the possibility of a representative sample was present. When this is the case and when the archeologist fails to give his comparisons the depth afforded by quantification, he is in grave danger of error. And even if his presence-and-absence tabulations are eventually shown to depict actual conditions, the demonstration of this fact must rest on just such added information as provided by quantification, association, provenience, etc. The tabulations themselves are but one part of the evidence, and of doubtful reliability at that!

Thus it is that when Steward criticizes Colton's taxonomic attempts by attacking the smallness of percentage differences between the various groupings (1941), he is hitting at a secondary phenomenon. Instead of analyzing the value of the lists themselves, he seems content to accept them. In fact, he says:

Were percentage tables [based on presence-and-absence lists] given for all classifications, the reader could ignore the formal classification and observe for himself the true relationships. (1941, p. 367)[108]

The reader might be able so to observe, but I doubt it. The real weakness lies, not in obfuscating the percentages, but in the source from which the percentages were derived.

Likewise, the dichotomy which Phillips sets up between "the stratigraphic and the analytic (McKern) methods" seems to hit beside the point. He says:

[the faults of Webb's Pickwick Basin report] lie almost wholly in the domain of interpretation and are the result of mixing the stratigraphic and the analytic (McKern) methods. In spite of all that has been said to the contrary, I believe that the two methods cannot be harmonized, one must give way before the other. . . . For once stratigraphy speaks so plainly it must be heard. No classifier could be happy in the contemplation of a mere focus which comprehends everything from a culture lacking even flint to one dominated by pottery. This is the focus to end all foci. Yet in all conscience what else could the authors do? The stratigraphy plainly offered no opportunity for a break-down *that could be expressed by trait lists*. This is the important point. Your archaeologist unhampered by a classificatory bias, would find no trouble at all in breaking the series down into sequent periods, each marked by the appearance of a new type of material. Persistence of the older types would not bother him at all. (1942, pp. 197, 198)

He seems unable to get away from the idea of "trait" lists. Why is it necessary even to have "a new type of material" before a series can be broken down? Why would it not be possible, and culturally significant, to recognize a break when the quantitative or qualitative relationships change? The cultural roster could remain exactly the same so far as presence-and-absence was concerned, but would it not be significant if, for example, the ratio of harpoons to fishhooks went from 75:25 in the lowest deposits to 25:75 in the upper levels? Would not that point at which it passed the 50:50 mark represent a possible point of division? What about a case wherein the quality of twined-woven sandals obviously improved from bottom to top within an archeological deposit? If the Midwestern taxonomists cry that this is not enough, that we are probably dealing with the evolution of a technique within a single human group, then let them not maintain that they deal only with "cultural factors." It is only by the assumption of a socio-political or "tribal" unit that this example can fail to call forth a division. Formally, the end-points are considerably different and should be so classified, if "cultural" factors alone weigh in the balance. According to the Southwestern system, if only it would recognize qualitative data, there would be no difficulty in separating the two end-points, because the space-time factor is not denied. The crux of this particular matter would, of course, be whether further evidence or the archeologist's explicit judgment seemed to warrant the break-down. Potentially and ideally it should be possible, but it is not so under the rigid tenets of a presence-and-absence system.

Therefore it does not seem probable that there is any unresolved conflict between the stratigraphic and the taxonomic methods. The trouble lies in the manner in which these tools are used by the archeologists. It is likely that much of the fault found, here and in other places, with the Gladwin-Colton and McKern systems would be eliminated if quantitative, qualitative, and other relational data were applied throughout the analytical procedure. In this fashion, cultural rosters made up of cultural and culture forms, types, classes, could be utilized for constructional and comparative purposes, and sequent groups of material could be assigned to different classificatory units, even though the actual cultural roster proved to be identical from bottom to top.

All this business of the objectivity of "trait" lists, and the adding and percentaging of "traits," is a fine instance of what Professor Sapir used to call "spurious accuracy." He made the point that because we feel we "must be accurate," we often limit ourselves in our analyses to those phenomena which are amenable to finite accuracy. This leads to an overemphasis of certain aspects and the neglect of others. The taxonomists are as aware as anyone that all culturally important data do not lie in the chemico-physical properties of the material nor in the mere presence or absence of objects at archeological sites. Yet because such things as quality, ratio, association do not readily lend themselves to tabular presentation and simple statements, they have been neglected, even shunned. The result is a warped picture of the culture and the cross-cultural relationships.

Furthermore, even the "trait" lists which have been established are suspect from the viewpoint of "objectivity." At the risk of seeming overly to dwell on one archeologist, I shall again turn to Griffin for illustrative material because his monumental work *The Fort Ancient Aspect* (1943) contains within its ample pages not only a classic example of the taxonomic method but also much detailed exposition to which specific reference can be simply made. He often speaks of the "objectivity" of the method which he employs (e.g., pp. 3, 303, 334, 335, 340). But, making the distinction between objective-subjective on the one hand and empirical-inferential on the other (see p. 123 above), we find that his method does not insure either objectivity or empiricism. To be sure, there is much which is of these orders, but also there is much which is no more objective or empirical than is to be found in the works of others following other methods. Intrinsically and of itself, the taxonomic method is no more objective nor based upon more empirical data than non-taxonomic methods.

In the table of non-pottery "traits" given following page 376, Griffin lists *Plain bone beads, long* and *Plain bone beads, short.* Empirically, it probably is a fact that there are some bone beads which are longer than others, but the decision as to the dividing line between what are to be designated as long and what as short is definitely not empirical. It is a matter of Griffin's judgment with regard to the significance of bead length within the cultural setting. The same can be said for his decision to make two categories instead of many. And finally, it has been his judgment which has brought about a subdividing of the bone-bead category and not of such categories as bone tubes, stemmed stone points, antler handles, etc. He has seen fit to give bone beads double weighting in his tabular lists, and this could have been done only on the basis of an inference as to the significance of the length of bone beads and the insignificance of length within other categories. As for his objectivity in so dividing the beads, one is in the dark because there is nothing in the text which will indicate the grounds on which he determined the significance of bead length or what actual lengths are designated as long or short. For this reason the division must be considered not only inferential but subjective. This lack of observational and explicit criteria makes it impossible for the reader to reproduce Griffin's results or to know on what basis they were achieved.

The same applies to the creation of others of his categories. He has distinguished between *side or corner notched knives, side notched points,* and *corner notched points,* in other words, between "points" and "knives" which display the same notching. Again the segregation is inferential and subjective. Thus, no matter how objective are the procedures applied to these categories, the results will still retain a strong subjective and inferential element. Basically, they will still be founded upon what the archeologist *thought* was important and significant. This point seems to have escaped Griffin because he says that he has used arbitrary divisions based on material of manufacture in order to "eliminate the use of subjective groupings based upon such terms as 'art' and 'ceremonial' " (p. 3). At the same time he tabulates specimens under such headings as *bone hair-spreader, whetstones, shell knives and scrapers, musical rasp,* etc., which beg no less interpretative questions than the terms *art* and *ceremonial.*

It is not conducive to a strong belief in the "objectivity" of his method, when we analyze some of his judgments upon which we can make a check after a fashion. For example, in Table XIV he lists the bell-shaped pestle from seven of the possible nineteen Fort Ancient sites, and in the text he says that "although the evidence is not clear, it seems likely that the Fort Ancient peoples may have had the bell-shaped pestle" (p. 231) and that "in spite of the fact that the bell-shaped pestle is listed as an aspect trait, its place in this culture is uncertain" (p. 197). In other words, seven out of a possible nineteen site-records is not enough to establish bell-shaped pestles within the aspect. On the other hand he lists stone hoes from eight of the nineteen sites and says:

The Iroquois used the wooden digging stick or more rarely an antler hoe instead of the stone hoe or shell hoe, as the Fort Ancient people did [*sic*]. (p. 231)

Here the stone hoe is credited with being a Fort Ancient implement on the basis of eight occurrences, while there was evidently considerable doubt as to the bell-shaped pestle on the basis of seven. I wish to emphasize that I am not holding in suspicion Griffin's judgments on these topics. What I am doing is trying to show that they are in fact judgments and that, therefore, his method is not the "objective" one he claims. Of itself, his method does not make his results any *more* objective or empirical (and it probably does not make it any *less* so). The mere putting of archeological data into lists instead of paragraphs does not make it more "objective," nor is this accomplished by the operations of adding, percentaging, or other mathematical manipulation.

The second point I wish to make, and one which is possibly even more basic than the last, is that the so-called culture classifications of the Southwest and Midwest are classifications neither of separable cultural entities nor of archeological materials in any cultural sense. Except by the odd chance of coincidence, there can be no connection between the groupings which result from taxonomic manipulations according to these systems and the aboriginal "tribal" or cultural groupings. Although the general tenor of explanatory statements (e.g., Colton, 1939, pp. 6-16; McKern, 1939) has been to the effect that, actually or potentially, the taxonomic units are equivalent to pre-existing socio-political or cultural units, there is no justification to be found for such a contention within the systems themselves. This is due to one fact: the taxonomic units, entirely or with but rare exception, are constructed from empirical types and classes, not cultural or culture ones. The attributes of quantity and quality, of provenience and association, and of their respective affinities have not been utilized in creating categories. Segregation has been accomplished on the basis of empirical attributes of a very restricted range and of significance more to the archeologist than to the bygone peoples. For example, Cole and Deuel say:

> To test this conviction [that both Woodland and Mississippi Patterns occur in Fulton County, Illinois], also to obtain a purely objective view [*sic*] of all materials recorded, the larger cultural complexes, such as pottery and projectile points, were spread out and separated into types *without regard to place of occurrence or association with other objects*. (1937, p. 39, italics mine)

And, although it was apparently not of his own doing, Griffin's analysis of Webb's Norris Basin pottery "was conducted without any knowledge of the other material found at the sites." (Griffin, 1938, p. 253)

How can it be expected that types, created with so little regard for cultural data, will, when classified, yield a picture of the cultural relationships that once existed? The mere fact that some types come from a single site or geographic locality is, of itself, no proof that they should be grouped together culturally. Camp sites and cave sites and other stopping places of more or less transient peoples can conceivably preserve within a very limited space the products of not a few separate cultural and political entities. Distinct strata, with or without interspersed sterile layers, will help the archeologist to discriminate in many cases, but what is to help him if there are no such aids and the deposits are found to be without a break from top to bottom? How can he be sure as to just what cultural entities he is dealing with, unless he analyzes the provenience and associations of his material for consistent and significant cohesions and separations? At some sites, such as small pueblos or individual pithouses, cohesion is quite apparent; but at a great many, as for instance the camp sites and shell heaps upon which much of the Midwestern classification has been built, there is the strong possibility that contiguity is due to historical accident rather than cultural relationship. To have reasonable assurance of the latter there is required more than formal similarity coupled with gross spatial propinquity. These may be profitable leads, but they cannot be expected to tell the whole story either from the point of view of cultural comparisons or cultural contexts.

In short, what the taxonomists are doing, for the most part at least, is grouping their material on the basis of purely chemico-physical similarities and saying that the resulting categories represent "cultural divisions," i.e., separable cultural entities which actually existed as such in past times. The Gladwin-Colton system avowedly uses the added criterion of space-time and, in Colton's case at least, identifies one of its categorical levels with former tribes (Colton, 1939, pp. 12, 71; 1942, p. 39). The McKern system professes to use only cultural criteria, but its advocates obviously believe that its categories are potentially representative of formerly existing units, cultural, linguistic, "tribal," ethno-geographic, etc. (Griffin, 1937a, 1937b, 1943, pp. 337-338, 1945a; McKern, 1943, pp. 314-315; 1944, pp. 445-446). Here I believe the Southwestern system has the greater possibility of attaining its goal, because the added factor of space-time reduces the likelihood of identifying chance aggregates as cultural or socio-political entities. Nevertheless, what the archeologists are really doing is putting together what seems to them to be similar in appearance, instead of combining what they have explicitly inferred was culturally cohesive in those bygone days from which their material derives.

In closing this chapter, I wish to bring up the often repeated criticisms of the similarities between Americanist taxonomies and the Linnaean classification of biology. Granting that the archeologists have for the most part applied their systems too rigidly and apparently often without a full awareness of the implications of their procedures, still it seems to me that a great deal of the criticism which I have heard and read has been beside the point and shows an almost equal inflexibility and a comparable misunderstanding.

For example, Brew has elaborated at some length the fact that cultural phenomena do not reproduce sexually and, therefore, are not susceptible of a genetic or biological classification in any literal sense (1946, pp. 46-57; see also Steward 1941, p. 366). To add weight to this attack, he makes much of the fact that, even in biology, the species concept which is the basis of the system is ill-defined and open to serious criticism. These arguments are definitely beside the point and add nothing to the force of his denunciation of archeological taxonomy. If, as Brew maintains, the relationships of cultural phenomena are incomparable to those of biology, if the two spheres are so distinct as to make the classificatory generalities of one impertinent to those of the other, then by the same token the classificatory deficiencies of one are not pertinent to those of the other! If it is held, for example, that the classification of European hedgehogs is completely separate from that of Anasazi pottery, it affects the latter not one whit to demonstrate, however conclusively, that the classification of the former is grossly in error. A case must be tried on its own merits, not on those of another jurisdiction. It behooves us then to examine the problems of archeological classification on the basis of archeological materials themselves.

It is a fact which can hardly be rightly disputed that culture relationships exist between cultural materials. If the word *genetic,* when applied to these relationships, bothers the archeologists and brings before their eyes bisexual images which are not warranted by the data, then by all means let us use other terms, say, *affinal, correlative,* or *legatary.*[109] But it cannot be denied that 1947 Ford cars owe many of their characteristics to ideas obtained from the appearance and performance of the Fords (and even Chevrolets) of previous years, or that the saddles of the Plains Indians are related to the saddles of the Spanish horsemen who came to America many years ago, or that the atomic bomb is an assemblage of many modes (culture ideas) and many cultural forms.

The significance of the above examples lies in the word *idea* and in the human factor. The culture relationships which do exist have been brought about through the minds of living beings, in the present examples through human agency. Inanimate products themselves do not reproduce, modify, copy, or influence one another culturally. It is the mediate agency of a mind that brings about the culture relationships between cultural products. Therefore, any classification which attempts to portray the relationships of human cultural materials must do so in terms of the people who made, used, or possessed those materials. We cannot say that Plains saddles are related to Spanish saddles unless we are willing to define what we mean by Plains Indians and Spanish people and unless we can prove or reasonably infer some connection, direct or indirect, between these human groups. In other words, we must be prepared to define, however crudely or exactly, the groups or individuals that acted as agents for the culture relationship. Since it will be a rare case in archeological research when a single individual can be identified as the agent, it follows that in our discipline a more general designation will usually have to be made, i.e., by groups of individuals.

Now, both in anthropology as a whole and in historiography, the human groups which seem to have given the most satisfactory returns to investigation are those based on one or more of the following criteria: biological heredity ("race," etc.), socio-political coherence ("nation," "tribe," village, "clan," family, etc.), cultural or linguistic heritage (Norse, Indo-European, etc.), and geographic propinquity ("European," "Midwestern," "Danubian," etc.). Therefore, either as a historian or an anthropologist, the archeologist has the criteria for several possible and demonstrably significant groups of people already set forth. He has at least one series of classificatory goals staked out for him: namely, to classify together in one unit all those cultural materials which can be shown or reasonably inferred to have pertained to such groups of people. This is to say that the cultural contexts which will have the more important results, if we may judge from current historiographic and anthropologic practice, will be those characteristic of biological, socio-political, cultural, linguistic, and/or local groups.

And these classificatory units are *inherent in the archeological material*, a contention which is at variance with the expressed views of several archeologists who have essayed theoretical discussions (e.g., Brew, 1946, p. 46; McKern, 1939, p. 312). The objects and other manifestations with which the archeologist deals were made, used, or possessed by individuals belonging to groups that had definite biological heredity, lived with more or less socio-political cohesion (unless the archeologist has discovered a hermit's den), had a specific cultural heritage, spoke as a mother tongue a particular language, and occupied a determinate geographic range. And whether or not these groups can be defined by archeological research does not alter the fact of their existence. For example, the fact that Berlioz, the composer, was of French nationality lies immanent in his musical compositions and provides, therefore, one way of classifying them. The fact that from a musical point of view, i.e., culturally, he was influenced by Beethoven is also inherent in his music and permits us to classify it among those culturally related to Beethoven or to the "German school." The facts that Berlioz spoke French and lived and studied in Paris give us other *inherent* ways of classifying his work. Thus, although it is the classifier who actually constructs the classification, as Brew has said (1946, p. 46), this does not controvert the fact that there are classifications which are inherent in the data. In archeological research, the student may or may not wish to seek and use them, but they are there. Although he is at perfect liberty to make his categories arbitrary, there are inherent ones if he wishes, and is able, to discover them.

Thus, as in the case of the typology and classification of objects and other individual manifestations, classifications of cultural contexts lie immanent in themselves and pertain to bygone people, not to the immediate world of the archeologist. The latter should realize that, potentially at least, he works on two levels. Empirically and "descriptively," he may group his findings to his own tastes and as "arbitrarily" as he wishes. But when he either professes or attempts to group them "culturally," i.e., with significance for the bygone culture under investigation, then he should try to group them according to the relationships pertinent to that culture, not to his own. It is a fact, as Brew states (1946, p. 46), that the data do not "fall into" types or classifications: they must be put there by the archeologist. But this does not mean that there are not inherent groupings which, with luck and conscious effort and by the use of reasoned but free interpretation, the archeologist may succeed in reproducing or approximating. The closeness with which his groupings fit past actuality will be one prime measure of his service to anthropological and historiographic studies.

This brings up another point which was mentioned at the beginning of this chapter and which is vital to an understanding of archeological theory. The empirical data with which the archeologist has to work consist of the material objectifications of culture traits and their empirical attributes. The archeologist who works in undocumented cultures has only three sets of these attributes upon which to base all his studies. They are (1) spatial relationships, (2) quantity, and (3) chemico-physical specifications. For example, most of his temporal relationships are inferences drawn from vertical or horizontal space, the associations of his material are purely spatial, his conceptions of cultural values are taken largely from relative quantity and from chemico-physical attributes leading to judgments of quality, his inferences as to use and function are taken either from spatial association or from the physical properties of shape, material, etc. His work is entirely a pyramiding of inferences based on these foundations, and there is no remedy for this situation. It is in the nature of the archeological materials, and the student might as well face it! The only recourse for him is to make his multitude of required inferences congenial to the empirical facts and as acceptable as possible to his own reasoned opinion and that of his colleagues.

Therefore the problem resolves itself into how, on the basis of these empirical data and with only an acceptable amount of inference, the archeologist is to construct classifications of archeological materials which will reflect cultural relationships as they existed among actual, pre-existing human groups. Since the broader and fuller experience of historiography and the anthropology of the living appears to have concentrated with advantage upon groups based on common biological, socio-political, linguistic, cultural, and geographic factors, it would seem best to follow suit, if only for the sake of the comparability of results and at least until the systems are proved impracticable for archeological research.

However, even a superficial check will show that some of the group criteria are, in fact, impracticable. In the first place, "racial" and other groups based on purely biological factors, as currently defined by the physical anthropologists, have proved too broad and inclusive to satisfy the requirements of "culture classification." Also, because Americanist archeology deals, for the most part, with non-literate and undocumented groups, there is little if any possibility of using linguistic criteria for classificatory purposes. Unwritten language does not "fossilize," i.e., it does not produce material objectifications to be preserved. Only in the case of the "direct historical approach," when the archeologist starts with a documented group, or in the case of a literate society such as the Maya hierarchy is linguistic evidence available. Statements as to specific linguistic affiliations of an undocumented people are inferences, usually of a highly unsupportable sort, and are based on cultural factors other than linguistic. Although it is perhaps legitimate to assume that a culturally homogeneous site, and one which appears to hold the remains of a relatively small social group, say a single house structure, formerly held people who spoke a single tongue, nevertheless when it comes to relating this site linguistically to some other site, the archeologist is on very insecure grounds. And this is true even if the sites seem to be culturally identical or very similar. In short and in general, neither biological nor linguistic classifications are satisfactory for Americanist archeology.

There seems to be at least some likelihood of correctly identifying the social character of individual groups, as for example the family connections of single house sites or the "clan" connections of Southwestern "unit dwellings." But here again, when it comes to projecting social inferences *between* such units, the procedure is precarious. Social or political organization is not objectified materially except through secondary phenomena such as house- and village-plan, "clan" devices and symbols. Therefore, as with language, the relating of bygone peoples socially or politically depends for any validity it might have upon the similarity of predominantly, if not wholly, non-social and non-political phenomena, i.e., a general cultural likeness in so far as it can be inferred from material manifestations.

Thus, whatever the case may be with regard to the characteristics of individual undocumented groups, whenever relationships are sought *between* them, the major dependence has to be placed upon cultural factors other than linguistic and socio-political. Similarities in the material objectifications of culture are taken to indicate cultural relationships, and the latter are often interpreted to include socio-political or linguistic, and sometimes even biological, relationships. But as McKern has said, "The only taxonomic basis for dealing with all cultural manifestations, regardless of occasional direct historical tie-ups, is that of culture type." (1939, p. 302)

Therefore it is the archeologist's task to abstract his empirical data (the spatial and quantitative attributes and relationships of his finds plus their chemico-physical specifications) and to construct from them a picture or definition of the "culture type" of the group of people whose remains he has found and aims to classify. The procedure by which this is to be done is more or less laid out for him by the nature of the archeological materials. In the first place, the archeologist is empirically given nothing more than a series of cultural remains grouped, i.e., localized, in space. The cultural materials at one geographic location, usually called a site, pertain to the people who occupied or utilized that location and can be so classified empirically without recourse to inference. Exceptions occur when, for example, the remains have been moved from their original locus by non-human action, as of water, glaciers, rodents, but such instances do not appreciably alter the generalization. Cultural materials "undisturbed" and *in situ,* represent the local group that made, used, or possessed them in the past. Since the local human groups represented by these localized finds are the only empirical ones with which the archeologist of non-literate and undocumented cultures deals, they are basic and constitute the starting point of all archeological taxonomy. On purely empirical grounds they may be marshalled into larger units based on geographic propinquity: all cultural materials within a certain valley or on a certain mesa or within a designated radius of a certain spot may be thrown together as representing the people who once were in that particular geographic region.

But for the delineation of cultural relationships such geographic taxonomy, although empirical, is often misleading and of little value. The archeologist who, because he finds Mousterian and Magdalenian remains in a single cave, would lump them together and seek cultural comparisons for this whole undifferentiated mass of material, would find himself in serious difficulties. To be sure, he might find another such series of material and thus make telling comparisons, but would not his conclusions as to bygone cultural groups and their relationships be mistaken? In other words, it is necessary for the archeologist to analyze the data from his individual locations or sites and to make a judgment as to what remains, if any, represent a human group which actually existed as a cultural unit in the past. This is to say that his primary obligation is to interpret his site in terms of the human group or groups which used it. This is nothing more or less than the construction of a cultural context for the site or its separable components. When this has been done and, if necessary, some definition made of the "culture type," then will come the time when comparative and taxonomic studies can profitably be initiated.

To put it most simply, the archeologist first separates his material empirically on the basis of space, defining a local human group; then he separates it inferentially on the basis of cultural cohesiveness, defining a cultural group; then he constructs a cultural context for this cultural group; and finally he compares this context with others similarly derived, typing and classifying them in order to bring out what he considers to have been their cultural relationships. In these procedures, two things should be emphasized again: first, that the primary concern of the archeologist should be directed toward a depiction of the culture of a human group represented at a single site or fraction thereof, not toward the placement of certain cultural manifestations in a broad panorama of archeological sites; second, that presence-and-absence trait lists, while they may prove useful tools, are neither the primary goals nor the vital factors in the present method that they are in the current taxonomic systems of the Southwest and Midwest.

As many others have pointed out, the criteria upon which taxonomic systems may be made (once the contexts have been constructed) can be widely variant depending upon the wishes, knowledge, compulsions of the archeologist. Furthermore, it is obvious that the criterion upon which the primary break-down is made will be of signal importance to the results (see Kluckhohn and Reiter, 1939, p. 152). But granting the premises of the present study, the purpose of all such systematization is to depict as exactly as possible the cultural relationships of culturally cohesive groups of people. Therefore, if any classification, no matter what its primary or other criteria, seems satisfactorily to reflect these relationships, then its use is justified. The particular system is but a means to an end and if, for example, one based on a primary break-down along ceramic lines appears to fill requirements, there is no cause to attack it because it is based on only one criterion. What the archeologist is trying to do is to find some classification which will correspond most fully to what actually were the cultural relationships of human groups in the past. If he comes to the conclusion that the similarities of even some "inconsequential" category, say stone axes, follows most closely what this and other evidence indicates were the actual relationships, then he would be vindicated in using a classification of stone axes to express broader cultural relationships. By doing this he is not saying that the most important cultural category is that of axes or that he is classifying cultural wholes. He is merely saying that a primary break-down on this basis seems to make the most sense, serves to provide him with the most productive leads, is congruent with the most empirical and inferential details, and depicts most exactly his opinion of what the cultural relationships actually were.

Nor is there any reason to believe that a classification which has proved valuable in one area or for one temporal period will prove equally practicable in another area or at another time. It is conceivable that at one time sandals will be found most sensitive, while at another they will become stable and apparently indifferent to cultural connections. It is possible that in one region the paste of ceramic products will be the conservative element, against which design will vary with foreign influence; in another area the reverse might prove to be the case. Therefore I do not believe that McKern is to be followed when he advocates the "standardization" of classificatory determinants for systems as broad as that which he proposes (1939, pp. 306-307). The archeologists, like other students of culture, must be prepared to assess their data and change their tenets accordingly. The formation of a rigid system and its mechanical prosecution is hardly warranted in view of what we already know of the nature and workings of culture.

Thus, with relationships which actually obtained to be depicted and human groups which actually existed to be categorized, the archeologist is faced with the problem of developing some method for the presentation of his hypotheses. To date, the most satisfactory way in which relationships in general have been depicted has been that of binomial classification such as is used in biology. But it is important to note that this method can be used to present only those relationships which have already been hypothesized by the classifier. Of itself it does not establish relationships. It serves merely as a tool, a filing system into which already classified data can be put for ready reference and as an aid to future study.

Therefore it is illogical for students of culture to belabor the binomial system because it was developed in the field ·of biology where sexual and bi-parental relationships are the rule. There is no reason to look upon it as the exclusive property of biology or to assume biological connotations when it is used. If viewed as a tool, the only problem is whether it can be of service in the exposition of cultural relationships and whether its mechanisms for showing ever widening circles of affinity can be of advantage to cultural studies. It becomes a question of whether the lineages which range from "mono-parental" to "multi-parental" and the asexual relationships characteristic of culture can be handled profitably with such a tool.

But actually, if we examine the way in which the Midwestern and Southwestern taxonomists apply the binomial system, we will find that it is quite different from the way the biologists use it. This rather important fact seems to have escaped both the taxonomists, who have failed to use it to defend their position, and the critics, who have thus been arguing largely at cross purposes. But what is more to the present point, it provides a means of adaptation whereby the binomial system can be, and has been, applied to cultural matters. First, however, it will be well to show just how the two applications differ.

In biology, the name of the lowest classificatory order, the species, is truly binomial, having two terms which cannot stand apart. These terms represent not only the specific characters but also the generic characteristics and affiliations as well. Thus the specific name *canadensis* when appearing alone may be indicative of many different groupings: the bighorn sheep (Ovis c.), the elk (Cervus c.), the Canadian goose (Branta c.), the columbine (Aquilegia c.). Only when the generic term is understood does the specific term have meaning. This brings about a considerable rigidity in nomenclature, because, before a species can be identified at all, it is already burdened with more or less definite and broad relationships. Should the hypotheses concerning these generic relationships be changed, the resulting disruption in terminology, as well as in the student's thinking, is proportionately great.

In archeology, on the other hand, the nomenclature is not binomial at all in any Linnaean or biological sense. Although the name of the lowest classificatory order consists of two terms as in biology, e.g., Orr Focus, only one of these terms stands for the characters of the specific group and neither represents the characteristics or affiliations of a higher order. The word *Focus* merely identifies the magnitude of the category and *Orr* designates the set of determinants. It is the same as if the biologists were to say "canadensis species." There are no automatic ties to a higher category, and when the system is expanded and the Orr Focus is affiliated with the Oneota Aspect, it is only by juxtaposition and is not inherent within the name *Orr Focus* itself. Therefore the archeological nomenclature is flexible, the units of classification being "free swimming" entities which can be attached and unattached to larger units without changing their given names or definitive characters.

I believe that it is this very flexibility which makes practicable the binomial system for cultural manifestations in archeology. It permits the classificatory assignments to be changed without changing names and without an undue amount of confusion to plague the archeologist. If one day he decides that the Orr Focus belongs in the Oneota Aspect and the next that it belongs in the Fort Ancient Aspect, he is not required to change his nomenclature or to rearrange other units whose relationships to the Orr Focus are proclaimed by their names. All he has to do is to shift the Orr Focus bodily into another pigeonhole and take care of the resultant gymnastics in his thinking when he deals with it. Taxonomy in archeology should be viewed as a system of working hypotheses which may be changed as the evidence warrants and opinion changes. It is illogical to cry with one breath that cultural taxonomy is incomparable to that of other fields, yet with the next to condemn it because it is not equally steadfast and sure! It is very possible, if not highly probable, that the very incomparability lies in its uncertainty and more tentative character, which in turn is due to the nature of its materials and the procedures required to handle them.

These same factors contrive to make archeological taxonomy a matter of judgment and not the automatic and "objective" outcome of manipulating cultural abstractions. The cultural contexts and their constituent elements have been established on the basis of large amounts of interpretation and hypothesis, and it is hardly to be expected that suddenly on the comparative level there will be a reversal so that mechanically applied systems will solve the problems. We can agree with Steward that

. . . strict adherence to a method drawn from biology inevitably fails to take into account the distinctively cultural and unbiological fact of blends or crosses between essentially unlike types. (1941, p. 366)

But the archeological method, whether drawn from biology or not, at the present time does not resemble the biological method except in so far as it attempts to depict the branching quality of relationships by the use of a dendritic or tree-like pattern. Brew has taken exception to this usage because of its biological overtones (1946, pp. 52ff), but it is not too much to point out that a dendritic pattern is not the exclusive property of biology, e.g., it is a characteristic of river drainages and the deposition of minerals upon stone. That it is also a characteristic of cultural relationships can be easily seen if one takes the trouble to analyze graphically such a body of data as given by Kroeber on the spread of the alphabet. (1923, pp. 263ff)

It is true that cultural derivations are often multiple and the dendritic pattern thus complicated. But this means nothing more than that the archeologist who would set a given manifestation upon some one "branch" or "stem" must decide which, if any, are the most fundamental and significant influences, either for his present problem or the cultural context as a whole. In a comparable instance, Leslie Spier found no difficulty in identifying Havasupai culture as fundamentally Basin, although it has obviously received strong influences from several other sources (1929, p. 219). Spier analyzed the data, made his decision, and assigned the culture to the category with which it seemed to him to display the most basic connections. The same can be done with archeological data, providing only that the bases for the decision are made plain for the evaluation of the reader. Trait lists and mathematical treatment may well be of service in clarifying the material, but alone they cannot be expected to solve the problem for the very reason that these relationships *are* multiple and an assessment of their relative importance is in the majority of cases a question of judgment, not of mathematics.

To me there seems no barrier to classifying a given cultural manifestation as a whole in one category and, either for other purposes or for a more detailed accounting, to classify its component parts with completely different units. For example, the cultural context of Component A as a whole might appear to have its most basic relationships with Component B, while at the same time its ceramic complex shows overwhelming influence from Component C. As long as the evidence is given, I can see no trouble in grouping Components A and B together when the intent is to show over-all relations. When, however, detailed ceramic studies are in order, Component A could be grouped with Component C. The same procedure can extend down the scale: when the data require, the ceramic complex as a whole might be grouped one way while some of its segments are grouped otherwise.

In short, as Brew has said (1946, pp. 46, 65), we need more, not fewer classifications. But there is little reason to expect that any rigidly applied, mathematical, "standardized" system will of itself be satisfactory for the presentation of cultural relationships. The archeologist *and* his system need to be flexible and able to change with the changing demands of his complicated and disconnected material. If so many judgments must be made throughout the process it comes to a question, not of denying and shunning them, but of seeing how explicitly and how soundly the necessary ones can be made, presented, and supported. On these grounds, then, there seem to be no substantial arguments against using a binomial system to depict cultural relationships as they are envisioned by the archeologist. If he will not apply it after the fashion of biology and then decry it because it brings biological connotations, but if he will adapt it to his own needs and at the same time keep it flexible, he may feel free to use it as a means. Let it carry him as far as it will, and then let him leave it. In a burning desert, let us not throw away our parasol because it is marked "Made in Japan."

CHAPTER 6

AN OUTLINE OF PROCEDURES FOR THE CONJUNCTIVE APPROACH

ALTHOUGH the important and distinctive features of the conjunctive approach lie in the mental attitude and the broad objectives with which the archeologist attacks his research, and although actual methods and techniques will differ in individual instances, nevertheless it is appropriate that some exposition be given of the practical means by which such an attitude may receive concrete expression and through which such objectives may be attained. In the following pages, then, an annotated outline of these means will be given. From the start, however, it must be recognized that any archeological scheme is, of necessity, subject to modification, elaboration, and even radical change in response to particular circumstances and the dictates of practicalities such as time and finance. Therefore, the outline to be set forth here has but one purpose: to provide a more or less concrete exposition of ideas basic to the conjunctive approach. Exhaustiveness is neither claimed nor achieved. The intent is merely to project some of the "flavor," some of the conceptualization behind this approach.

The concrete examples used in the following pages will be found to come predominantly from my own, unpublished work. I do not wish this fact to convey the impression that I consider myself to be the only archeologist to have attempted such studies. I have already cited others whose work follows the lines here advocated. The purpose of drawing from my own researches has been to provide would-be critics with something tangible to analyze and cite, inasmuch as my archeological writings have heretofore been very few. In view of my many remarks on the published work of others, I felt that not so to provide would open me to justifiable accusations of hiding behind the skirts of non-publication.

Table 4 gives the levels and sub-levels of procedure that characterize the conjunctive approach. While in general the levels are sequentially arranged according to actual procedure, it is obvious that much latitude may be allowed in this regard. For instance, the studying of data may proceed together with its collection, rather than after, as for instance in the case of material which cannot be removed from the field or which is destroyed during excavation: e.g., Maya buildings and occupation levels within a shell mound. Nor are the headings mutually exclusive or segregated according to cultural criteria. They are inclusive and descriptive, representing merely a working scheme to suggest, not dictate, the mechanics of archeological research.

In the following analysis of Table 4, and hence of the conjunctive approach,

TABLE 4

A. Problem
B. Data
    1. Collection
        a. Local cultural
            1) Artifacts
            2) Cultural refuse
            3) Deposits
        b. Local human biological
        c. Contemporaneous geographical
            1) Geological
            2) Meteorological
            3) Floral
            4) Faunal
        d. Non-local human
            1) Contemporaneous
            2) Pre-local
            3) Post-local
        e. Non-contemporaneous geographical
            1) Pre-local
            2) Post-local
    2. Study
        a. Criticism of validity of data
        b. Analysis
        c. Interpretation
        d. Description
    3. Presentation
C. Local Chronology (chronicle)
D. Synthesis and Context (ethnography or historiography)
E. Comparative (ethnology)
    1. Cultural
    2. Chronological
F. Study of Culture, Its Nature and Workings (anthropology)

the category *Problem* will be treated first. But from that point onward, the table will be discussed in reverse order. The reason for this reversal is plain. The type of data to be collected and the very manner of collecting depends on the kind of information which it is desired eventually to utilize when the time comes for synthesis and study. Thus, if there is given an idea of the information which the conjunctive approach aims to include in its cultural contexts, the required data and the means for collecting them can be more easily visualized. If, for instance, it is shown that sound inferences as to modes and configurations can be abstracted from particular archeological data, then the means can be sought whereby these data and others like them can be brought to light.

A. PROBLEM

It has been said, and it is true, that the problems which have brought students to the field of archeology and to their respective sites have been widely varied. Given this range, it is natural that the approaches to, and the results of excavation should also show considerable variation. Natural or not, this state of affairs when reflected in the actual collection of archeological data is not only unsatisfactory—it is also positively disastrous. Personal problems and objectives which are pursued at the expense of collecting other data are unwarranted.

The archivist and the experimental scientist may with impunity select from their sources those facts which have for them a personal and immediate significance in terms of some special problem. Their libraries and experimental facilities may be expected to endure, so that in the future there may be access to the same or a similar body of data. If, however, it were certain that, after the archivist's first perusal, each document would be utterly and forever destroyed, it would undoubtedly be required of him that he transcribe the entire record rather than just that portion which at the moment interests him. He would have difficulty in justifying his research if, knowingly, he caused the destruction of a unique record for the sake of abstracting only a narrowly selected part.

The gathering of data from archeological sites, in nearly every instance, involves the destruction of the original record. Only to the extent to which that record is transposed to the archeologist's notes is it preserved for study either by the collector himself or by other students. A good axiom for archeologists is that "it is not what you find, but how you find it," and it is superfluous to point out that "how you find it" can be told only from notes and not specimens. An archeological find is only as good as the notes upon it. Therefore only one objective can be sanctioned with regard to the actual excavation of archeological sites: that of securing the most complete record possible, not only of those details which are of interest to the collector, but of the entire geographic and human environment. That which is not recorded is most often entirely lost. In such a situation, selection implies wanton waste.

It should not be understood that the above remarks indicate a protest against special problems or specific objectives in archeological research. The case is distinctly otherwise. What the statements do mean, however, is that questions of problem and objectives, in so far as they are limiting and abridging factors, should be confined to two stages in the procedure of investigation and, above all, that they should not inhibit the excavations themselves.

As the first of these stages, the choice of area of investigation and of the sites to be dug should be made with reference to specific problems. And the word *should* is used advisedly. These problems may be of many sorts and by their nature will indicate the type of final conclusions to be expected from the investigation. The archeologist's interest may be in art or architecture, in philology, or in the corroboration of myths and legends. His interest may be purely chronological, being directed toward the sequential arrangement of the data or toward the determination of specific dates for certain manifestations; it may be historiographical, leading him to construct temporally sequential series of cultural contexts or to describe the culture of a given area at a given time; or it may be anthropological, leading him to select his area and site with a view to testing some hypothesis as to the nature and workings of culture.

But after the selection has been made and when the actual excavation is begun, there can be only one objective: to exploit fully and without abridgement the cultural and geographic record contained within the site attacked. There is no justification in discarding or failing to record projectile points, for example, because of a single-minded concern with ceramic chronology. No more is there justification in neglecting the local, the peculiar, the atypical data, just because they are not useful for comparative purposes *outside* of the site. Within his broadly given cultural and geographic universe, the archeologist is a technician concerned with the production of data, and, although he should be aware of the concepts and goals of many disciplines, he should not be restricted in his exploitation of the site by the dictates of any of them. Time will come in his study and analysis when these factors will again assume the major role, but when he puts spade to ground the archeologist should be dedicated to an exposition unconfined except by the broadest stretch of the cultural and geographic frame of reference. This is what makes archeology a technique and the archeologist, as archeologist, a technician. His particular problems are concerned with the production of data. When he makes use of these data to some purpose, he becomes affiliated with the discipline whose concepts he employs and whose aims he serves.

Likewise, the archeologist is obligated to preserve, whether in publication or some permanent repository, the full body of his empirical data and records. Since he has destroyed the original record, his transcript and the recovered specimens are the only substitute. The archeologist has no more justification in submerging part of the record than he would have had in destroying, without record, a part of the original site. Practical considerations such as space and money have sometimes been blamed for the failure to preserve the record fully. However valid these factors may be, the extent of their victory over the ideal of full preservation is a measure of the defeat of the very excavations which have been accomplished.

With regard to the publication of the record, practical considerations enter the picture. But whatever the means of accomplishment, one thing is certain: it is incumbent upon the archeologist to publish the empirical bases for all his inferences in order that the reader may judge for himself their acceptability. Conclusions unsupported by adduced empirical data carry the implication that they are to be taken at face value, without criticism or doubt. It is a dubious procedure to put the contributing evidence out of reach of interested students. This topic will be examined at somewhat greater length below; it is enough that it be mentioned here.

The second stage of procedure wherein special problems may determine the nature of archeological research comes after the empirical record has been gathered. The archeologist has fulfilled his obligation by transposing the record from the ground to some form, both permanent and available. From this point onward, his own personal interest may again take possession and guide his further use of the data. Perhaps he wishes to study the chronological development of art forms. Perhaps he wishes to write history and construct a cultural context. Perhaps he wishes to study culture itself and also construct a context in order to examine its internal and external relationships. Whatever his interests, they may again take over.

F. STUDY OF CULTURE, ITS NATURE AND WORKINGS

That the study of archeological materials can, in fact, give insights into the modes, archetypes, and configurations of bygone cultures is contrary to the expressed beliefs of many anthropologists. Boas, Griffin, Kidder and Thompson, Lowie, Speck, among others, have made statements to the effect that archeology deals only with the material aspects of culture and cannot aspire to information regarding non-material aspects.[110] But if anthropology, as the study of culture, is to be able to generalize fully, to base its conclusions on the broadest foundations, it cannot be satisfied with data gathered only from the shallow depth provided by the ethnographic reach. To quote Randall's very pertinent remark made in a somewhat different context:

When one has reached an understanding of what materials are furnished by the world around him, and what resources he can hope for inside himself, it still remains for him to appraise the past as it is left to operate in the present. . . . (1940, p. 6)

Anthropology cannot afford to reject the help of other disciplines, archeology included. It should at least attempt to give its statements as much perspective as possible, and the discipline of archeology should attempt to help in this project. This can be done, in one way, by making full use of the archeological record within the limits, not of dogma, but of demonstrated value. And "demonstrated value" calls for just that, *demonstration:* attempts to push archeological methods and techniques to their utmost, willingness to excavate and record and describe with thorough utilization of the empirical data (both specifications and affinities), and then a willingness to provide an interpretation for the finds.

This last has been called "sticking the neck out." But such a reaction to interpretation is unjustified. Once the empirical information has been presented, the archeologist has his right as well as his duty, as the man on the job, to give his understanding of the data. This understanding is open to criticism only on logical and empirical grounds. The fact that an interpretation has been offered is definitely not open to criticism *ipso facto*. Nor is it subject to refutation on the grounds of alternate opinion except in so far as this alternate opinion is itself founded upon more acceptable evidence than, or better and more economical use of, the evidence *originally adduced*. In other words, reason and argumentation, not polemic, should be the resort of the critics. As Mandelbaum put it:

No sociological understanding of the conditions under which the statement was made bears the slightest resemblance to an estimate of the truth or falsity of the statement itself. [After the truth or falsity is judged by recourse to other statements of fact, we may reexamine the original statement in the light of the stater's background to ascertain how or why he made a correct or false statement.] (1938, pp. 183-184)

With the proper and sensible proviso that conclusions are based on "the facts at hand" and are subject to revision in the light of fuller and better data, it is a premise of the conjunctive approach that interpretations are both justified and required, when once the empirical grounds have been made explicit. Why has revision been such a bugbear to archeologists? Other disciplines are constantly reworking their hypotheses and formulating new ones upon which to proceed with further research. When these are found to demand modification and change they are altered. Why should archeology assume the pretentious burden of infallibility? Why is it not possible to project hypotheses, specifically labeled as such, and then to go on from these toward testing and answering the questions thus raised? Why should every archeological hypothesis have to stand and be correct for all time?[111]

Furthermore, as I have already said with specific regard to pottery taxonomy (Chapter 5, pp. 128ff), I do not believe that criticism merely on the grounds of too few data will hold water. If the data are conclusive enough, even a very few will serve to establish a point. A most pertinent statement is offered by Cohen and Nagel:

In a well-known passage, Mill remarks that often a very large number of verifying instances is insufficient to establish firmly a generalization (for example, that all crows are black), while a few such instances are sufficient to win our assent to others (for example, that a certain type of mushroom is poisonous). (1934, p. 279)

If the evidence will not bear the weight of the interpretation, it is not merely that it is too scanty, but because it is first of all too poor and *then* too scanty. For example, if we should infer the presence of the atlatl from a single, rather heavy, chipped stone point found in some pithouse, there might be understandable reasons for doubt because of the ambiguous nature of the criterion. But the fact that only one was found could not rightly be the reason, because if a single unquestionable atlatl hook had been found, there could have been no doubt at all. And finally, even if the data are not "good enough and conclusive enough," if they are all the archeologist has, then he has not only a right but also an obligation to do what he can with them, of course describing their nature and limitations. A policy of wait-until-all-the-evidence-is-in can stunt the growth of archeology to a dangerous degree. The man on the job has tremendous advantages over students who might wish, at some later time, to make use of his specimens and records.

Returning from this brief digression on critical standards and assuming for the moment that archeology can produce information pertinent to the study of culture itself, it may be required to show that such information is of a sort sufficiently important to justify its derivation and presentation. It has been my experience on several occasions to be forced to answer challenges to the effect that: "Such material is much more easily obtained, and in much greater detail and quantity, from living groups. Why struggle to derive it from the archeological records?" A few answers to this question may be given here in cursory fashion.

Granting that information as to the nature and processes of culture might more *easily* be abstracted from living groups, it still remains that nothing has been granted as to the *adequacy* of such treatment. The information may hold true for living groups, but nothing is thus proved as to its applicability in the past. Whether the same conditions existed then or are recent developments, whether specific aspects are due to demonstrable borrowing or are native as far back as we can go: these are vital questions not to be answered with data from a single time-plane. Furthermore, "as far back as we can go" does not end with the memory of the oldest living informant or the most ancient written document! Despite the interest and importance of cultural data from a shallow time-depth, statements of fact, without information as to how the facts got that way, have a faculty of badly misleading the investigator and of being highly inadequate therefore (see: Lesser, 1935; Miller, 1939, pp. 39ff.). What boots it if two endpoints in our particular way of looking at things are similar, if actually they are the products of entirely different biological and/or social stimuli? For some purposes a bionomic classification which groups together whales, sharks, and fishes is of value, but does this exhaust the possible and significant ways of viewing them? Many anthropologists and a host of biological taxonomists have shown that this is not so. By the same reasoning, then, it is maintained that the study of culture is potentially a gainer from the use of the archeological record, providing only that the record is capable of producing the pertinent information.

The crucial test is whether data on the nature and workings of culture and particularly on the non-material aspects of cultural phenomena can be derived from archeological material. The following examples are given to demonstrate that such derivations can be made and to give an idea of the sort of information which archeological data will produce when viewed with a certain attitude, i.e., that designated here as the conjunctive approach. The examples are not finished pieces of research, and represent some of the first attacks upon a difficult and complex problem by one individual. Consequently they may seem to be isolated instances rather than integral and widely connected parts of detailed contexts. However this may be, the reader is asked to imagine them as actually in context and to visualize what the picture would be if all aspects of the local culture manifestation had been similarly treated.

During cave excavations conducted for the U. S. National Museum in the State of Coahuila, Mexico, one small burial cave was found to contain a number of large fragments of plaited mats and several coiled baskets in addition to its other contents.[112] Although the cultural relations of this site are not definitely established as yet, it appears probable that the contained artifacts and skeletal material are related to similar finds in the Laguna District of Coahuila immediately to the south. The latter area has produced the justly famous Palmer collection, lodged in the Peabody Museum of Harvard, and one burial bundle housed in the U. S. National Museum. This latter bundle I have studied in detail, and the Harvard specimens I have examined superficially.[113]

When the material from the northern burial cave and the presumably related finds from the Laguna District are examined, one thing is immediately apparent: although clearly demonstrating a mastery of the various techniques of manufacture and indicating a strong tendency toward decoration, the fabrics display a startling and pervasive lack of regular pattern or design. Symmetry and regularity in the over-all use of decoration are absent. The areas in which variation of weaving technique and use of color have been employed to create decoration appear to be placed with no regard for design unity or symmetry. Even within the techniques themselves, although mechanically they are extremely well executed, there is no consistency: spacing, weave-counts, and measurements vary at random in all but an insignificantly few instances. Plate 1 will give visual support to these contentions.

In direct contrast to this lack of symmetry, to this unconcern with over-all patterning, is the use of decoration among the San Juan Basket-Maker. Plate 2 will indicate the high development of a sense of design found in Basket-Maker materials. Here there is a definite conceptualization of a decorative whole adapted to the structural whole. The apparent "need" or desire for decoration is channeled by what seem to be the dictates of a visualized entity which applies both to textile fabrics and to the obviously derived treatment of ceramic products. In other words, whatever the origin, whether in the mechanics of weaving technique or otherwise, the people represented by the Basket-Maker remains possessed a conception of decorative wholes in their textile and pottery complexes.

This difference between Coahuila and San Juan textile decoration cannot be accounted for on the basis of differing techniques or materials. Although these vary between the two regions, the mechanical excellence and control exhibited in all the specimens rule out the possibility that the decorative idiosyncracies of the Coahuila people are attributable to their lesser abilities as artisans or to any relative intractability of their materials. For example, it surely is a fact that plaiting is a simpler technique than either twining or coiling and no less regular; yet the Coahula plaited specimens, while showing remarkable versatility and control in technique, nevertheless are decoratively the most irregular of all and cannot be compared in this respect with the twined and coiled textiles from Basket-Maker sites. Also, an analysis of Coahuila netting shows that there is an exceptional control of technique and that the irregularities of design arise from a failure to perform regularly the purely mechanical functions of counting rows, choosing colors, etc., and not from failures of manipulation. The fact that a few Coahuila textiles show regularity, at least in small sections, indicates that they could do this sort of work. That they did not do so more often conveys the idea that they were not concerned with producing regularity. I feel it is making only a permissible judgment to state that both areas show an equal control over their media and that the difference in textile decoration is due to other factors than techniques or materials.

It seems merely to be a fact that one group had, and the other did not have, the inclination, the conceptualization, the uniformity of culture ideas, in short the configuration, which resulted in the construction of over-all designs on textile fabrics. What has been demonstrated from this set of archeological details, I believe, is a culture configuration in the sense in which Kluckhohn has used the term. He says:

To a considerable extent patterns are arrived at by simple abstraction from trends toward uniformity in statement and deed. . . . Configuration looks to an *inner* coherence in terms of the large structuralizing principles which prevail in the *covert* culture. Patterns are forms; configurations are, so to speak, interrelationships between forms. (1941, p. 126; see also: Kluckhohn, 1943)

PLATE 1

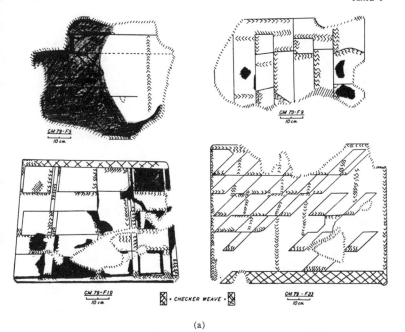

(a)

(b)

a) Twill plaited mats from Cave CM 79, Coahuila, Mexico
(Black splotches represent areas covered by red paint.)
b) Textile of knotless netting from Coyote Cave, CM 88, Coahuila, Mexico
(Actual colors not represented.)

PLATE 2

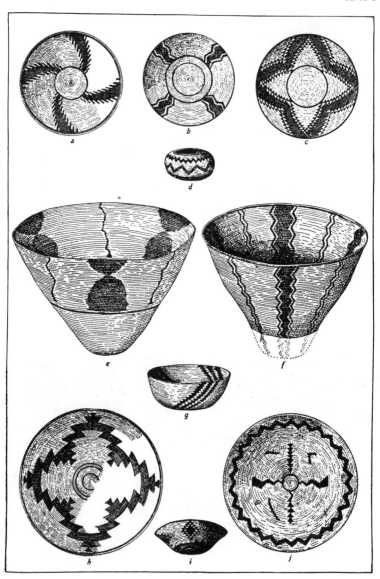

Basket-Maker basketry from Northeastern Arizona. (From "Basket-Maker Caves of North-eastern Arizona," by Samuel J. Guernsey and Alfred V. Kidder, *Papers of the Peabody Museum, Harvard University*, Vol. VIII, No. 2, 1921. Plate 24.)

The pattern for the San Juan is over-all design fitted to the structure of textile fabrics (and ceramics). The structuralizing principle which holds the pattern together is the configuration which may be verbalized as "regularized decorative wholes." The reverse configuration was present among the people who produced the material found in the Coahuila caves, i.e., "unconcern with regularized decorative wholes."

It should be pointed out that these configurations, as they appear from the textile data, may be incomplete. It is possible, if not probable, that the currently envisioned ones represent but parts of broader configurations which structure other patterns of Basket-Maker and Coahuila culture. In fact, if the modern Pueblos are to be viewed as the cultural decendants of the San Juan Basket-Makers, it seems highly probable that the configuration, to which their ancient textile patterns are but a partial clue, is actually something like "symmetry and regularity of wholes." Pottery design and turquoise mosaic, pilastered kivas and the D-shaped pueblo form, the uniformity and symmetry of ceremonial and social patterning among the recent Pueblo peoples, these and many other cultural items of the Anasazi and their cultural descendants lend weight to the belief that the pattern of over-all design on Basket-Maker textiles was supported by a broad structuralizing configuration which entered into other patterns as well. Here then, if the analysis has been correct and holds up in the light of further evidence, is a cultural configuration of considerable temporal persistence, and concrete evidence has been adduced from the data of archeology to the hypothesis, offered by Boas and others (Boas, 1934, p. xiii; Kluckhohn, 1941, p. 127), that culture configurations often have a remarkable permanency as compared with specific content which shows more frequent change.

The implications of this analysis for the definition of Coahuila culture are also important, but more study will have to be done upon other aspects of culture in this region before a clearer understanding of these implications will be possible. For example, does the configuration of "unconcern with regularized decorative wholes" also imply the absence of regularity and symmetry in other patterns? Or were there compensatory adjustments to counterbalance, with regularity in other patterns, the lack of it in textile decoration? The test lies in a fuller knowledge of the culture, and this will come only with further excavation and more extended study of documentary sources. But one point seems established: there is a marked difference in a broad culture configuration between Coahuila and the San Juan, and thus it is expectable that more than one cultural pattern is different in the two areas. These observations, taken in conjunction with other information, reduce the possibility that the Basket-Makers and the people of Coahuila were closely related culturally or are to be included within a single category in any classification which professes to depict the more detailed cultural relationships of human groups. In short, it is very doubtful that the

Coahuila people possessed a "north Mexican form of Basket-Maker culture." (Roberts, 1932, p. 16; see also: Guernsey, 1931, p. 112)

The next example has to do with the twisted fiber cordage from two locations: six caves in northern Coahuila[114] and Lovelock Cave, Nevada (Loud and Harrington, 1929). At the latter site, "twine" was usually twisted with a right twist (see definition in Amsden, 1930): out of 1,973 specimens only 14 were twisted to the left. Furthermore, when the ancient inhabitants of Lovelock twisted two or more two-ply cords together to make what may be termed compound cord, in all cases the basic cords were of normal (right) twist. But since it seems to be a mechanical principle of string-making that the direction must be reversed in each successive twisting (Roth, 1924, p. 112), the final product of Lovelock compound cord was twisted to the left, which produced a contrast with the normal. Their two-ply and their compound cordage are thus of different spirals and different final appearance.

TABLE 5

		Initial Twist	Final Twist	Final Appearance
Lovelock	Two-ply.....	—	right	different
	Compound...	right	left	
Coahuila (CM 95)	Two-ply.....	—	left	same
	Compound...	right	left	

The specimens from Coahuila were twisted with a left twist in all but one of the sixty examples studied. A quick survey of cordage from other regions of the state indicates that this practice is the usual one throughout the area. In making compound cords, however, the basic two-ply strings were first twisted to the right, i.e., abnormally, so that when these were combined, through the mechanical principle of reversing the direction of the spiral, the result was a compound cord with a left, or normal, twist. Thus in Coahuila, two-ply and compound cords were of the same spiral and the same final appearance.

Although the numbers of compound specimens in this example are probably insignificantly few (eight from Lovelock including what seems to be a falsely identified exception; four from one Coahuila cave, CM 95), this should not affect the implications of the results. In the first place, the four and eight specimens comprise the total number of compound cords reported from the respective sites and, therefore, represent a 100 per cent conformance within a total universe, not a sample. Secondly, although this fact would appear to suggest some actual validity for the data, in the present context the idea is the important thing, not the eventually established truth of the conclusions. The example has been given to show what sort of information may be derived from archeological materials, and not to reach any verdict or solve any specific problems with reference to Nevada or Coahuila cave cultures.

To continue with the analysis: it seems that, as in the case of textile design stated above, there are two conceptualizations, one being the opposite of the other. It appears that the Coahuila people, when they desired a strong compound cord, visualized the whole process and reversed their normal procedure at the start so that the final product would conform to their idea of how finished cordage should be twisted. The Lovelock people, on the other hand, appear to have been unconcerned with the final form and merely continued their usual procedure one step further and, by the machinations of technique, came out with compound cords having a spiral different from the majority of their cordage. One group visualized compound cord and allowed for it from the start; the other merely put together several two-ply strings to make a stronger twine. The Coahuila people would seem to have had an ideal pattern for string, and they saw to it that the final product conformed, whether it was two-ply or compound. There was a sense of order, a conscious or unconscious structuring of a pattern.

How does this configuration, with its implications of regularity, affect the formerly identified Coahuila (textile) configuration of "unconcern with regularized decorative wholes?" To mention but one thing, it points to the probability that the latter is not part of an otherwise possible, broader configuration such as "unconcern with regularity and symmetry." In this fashion it serves as a check or balance, a modifier of the first conclusion. Just exactly what the two, somewhat opposed, configurations do mean in relation to one another and to the culture as a whole is a problem which must wait upon more, and more comprehensive, data. But it is to be hoped, indeed expected, that when enough of these structuring ideas have been defined on enough evidence, they may be weighed against one another to arrive at an acceptable insight into the covert culture of the Coahuila Indians. The importance of this outcome, for historiographic depth and for the study of culture itself, needs no elaboration.

In the south-central, mountainous portion of the Southwest, Haury and others have uncovered materials which they have designated as the Mogollon culture (Haury, 1936b). This is characterized in its earlier, more diagnostic periods by a ceramic tradition of polished brown ware which, when painted, displays a red pigment. After a period of time, the Mogollon is thought by some to have developed into the Mimbres culture with the aid of influences from other areas. One of the elements by which the Anasazi influences are recognized is that of black-on-white pottery.

As transitional between the black-on-white ceramics of the later and the red-on-brown ceramics of the earlier phases, the pottery type known as Three Circle Red-on-white is found. Haury says:

The adoption of a white background and the appearances of small unpainted zones in the decorative field is doubtless to be attributed to the influence of northern potters. . . . (1936c, p. 21)

If this hypothesis is accepted, what are the implications of the existence of the pottery type called Three Circle Red-on-white? Concerning its value Haury makes but one remark:

For this reason [its short temporal span], and because it did not represent a stage when other traits, as architecture, had attained a characteristic development, Three Circle Red-on-white has not been accorded the same value as other types, namely, as a basic component of a phase. (1936c, p. 20)

That is to say: since there is little or no value to be found in the type for taxonomic purposes, it is to be accorded no further attention. To date, as far as I have been able to learn, there has been no analysis of the intra-cultural meaning of the Three Circle pottery type.

The ceramic tradition of the Mogollon culture included the use of an oxidizing firing atmosphere which produced a brown surface color and a red decoration. The Anasazi tradition included a reducing atmosphere which produced a white or gray surface color and black decoration. Assuming the actuality of Anasazi influence upon the Mogollon, what inferences may be drawn from the pottery sequence in the latter culture: Mogollon Red-on-brown>Three Circle Red-on-white>Mimbres Bold Face Black-on-white? The first two types are closely related as Haury has said (1936b, pp. 94, 96), but this affinity is marred by the white surface on the later one. This is most probably due to the northern influence. But Three Circle still carries red paint and is still fired in an oxidizing atmosphere using an iron-free slip to achieve the white surface. The inference is clear: at the incidence of Anasazi influence, the Mogollon potters acquired a desire for white surface and a contrasting paint, but they attained their results by variations upon their own techniques of manufacture. Later, possibly through closer contact and a transference of a knowledge of pigments, or by their own experimentation to obtain a more exact copy of the northern ideal, the Mogollon potters attained, in their Mimbres Bold Face Black-on-white, the black decoration characteristic of northern wares. But here again, their own oxidizing technique was employed, and a reversion to red decoration was occasionally achieved by the expedient of changing firing conditions and/or paint composition.

In the case of Three Circle Red-on-white, perhaps the Mogollon people had tried to produce a black but had failed and were forced to retain their original color. Perhaps they were impressed only by the white surface and were not interested in producing black paint at all. Perhaps something in their own culture, color symbolism for example, erected a barrier against the initial acceptance of the color *black*. Whatever the answers to these questions, the importance of Three Circle Red-on-white is not to be judged solely on its lack of taxonomic value. If the above hypotheses are acceptable, here is an archeological example of the persistence of techniques of manufacture during a radical change in decorative style. It is a case to parallel that which W. W. Hill cites for ethnographic data when he says:

However, they [the ceremonial examples cited] do seem to indicate not only a stability of the religious aspects of the culture but also that any changes which are made and attempted will be within the ideology of the existing pattern. (1939, p. 260)

Spier and Wissler have both pointed to the fact that often a cultural phenomenon is taken over by a group which then proceeds to make use of it according to the patterns and configurations with which it itself is familiar instead of those which have influenced the donor group (Spier, 1921, pp. 500, 511-516, 520-521; 1929, pp. 220-221; Wissler, 1915, p. 38). Also an archeological example of the workings of stimulus diffusion has been illustrated (see Kroeber, 1940).

For some years the area around Flagstaff, Arizona, has been recognized as the meeting place of several ancient culture streams (Colton, 1939). The Museum of Northern Arizona has been working on the archeological problems of this region with a rare and exemplary consistency, and it is very apparent that the purpose of its investigations has been to place the many sites and components in taxonomic categories relative to each other. Except for brief sentences in rare publications, the approach has been purely comparative, and the cultural contexts and their implications for the nature and workings of culture have been left strictly alone.

However, there are other ways of looking at the data and an example will be given here. In one of his latest papers, significantly entitled *Archaeology and the Reconstruction of History* (1942), H. S. Colton, of the Museum of Northern Arizona, gives some very provocative information on the diffusion and persistence of "traits" over the frontier between two of his taxonomic categories (Branches) which he identifies as "tribes."

1. The traits of the Kayenta [Branch] and Sinagua [Branch] which did not diffuse are: (a) earth lodge shape . . . (b) two post roof support absent in Kayenta, present sometimes in Sinagua; (c) ball court absent in Kayenta, present in Sinagua; (d) sipapu . . . (e) method of shaping pottery . . . (f) axes . . . (g) black pottery paint . . . (h) firing atmosphere . . . (i) inhumation flexed in Kayenta, extended in Sinagua.

2. Traits that seem to have diffused from the Kayenta to the Sinagua, 900-1100

A.D., across the border are: (a) ventilators; (b) deflector; and (c) good masonry construction. After 1100 the masonry, multifamily pueblo was accepted by the Sinagua.

3. No true Sinagua traits seem to have crossed the border to the Kayenta between 900 and 1100 A.D. . . . . After 1100 A.D., the use of white paint on red pottery crossed to the Kayenta.

4. Certain traits are shared by both the Kayenta and Sinagua, 900-1100 A.D.: (a) earth lodge entered through a hole in the roof; (b) four post roof support . . . (c) coiled and bundle basketry; (d) cotton textiles woven on a loom; (e) grooved metate; and (f) burial offerings. (1942, p. 37)

Taking all these data at their face value for the moment, here is a set of facts begging for attention. Colton addresses them with the purpose of "reconstructing history" which apparently means to him the chronological arrangement and taxonomic ordering of his units. But one can also view them as exhibiting examples of differential diffusion and acceptance of culture traits (meaning *ideas*). One might make an analysis of what traits were borrowed, what their character might mean with regard to culture processes, and what meaning hypotheses developed on these foundations might have for the individual cultural entities involved.

Looking over the examples in Colton's paragraph No. 1, i.e., those that did not diffuse, two common denominators appear: religion (sipapu, ball court, burial posture, if we proceed on assumptions current in the Southwest today), technique of manufacture (method of smoothing pottery, firing atmosphere and its connected feature: paint color). Respecting axes, lodge shape, and roof support, we advance with less assurance. It may be that they belong with the category of technique. But on the other hand it may be that roof support has religious import as among the Pawnee and that the shape of the lodge has religious sanctions, as is presumably the case of the Anasazi (Kayenta) house-kiva complex before about A.D. 1300 (noted by Colton but to another purpose, 1942, p. 38).

When we come to the examples which did diffuse from Kayenta to Sinagua, i.e., Colton's paragraph No. 2, something else is seen: they are all practical and *de novo* improvements on house form. There were no conflicting practices already established and, if we argue from the fact of their very obvious efficiency, the traits were perfectly capable of being taken over without any of the original religious connotation which they might have had. Of course, the same reasoning could possibly be used in the case of the ball game: that it could have been taken over without any religious features; but the mere fact that it was not diffused may indicate that these features were strong enough to prevent its transmittal or acceptance.

Here are a series of hypotheses erected on none too plentiful empirical evidence, yet if they should lead to more intensive studies or if they should come to be fully accepted, they would have a far-reaching influence on the cultural picture of the ancient Southwest. For one thing, they would greatly broaden and strengthen the criteria upon which the Kayenta and Sinagua Branches are separated. If their religious conservatism was of such a nature as to prevent the interchange of ideas, then it is a justifiable inference that their religions were different. If their religions were different, it is doubtful whether the two branches could rightly be thought to represent an ethnic entity which actually existed in the past. Also assuming the conservatism of motor habits and methods of manufacture as opposed to the changeability of end-results, we again find grounds for segregating the two branches. Or reversing the assumption and admitting their distinctiveness, we have found evidence to substantiate the conservatism of methods of manufacture and the mobility of practical and efficient ideas. As always in any discipline which, like archeology, progresses by the method of "successive approximation," the need is for more data and for more intensive, yet broader, study upon them.[114a]

Four examples have been presented: two demonstrated how non-material traits, even implicit culture, may be derived from archeological data, and two showed how certain concepts as to the workings of culture may be tested and given temporal depth. The examples have further indicated that analysis of archeological data along such lines can be made without having or using a complete cultural context. Immediate context for the cultural segment under investigation is required or at least the material must be handled with regard for its context whether it is explicitly given or not, but within these limits, almost any cultural analysis will offer hints and leads for continued study. However, the method is one of "successive approximations," and the acceptance of the results will depend to a large extent upon the breadth and depth of the context from which the data have been drawn.

Thus, in the above pages, two configurations were shown to lie within the decorating of textile fabrics and the making of cordage as practiced by the ancient people of Coahuila. But the first was modified by the second and both are expectably subject to modification by other configurations yet to be discovered. Eventually it will require an analysis of the whole available culture roster before there will be even a modicum of certainty that further knowledge will not change the picture. The point here is: a start may be made upon data that are incomplete, and a definite effort should be made from the beginning to study the data from a cultural (not merely an empirical) angle, but it is understood that the results will be in the form of tentative hypotheses and guides to other lines of investigation and are expected to undergo progressive correction, although perhaps not radical change, as research proceeds.

E. COMPARATIVE

Under this heading is included the study of the relationships between cultural contexts as wholes. Although it may utilize comparisons of elements or cultural complexes, its major objective is to place a given synthesis in its proper temporal and cultural position with respect to the broad picture of human life in the surrounding territory. At this point in the procedure, interest has gone beyond the mere comparison of individual objects and culture traits and is focused on ascertaining the connections of cultural entities as manifested at sites, cohesive components thereof, and areas.

These relationships are at the same time cultural and chronological, but for the purpose of study and in actual practice they can, and often must, be treated separately. It may be possible in one instance to discover the cultural relations of a site and not be able to define its temporal position with regard to other materials. Similarly it may be possible, through the presence of diagnostic elements, relatively or absolutely to date a site, while at the same time it is impossible to recognize its over-all cultural affiliations. The ideal, of course, is success in both directions, but failure along one line need not make for failure along the other. There are, in practice, two problems, the solutions of which may be separate operations but the results of which are sought for a single purpose, the writing of archeological ethnology.

In regard to such comparisons, the conjunctive approach has two tenets: (1) that they should be based upon cultural rather than empirical categories, and (2) that quantitative analysis is absolutely necessary in order that warpings and errors be eliminated as much as possible. This is to say that trait lists, consisting of descriptive categories and based on mere presence and absence, have only a very limited function in these comparisons.

As an example, the cave material from the Southwest and northern Mexico may again be used. For a long time, the list of similar items to be found in such sites (atlatl, grooved club, coiled basketry, sandals, twined bags, etc.) either confused and troubled the archeologists or led them to believe that all these manifestations belonged to a single culture which could be given the name Basket-Maker.[115] Although the comprehensiveness of this "culture," to my knowledge, was never defined, it is plain from their writings that many archeologists viewed these similarities between the sites, not as the reflection of a basic, broad, and ancient connection, but as indicating relationships much closer in both time and culture. In one of the most recent instances, R. R. Zingg is most certain in his assertion of "Basket-Maker" affiliations for material from Chihuahua, Mexico, on the basis of nine such items (1940).

Although this position is not now held by all Americanists, nevertheless it is revealing that it should ever have been held at all, because it demonstrates very clearly the pitfalls of basing comparative studies on presence-and-absence trait lists and incomplete and unweighted cultural inventories. To quote from my review of another of Zingg's papers:

In fact, it appears possible, and even probable, that Lovelock material is not Basket-maker I or Basketmaker at all, if by Basketmaker we mean Basketmaker II of the San Juan. The former depicts a littoral, hunting, fishing, and gathering culture quite apart in economy, in the weighting of its techniques of manufacture, and in its artifacts from agricultural Basketmaker. To equate these two economies under a single cultural designation would appear to be misleading, and the disharmony is even greater when the desert gathering cultures of southeast New Mexico and Texas are included. If Dr. Zingg had re-analyzed the available cave material, I feel sure that he would have rejected the current belief that the presence of the atlatl, coiled basketry, twining technique, curved club, sandals, etc., indicates a cultural identity with San Juan Basketmaker or any other specific group. These few generic similarities of rather wide distribution have overshadowed for many years the detailed and very real differences in cultural materials from cave sites. There has been little or no consideration of total culture-rosters, and no extensive and determined effort has been made to weigh the predominance of various traits within, and between, sites or groups of sites. (Taylor, 1943, pp. 309-310)

Basic to this viewopint is the axiom stated by Clark Wissler that:

. . . we may take it for granted that wherever there are sharp differences in peoples as to such fundamental necessities as housing, clothing, and feeding, there will like-wise exist differences in beliefs and ideals, so great and having so much originality of form, that the whole life complexes of these people must be taken as distinct cultures. (1923, p. 3)

Therefore what is necessary is that we compare, not individual items either separately or in groups, but rather cultural contexts and/or broad cultural complexes as wholes. These entities can be isolated for study only by using cultural categories as opposed to empirical ones and by employing the rectifying factors of quantification, each to the extent of their availability. Many individual items may be expected to have wide distributions and thus to bring about a leveling of cultural inventories if viewed from a presence-and-absence basis. But when these items are taken in conjunction with, and in relation to, their cultural matrix (and quantitative analysis is one of the best means to show this relationship), they may be expected, and indeed are found (as in the textile industry example given in Chapter 5 of the present study, pp. 134ff), to show differences that are locally and comparatively significant. A determination of the meaning of these differences is not always possible, immediately or ultimately, but this is no reason for their neglect, and offers, in many cases, a further source of archeological problem. The investigation and possible solution of such problems cannot help but enrich the productions of archeological research.

D. SYNTHESIS AND CONTEXT

In order to provide the materials for such comparisons as proposed in the preceding section, it is obvious that the synthesis of data from individual archeological sites will have to be both cultural and quantitative. There is a place in the procedure of archeological research for empirical, descriptive categories, but that place is not here. Headings such as "Artifacts of Wood," "Artifacts of Stone," etc., have no place in a cultural context. Ethnographies and histories are not written by the use of such rubrics, and it is not a quibble to insist that the viewpoint expressed by presenting data under the headings "Artifacts of Stone" and "Artifacts of Wood" is quite different from that indicated by "Exploitation of the Mineral Environment" and "Utilization of Wood."

It may be argued that in a great many cases the cultural use, function, meaning of an archeologically derived artifact is unknown and even unknowable. This is true and will reduce, more or less, the amount and detail of the data from which the archeologist can construct his cultural context. But there are many ways of viewing and categorizing the cultural materials, and it will be a rare find that is not amenable to some analysis, be it from the angle of material of manufacture, technique of manufacture, general use such as transportation or food or art, etc. By analyzing a puzzling form in one or a number of these possible ways, it is very probable that at least some information can be gleaned from it, by which the cultural context can be augmented. Perhaps the information will not be an aid to an interpretation of its actual use or function, but it should be remembered that an artifact is but the end-product of a mental process and that it is made of something and by some means. It is assumed that these contingent factors will have left some mark upon the find, which will be in addition to its use. Even use, of whatever sort, probably has left some signs upon the artifact, e.g., scratches, smoothed areas, beveled edges. For example, in the Coahuila cave CM 68 (Frightful Cave), evidence on the cutting methods, and thus to some extent on motor habits also, was obtained from an analysis of a multitude of cut twigs and agave stalks whose use, if they were not merely blanks or rejects, has not been ascertained. And the implications of the method of twisting fiber cordage, the specific use of which was not indicated, have already been discussed (pp. 162f above). It is hardly coincidental that a most pertinent statement has come from one of the few archeologists who has presented his material under broad cultural categories and written what, in effect, is an archeological ethnography (Clark, 1940). Grahame Clark says:

Archaeology is often defined as the study of antiquities. A better definition would be that it is the study of how men lived in the past . . . . [the archaeologist] has to rely upon circumstantial evidence and much of his time is taken up with details which may appear to be trivial, although as clues to human action they can be of absorbing interest. (1939, p. 1)

A suggestion may be put forward with a view to aiding the archeologist construct a cultural context or at least broaden the base of his thinking and research along cultural lines. This is that before, during, and especially after his field work he go carefully, heading by heading, through the *Outline of Cultural Materials* (Murdock *et al.*, 1945) or some other compendium of cultural items, e.g., *Notes and Queries on Anthropology* (Royal Anthropological Institute, ed. 1929).

The purpose of such a procedure would be to refresh the archeologist's memory on cultural topics and to awaken him anew to the implications of his data. In the field this should result in a sharpened sense of problem and a broader envisioning of profitable leads for investigation. But the greatest potential advantage would accrue to the laboratory analysis and to the construction and writing of a cultural context. With his data at hand, the *Outline* beside him, and starting with heading No. 1, the archeologist asks himself: "Are there any of my empirical data which could serve as the basis for an inference on this subject? Can I orient my way of viewing the material so that I can see light on this topic? With respect to the empirical data and general cultural hypotheses, is it likely or unlikely that this element was present among the people I am investigating?" In addition to helping the archeologist to establish a cultural outlook, such compendia will aid him in the construction and actual writing of his context by offering him ready-made outlines that are based on cultural categories. It devolves upon him to fill in these outlines as best he can, using his empirical data and explicit inference.

Finally, brief mention may be made of another source of inspiration for the archeologist who would attempt to write ethnography-of-the-more-distant-past: the "universal culture pattern." Murdock has given a considerable list of items "which occur, so far as [the author's] knowledge goes, in every culture known to history or ethnography" (1945, p. 124). If, therefore, we may take it as probable that these items occurred in archeological cultures as well, the archeologist has been provided with not a few basic assumptions, and it remains for him to examine his material to see if he can discover the particular form which these generalized "universals" took in his particular culture. About many of them he will be unable even to make acceptable inferences, but if his viewpoint is thus broadened and the scope of his analyses enlarged, it is to be expected that more will be forthcoming than if he should continue to treat his finds as *Objects of Stone* and *Objects of Bone* and leave it at that. If he accepts Murdock's hypothesis, he knows that these items existed in some form or other, and that is half the battle!

It is possibly gratuitous to remark that the ethnographies of local peoples will also serve as guides for the investigation, construction, and presentation of an archeological cultural context. Although they are rarely so used, these ethnographies have more value to the archeologist than merely to provide support for interpretations of the use and function of artifacts or to supply leads as to cross-cultural relationships.

But the utilization of cultural categories of itself is not enough. The information within them must be evaluated, weighed, and given balance by the use of quantitative and qualitative data and by taking into account the natural and cultural matrix within which the culture operated. It is of little help to a cultural context to state, as so often is done, that "among the rubbish in the cave there occurred many pieces of worn-out and discarded mats" (Kidder and Guernsey, 1922, p. 98), or that "there are several forms of ax heads" (Roberts, 1940, p. 119) and then fail to give any figures on the number of forms recognized or the quantities of specimens in each category. What it is vital to know is how many pieces of matting there were and of what weaves, the relative frequency of each ax type and how the category of ax heads (with its quantified subdivisions) compares with, say, mauls or hoes or cutting tools in general. For example, it would be important for a cultural interpretation to know whether a site contained a great number of pottery bowls while at the same time it was deficient in jar forms. In such circumstances, the archeologist might be expected to look for storage facilities in other directions, to explain why storage was not needed, to discover a nearby and constant water supply, etc. Many problems and interpretations can be derived from equalities or inequalities in the numbers of such things as basketry trays and bowls, the amount of netting that could have been used for carrying compared to the number of carrying baskets, the relative number of ulna and metapodial awls. Bennett has noted the apparent withdrawal and fortification in Late Middle Mississippi times in the Mississippi Valley and suggests the possibility of warfare (1943a, pp. 37-38). Yet to my knowledge there has been no study of the sizes and numbers of projectile points in order either (a) to help identify the type most prevalent, assuming a war condition to have existed, or (b) to check on the hypothesis of warfare, assuming that a small point or some other specific type was used primarily for fighting. The mere listing of types and their descriptions does not provide all possible data, or even enough. What is needed is a weighted and balanced picture (as far as the empirical data will permit), and one method of obtaining this is by thorough quantitative analysis.

During the excavation of the Coahuila cave site CM 68, it was decided to make a count of the fiber quids or "chews" which occur so numerously in the deposits of most caves but which, to my knowledge, had never been subjected to analysis.[116] After the count had proceeded for a short time, it became evident that there were two types of quid present. One seemed to have been chewed around-and-around in the mouth, giving it the appearance of a wad of chewing gum. The other had been merely gnawed as one would bite the leaf of an artichoke, i.e., by squeezing, sucking, and chewing one end while retaining the other end in the hand. It was then decided to continue the count, using these two types as a basis of distinction. In all, somewhat over 20,600 quids were typed, counted, and their frequencies plotted according to horizontal and vertical strat-blocks within the cave. The graph resulting from this manipulation showed a startling and definite modality. Although the gum-chewed quids exhibited a considerable numerical superiority in the total count and in the great majority of blocks, there were blocks in which the artichoke-chewed quids approached parity with the round type and even surpassed it in some cases. By plotting the percentage of round to long quids for each block, a definite bimodal curve appeared: there were two distinct peaks showing the greater frequency of the long artichoke-chewed type. This was an empirical fact, and possible correlations were sought for it.

It was found that the peak frequencies of the long type were spatially correlated with the two major fire-rock areas within the cave, or rather that they were just to the inward side of the cave from these cooking areas. Here again was an empirical fact; it remained to be explained by inference. The most satisfactory interpretation which has been projected to date suggests that the former inhabitants, when their feast of agave or sotol was baked and ready for eating, clustered around the opened rock oven-pit and grabbed leaf after leaf to extract just the "cream" from each, tossing them quickly away to grab another. When, however, they went away from the source of supply or when the urgency of a community and somewhat competitive repast was not upon them, they chewed their quids around-and-around to extract every bit of sweet nourishment contained therein, spitting out the spent quids generally over the whole length and breadth of the cave.

The analysis might end here, or it might go on. There are implications of hunger in the picture thus drawn. Are there other signs in the culture of a marginal subsistence? The fecal specimens found throughout the site, although they have not yet been reported upon by competent authority, seem to contain a superabundance of woody and coarse fibrous materials, possibly indicating a starvation diet mainly dependent upon vegetal foods. On the other hand, for people willing to subsist on agave, sotol, lechuguilla, and other such plants, there would seem to have been no lack of food. But the availability of nourishment from these plants seems to be seasonal (at least in the present day and with modern tastes), and this fact might give a clue to the problem. In any event, the leads given by this one quantitative study and the cultural and geographical researches thus called forth are ample evidence that presence-and-absence lists do not exhaust the potentialities of even the simplest archeological data. The cultural conjunctives *within* a site are a vast source of problem as yet hardly tapped by those whose concern is with relationships *outside* the site.

Another analytical attack is from the standpoint of quality. This is not an empirical criterion like quantity, but so long as the archeologist is explicit as to the standards he sets up, there is nothing to prevent its use. To take an example from ethnography and one which could receive investigations and testing in the archeological field, the question may be asked whether it is a function of the group's interest or some configuration of their culture that the Navaho have assimilated and improved upon Pueblo weaving, while they have made a very poor showing indeed at the art of pottery decoration. If Reichard's suggestions are correct, the Navaho entered the Southwest with a knowledge of both weaving and ceramics (1936, pp. 162-177), but Navaho weaving in its recorded form is undoubtedly of Pueblo inspiration in the great majority of its features, as Reichard very clearly shows, and the painted decoration of Navaho pottery seems also to be due to Pueblo influence. In these circumstances, then, the differential emphasis, integration, and excellence of the two techniques among the Navaho are all the more significant.

Likewise, if from an archeological site (in Coahuila this is somewhat the case) the artifacts of wood and fiber show a considerable degree of craftsmanship while stone work is unelaborated, even crude, does not this fact have a bearing on the cultural picture to be derived and also, indeed, upon the comparisons to be made between sites and areas?

And what about conjunctives between the people and their environment? To what extent do artifacts and other cultural items represent the full range of possibilities offered by the natural surroundings? Are there plant and animal forms identifiable as having lived at the time of occupation but which are not found to have been culturally utilized at the sites? How much of the empirical data along these lines appears attributable to the vagaries of preservation and excavation and how much to actual bygone conditions? (This is a problem to face, not one to dodge by bemoaning the inadequacy of the archeological record.) How do the potential and actual utilizations of the mineral resources compare? Did the people go distances for a substance, a like or substitute form of which existed in the neighborhood? Along the latter lines, the results and implications of Anna Shepard's work on Rio Grande and La Plata pottery shows what can be done (1936, 1939, 1942).

An example may be cited from Coahuila. Plate 3 gives the vertical and horizontal distributions of a land snail and of piñon nuts in Frightful Cave.[117] *Humboldtiana* is a rare form and has been found in the higher, more moist regions of the Sierra Madre of Mexico under conditions quite different from those prevailing in the Coahuila desert today (Pilsbry, 1939, pp. 397-398).[118] The evidence from snails, then, indicates the presence of a form which was disappearing because of increasing aridity in the region. The presence of piñon, on the other hand, seems to require another interpretation. These trees are found today only on the tops of the higher, and therefore more moist, mountains.[119] Here is a case of a life form, which requires more moist and cooler conditions than exist today in the vicinity of the cave but which increases, rather than decreases, its representation in the deposits from bottom to top.

Taking these data and having other evidence for a growing aridity in the Coahuila desert, it seems that the upward decrease of *Humboldtiana* is a function of this climatic shift. But the increase of piñon cannot be accounted for on this basis, since it directly contradicts the assumption of increasing dryness. If not controlled by the environmental factor, it seems that the utilization of piñon in the upper levels of Frightful Cave is a cultural phenomenon. Surely if it were present and used for food in the drier and later stages, it must have been present in the earlier and more moist stages *but was not used for food by the people.* Here, then, is an instance of failure to make full use of the environment.

In addition to the study of objects and their relationships, the investigation and interpretation of what may be called the "cultural matrix" is also an integral part of constructing a cultural context. Under this heading would come the sequential development of a pueblo structure, a mound, a village site, or the deposits within a cave. The fact that a people were accustomed to strew fiber rubbish around their cave dwelling or to make definite occupation levels in an open village by the importation of clay for flooring is as much the result of cultural behavior as is the shape of a stone ax. While such factors may be of little importance for direct comparison with other sites, they nevertheless constitute basic and important information on the life at the particular site in question. The growth of a pueblo structure is as much a part of the cultural picture as the forms of metate or the number of pottery bowls—in fact it would appear to be more basic and not the secondary, by-the-way evidence which it seems to be in most reports of Americanist archeology.

An example of what may be done along these lines will be offered here. Indulgence must be asked for it, however, because of several factors which contribute to make it far from an ideal one: both excavation and analysis were made before the ideas comprising the conjunctive approach had taken definite form; the excavation was not completed; the work was done by students under supervision which was not as close as it might have been, due to other duties having call upon my attention. Nevertheless it does indicate the potentialities, if not the utmost success, to be expected. It consists of the interpretation of the growth of two pueblo rooms in site Bc 51 in Chaco Canyon, New Mexico.[120] Plate 4 will illustrate the text.

The construction of Room 26 began by the excavation of its floor space some 2 feet 3 inches below the then surface. Evidence from Rooms 28 and 24b indicate that there was an extensive excavation providing space for several rooms (the implications of this fact for group or family activity would possibly be clarified by examination of other data such as artifact styles, fragments of single vessels found in several rooms, etc.). This excavation cut at an angle through a top, culturally sterile, wind- and/or water-laid sandy stratum and into a cultural fill lying in what appears to have been an old pit structure. Floor excavation went to, or a little into, the blue-yellow clay of the native earth.

The construction of the east wall was begun with only one course of masonry as a facing against the excavation but was increased outward to two courses some 16 inches above floor level. This was probably controlled by the angle of the original foundation excavation which, in turn, was a function of the use of digging sticks. With the use of such instruments, the sides of a pit are more apt to be sloping than straight. The east and south walls were built as one job, the former abutting the south wall of Room 24b and the latter the west wall which serves both Room 24b and Room 26. Thus Room 26 was built after the former.

With the exception of the north, the walls were built very high, yet there are no indications of vigas or other roof construction in them. From this it might be inferred that, after abandonment and some filling, the walls had been re-worked and extended upward, covering beam-holes and other evidence. But despite evidence for the reuse of the area (see below), there is no definite sign that the walls were ever re-worked. Perhaps the ceiling was actually over 9 feet high. The walls were plastered to a thickness of about one-half an inch, but no layer count was made.

The floor showed no trace of a fire-pit, nor was there any burned area to indicate that fires might have been made in the room. Pit A was apparently lined with thin plaster, and 3 inches from its bottom it contained a turquoise inlay pendant. Pits B, C, D, and E were well plastered and well executed as to shape. Pit E served as a pot-rest and contained a large corrugated jar fitted with a stone pot-lid. The locations of a Gallup Black-on-white bowl and another corrugated jar correspond to the location of Pits B and C respectively, which were probably pot-rests also.

The abandonment of Room 26 seems to have been caused directly, or was at least hurried, by the buckling of the north and west walls. The final northward collapse of the former was probably the final consideration. This wall not only collapsed and split in the center but also pulled away from its junction with the east wall as much as 10 inches at the top. That this happened before abandonment, or at least before any appreciable fill had accumulated, is suggested by the absence of local down-dropping in the fill of Room 26.

With abandonment, Room 26 began to fill with debris. At first, culturally sterile sand blew in or was washed in and covered the floor. Then cultural material began to be deposited over a considerable area of the room. The amount of adobe clods and rock, which might indicate roofing materials, was very small and confined almost entirely to the north end. No evidence of any roof supports

PLATE 3

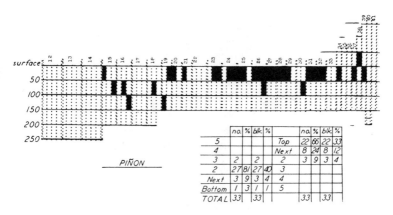

PIÑON

	no.	%	blk	%			no.	%	blk	%
5					Top		22	66	22	33
4					Next		8	24	8	12
3	2		2		3		3	9	3	4
2	27	81	27	40	4					
Next	3	9	3	4	5					
Bottom	1	3	1	1						
TOTAL	33		33				33		33	

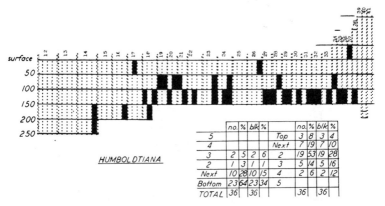

HUMBOLDTIANA

	no.	%	blk	%			no.	%	blk	%
5					Top		3	8	3	4
4					Next		7	19	7	10
3	2	5	2	6	3		19	53	19	28
2	1	3	1	1	4		5	14	5	16
Next	10	28	10	15	5		2	6	2	12
Bottom	23	64	23	34						
TOTAL	36		36				36		36	

Distribution of *Humboldtiana* and piñon shells in Frightful Cave, CM 68, Coahuila, Mexico

This chart depicts three-dimensional distribution. The vertical depths are indicated vertically in centimeters. The horizontal meter-blocks from front to back of the cave are represented from left to right by the numbered sections between double-dotted lines. The horizontal meter-blocks from the center of the deposits to the west wall of the cave are represented from left to right by the single-dotted subdivisions within each numbered section.

In the summary tables, the numbers of specimens and blocks are identical because the data were gathered only on a presence-and-absence basis according to stratigraphic blocks. On the other hand, specimen percentages are figured according to total presences listed, while block percentages are figured according to the maximum possible blocks within the respective stratigraphic levels.

The lack of specimens from the front of the cave is only apparent. This is due to the fact that tabulation of these types was not begun before Line 14.

PLATE 4

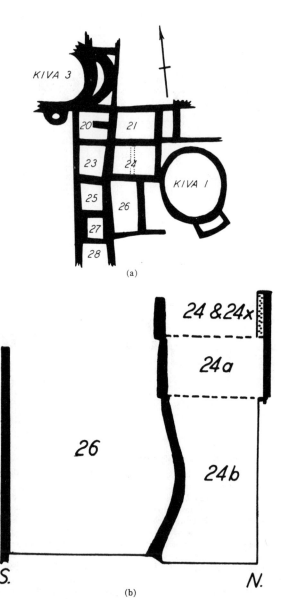

a) Plan of the south-central portion of Bc 51, Chaco Canyon, New Mexico (schematic)
b) Section through Rooms 24 and 26, Bc 51, Chaco Canyon, New Mexico
(vertical exaggeration is three times)

larger than finger-sized impressions in clods was found. The cultural fill, composed of ash, sand, sherds, artifacts, as a loose and unconsolidated mass, banked up against the south wall to a height of 5 feet. It appears that the angle of repose controlled the amount of deposition and, when the angle became too steep, increments slid downward and northward. The result has been that the fill of the north end was found to be either horizontal or dipping slightly back toward the south. These facts indicate that the deposition was cumulative and not the result of short-term, purposeful action. But before the north end filled to more than 2 feet above the floor, a dump of almost pure sand, containing relatively little cultural material, was thrown in, obviously for the purpose of leveling off the partially filled room.

At the top of this dump were found several features which further substantiate the hypothesis of intentional fill by giving a reason for its deposition. A stone-sided fireplace and a corrugated jar set in stone slabs and covered with a pot-lid were found at what had evidently been two separate levels of occupation upon the room-fill. The top of the fire-pit was on a level with the floors of Rooms 24 and 24x, and the pot-lid was even with the floor of Room 24a. Roofing material on the upper portions of the fill of Room 26 and below the south wall of Rooms 24 and 24x indicates that the destruction of the roof of Room 24a was effected after the use of the slabbed jar and before the construction of both the fill fire-pit and the south wall of Rooms 24 and 24x. These correlations lead to the conclusion that the area of Room 26 (abandoned and filled) served as an open-air adjunct first of Room 24a (slabbed jar) and then to either or both Rooms 24 and 24x (fire-pit). The south wall of Rooms 24 and 24x was built out over the fill of Room 26.

Above the level of the fill fire-pit, the deposits at the time of excavation showed much re-working and disturbance. Aside from the obvious slope wash of later years, there is nothing that could be determined concerning them. There is no evidence of any superstructure on this room.

Turning to Room 24, it is found that within the horizontal area designated by this number on the original survey of the site, there were actually four rooms on three levels. The lowest of these, Room 24b, had not been completely excavated when this analysis was undertaken, and the information from it is less complete than from Room 26 and the other Rooms 24. Nevertheless, its career can be outlined with a reasonable enough fullness to permit its inclusion to round out the picture.

The floor of Room 24b was laid in the same excavation as that of Room 26. The floors of the two were made as one continuous piece of construction separated only by a low, rounded clay sill which also served as the foundation for the party wall between the rooms. The floor of Room 24b was slightly lower than that of Room 26 due to the dip of the native earth which acted as the base of room excavation; the same control influenced the floor level of Rooms 28 and 29.

Three walls of Room 24b were constructed clockwise from the northwest corner, while the west wall was carried directly south from that point. The south wall was finished off by an abutment against the west. This latter was not ended here but was continued southward without a break for two more rooms. Rooms 24b, 26, and the unnumbered one immediately south of the latter were, thus, all part of a single sequential construction, starting at the north end.

Both the west and north walls of Room 24b were found to be in poor condition, bulging inward at precarious angles. The west one was plastered and then chinked with stone spalls through the plaster. Sherds were set vertically as chinking in the angle of the northwest corner. Due to incomplete excavation, the floor features are not sufficiently known to be discussed. The abandonment of Room 24b was caused, or hurried, by the imminent collapse of the south, west, and north walls. Possibly the south one actually sagged before the room was entirely deserted. But the increased dip in the fill near the wall indicates that the party wall did not completely give way until some time after abandonment. The first deposits in the deserted room were laminated sands. Upon these were found several metates surrounded and covered by adobe clods and other evidence of roof material. It seems, therefore, that the roof held for some time and that it eventually fell or was torn down, causing the metates to fall together with the roof debris. The impressions of wood found in the clods are not large, and once more there is no evidence of beams having been set in the walls. In view of the obvious re-workings and superposition of the rooms, such beam holes might have been obliterated, but the similar conditions of Room 26 throw doubt upon this interpretation. As the fill was building up, many manos became incorporated in it, suggesting that it might have served as a depository for the refuse from some nearby working area. The horizontal bedding of most of the fill may indicate purposeful action of relatively short duration, but at least two layers were definitely deposited as a single action: shale and yellow sand were brought in and dumped for the purpose of leveling the room area preparatory to laying the floor of Room 24a.

Over the fill of Room 24b and on top of the prepared layers, a clay floor was laid within the limits of the still-standing walls of the old room area. A stone-sided fire-pit was constructed in the center of this Room 24a merely by digging a pit through the finished floor and into the soft fill beneath. The floor was also plastered—at least six times during the occupancy of the room. In order to complete the rectangle of the new room, a piece of wall had to be built to replace the badly bulged and collapsed segment of the old south, party wall. The new piece was dove-tailed into the eastern portion which was still standing, and in order to make a straight line and a rectangular room it was built out over the fill of

Room 26, which deposits had bulged into the area of Room 24b with the sagging of the party wall. There was evidence of a door at the west end of this new segment of wall, and, if this fact could have been more firmly established by excavation, it would have lent a good deal of support to the hypothesis of an outdoor occupation level containing a slabbed jar, lying on the fill of Room 26, and connected with the occupation of Room 24a. The height of the walls of this room is unknown since their upper parts were destroyed with succeeding renovations.

At some time after the floor was laid and after one or more plasterings, the threatened collapse of the west wall prompted the occupants of Room 24a to erect a support. Two buttresses 18 inches high were built against it. The south one was made of adobe with an occasional sherd, pebble, or twig; it blocked what may have been the door to the fill occupation-level over Room 26; this opening, door or otherwise, was closed by a thin stone facing on the indoor side. The north buttress was of similar composition but was faced with one whole and one fragmentary metate. The buttresses were not tied into the wall and are now found to be separated from it by distances up to two inches at all points. After these features were in place, occupation continued for a time, and the occupants kept on plastering their floor—but not beneath the buttresses.

Eventually, however, Room 24a was deserted. This may have been due to an increase in the danger from the west wall, although it seems rather unlikely in view of the buttresses. It was more probably due to some trouble with the north wall, which was ultimately torn down to the floor, while the three others were demolished only to the height of the buttresses. The room was filled to the latter level with the resulting debris. The floor of the next room, Room 24x, was laid directly upon this fill.

The demolition and filling of Room 24a and the construction of Rooms 21 and 24x were connected operations. The south wall of Room 21, which was to be the party wall between it and Room 24x, was built before the filling of the old Room 24a and served to hold back the fill and permit the lenses of debris to lie horizontally. But the construction of this and the east and west walls of Room 24x was a single piece of work without breaks or abutments. On the other hand, the east and west walls were built after the party wall since they were placed over the fill which the party wall retained in horizontal position and over the buttresses and wall-stubs forming the western limits of Room 24a. The walls of Room 24x, the south wall of Room 21 (but not its other walls, a fact which throws light on the contemporaneity of various masonry types in Chaco Canyon), and the bracing wall built inside the neighboring Room 23 are all of the same excellent workmanship and stand in contrast to the poor, weak walls of Rooms 26, 24b, and 24a. Probably all of them were laid up at the same time and to remedy the same condition: the buckling of the walls inherited from

Room 24b. On the west side of the party wall between Rooms 24x and 21, a window with a sill joined the two apartments.

The destruction and abandonment of Room 24x was caused by the building of Kiva 1. This operation disrupted part of the east wall and part of the floor. The occupants were forced to move their east wall farther westward and thus reduce the size of their room. In making this new and smaller Room 24, they not only changed the east wall but also erected a facing against the party wall shared with Room 21. This facing consisted of a wall in the better-style masonry about 4 inches south of the old wall, and the intervening space was filled with rock and adobe rubble. At this time or possibly earlier, the connecting window was blocked with masonry. The space between the new east wall and Kiva 1 was filled with debris from the old east wall. After the final abandonment, Room 24 filled with its own detritus.

The above example has been an interpretation (not the raw data) of building operations only. It has made no attempt, except for two parenthetical remarks, to go into the broader implications or to bring to bear the weight of other finds associated with and within the rooms. Nevertheless, I believe that the potentialities should be perfectly obvious. Combine such studies with the other cultural and natural data, with similar analyses of other rooms, with interpretations of the relationships and affinities of all these factors, and there will result a picture of the site and the life of its people that is historiography every bit as much as a report on a living group or a documented society. It may not be as complete or as sure in certain aspects, but these differences are of degree and not of kind. Archeology can "do" historiography, can construct cultural contexts, but not when it is concerned only with data that are of *immediate* comparative significance *outside* the site.

It is also true that, should the archeologist come to view his sites as units which contained people with a past and a cultural context to be investigated, then extra-local comparison itself will be better grounded, and a wealth of problems, interpretive and descriptive, will develop to inspire new research. According to the conjunctive approach, the first and most important task is the construction of this context. As has been very clear from the above examples, extra-local comparisons are vital means to this end, but until the cultural picture has been developed from the latent image in the ground by the use of interpretation and all the data, they will remain just that: means, not ends. If the conjunctive approach is to come up for trial, it must rest its case on the primacy of the cultural context, first of components and sites and then of areas, "culture areas," temporal groupings, or whatever. What does it gain us to know that one culture came after another and was in some way related, if we know little or nothing of either culture as it existed in the past among the people to whom it belonged?

C. LOCAL CHRONOLOGY

Since the chronological relations of one cultural context to another have already been taken up under the heading *E. Comparative,* the purpose of the present section is to provide for the analysis of chronological relationships within a single site. This step is important whether the site prove to contain one or several cultural entities. In the first instance, the development and change through time exhibited by a single component will be one of its most important aspects, culturally speaking. In the second, a time differential may be one of the important diagnostic features belonging to different components and, once established, will aid in the interpretation of the separate contexts themselves and their interrelationships, if any.

The analysis of room sequence in the Chaco Canyon site Bc 51 given above will serve as an example of what information is sought under this heading. The various building periods of a pueblo are crucial to an understanding of the structure as a whole and of the life that was led in it. The temporal relationships of varying pottery styles, of a mound to a nearby village, of obviously distinct complexes within a midden or shellheap are complicated problems in themselves, and their solutions, although they may be aided by comparative material from outside, are primarily to be attacked from within, from data found at the site itself. For this reason, local chronology has been given a separate heading in this outline of the conjunctive approach.

B. DATA

What is asked by the conjunctive approach with regard to the collection and study of the data should be apparent from the foregoing summaries of chronology, synthesis, and comparison. Therefore the contents of the following pages are to be construed as leads and suggestions. They are intended to give an idea of the sort of information sought, not to outline or define the range of desirable data.

1. COLLECTION

a. Local cultural

The cultural material of a site, all of it, is included under this heading. In many cases, the artifacts, the cultural refuse, and the deposits will be difficult, if not impossible, to distinguish as separate categories. This is to be expected and in no way affects the break-down, which has been made for the sake of clarity and description and with a view to aiding the visualization of what kinds of data may be collected.

Two generalized ideals may be stated with reference to the collection of cultural data. The first is that excavation and recording produce more satisfactory results when executed according to the units by which the deposits were formed, i.e., by occupation levels, by refuse layers, by periods of construction, by periods of natural deposition, etc. The placing of finds in relation to some arbitrary, stratigraphic system causes the loss of much important, even vital, information. Many of the more significant associations of the material will be lost or badly obscured if left to be extracted from the assemblages of gross and often culturally unrelated blocks in a stratigraphic grid. In other words, that *deus ex machina,* the stratigraphic method, if used mechanically and alone, will fail to provide the detail necessary to construct the fullest possible cultural context. It is realized, of course, that this ideal will meet with many practical obstacles. But as a mark to be aimed and shot at, it constitutes one of the tenets of the conjunctive approach.

The second is that all cultural materials, i.e., all phenomena that were used, made, modified, or possessed by the human beings under investigation, directly or indirectly, consciously or unconsciously, should be preserved for study or fully recorded in the field when preservation is unwarranted or impossible. By this procedure alone can there be achieved acceptable distribution studies, quantitative analysis, and weighting of segments within the cultural whole represented by the site or component. Here again, practicality will often and drastically alter the ideal which, nevertheless, has its important function and deserves to be kept well in mind, to be adhered to as closely as practically possible.

1. *Artifacts:* An artifact may be defined as any material construct made or modified by the conscious agency of man. Dwellings as well as ax blades, pictographs and temple mounds, bedrock mortars and furrowed fields are artifacts. The relation of an artifact to a culture trait is that of the material objectification of a mental concept. It follows, therefore, that a fragmentary artifact represents a trait as much as does a whole specimen and should receive similar treatment and weighting. In other words, matting fragments represent the same culture trait as complete mats and should be preserved or recorded equally. This does not mean, of course, that fragments are to be counted as wholes. The significance of fragments for the context is a problem to be solved in terms of the actual conditions at the site, not hypothetical or generalized ones. But the fact that detailed and complete information often may not be forthcoming from a fragmentary artifact does not alter the cultural factor. In fact, its very fragmentary nature may be indicative of a culture trait not present in the complete object. The cultural interpretation of whole and partial specimens may be different, complementary, or overlapping, but nonetheless both represent culture traits and are grist to the archeologist's mill.

2. *Cultural Refuse:* Cultural refuse may be defined as the debris or residuum from the cultural activities of man. Included in this category would be such things as food refuse, the detritus from the manufacture of artifacts, the fire-fractured rocks from a pit-oven, etc. Even the fecal specimens that are often found in sheltered sites may be considered here, representing as they do the dietary residue. Once more, complete recovery and recording is the ideal, but

here there is even less chance of attainment than with respect to artifacts. In certain midden and cave sites, the very mass of refuse is so tremendous that full recovery is entirely out of the question. As a bow to expediency in such cases, it is suggested that if presence or absence is noted for the whole site or an acceptably large portion and according to reasonably small units of deposit, a satisfactory and representative sample will be obtained. This system is based on the assumption that the relative proportions of the forms in question will be reflected areally as well as quantitatively, but an analysis will have to be made for individual sites to ascertain the validity of this generalization in each case. Such analysis is one of the tasks to be handled under the sub-heading *Criticism* in the section on *Study* (see p. 193).

But this concession to practicality may be overworked to the detriment of the context. Much information that is often discarded may be saved for study if its value is recognized and an effort made to lighten the burden of preserving it. Specimens that can be identified may be tabulated in the field for each unit of excavation, either on a presence-and-absence basis or by some relative designation such as "abundant" or "scarce." Unidentified specimens which, however, can be typed, may be similarly treated and several examples saved for future identification. All untyped and unidentified specimens should be retained, and they will probably not amount to a number too great to handle. In the excavation of Frightful Cave, for instance, although working with the bare minimum of a crew, it was possible to make presence-and-absence charts throughout the site for the more common vegetal forms and to save the less common and untypable ones, while at the same time every identifiable animal bone was saved and the unidentifiable ones recorded as "small, medium, or large." The value of these records is demonstrated, among others, by the examples of snails, piñons, and fiber quids given above.

3. *Deposits:* Here may be included such information as the details of mound structure, the manner in which cave deposits were built, the nature of fill in a pueblo room, etc.—in other words, the character of what above was called the "cultural matrix." The formation of deposits within an abandoned room in a pueblo carries cultural implications over and beyond the fact that the deposits are the resting place for a certain number of artifacts. The cited example of site Bc 51, Chaco Canyon, should be ample argument, e.g., the nature of the fill indicated intentional leveling for an outdoor occupation area and also suggested the relative time of abandonment of certain rooms, thus helping to round out the cultural picture by the addition of temporal factors.

b. Local Human Biological

Three sets of data may be included under this heading: the physical attributes of the people under investigation, their mortuary customs, and the cultural implications of these characteristics for other categories of the cultural whole.

The first requires either competency on the part of the archeologist or the services of a physical anthropologist. The second would seem to be obvious, yet it is often a much neglected topic. For example, in three of the most recent and compendious of publications on Mississippi Valley archeology (Griffin, 1943; Ritchie, 1944; Webb and Snow, 1945), there is almost no information to be gained as to what cultural objects were found with what burials. Usually the orientation, the body posture, the sex or age (if identifiable), and the presence or absence of "grave goods" are noted. These aspects seem to have comparative significance as criteria of units in the McKern classification and are therefore given. But one looks in vain in the vast majority of cases for descriptions of the actual artifacts found in the graves. In the Ritchie citation, for instance, grave goods are listed by type in the photographs of certain burials, but in the text the contents of specific graves are not given except incidentally. In other words, the attempt has not been consistently made to associate the sex, age, physical attributes and pathology, posture, orientation, location, and associated cultural material in all possible examples.

With regard to the cultural implications of such data, even less is usually given. For example, Webb says:

Burial practices and the resultant traits which point to them may thus be conceived as the social act of the body politic, in contrast to, for example, the manufacture of a particular type of artifact. . . . (Webb and Snow, 1945, p. 167)

If this is true, and if Webb and his colleagues were actually interested in depicting the life of the social entities that lived in their areas in the past, it seems impossible that they would not have made a more concious effort to give the complete picture of burials as found. The cat is let out of the bag, however, when on the next page Webb says:

If this be true [that burial customs change more slowly than the material aspects of culture], similar burial traits should be of prime importance in establishing close connections between peoples. . . . (p. 168)

Obviously, his interest in the "social act of the body politic" was not for the purpose of understanding the culture of that body, but for comparative purposes *outside* the site.

But there are other ways of looking at the data. Why have there not been studies of the burial offerings associated with individuals of a given age or sex? Is it not worthy of further thought that a seventeen-year-old girl was buried with a large celt in addition to some six other artifacts (Lewis, 1943, p. 310)? Likewise, Ritchie finds a female buried with a harpoon (1944, p. 282). These facts lead the inquiring archeologist to ask: If the grave goods belonged to the deceased, what do they imply; if they did not belong to the deceased but were donated by others, what are the implications? The need is obviously for more information in order to tell whether these instances are atypical or of common occurrence. Comparative data are called for, not for classificatory purposes alone, but also so that the cultural significance of such finds may be clarified by evidence from several sources. In another place, Ritchie makes the observation that, although previously they had been rare, "beginning with the earliest [European] contact, grave goods were lavished upon the dead" in Iroquois sites (1944, p. 26 fn. 1). Proceeding from the knowledge of the importance of women among the Iroquois at least in post-contact times, it would be interesting to know whether the abundance of grave goods had any correlation with the sex of the person interred. Furthermore, many physical characteristics have cultural factors and connotations as well, e.g., knife marks on skulls indicating scalping, death rates and pathology indicating war and dietary deficiencies, the possibility that an analysis of fecal specimens may shed light upon diet, season of occupation, as well as the biological attributes of metabolism and endo-parasites.

In short, if the physical remains are looked upon as bearing in themselves and their associations the evidences of cultural activities, capable of variation and indicative of other cultural features, they can be studied with profit to one interested in the cultural context. It is assumed, as in other phases, that the burial complex was more or less integrated within the general culture and will therefore not be an isolated phenomenon divorced from other cultural complexes. If this assumption is conceded, then it follows that the burial complex will have implications for those other aspects with which it was integrated. Similarly, granting that culture has an effect upon physical constitution and biological functioning, it follows that, whether they can be recognized or not, there must be reflections of cultural life in the physical characteristics of a people. It remains to see whether or not they can be acceptably demonstrated from archeological data. The challenge is there to be met.

c. Contemporaneous Geographical

In order properly to evaluate a given culture, it is necessary to know what possibilities were offered it by the geographic as well as by the cultural environment. Until there is some idea as to the potentialities of the natural surroundings, it is very difficult to understand just how culturally significant a certain trait really is. For example, it will make considerable difference in the analysis of a culture if it is found that clay was present and not used for pottery, that clay was not available, or that clay was not available in the vicinity but was brought from a distance for use. Shepard's work on the pottery of Pecos (Shepard, 1936) is an outstanding instance. Before she demonstrated that certain pottery types had been constructed of clay not native to the Pecos valley, it had been assumed that these vessels were the products of local potters. When it became apparent that they must have been made in another area or that their ingredients must have come from a distance, the cultural meaning of the vessels changed. The implications for inter-pueblo relations, for industry, for culture conservatism, and many other facets had gone unrecognized because of a lack of information on the potentialities of the geographic region.

Similarly, before it was established that edible fish were native to the salines and marshes of the Cuatro Cienegas region of Coahuila, the absence of fish bones (with the exception of one artifact) from the deposits of nearby caves was regarded as an environmental deficiency. But when fish were found to have existed in those waters at the time of the first Spanish *entrada,* and when cultural comparison showed that the Coahuila culture without fish remains is comparable to the Pecos River cave-dweller material which includes fish remains, the meaning of the data changed. It can no longer be assumed that the lack of fish bones is due to environmental causes. In fact, it becomes highly probable that this condition is attributable to cultural factors.

The extent to which a society utilizes its natural surroundings is one of its most particular and significant aspects. But utilization means more than merely that which concerns the subsistence economy or material items. It also means the degree to which the environment enters into the ideas and other non-material aspects of the cultural picture. A quotation from A. I. Hallowell may be given at some length because it so well expresses this point:

Man's psychological responses to the physical objects of his external environment can only be understood . . . in terms of the traditional meanings which these latter have for him. He never views the outer world freshly or responds to his fellows entirely free from the influences which these meanings exert upon his thought and conduct. Celestial and meteorological phenomena, for example, or the plants and animals of man's habitat, even its inanimate forms, are never separated as such from the concepts of their essential nature and the beliefs about them that appear in the ideological tradition of a particular cultural heritage. Man's attitude toward them is a function of reality as culturally defined, not in terms of their mere physical existence. Thus, to treat the physical environment in which a people lives independently of the meaning that its multiform objects have for the people involves a fundamental psychological distortion if we aim to comprehend the universe which is actually theirs. While useful in certain kinds of analysis, even the assertion that two peoples occupy the same natural environment because the regions inhabited by them exhibit the same climatic type, the same topography and biota can only have significance in the grossest physical sense. It is tantamount to ignoring the very data which have the most important psychological significance, namely the differences in meaning which similar objects of the phenomenal world have for peoples of different cultural traditions. Consequently, the objects of the external world, *as meaningfully defined* in a traditional ideology, constitute the reality to which the individuals habituated to a particular system of beliefs actually respond. As applied to the sphere of ecological relations, for example, an inventory of all the natural resources of a specific human habitat does not necessarily correspond to the "natural resources" of that habitat.

The physical objects of the environment only enter the reality-order of the human population as a function of specific culture patterns. It is the knowledge and techno-logical level of the culture of a people that determines their natural resources, not the mere presence of physical objects. To people without a tradition of pottery making the presence of clay in their habitat is no more a natural resource than was the presence of coal and iron in the habitat of the pre-Columbian Indians of eastern North America. (1935, pp. 20-21)

A series of data which, in my estimation, has been inconceivably neglected by the students of Americanist archeology is to be found very pertinent to this point. I speak of the life-forms depicted upon the pottery bowls of the Mimbres region in southern New Mexico. These forms certainly reflect an interest in the natural and human environment, but here the question of significance is: an interest in what aspects of this environment? A tabulation of some published life-forms reveals the following data:

TABLE 6

Humans	65	Parrots	6
Birds (type?)	53	Snakes	2
Fish	50	Snails	1
Insects	30	Scorpions	1
Rabbits	24		
Mountain sheep	21	SUMMARY	
Antelope	20	Birds	96
Turtles	19	Humans	65
Swallow-like birds	17	Deer, sheep, antelope	57
Carnivores	16	Fish	50
Deer	16	Insects	30
Turkeys	14	Frogs and lizards	26
Frogs	13	Rabbits	24
Lizards	13	Turtles	19
Quail	6	Carnivores	16

Discounting for the moment the possibility of error in a few identifications and the failure to list some doubtful forms, the above table may serve as a representa-tive sample.[121]

The life-forms on the pottery do not correspond quantitatively, nor typo-logically as a whole, with the animal remains found at Mimbres ruins (e.g., Cosgrove and Cosgrove, 1932, pp. 3-5; Nesbitt, 1931, p. 19). Nor do they corre-spond, very closely at least, with the diet of Pueblo people as it is generally recognized. Insects, reptiles and amphibians, carnivores, and finally humans are not within the range of food usage. As for fish, the picture presented by the ethnographic accounts is neither complete nor very clear, but it is safe to say that this article of diet was never important and is actually taboo among the

Hopi and Zuni. It is probable that neither parrots nor scorpions were eaten, and the relative numbers of swallow-like and other small birds are quite surely out of proportion to any food utilization they might have had. There remain only rabbits, snails, and herbivorous quadrupeds to represent the food quest. But among these, rabbits occur less frequently upon the pottery than do humans, small birds, fish, and insects; deer occur less than insects, turtles, and swallow-like forms; antelope and mountain sheep less than insects, fish, humans, and small birds. It is apparent that the decoration of Mimbres pottery was influenced by other considerations than the food quest.

Nor does it appear that clothing or other utilitarian arts were the vitalizing factors. Little or no vegetal material is depicted and the hide-producing forms, such as deer, antelope, sheep, and rabbit, have been shown to be of less numerical importance than the non-hide-producers. The predominance of birds might point to an interest in feathers for dress or ornamentation, but this still does not explain the prevalence of fish, insects, and turtles. In the light of these facts, it seems highly probable that the non-utilitarian forms, as well as those which might be thought at first glance to have some practical significance, actually contain an esoteric, non-material import and indicate the concern of the Mimbreños with environmental aspects other than subsistence and material things.

Another lead may be suggested. Throughout the Southwest among the living Pueblos, the potters are predominantly women. However, with the exception of delineations of childbirth, the scene which is so similar to the Aztec manner of showing sexual intercourse (Cosgrove and Cosgrove, 1932, plate 225e; Nesbitt, 1931, plate 25a), and a very few other possibilities, all human figures on the examined Mimbres pottery are male, and depict purely male activities. The same correlation can be noted for the non-human figures: there is a concern with usually masculine occupations, with game and the hunt or with ritual as implied by parrots. Perhaps the presence of fish, reptiles, insects, and the like indicates female participation, but the dominance of male-connected activities where the identification is sure would appear to make this unlikely. Furthermore, the tendency toward geometric design and stylized rather than natural life-forms in the Southwest where female artisanship is undoubted makes the uniqueness of Mimbres artistry all the more suggestive of male authorship for at least the life-forms. Whether the making of pottery and the drawing of the geometric designs which appear on Mimbres pottery were also the work of men is another problem which, together with the testing of the above hypothesis, should prove an interesting study. A thorough and careful analysis might lead to acceptable inferences as to the religious ideas and organization of the Mimbres people.

When it comes to the identification of animal bones found in archeological excavations, the amount of information to be sought does not end with a specific or generic designation. The age, sex, and part of the organism are also important aids to the interpretive work of the archeologist. For example, the age of the individuals can often provide information on seasonal occupations and food preferences. Immature birds and mammals are alive only at certain seasons of the year. Similarly, migratory birds are present in given localities only at times definable within relatively narrow limits. Should numbers of bones thus reduceable to seasonal limits be found within particular strata, it would be possible to date the deposits to their season. With this as a known factor, inferences could be made as to the significance of consistently associated materials: buffalo bones appearing with young birds would indicate a spring hunt, a ceremonial object with goose bones in New Mexico would mean either a spring or late fall ceremony, etc. Such seasonal data might also lead to hypotheses as to the seasonal occupancy of shell mounds and caves, which would, in turn, lead to modification of ideas concerning the length of occupation, nature of the human groups using the sites, meaning of the absence of certain expectable artifacts.

Of course the same procedure is applicable to vegetal remains. Plants ripen and produce edible seeds only at definite times during the year. Piñon nuts are available at specific times which are not the same as those when the maguey stalks are ready for roasting. If these two forms are associated in a cave deposit, what does it mean? Were the nuts stored and, if so, where? If they were stored in the cave, does it mean that the people lived in the cave permanently or that, being migratory, they returned to the cave and their cache of nuts at the time when the maguey sap began to run? What evidence for caches is there in the cave itself? What indications are there of permanent or intermittent occupation? If the people could count on their cache of nuts being safe in the cave from the fall until spring, what implications does this fact have for the human groups occupying this region? Might it signify hunting and gathering territories, or possibly the sole use of transient stopping places by certain nomadic groups? Or does it merely mean that they took the chance of hiding the cache well enough to escape notice until they returned? Whatever might come of such speculation and the analysis and testing that should follow, the point which I wish to raise is that there is more to the presence of piñon nuts and burned maguey stalks than just their existence in the cave.

The climates under which bygone peoples lived are also of importance in the construction of a cultural context. The fact that biological forms appear naturally in constellations, that there are such things as ecological groupings, that a certain biota is indicative of certain climatic and physiographic conditions can be of great assistance to the archeologist bent upon obtaining a picture of past actuality. Success along these lines will depend upon his collections of floral, faunal, and geologic materials and upon thorough analysis by competent specialists.

d. Non-local Human

There should be no need to point out the importance of obtaining cultural and biological information on the human societies that lived in the neighborhood of a site at a time either before, during, or after its occupation. But it should be mentioned that the value of this perception lies not only in its use for comparative studies and the interpretation of use and function, but also for the insight it gives into other, possibly more obscure, cultural aspects. Just as knowledge of modern Hopi (or Keres?) culture will be of help in interpreting the murals found at the ruined pueblo of Awatovi, so will other, perhaps less obvious and more far-fetched, information serve to clear up problems (and to lead onward to new ones) that otherwise might not be answered on purely archeological grounds.

For example, within the Coahuila site called Frightful Cave, there were found nearly a thousand sandals made of plaited fiber. Some of these are long and some short, obviously having been made for feet of different sizes. But what sizes? Perhaps it would be possible merely to measure the length of each sandal and assume that this dimension represents the length of the foot which wore the sandal. But the wear on individual sandals shows that they were made somewhat longer than the feet which wore them. But how much longer? A short and informal study of the living Mexican, sandal-wearing population of the region demonstrated that their modern sandals extend, on an average, one-half inch both before, behind, and beside the foot. Some questioning elicited the statement that this extension is necessary so as to protect the foot against rocks and cactus over which one is constantly traveling in desert and mountainous country. A broader extension would make the sandal too clumsy and unwieldy. A test of a sample lot of the archeological specimens shows that, when heel and toe depressions are present, they also range closely around a point one-half inch from their respective margins. With these data, it will be possible to estimate the range of actual foot size among the bygone people of the area and to make some hypotheses as to stature and age-group of the population, e.g., adults, adolescents, children. If it is assumed that the proportion of these age-groups within the cave as a whole reflects their relative numbers within the bands that occupied the cave, some idea will be forthcoming as to the constitution of these bands.

Ethnographic accounts, documentary sources, other archeological reports, the habits, customs, practices of living groups, all provide valuable hints and leads. Going on the assumption that an interpretation has more chance of being correct if it corresponds with some known practice of similar or neighboring societies than if it finds no parallel in any known human group, the value of non-local information on cultural or physical subjects is plain.

e. Non-contemporaneous Geographical

The value of the information included under this heading is of a rather special and restricted kind. In most instances, it has to do with such things as the physiographic changes which might have caused a site to be occupied or abandoned and the geographic factors which may have kept earlier or later people from using the same location. These data are often difficult or impossible to secure, and even then they may be of little significance either for constructing a cultural context or for comparative purposes. It is probably not an overstatement to say that this is the least important category into which pertinent data fall.

One final point may be mentioned in connection with the whole matter of the collection of archeological data. I believe it is possible to say without injustice to any particular field worker that, however carefully the archeologist preserves his findings either in the form of notes or specimens, he always finds that there is information which he needs for his analysis but which he does not have in his records. Critical details will beg for elaboration and clarification during laboratory study, but there will be no way of bettering the situation. Only experience and the failings of former jobs will tell the archeologist what he should be on the lookout for in his next investigation. For these reasons there is only one axiom to be remembered: when in doubt, preserve! Many things which may seem trivial and merely an added burden at the time of excavation may turn out to be of great importance to a full-blown cultural picture. It is worth preserving these data at the expense of a little extra labor and the following out of a few blind leads. When in doubt, preserve!

2. STUDY

In the preceding pages, the type of materials to be collected and some of the reasons for collecting them have been given. Therefore, the character of the study upon them has been implicit in the whole discussion. Briefly, study should be detailed and go beyond the mere requirements of a comparative approach. For comparative purposes, it may be sufficient to know that two basketry trays found at two sites are descriptively similar in their gross features of materials, technique of manufacture, and design. But in order to extract as much of the cultural significance as possible from the tray at one particular site, it is necessary to notice its charred pitting indicative of live coals, the extent to which it is pitted, the sources of its component materials, the quality of manufacture, the presence of dried mush in its crevices. Two superficially similar bone awls may be found to have entirely different types of scratches on them, or their points may be sharpened or worn in contrasting ways. The direction of beveling on stone points may be consistent in specific associations, sites, areas, and thus indicate handedness among the people or some culture norm over and above shape, material, and other gross attributes. The wear on the bottom of a certain pottery bowl, in contrast to the wear on the bottoms of other like forms, may be indicative of the length and manner of its use. Errors in weaving technique may not have extra-local comparative importance, but they have a cultural and individual significance, especially if carelessness in weaving is in opposition to care in some other technical process or if only a few textiles show poor workmanship while the majority are well fashioned.

Once more it may be asked: what good is it if a cultural item is found to have counterparts in other sites, if nothing is known of the significance of that item within its own cultural context? Of what value is it if a comparative study demonstrates temporal and cultural relationships between sites, while little or nothing is known of the culture of those sites? What is the purpose of working out the distribution of flanged bowls in the Maya area? If the answer to this is that it will tell us the temporal and cultural relationships which existed between certain Maya sites, we may continue to ask: what is the purpose of learning which sites are later than others in the Maya area and which had cultural relations with which? Is it not for the purpose of understanding the nature, the change, the growth of Maya "civilization"? If this is granted, the next question is: How can we understand the nature, change, or growth of anything about which we know only superficials? Would it not be wiser, in addition to learning the spatial location of flanged bowls or plumbate ware, also to make every effort to learn their materials, techniques, use, function, meaning, in other words their places within the cultural whole?

From the foregoing, it is apparent that not only will the archeologist have to study his material with finer perception, but also he will have to employ the services of many other scientific specialists in order to secure the information which he needs for his purposes. In order that materials of manufacture may be identified and traced to their sources, in order that the more complicated techniques may be recognized, in order that the environment and its utilization may be understood, the archeologist will be forced, except in relatively rare cases, to call upon the aid of colleagues in other disciplines. If a society consistently used a particular wood for its projectile foreshafts or if it obtained its pigments or clay from distant deposits, these facts are in addition to the information on trade and contact relations. They are of importance for a picture and an understanding of the culture itself. Therefore, the identification of all possible materials and techniques is a goal which should be constantly in mind and consistently sought. This is a hampering requirement, but the information is vital. I shall refer to the practical aspects of this problem at a later time in this chapter.

a. Criticism

As the term is used here, criticism involves the making of judgments as to the validity and applicability of the archeological finds. Is there any doubt as to provenience; is there any indication of disturbance, reversed stratigraphy, or other movement in the deposit after primary deposition? Can a find be accounted for on other grounds than human agency? Does an increase in, say, piñon shells signify a cultural phenomenon, or is it a function of environmental change? Criticism in many instances will have to come after analysis and interpretation, but usually it is one of the first avenues of attack upon archeological materials.

b. Analysis

Analysis involves the study of archeological data in terms of their empirical attributes, including their provenience, associations, and specifications, in other words their empirical "forms." Analysis also includes the typing and classifying of forms according to their empirical attributes and affinities. With regard to cultural data, form is the most obvious feature, being empirical, and the most readily comparable. It is not to be wondered, then, that it has received the bulk of attention by archeologists since that time when they became conscious of the "objective" method and eschewed the free and easy interpretation of the earlier workers.

But form may be misleading even in comparative studies, and most certainly it is a very superficial aspect of any cultural item. It is a prime requisite for further investigation, but it should not be the end-point of archeological study. Form is actually only the outward shell of the matter. The kernel lies inside.

c. Interpretation

Interpretation involves the study of archeological data for the purpose of discovering their technique of manufacture, use, function, and the idea or ideas which lay behind them. It also includes the typing and classifying of cultural phenomena on the basis of groupings which are inferred to have been pertinent to the culture and people under investigation. It is at this point that the cultural conjunctives, the relationships between the archeological data of a society or cultural entity, play their important part. Often this interpretation is neither easy nor the means obvious, but if archeology intends to attain the level of context, if it professes to become either anthropology or historiography, this is an essential step in the process. Archeology should not deal only with empirical form.

d. Description

Description follows analysis and interpretation in this outline because the determination of the attributes which are considered important enough to describe depends upon these two preliminary steps. It is impossible to describe fully and "objectively" even the simplest object. Analysis and interpretation are necessary, therefore, in order to distinguish those features that are important (and those that are not) within the given frame of reference which, in this instance and speaking broadly, is that of human culture.

3. PRESENTATION

Presentation of the mass of detailed, descriptive data gathered by their research is one of the major problems faced by all archeologists. The greater amount of both data and detail demanded by the conjunctive approach only adds to the difficulty. It has already been maintained that these data should be preserved in their entirety and that the empirical bases for all published interpretations and inferences should be given to the reader. Archeology, as well as other disciplines, must endeavor to make its findings cumulative.

In view of these needs and their attendant problems, it is evident that special methods and techniques for handling this wealth of detail will have to be developed. And once more it seems that compromise will have to be effected between the ideal and such contingent factors as finances, space, time. This will be so either until the archeologists work out means to present the mass of material or until more abundant subsidies and publication facilities are available to them. Nevertheless, it may be possible to make some practical suggestions as to ways in which the ideal may be approached, even ultimately attained.

First, it should be remembered that the presentation of the detailed descriptive data is primarily for the specialist who wishes to check or follow out the archeologist's conclusions or who seeks material for further comparison and study. For those whose interests lie solely in the broad cultural picture and not in intensive study, the cultural context should be sufficient. Therefore the publication of the descriptive data themselves may be as technical, as abbreviated, as tabular, in short as "dull and uninteresting" as demanded by the dictates of practicability, yet consistent with the limits of clarity and fullness. There is no call upon the archeologist, at least in his sections devoted to the evidence, to attempt a work of literary art.

The presentation falls roughly into three divisions: excavation procedure, description, and interpretation. In practice, these will often overlap and may be impossible to treat separately. For example, it is often impractical to divorce the account of excavation procedure from the description of the deposits excavated or the cultural features, such as caches or fire-pits, found during the course of the work. On the other hand, there is one point which should be strictly observed: to make explicit and clear what is interpretive description and what is description of an observational order.

a. Excavation Procedure

This section is primarily concerned with the archeological deposits and how they have been handled by the archeologist. It is designed to provide the means for a critical judgment and analysis of the methods and techniques employed by the excavator to obtain his data. It may be profitable, in some cases, to include the provenience and details of association of the material found during excavation. In other cases, especially when there is a large quantity of findings, it may be better merely to recount the excavation methods and to leave the description of deposits and their contents for separate treatment.

b. Descriptive Section

This is concerned with the nature of the deposits and their contents or, in the case of unburied material, with the particulars of these phenomena. The section is purely and admittedly empirical and descriptive and therefore can best be served by the use of descriptive rubrics. Here is the spot in an archeological report where such headings as *Bone Artifacts, Objects of Shell, Pits*, etc., have their proper place. In fact, special care should be taken that no interpretive question is begged by the use of cultural, i.e., inferential, headings, the implications of which have not been thought out and explicitly demonstrated. Here the concern is with empirical form, type, and class.

Furthermore, description should cover the full range of variation. Purely typological exposition, even when accompanied by quantitative data, is not sufficient. Cultural phenomena are amenable to categorization only within limits, and variation is one of the most characteristic and one of the most significant factors about all culture. It is this fact that has given rise to Linton's valuable concepts of ideal and actual patterns (1936b, pp. 99ff, esp. p. 101). The archeologist is dealing with the results of actual behavior, with the objectifications of actual patterns. There is every expectation that these will show variation, and variation of a culturally significant sort. If, therefore, the archeologist completely replaces these actual phenomena with generalized patterns of his own, he is not only obscuring the picture but also throwing away some of his most realistic and precious data. While it is true that he should attempt to abstract the ideal patterns inherent in the actual patterns of his material, he should not completely submerge his observational data in a classification of his own devising. If he presents only his own groupings without indicating the actual variation, no matter how closely his categories may correspond to the ideal patterns of the culture under investigation, he is at best losing much of the significance of his material and at worst may be seriously warping his picture of the culture.

It is suggested, therefore, that the archeologist present his empirical categories and then proceed to indicate the range of variation and the specific details of the finds which come under that heading. For example, after giving a typological description of "triangular stone points" covering the specifications and affinities of the type as a whole, there should be added the dimensions, petrography, and other individual features of each specimen. Many of these data can be tabulated or given in predesignated outline form.

c. Interpretive Section

This has to do with the techniques of manufacture, use, function, the culture ideas, and the meanings of the archeological material. Analysis and discussion along these lines may be segregated in a separate section or incorporated with the preceding one, either following or being interlarded with the pertinent empirical data. Close physical proximity of these two aspects within the body of the report need be no cause for confusion, so long as the observational and interpretive details are explicitly identified.

At this point in the account, the interpretive groundwork for the subsequent cultural synthesis should be the first concern of the author. It will save much lengthy, disconcerting, and highly parenthetical discussion when it comes time to develop the cultural context if the interpretive analysis, the weighing of evidence, the arguments pro and con are all finished and at least some conclusion, negative, neutral, or positive, is reached at this early stage in the report.

It is, of course, realized that in order to accomplish this purpose, extra-local comparisons of artifacts and other individual items will have to be made. And this is the best place for them to be made. In contradistinction to the comparisons made on the basis of cultural contexts or extensive cultural complexes, those to be made at this place are of single items or categories. The full range of distribution may be treated here and hypotheses as to relationships made on more tenuous and far-flung likenesses than would be advisable to use for the comparison of larger cultural units such as complexes or contexts. In other words, in the presentation of the empirical and inferential analyses of individual finds, comparative studies of individual finds and categories are also in order.

One last point may be mentioned. There is a definite and urgent need for some method of reference whereby each and every find can be identified during the course of an archeological report without having to be redescribed or identified at length at each citation. It should be possible to discuss the finding of a given stone point and to give its associations in the section on excavation procedure, to describe its form in the descriptive section, and to make use of its cultural implications in the final section on cultural synthesis, without being forced in each instance to make long, detailed, and repetitive identification. It is of the utmost importance that the reader be made aware that the description on page so-and-so refers to the same point whose provenience is given on page such-and-such and which is utilized for cultural interpretation on yet another page of the report. The failure to provide such cross checks is one of the most confusing and frustrating features of current publications on Americanist archeology.

A remedy for this situation may be suggested. As an appendix to the archeological report, a serial catalogue of finds may be given, listing, after a serial number and short identifying tag such as "stone point," "mano," "foreshaft," etc., the provenience of the item. In order to kill several birds with one stone, other data might also be included, specifications such as dimensions, material of manufacture, etc., and even an index to the textual citations of each item. By such a catalogue and with constant reference whenever a find is mentioned in the report, the data will be "brought down to units" capable of being assembled and reassembled any number of times and in any number of ways. The individual items and their potentially significant variation from the categorical norm will not be smothered in a welter of taxonomy and more or less arbitrary groupings made by the archeologist. Such a method would help to preserve and keep to the fore the associations and relationships, the all-important cultural conjunctives, which are vital factors in the construction of cultural contexts.

The system advocated here is a modification of that employed by ethnographers to refer to information received from certain, specified informants (e.g., Kroeber, ed., 1935b; Wyman and Kluckhohn, 1938), but an archeological illustration may be taken from the records of the U.S. National Museum Coahuila Expedition of 1940-1941. As part of the laboratory work, the field catalogue was transferred to an "Accession Book" wherein the specimens of each empirical grouping such as stone, bone, fiber, shell, were listed serially for each site excavated. This record is such that it can be transferred directly (with only minor corrections) to an appendix of the final report. By using this roster in writing the sections in the body of the report, it will be possible to proceed generally as follows:

In the .50-1.00 m level of block E 16, at a point .30 m from the west wall [etc.], a bone artifact (Z-21) was found lying just two inches north of a charred tray of coiled basketry (F-523). . . .

then in the Descriptive Section under *Bone Artifacts:*

Z-21: a bone point .01 m wide, .20 m long [etc.], from its appearance and its proximity to the basketry tray (F-523), it may be interpreted as an awl. . . .

then in the cultural context under *Textile Industry:*

. . . for use in basketry, the people of Frightful Cave employed rather long, thin awls made of deer metapodial worked down to sharp but short points (Z-21) . . . .

It might be possible, if the descriptive and interpretive sections had been handled fully and clearly, to forego numerical identifications in the writing of the cultural context. Such a practice would make for easier reading and a more vivid picture and would, in fact, be the ideal presentation. However, a compromise course, one in which the least obvious points would be clarified by reference, might serve expediency, clarity, and accuracy.

In closing this account of the conjunctive approach, a word may be said about practical considerations, which in the usual run of archeological affairs mean financial considerations. It should be evident that the requirements of such detailed and intensive work, both in the field and in the laboratory, will demand not a little revision of the expenditure of archeological funds. Assuming a more or less constant budget, how can the work be done and the money to do it with be balanced? A few ideas may be put forward along these lines but, whether they prove satisfactory or not, it remains a fact that the detailed work must be accomplished—otherwise the archeologist may as well shut up shop as a historian or anthropologist.

The first and major solution is, I believe, to excavate less extensively and more intensively for shorter periods of time. If the data are extracted with anything like the proper refinement and if they are studied in the necessary detail, the product of a very brief excavation will occupy the efforts of the archeologist and his assistants in the laboratory for a remarkably long time. But when the job is done, the ensuing report may be expected to provide more valuable and better grounded information than one resulting from a longer and less intensive excavation with a more hurried and superficial study.

Such intensive field work requires an increased amount of supervision. Two solutions are offered for this problem. First, the professionally trained personnel should work more than my observations have led me to believe they are accustomed to do at present. An effort should be made to make the most of every member of the trained staff during the period of actual field work which, however, should be short enough to forestall "going stale." Second, and perhaps more congenial to expedition directors, a plan should be worked out to attract more (and the more serious) students to the field, either to act as laborer-technicians or merely to supervise other labor. Such students would receive no remuneration.

Experience in archeological techniques should not be looked upon either by the student or by the professional and academic group as a side-line which can be picked up in desultory fashion. It is only by continued and broad experience that the archeologist learns to recognize what is significant and how to record, concisely and completely, those data which he will require for his cultural interpretations. Just as he should be conversant with culture in the ethnographic realm, so he must become familiar with culture viewed archeologically. The data seen from each of these two angles are different to such an extent that proficiency in one does not necessarily or automatically indicate proficiency in the other. Relationships of cultural phenomena in the ground often appear quite different from those that are observed or described in actual practice among living peoples. Experience, and the imagination born of experience and reading, are essential parts of the professional's repertory, and it should be made possible for the student, and attractive to him, to obtain as much of both as he can before he attempts to do his own work. Archeological field work of an intensive sort should not be considered a vacation; perhaps it is a change, but is hard and tedious work and deserves recognition as such.

Therefore, it should be possible for a student to earn academic credits by diligently performing archeological work under an accredited professional and according to the same standards set up for other scholastic performance by the student's institution. What is being advocated here is a system of archeological apprenticeship, whereby the student is given the incentive of academic credit for field work under proper direction. Such a system would relieve the pressure on archeological budgets and would develop a pool of student archeologists with considerable broad and practical experience.

What is perhaps even more important, it would involve passing judgment upon the professional archeologists themselves. In other words, it is to be presumed that an academic institution or department would give credit only for work done under what it considered to be competent and exacting direction. In this fashion, only the better-regarded archeologists would be able to obtain the desired student help and a practical premium would be placed on "good" archeology. This would serve to improve the field from the professional as well as from the student level and would expectably bring about a stiffening of professional standards which current book reviews and criticisms do not seem able to do. If it came down to awarding academic credit, I believe a more rigorous judgment would be passed, assuming the institution to be jealous of its standards.

Concerning the laboratory study of the excavated material, three points may be raised, two of which are similar to the above. If it is granted that the time in the field should be utilized to the utmost, then much study and analysis can be accomplished there by the personnel of the expedition. Trade-union hours have little place in the schedule of archeologists in the field, and the day does not need to end when work in the trenches is through. On the supposition that the effort will not carry on unduly, it can be asked of the personnel that they exert themselves to the maximum for the duration. It is needless to mention that this field study is also of great advantage because of the problems it raises and the leads it gives toward further and more pertinent investigations. Second: when students are available and can be supervised, they may be used in the "home" laboratory as well as in the field. Academic or publication credit may be provided or even the allotment of small subsidies which, nevertheless, would be less strain on the budget than the extended services of some salaried professional, e.g., the expedition director or a specialist.

And third: some arrangement should be made on a broad and long-range basis so that the costs of special laboratory investigations such as dendro-chronology, petrography, serology, botanical identification, can be underwritten by philanthropic institutions as a regular and recognized part of their programs. The dependence of archeological research on such identifications and special studies is understandably greater than that of other anthropological sub-disciplines, and so crucial a factor in its success or failure that too much emphasis cannot be laid upon such help. Yet one of the worst blocks that faces the archeologist is his inability to get identifications and pertinent information on his varied materials within a reasonable time or with the necessary detail.

The main reason for this situation seems to be that the specialists have been doing the work as an incidental, rather than an integral, part of their own research. For the most part, the identifications and other studies have been done without charge, as a favor to the archeologists or to their institutions, and apparently often as "spare time" projects. To my knowledge some specimens have been in these channels for five years and more! This unhealthy situation might be remedied, I believe, if the specialists could be led to look upon this work as a personally rewarding part of their own regular research program, not merely as a favor or service to another discipline. What is necessary is to demonstrate that there is something of value in it for them. If they can be convinced that the work is a joint project of mutual benefit and if they were given enough financial support to enable them regularly to devote time, then I believe that the block would be well on its way out.

There are at least three means of promoting this attitude among the specialists. First is to bring to their attention the fact that archeological sites have preserved, and are producing, materials of great importance to their own studies, e.g., materials from that twilight zone between the modern and the strictly paleontologic. Here are the immediate forerunners of modern forms and all given to them, often dated to the year over a long span of time, with no expense to their own budgets. Second is to encourage the specialists to conduct investigations and to publish papers along the interests of their own professions, based upon the archeologically derived materials. In the past, it seems that much of the work was viewed merely as wearisome identification for another discipline, for which at best they were allotted an appendix and many times only a footnote of acknowledgment in journals which their colleagues would never see. In place of this, they should be encouraged to publish in their own periodicals, under their own names, and on topics pertinent to their own interests, the only proviso being that they furnish either there or separately the data needed by the archeologist. Third is to collect the materials from archeological sites in such a manner that they can be utilized by the specialists, not only for identification purposes but also for their own investigations. This means (a) the collections must be adequate samples or total universes, not representative specimens, in order to permit conclusions; (b) the collections must be in as good physical condition as possible (clean, labeled, boxed, etc.), so that too much work of a purely preparatory nature will not have to be done by the specialist; (c) the catalogue should be as detailed as possible and available to the specialist.

One of the major problems in implementing the above proposals is that of finances. And here is a function which a central agency or clearing house, so long needed in Americanist archeology, could perform to the undying gratitude of the profession. To my mind, there is a definite and urgent need for an organization with little operating costs to put all its funds into services, and forego the impressive but non-utilitarian aspects of a large and beautiful plant. And one of its major functions would be to subsidize the technical research requirements of institutions actively engaged in archeological excavation. I do not mean that it should merely have money available on application for such projects. It would best assist in breaking the technical stranglehold on archeology by conducting a permanent project of subsidization, not by employing and housing a stable of specialists on any premises but by providing them regular, yearly grants to be expended either in the field or in their own laboratories on projects sent to them through the central agency. In the first place, this would eliminate the overhead of many laboratories and specialists. It would also permit the latter to remain in familiar and established surroundings, to plan their yearly work, and to regard the identification and study of archeological specimens as an integral part of their research program. The agency on its part would make it generally known that it was in a position to subsidize a certain amount of research by specified specialists; it would solicit projects; with the participation of the specialist, it would select those that seemed the most worthy and filled best the requirements established for collections; and it would forward a note to the specialist that such-and-such a collection was coming to be worked on under the year's allotment.

The archeologists would get better service. The specialist would benefit by being able to plan for himself and/or his students. The agency would be able to some extent to raise the standards of archeological collecting and bring home to the archeologist the fact that there is more to the cultural picture than architecture and potsherds.

In the preceding pages, a summary treatment of the ends and a few of the means of the conjunctive approach have been offered. An archeological report according to this viewpoint has been outlined as consisting of, first, a statement of problem; second, a description and interpretation of the findings; third, an analysis of local chronology; fourth, and of most concern, the construction of a cultural context; fifth, the study of extra-local relationships of the material as a cultural entity; and a possible sixth, the study of the cultural context and its relationships in terms of special problems such as culture itself, art, architecture, ceramics, etc.

Once more it should be pointed out that the conjunctive approach is a conceptual scheme made explicit in a set of goals which, in turn, are best attained by certain means. This scheme is one which views archeological data as cultural data. It considers the writing of history to be the construction of cultural contexts with due regard for time, not merely the arrangement of events and cultural phenomena in temporally sequential order. It considers the writing of anthropology to be concerned with the nature of culture and cultural dynamics. It believes that even the fullest attainment of the objectives apparent in a purely comparative approach will not provide adequate material for the writing either of history or of anthropology. And it does *not* believe in the conception of archeological prestige which is apparently held by those who pursue the comparative approach, i.e., that it is more praiseworthy to dig much material from the ground than it is to make a full study of the material already excavated.

The conjunctive approach is not concerned as to whether the particular archeologist has for his objective historiography or anthropology. But it does believe that, to justify itself as a social science as opposed to antiquarianism, archeology must at least write history, must at least construct the fullest possible cultural contexts. Beyond this point, it recognizes the personal inclinations of the individual, either to stop or to go on to another level of procedure, be it the study of culture or any segment of the cultural whole: sociology, art, economics, mechanics, or whatever.

NOTES

CHAPTER 1

[1] Cambridge University makes the distinction between General Archaeology which is handled under the Faculty of Archaeology and Anthropology, and Classical Archaeology which is under the Faculty of the Classics (Cambridge University, 1937, pp. 579-582). The same separation is found at Oxford (Oxford University, 1935, p. 394). Both aspects are treated together at London and Edinburgh, while, at Liverpool, archeology means only "Mediterranean" archeology (University of London, 1939, p. 39; University of Edinburgh, 1939-1940, pp. 205-206; University of Liverpool, 1938, pp. 210-211).

At the University of Paris, "general" archeology is under the Institut d'Ethnologie, while Classical archeology is found in the Institut d'art et d'archeologie (University of Paris, 1939-1940, pp. 181-182, 185-186).

At Yale University, the Undergraduate Schools state: "For a major in archeology or Ancient History or Classical Civilization the prerequisite is Classical Civilization 10 . . . or a college course in Greek or Latin." In the Graduate Schools, Classical Archaeology is listed under Classical Languages and Literature; Greek and Roman sculpture is listed under Archaeology III; "prehistoric" and Americanist archeology is listed under the Department of Anthropology (Yale University, 1939, pp. 137, 183-184, 189-190).

At Columbia University, the Department of Fine Arts and Archaeology and the Departments of Greek and Latin offer archeology; under this heading there is the statement that "Students interested in primitive archaeology should consult a representative of the Department of Anthropology. . . ." Far Eastern archeology comes under History, Japanese, Chinese; Mediaeval and Renaissance archeology under History; Near Eastern archeology under Semitic; "primitive" and "prehistoric" archeology under Anthropology (Columbia University, 1940, pp. 17-38).

At the University of California, the Department of Art includes Group C which is titled "History of Art and Archaeology"; the Classics Department includes Classical Archaeology, Greek Mythology and Archaeological Discoveries, Classical Antiquities, Greek Scenic Antiquities of the Fifth Century B.C.; the Anthropology Department includes Prehistory and Americanist archeology (University of California, 1940, pp. 157-161, 165-169, 199-203).

At Harvard, Pennsylvania, Chicago, and Wisconsin this same separation of "prehistoric" and "primitive" from other archeology is to be found. At Princeton, archeology is found under *Art and Archaeology.* (Harvard University, 1941, pp. 186 *et seq.*, 196, 244; University of Pennsylvania, 1940, pp. 70-73, 114-115, 116, 133; University of Chicago, 1940, pp. 214-223, 322-328, 367-380; University of Wisconsin, 1940, pp. 104, 173; Princeton University, 1941, pp. 67 *et seq.*).

In all of the above, the latest pre-War announcements available have been used.

Although the Archaeological Institute of America was founded with the explicit intent of having "no narrow local interest" (1st Annual Report, 1880, p. 8), the subsequent history of its membership and publications clearly shows the disruptive effects of the primitive-Classical dichotomy. From the very first, the Papers of the Institute were divided into an American Series and a Classical Series. The *American Journal of Archaeology and of the History of the Fine Arts* (subtitle dropped after 1896), stated to be dedicated to furthering "the interests for which the Institute was founded" (Vol. I, 1885, p. ii), has been from the start primarily an organ for archeology other than Americanist, predominantly "Mediterranean." On the other hand, within the Institute, the American School of Prehistoric Research and the School of

American Research (at first the School of American Archaeology) have had definite ties with the anthropological segment of archeology in the United States.

The *American Anthropologist,* although publishing from time to time articles in the "Mediterranean" field, has been overwhelmingly concerned with "primitive" and "prehistoric," i.e., "anthropological" archeology. *American Antiquity* has been professedly Americanist and the professional membership of the Society for American Archaeology has consistently over-lapped that of the American Anthropological Association to a most significant degree. The overlap with those professional archeologists who support the *American Journal of Archaeology* is proportionately and significantly small. The same may be said for the overlap with sup-porters of those Classical, Philological, Oriental, and Historical Journals that carry papers re-sulting from archeological research.

² Frazer, 1898; Thompson, A. H., 1935. "Throughout the length and breadth of Italy, memories of ancient greatness spurred her children on to emulation. . . . It was while gazing on the ruins of Rome that Villani felt impelled to write his chronicle. Pavia honored Boethius like a saint. Mantua struck coins with the head of Virgil, and Naples pointed out his tomb. . . . It is, however, more to the purpose here to notice that in Italy this adoration of the antique world was common to all classes; not students alone, but the people at large, regarded the dead grandeur of the classic age as their special heritage." (Symonds, 1908, pp. 29-31; *see also* pp. 149ff., 152ff.)

³ Burckhardt, 1860, esp. pp. 90ff; von Martin, 1932, esp. pp. 20ff., 53ff.

⁴ "Winckelmann is justly regarded as the founder of the science of archaeology, for he was the first to study ancient art from the historical—which is in this instance the scientific—point of view" (Fowler and Wheeler, 1909, p. 13). *See also* Winckelmann, 1763-1768.

" 'Archaeology of the spade' and its results form the subject of this volume. By the term archaeology is meant the archaeology of art; the products of civilization in so far as they express no artistic character will only be mentioned incidentally. . . . My main object has been to give an account of the rise, the diffusion, and the deepening of our knowledge of Greek art." (Michaelis, 1908, p. xiii)

⁵ "Simple tomb-robbing gave place to a systematic search for ancient works of art, while the profound respect of Renaissance engineers for classical builders and the growing interest in ancient inscriptions led to an increasingly careful study of everything uncovered. . . . In all these regions [the "Mediterranean" area] the investigators were dealing with highly civilized cultures whose history was already partially known. They centered their investigations at first on the finding of inscriptions and objects for museum display" (Linton, 1936a, pp. 306-307). *See also* Wissler, 1942, esp. p. 190.

⁶ Barnes, 1936, pp. 226-227, and Shotwell, 1929, p. 596, give the historians' point of view concerning these men. See *Encyclopedia Britannica,* articles "Antiquary," "William Camden," "Sir Robert Cotton," "Matthew Parker," "John Leland." *See also* Hearne, ed., 1720. This is a posthumous collection of the products of the society. *See also:* Prothero, 1909.

⁷ For "these dull volumes": Dugdale, 1655-1673, 1656; Tanner, 1744, posthumous.

⁸ Anonymous, 1718-1747. This represents probably the first published work by the recon-stituted Society. *See also:* Anonymous, 1800. This is the charter of the Society, which was not granted until 1751. *See also:* Cust and Colvin, 1898.

⁹ Beers, 1901; Kendrick, 1927, esp. Chap. I; Piggott, 1937.

¹⁰ Fairchild, 1928.

[11] Early beliefs about stone artifacts: Boule, 1921, pp. 1-27; Cartailhac, 1877; Evans, 1897a, esp. Chapters III and IV; Hamy, 1906.

Antiquarian research in England after 1750: Borlase, 1764; Boys, 1792; Douglas, 1793; Grose, 1773-1787; Hoare, 1812-1821.

[12] Clark, K., 1928; Summers, 1941. Products of this influence: Britton, 1835, 1836; Pugin and Willson, 1850. *The Antiquary* (Sir Walter Scott, 1816) is a contemporary picture of the type of individual engaged in these pursuits.

[13] Leeds, 1936, contains a valuable bibliography; Neville, 1852; Wylie, 1852.

"One object aimed at when this book first appeared, was to rescue archaeological research from that limited range to which a too exclusive devotion to classical studies had given rise; and, especially in relation to Scotland, to prove how greatly more comprehensive and important are its native antiquities than all the traces of intruded arts." (Wilson, D., 1863, preface)

"To each of these classes [of Ancient British and Celtic remains] I propose devoting a few pages, so as to give a general insight into the remains of that, and subsequent, periods of our early history" (Jewitt, 1877, p. 1). "Its [the book's] object is to give a sketch of that part of our history which is not generally treated of, the period before Britain became Christian England. . . . Every article which, as just stated, is turned up by the spade or the plough, is a record of that history. . . ." (Wright, 1885, pp. v-vi)

"Thus we are attempting to push back the history of Sussex beyond the coming of the South Saxons, beyond the Romans, beyond even the 'Ancient Britons'." (Curwen, 1937, p. 2)

Similar opinions in: Clark, G., 1940, p. 2; Hunt, 1884, p. v.

[14] For history of development and bibliography: Cochet, 1855; *Encyclopedia Britannica,* article: "Quicherat"; Reinach, 1898.

[15] Šimek, 1914; Stocký, 1924.

[16] *Encyclopedia Britannica,* article: "Antiquary"; Stemmermann, 1934.

[17] American Antiquarian Society, 1820, p. 27; Beltz, 1927; MacCurdy, 1924, Vol. 1, p. 13; Muller, 1897; Nelson, 1937, p. 83; Undset, 1887.

For development of archeology in other areas: Heierli, 1901 (Switzerland); Menghin, 1917-1918 (Balkans); Pigorini, 1874 (Italy); Tallgren, 1922 (East Baltic).

[18] "The history of Europe begins outside Europe. Its civilization is so deeply indebted to the older civilizations of Egypt and South-Western Asia that for the study of its growth the early history of those lands is more important than the barbarous life which Celts, Germans, and others lived within the limits of Europe." (Cambridge Ancient History, 1923, Preface to Vol. I, p. v)

Childe, 1925. In his Preface to the first edition, Childe is more cautious than the above quotation, but in the Preface to the edition of 1939 he has become convinced of the magnitude of Oriental influence upon European civilization.

"Before it was Romanized, before it was Hellenized, the ancient world was Aegeanized." (Henri Berr in Glotz, 1925, p. vi)

"This book is an attempt, based on the findings of archaeology, to trace in outline the early foundations of human culture in Europe (p. 1). What, then, of human culture in what we know as Europe? Its long-drawn-out genesis, however remote its inception, leads at last to our own civilization: its prehistory comes ultimately to lie directly behind the historic records of our own doings [p. 4]." (Hawkes, 1940)

[19] Evans, 1897b; MacCurdy, 1924, pp. 17-18.

[20] White, A. D., 1910, esp. Chapters VI-X. For an earlier rebuttal by reassertion *see* Augustine's *De Civitate Dei*, A.D. 413-436.

[21] Huxley, 1871; Osborn, 1929, esp. pp. 127-130.

[22] Evans, 1897a, pp. 526ff; Prestwich, 1899, p. 119. This is an interesting letter crediting Boucher. *See also:* Schorr, 1935, pp. 437ff.

[23] Dieserud, 1908; Haddon, 1934; Honigsheim, 1942; Lowie, 1937; Marett, 1934; Myres, 1916; Penniman, 1935.

[24] Boyd, 1934; Haven, 1855; Mitra, 1933; Nelson, 1937; Wissler, 1942.

[25] Adair, 1775; Barton, 1797; Bureau of American Ethnology, 1907, articles: "Lost Ten Tribes", "Popular Fallacies"; Fowke, 1902, Chapters III, IV; Henshaw, 1905, pp. 104-105, 111-112.

[26] Chamberlain, 1907, pp. 499-500; Jefferson, 1788, p. 105.

[27] Fowke, 1902. The titles indicate the purpose and interest of these works: Delafield, 1839; Drake, 1832; Haywood, 1823; McCulloh, 1829; Priest, 1835.

[28] Beckwith, 1855; Emory, 1848; Hughes, 1848. This is Doniphan's expedition. *See also:* Simpson, 1852; Whipple, 1856.

[29] "The same work which in Troy has been done by running a section through the massive earth heaps, and in Europe by excavation in caves and gravel beds or shell heaps, has been done here by traveling over the whole continent. In fact, the work has been done by traveling rather than by digging" (Peet, 1879, pp. 212-213). *See also:* Mitra, 1933, Sec. III.

[30] Hayden, 1867-1883. This became the U. S. Geological Survey in 1879. *See also:* Powell, 1877-1893; Wheeler, 1875-1889 (Archaeological volume, VII, 1879).

[31] A list of first contributions and of those which first contributed to the author's future fame: Brinton, 1866a and 1866b; Mason, 1873 (*see:* Hough, 1898, for obituary); Morgan, 1849, 1851, 1871; Powell, 1875a and 1875b (*see:* Dellenbaugh, 1918, and Hobbs, 1934, for appreciations). Putnam became Curator of the Peabody Museum of Harvard University in 1875 and eleven years later was appointed Peabody Professor of Anthropology. (*See:* Kroeber, 1915, for obituary.)

[32] Bureau of American Ethnology established 1879; first *Annual Report,* 1879-1880, published at Washington, 1881. The Archaeological Institute of America organized 1879; first report 1880. American Association for the Advancement of Science, first permanent Subsection VI, Anthropology, of Section B formed probably 1875; first transactions 1876; Section H, Anthropology, formed at 1881 meeting. Anthropological Society of Washington founded 1879; became American Anthropological Association 1890. American Ethnological Society reorganized as Anthropological Institute in 1871. Congrés International des Américanistes, 1st session, Nancy, 1875.

CHAPTER 2

[33] Brinton, 1892; MacCurdy, 1899, 1902. In his "On Limitations to the Use of Some Anthropologic Data" (1879), Powell lists Archaeology as his first subheading.

For the relation of archeology to anthropology at the Peabody Museum of Harvard under Putnam, *see* Kroeber, 1915, esp. pp. 714-715.

[34] "Southwestern archeology has long occupied a prominent place in North American anthropological researches." (Roberts, 1935, p. 507)

". . . . the anthropologist has taken as his particular field the study of languages and cultures of nonliterate peoples (ethnology), of prehistoric cultures (archaeology), and of human evolution (physical anthropology)." (Strong, 1936, p. 364)

"And to archaeology, that branch of anthropology which deals with prehistoric peoples, is delegated the task of recovering as much as possible of the story of the rise and spread of early cultures and of their flowering into the various historic civilizations." (Kidder and Thompson, 1938, p. 494)

[35] "To the writer, ethnology and archaeology, far from being isolated studies, are actually two inseparable means to an essential end—the attainment of the most complete understanding possible of human culture at all places and in all times." (Strong, 1935, p. 6)

"The ultimate goal of American archaeology, which is to contribute to the knowledge of human experience, can be. . . ." (Guthe, 1942, p. v)

"Although the immediate and obvious purpose of archeological work is to fill out our factual knowledge of man's past, its ultimate purpose is to give us an understanding of the processes involved in the growth, flowering and collapse of civilizations and the factors which may be responsible for these." (Linton, 1945c, p. 9)

[36] "For the reconstruction of history, with its story of successes and failures, should be, in the last analysis, the end and aim of archaeology." (Mera, 1935, p. 33)

"To reconstruct history, which is the main objective of archaeological study, the archaeologist must. . . ." (Colton, 1942, p. 39)

"In this brief paper we will attempt to reconstruct the history of the Mississippi Cultures. . . ." (Bennett, J. W., 1943a, p. 34)

"The archaeological objectives [of the Rainbow-Bridge–Monument-Valley Expedition] were directed toward the most complete reconstruction possible of the human history of the region." (Beals, Brainerd, Smith, 1945, p. 4)

See also: Colton, 1943b, title; Holmes, 1919, pp. xvi, 2, 18.

[37] "In anthropological parlance, the terms 'history' and 'historical' have, so far as I can see, never been satisfactorily defined." (Malinowski, 1944, p. 20)

In the course of reading for this study, relatively few references have been found dealing at any length with the relations of anthropology to history. Not one of the authors was specifically an archeologist. *See:* Barnes, 1924; 1925, pp. 21, 34; 1936, p. 256; Boas, 1936; 1938, pp. 1, 5-6; Brinton, D. G., 1896b; Bury, 1906, pp. 46-47; Fellows, 1896; Kroeber, 1923, pp. 5-6, 10; 1935; 1936, esp. pp. 327-333; 1943, pp. 294-295; Olmstead, 1927; Rivers, 1920, esp. pp. 78-79; Teggart, 1919; Wallis, 1917; Wissler, 1923, pp. 246, 279.

[38] "The anthropologist seeks to unite all that can be known respecting man into a comprehensive science, and to study the innumerable correlations which bind the most incongruous actions and thoughts together in harmony." (Mason, 1884, p. 367)

"The science of anthropology, in its widest sense, embraces all the materials bearing on the origin and history of mankind." (Munro, 1894, p. 885)

"I use the term anthropology in the sense in which it had been adopted by this association [the American Association for the Advancement of Science], that is, to include the study of the whole of man, his psychical as well as his physical nature, and the products of all his activities, whether in the past or in the present." (Brinton, D. G., 1895, p. 241)

"Anthropology was defined to be the science of man, and included everything related to man, his physical, intellectual psychologic characteristics; and these extended through all ramifications." (Wilson, T., 1899, p. 332)

"What, then, is this manifestation of omniscience called history?" (Beard, 1934, p. 219) *See also:* Linton, 1936b, title.

[30] Linton for one, while maintaining that anthropology is the potential synthesizer, has also said in the same paper that "Anthropology is by no means the only discipline which has concerned itself with the study of man." (1945c, p. 16)

[40] "If history is to reach its highest development it must surrender all individualistic aspirations and recognize that it is but one of several ways of studying mankind. It must confess that, like geology, biology, and most other sciences, it is based on sister sciences, that it can only progress with them, must lean largely on them for support, and in return should repay its debt by the contributions which it makes to our general understanding of our species." (Robinson, 1912, p. 74)

"Every science which deals with human phenomena is in a way an implement in this great factory system, in which the past is welded together again." (Shotwell, 1929, p. 596)

"The 'Study of Man' is certainly a somewhat presumptuous, not to say preposterous, label when applied to academic anthropology as it now stands. A variety of disciplines, old and recent, venerable and new, deal also with inquiries into human nature, human handiwork, and into the relations between human beings." (Malinowski, 1944, p. 3)

Langlois and Seignobos (1898, pp. 310ff.) say that Universal History is a collaboration. Both Berr (1911) and Bury (1909, esp. p. 33) hold that to "reconstruct" history, data from other disciplines than history must be used. Ware's criticism of the New History (1940, esp. p. 5-8) is that it attempted too much and was neither selective nor organized enough.

[41] "Our understandings of the world are still too fragmentary, still lacking that continuity necessary to permit us to understand the role of Man on the earth. The solution of the problem with which it is concerned, which touches at the same time philosophical history, sociology, and natural history, must needs be preceded by the elucidation of a multitude of other particular scientific questions. The philosophy of history will be the crowning of human knowledge." (Majewski, 1908, p. 20)

"For the purposes of this study—not necessarily for others—it is legitimate to define philosophy as a residual category. It is the attempt to achieve a rational cognitive understanding of human experience by methods other than those of empirical science." (Parsons, T., 1937, p. 21)

[42] "History deals always with the progress or decadence of a unitary being which persists as an individual in spite of changes; it never deals with a collection of sequent but unrelated events. Unless this were the case, any fact would be of equal importance to the historian with every other fact; selection can take place only with reference to a universal." (Sabine, 1906, p. 13)

"The unity of any history is the creation of an artist, and is arrived at through the selection from given data or materials of such facts as are in harmony with the artist's conception or purpose." (Teggart, 1925, p. 40)

". . . . any selection and arrangement of facts pertaining to any large area of history. . . . is controlled inexorably by the frame of reference in the mind of the selector and arranger." (Beard, 1934, p. 227)

"The idea of history only emerges with the search for certain connections, the essence of which is determined by the value which we attach to them. It makes no difference whether we think of a history which is the result of researches strictly critical in method or of sagas or epics belonging to former phases of civilization." (Huizinga, 1936, p. 5)

See also: Beard, 1935, esp. pp. 82-83; Croce, 1921, esp. Chap. 1; Pareto, 1935, Vol. I, p.

318; Parsons, T., 1937, pp. 28-30; 1938. For a contrary view which, however, does not seem to be sound in this particular regard, *see:* Mandelbaum, 1938.

[43] "The more comprehensively, profoundly, penetratingly, and, in a word, truthfully, historians deal with their themes, the more entitled are they to rank as historical philosophers." (Flint, 1893, p. 13)

"The philosopher, on the other hand, is burdened by the double task of weighing the conclusions of all the sciences, and of taking into account, also, the personal data [of subject and author] which every science officially omits and every philosophy tacitly builds on." (Schiller, 1934, p. 235)

"Now has the work [Social and Cultural Dynamics], in its choice of materials, its principles, methods and aims anything to do with what is called Cultural History? Of the semi-historical disciplines which it resembles, it is nearest to what often is styled Philosophy of History. Since almost all great sociological systems are a brand of philosophy of history, and since most of the great philosophies of history are a sort of sociology of culture change, I do not have any objection to the use of this name by anyone who fancies it to describe the present work." (Sorokin, 1937, p. x)

Coulborn and Dubois agree with Sorokin and call his work a "philosophy of history" (1942, p. 501). Coulborn (1941, p. 45) also identifies the writings of Toynbee, Spengler, Ortega y Gasset, Pareto, and Croce as "philosophy of history." *See also:* Giddings, 1922, esp. p. 66.

[44] ". . . . history *par excellence,* human history, what has happened within the sphere of human agency and interests, the actions and creations of men . . . . or which have been produced by men. . . . History is all that man has suffered, thought, and executed—the entire life of humanity—the whole movement of societies." (Flint, 1893, p. 8)

"Whatever history may or may not be, it always concerns itself with man." (Robinson, 1912, p. 74)

"All are agreed, for instance, that the term 'history' should be limited to substantially human affairs." (Shotwell, 1922, p. 5)

". . . . while the name 'historian' is applied only to those scholars who devote themselves to reconstructing the past of the human race." (Salvemini, 1939, p. 4)

[45] "Historiography: 1. The art or employment, or a work, of a historiographer; the writing of history. 2. The study and criticism of the sources and development of history, as a branch of knowledge." (Webster's *New International Dictionary,* 2nd ed., 1937)

A list of writers who use the first meaning includes: Barnes, 1936, esp. pp. 251-260; Beard, 1935, pp. 86-87; Beard and Vagts, 1937, esp. pp. 461, 482; Burton, 1938; Childe, 1937, pp. 4ff.; Cohen and Nagel, 1934, p. 325; Croce, 1933, p. 230; Hearnshaw, 1931, p. 776; Kroeber, 1944, p. 23; Lynd, 1939, p. 131; Merton, 1936b, p. 157; Robinson, 1912, pp. 16, 47; Shotwell, 1929, p. 596; Teggart, 1925, esp. Chap. III; Zilsel, 1941, pp. 572, 578.

Only three sources have been discovered that use the second meaning: American Historical Association, 1945, p. 73, although on later pages in this same publication *historiography* is used with the first meaning (*see:* pp. 80, 81, 87); Becker, C., 1938, p. 20; Meadows, 1944, p. 53.

[46] Ueberweg designates two: objective, as the process of the development of nature and spirit; subjective, as the investigation and writing (1872-1874, Vol. I, p. 5). Bernheim designates three meanings: events themselves, the art of writing, and *Geschichtswissenschaft* or discipline (1903, pp. 2, 126). Shotwell designates two: the events; the record of events (1929, p. 594). Hearnshaw designates three: actual course of events; narrative record; and enquiry

or learning by enquiry (1931, pp. 775-776). Carl Becker designates two: the events; the ideal series which is held in memory, i.e., the record (1932, p. 222). Steefel designates three: the past itself, the record, the discipline (1937, p. 305).

[47] These levels are essentially those noted by Goldenweiser (1933b, p. 7), although he does not mention the level of problem. Teggart, however, says: "Science is, fundamentally, a method of dealing with problems, and the initial step in any scientific undertaking is the determination of the problem to be investigated." (1918, p. 1)

"The facts now dead once lived; unless they have become alive to you you know them not. The investigation of facts, the study of their relation, the reproduction of their form and motion, these constitute history, and every great historical work must be judged by these tests." (Guizot, quoted in Gooch, 1913, p. 190)

"There seems to be just one qualification necessary: it must be that past *viewed historically,* which means that the data must be viewed as part of the process of social development, not as isolated facts. For historical facts are those which form a part of that great stream of interrelation which is Time." (Shotwell, 1922, p. 5)

See also: Berr and Febvre, 1937, p. 363.

[48] "But if the life of every society belongs to history, much more does the life of that highest and sovereign society which we call a state or nation." (Arnold, 1842, p. 6)

"The military and political course of a community with which history is chiefly engrossed. . . . Public office and influence—the making of history—. . . ." (Schouler, 1896, pp. 29, 36)

"Wars and the administration of public affairs are the principal subjects of history." (Gibbon, quoted in Rhodes, 1909, p. 126)

See also: Gooch, 1913; Langlois and Seignobos, 1898; Nevins, 1938.

[49] Barnes, 1925, pp. 5, 28; Dow, 1899; Eggleston, 1900; Gooch, 1913, esp. Chap. XXVIII; Jameson, 1891; Kraus, 1937; Langlois and Seignobos, 1898, p. 297ff.; Pirenne, 1923; Robinson, 1911; 1912; 1930; Schlesinger, 1925; Simkovitch, 1929-1936; Teggart, 1916; Ware, 1940.

[50] "The third fallacy of common-sense sociology is the implicit assumption that any group of social facts can be treated theoretically and practically in an arbitrary isolation from the rest of the life of a given society. . . . This does not mean that it is not possible to isolate such groups of facts for theoretic investigation or practical activity, but simply that the isolation must come, not *a priori,* but *a posteriori,* in the same way as the distinction between the normal and the abnormal. The facts must first be taken in connection with the whole to which they belong, and the question of a later isolation is a methodological problem which we shall treat in a later part of this note. . . ." (Thomas and Znaniecki, 1918, pp. 10, 11-12)

"Indeed, the essential work of the historian is to bring these episodes to light, to show the relations existing between events and in relating to explain them. Thus it appears that history is the expository narration of the course of human societies in the past." (Pirenne, 1931, p. 441)

"History is an integrated narrative or description of past events or facts. . . ." (Nevins, 1938, p. 22)

[51] History is "distinguished from *annals* and *chronicles,* which simply relate facts and events in strict chronological order" (Webster's *New International Dictionary,* 1926). *See also:* Teggart, 1925, p. 17.

[52] "Historical analysis moves differently [from theoretical]. It notes not similarities among discontinuous particulars, but contiguities of particulars in space and time. It desires to see the observed occurrence as a part of a larger, unobservable, but still unitary occurrence. Every natural occurrence, however small, has a temporal as well as a spatial dimension; and in this way even observed occurrences are short histories. These short observed histories have a historical context, they are parts of a larger but still particular spatiotemporal pattern; and it is the historian's purpose to reach, by hypothesis based on observed occurrences, a knowledge of this larger history." (Miller, 1939, pp. 6-7)

See also: Coulborn, 1944, pp. 56-57.

[53] See: quotation from Miller in Note 52 above.

[54] "The rarity of recorded events in primitive life has helped to force anthropologists into recognition of the forms or patterns of culture, and from this into a clear recognition of culture as such. In short, they discovered culture. To be sure, this was long after intelligent historians had known the fact; but these took it for granted and tended to deal with culture indirectly or implicitly, whereas anthropologists became explicit and culture-conscious." (Kroeber, 1936, p. 331)

The editors of the Encyclopaedia of the Social Sciences, while giving the "anthropological attitude" the first place among the contributions of anthropology, nevertheless state that the concept of culture is "of first rate importance" and in fact note that the "principal positive theoretical position" of anthropology in the first decade of the 20th century was the "glorification of culture." (Vol. I, pp. 202-203)

Redfield notes that the concept of culture was developed at the hands of the anthropologists. (1940, pp. 738-739)

[55] The articles of Leslie White, while designed to clarify different problems, will give ample evidence of this contention.

[56] ". . . . on account of the uniqueness of cultural phenomena and their complexity nothing will ever be found that deserves the name of a law excepting those psychological, biologically determined characteristics which are common to all cultures and appear in a multitude of forms according to the particular culture in which they manifest themselves.

". . . . When I thought that these historical methods [acculturation and dissemination] were firmly established I began to stress, about 1910, the problems of cultural dynamics, of integration of culture and of the interaction between individual and society." (Boas, 1936, ed. 1940, p. 311)

[57] "Thus, the scientific quota in all anthropological work consists in the theory of culture, with reference to the method of observation in the field and to the meaning of culture as process and product." (Malinowski, 1944, p. 5)

The "process and product" of Malinowski may be equated with what Teggart called "change" and "conditions" (1925, p. 105). Lesser (1939) has shown that, despite the disclaimer, the anthropologists have in fact abstracted and used "laws."

[58] It is agreed with Murdock (1932, p. 200) that anthropology and sociology both treat of culture itself. But it is further held with Znaniecki (1934, pp. 95ff.) that sociology is not the study of the full range of cultural phenomena.

Abel (1930) denies an interest in culture and says that social life is entirely in terms of inter-individual behavior. Ogburn (1937) is at great pains to show the importance of culture for sociology. Brown (1944) says that from a biological, cultural, and "human nature" standpoint, anthropology and sociology are the same; he seems to imply that the difference between them lies in the fact that the data of anthropology consist of the "primitive."

[59] Caird recognizes Europe and the Mediterranean basin as within the scope of historiography but claims that, outside this pale, men "had no history any more than herds of cattle." (1899, pp. 260-261)

"Anthropology is the study of primitive peoples. . . . What anthropologists find in the study of primitive people is a natural and well-nigh inexhaustible laboratory of custom, a great workshop in which to explore the major role it has played in the life-history of the world." (Benedict, 1931, p. 805)

"If it is possible to differentiate between anthropology and the allied science of sociology, one would say that anthropology is more concerned with the simpler peoples, whereas sociology coordinates both the simple and the complex civilizations, and studies the principles which underlie them both." (Driberg, 1932, p. 15)

". . . . anthropologists have taken as their primary fields the study of human origins, the classification of human varieties, and investigation of the life of the so-called "primitive" peoples." (Linton, 1936b, p. 4)

". . . . the anthropologist has taken as his particular field the study of the languages and cultures of nonliterate peoples . . . . of prehistoric cultures . . . . and of human evolution." (Strong, 1936, p. 364)

"Without either past, or a body of documents, how may one claim to an historian?" (Redfield, 1937b, p. 171)

"The specific task as well as the real value of ethnology consist in the methodological application of *these* means, not only to understand the conditions existing among the primitive peoples today, but also to recognize in them witnesses and survivals of the oldest development of mankind and thus to reach back over the epochs of written history . . . . in a word, to change juxtaposition of culture circles into succession of culture layers." (Schmidt, 1939, p. 13)

[60] Benedict, 1934, pp. 16ff.; Goldenweiser, 1933a, esp. p. 132; Kroeber, 1923, p. 6; Linton, 1936b, pp. 4-5; Mead, 1928, pp. 7-8; 1930, pp. 3-4.

[61] Davis, Gardener, and Gardener, 1941; Embree, 1944; Leighton, 1945; Lynd and Lynd, 1929, 1937; Powdermaker, 1939; Warner and Lunt, 1941; West, 1945.

[62] ". . . . [the relation of ethnography of "primitives" and of social history] to social practice is only mediate; they can help the practitioner to solve actual cultural problems only to the degree that they help the scientist to understand actual cultural life." (Thomas and Znaniecki, 1918, p. 18)

"While nature in its historical pattern is everywhere individual and unique, certain aspects or characters of historical fact can be repeated elsewhere; and it is these repeatable characters that constitute the structures defined by theoretical analysis. Yet the fact that these characters can be repeated elsewhere does not make them less instrinsic or proper to the historical developments bearing them; and this means that all structural pattern is ultimately rooted in particular historical fact." (Miller, 1939, p. 9)

Ellwood (1944, p. 14) calls cultural anthropology "fundamental to all the other social sciences" because culture dominates social life. While this would seem to be true, it still holds that historiography is basic to any historical discipline dealing, as it does, with actuality.

[63] For example: Brinton, Crane, 1938, esp. Chap. I; Buckle, 1876; Cheney, 1924; Toynbee, 1934-1939.

[64] Kroeber's intellectual debt to Rickert is stated in his *So-Called Social Science* (1936, p. 339ff.). A particular passage from Rickert may be noted in this special connection, however: "Empirical reality becomes nature when we regard it in terms of the universal; it becomes history when we regard it in terms of the particular individual." (Rickert, 1896-1902, p. 227)

"Orthodox history still regards the comparative beyond its proper jurisdiction." (Kroeber, 1943, p. 294)

". . . . as historians, our real task is with history, not with its application; but when troubles come upon us, the question will always emerge—it will not down—whether it belongs to the historian, even if not strictly *as* a historian, to find in all these facts and developments, assuming them to be accurate, any lessons of value that may be practically useful." (McIlwain, 1937, p. 223)

See also: Rickert, 1898; Znaniecki 1934, pp. 21ff. For other opinions, *see:* Collingwood, Taylor, Schiller, 1922; Droyson, 1882, esp. p. 7.

[65] "Hence it may be argued that the action of the individual wills is a determining and disturbing factor, too significant and effective to allow history to be grasped by sociological formulae. The types and general forms of development which the sociologist attempts to disengage can only assist the historian in understanding the actual course of events." (Bury, 1909, p. 38)

"While historical knowledge to be scientifically valid must, therefore, be controlled by classificatory and nomothetic knowledge, the latter is obviously dependent on historical data. Not only is the study of particular systems and individual changes a necessary condition of all inductive generalizations, but the ultimate significance of these generalizations is that they help understand such particular systems and explain such individual changes as have not yet been investigated." (Znaniecki, 1934, p. 25)

"Theoretical and historical analysis are, accordingly, coordinate methods in scientific inquiry. They are equally essential, and neither is to be subordinated to the other." (Miller, 1939, p. 27)

"Ordinarily the business of history is the narration of a sequential series of events in their connections or coherences, with culture as a context.

"The anthropologist's situation is essentially the reverse: he deals with culture as such, in a context of history." (Kroeber, 1944, p. 4)

CHAPTER 3

[66] Kidder, 1915; Nelson, 1914; Spier, 1917, 1918, 1919.

[67] See: *Who's Who in America*, 1944-1945, p. 1149; *National Research Council*, 1940, p. 78.

[68] "The Section [dealing with Maya archeology] is engaged in studying the career of the Maya Indians, from the earliest times to the present. Its primary objective is of course to learn the facts of Maya history." (Kidder, 1934, p. 81)

"The aim of the study of New World archaeology is to reconstruct the history of the Indians throughout both the Americas, and from the earliest times to the period when the arrival of Europeans put a final stop to native development." (Kidder, 1936a, p. 46)

See also: Kidder, 1930c, p. 391; 1933, p. 81; Thompson, 1939a, p. 1.

[69] "But shall we be able to digest our masses of raw data in such a way as to reach understanding of the all-important whys and wherefors of Maya history and by so doing contribute toward comprehension of the infinitely complex interaction of those biological, environmental and social factors which govern the evolution of man?" (Kidder, 1935b, p. 114)

"Fuller knowledge of the Indian's history can bring us nearer to understanding the laws of cultural evolution." (Kidder, 1940a, p. 535)

See also: Kidder, 1931b, p. 101; 1933, pp. 82-83; 1937c, p. 160.

[70] No provenience or ceramic association is provided for projectile points and knives which constitute the bulk of the stone work; only one (odd) specimen out of 325 drills is identified with ceramic period; nor are such data provided for awls which form the bulk of the bone-work. Yet, in the same publication, Kidder says: "But specimens . . . . have also suffered shameful neglect. By this was meant, of course, that the study of specimens, which naturally includes thinking about what they mean, has by no means kept pace with their accumulation. Yet upon artifacts, their nature, their distribution and their position in the ground, rests the entire study of archaeology; they constitute practically the only evidence we shall ever have regarding that part of man's career which is unrecorded, or insufficiently recorded, by the written word. . . . We dig, or at least we ought to dig, for the purpose of recovering facts to elucidate the history of vanished civilizations; and those facts should obviously be made of record for the use of other students. Only by doing so can we build up a corpus of information sufficiently large to permit valid generalization." (1932a, p. 8)

[71] The "major works" consist of the *Publications* (P) and *Contributions* (C); the "minor works" of the *Notes* (N) and the *Theoretical Approaches to Problems* (T).

	MAJOR WORKS	MINOR WORKS
Descriptive		
Reconnaissance and brief excavation	P-444, 543 C-8, 9, 15, 40, 41	N-3, 14, 32, 57, 59
Site reports	P-477, 506 C-35?	
Ceramics	C-5	N-2, 15, 30, 35, 36, 37, 60
Artifacts	P-472 C-16, 24, 26, 37	N-1, 9, 16, 17, 21, 25, 27, 29, 31, 40, 47, 52, 54, 55
Buildings	P-454 C-7, 17, 19, 20, 27, 43	
Topical synthesis	P-471	
Epigraphy, Calendar, and Chronology	P-437 C-14, 21, 22, 42	N-7, 18, 20, 22, 24, 28, 33, 34, 38, 39, 45, 49, 50, 56, 58 T-2
Interpretive		
Religion	C-10	N-12, 19
Cultural inferences	C-6, 11, 29, 36	
Topical synthesis		N-61

[72] Brainerd, 1940; Kidder, 1930a, p. 103; 1932b, p. 97; 1945b, p. 591; Roberts, H. B., 1931; Smith and Kidder, 1943, pp. 162-163.

[73] For a similar case, this time leaving reconnaissance for mound excavation, see *Explorations in the Motagua Valley, Guatemala.* (Smith and Kidder, 1943)

[74] Pollock says that the Casa Redonda was chosen because it was round, and round structures are rare (1936a, p. 131). R. E. Smith says Structure A-I at Uaxactun was chosen because of its several superimposed pyramids which gave a chance for pottery, burial, and architecture sequence and also because of the prominent part it played in the group. (1937, pp. 193, 196)

A. L. Smith says that Structure A-XVIII at Uaxactun was of impressive height, one of the oldest and one of the highest and best preserved; he says it was desired to know if it had been residential; it was also important to clear because Tikal was visible from its summit. (1937, pp. 4-5)

Trik says Temple XXII at Copan was selected because the main room contains one of the finest compositions of Maya sculpture. (1939, p. 87)

At Benque Viejo, Thompson stated his intention to be the bridging of the ceramic gap between Uaxactun, San Jose, and other sites (1942a, p. 1). At San Jose, his purpose was to attack a small site which he thought woud prove to be more typical and more in keeping with the more recent tendencies in history, which decry pomp and circumstance; also such a site was thought to provide better opportunities of getting data on every facet not destroyed. (1939a, p. 1)

Smith and Kidder say that San Agustin excavations were instituted because the site showed long occupation and trade with Guatemala and Honduras and also because the remains were of a type not previously reported from the Maya area. (1943, p. 109)

Ruppert says that the Mercado at Chichen Itza was attacked because it was a type of structure not excavated before and because it presented new features not encountered elsewhere. (1943, p. 229)

[75] Yet Kidder once said: "The museum attitude, in other words the valuation of an object for what it looks like instead of for what it tells, has been a most serious brake upon the wheels of archaeological progress, for archaeology is a historical discipline, it seeks to reconstruct the past of peoples who have left no written records, and its documents are the material remains left by vanished populations. The selection from such remains of a few pieces of outstanding appearance, to the neglect of everything which is not handsome or unusual is therefore a perfectly fatal perversion of emphasis." (1932a, pp. 6-7)

[76] "Most of us have worked, I think, too much in restricted fields; and in those fields we have perhaps devoted ourselves too exclusively to site excavation. The comparative methods of ethnography might well be given greater consideration by archaeologists. Nordenskiöld's results achieved on the basis of the scanty South American data, show how much can be accomplished by such means." (Kidder, 1936c, p. 146)

[77] Kidder, 1931b, p. 101; 1932b, p. 91; 1933, p. 82; 1934, p. 81; 1939, p. 235. Kidder and Thompson, 1938, p. 494; Morley, 1943—in the first nine pages, the "rise and fall" motif is memtioned four times.

[78] "If the archaeologist, however, is forced, or forces himself, to digest and publish his results, the specimen-complex still vitiates his work, for he chooses for description and particularly for illustration his handsomest articles (which like as not are far from representative) or his unique finds (which may very well be the handiwork of the village idiot) and leaves utterly out of account the common, everyday, typical tools and vessels which, properly classified and compared with similar objects from other areas or other chronological horizons, alone can supply him with data as to the cultural relationships and cultural changes which should be the real objective of his excavations. He still acts as a connoisseur rather than a student of prehistory." (Kidder, 1932a, pp. 7-8)

Compare also: "One must recognize that the manifestations of the Maya hierarchal religion—glyphs, stone temples, stone sculpture, and, probably, ball courts—are due to extraneous influences, and it is the underlying local cultures which must be compared." (Thompson, 1939a, p. 6)

[79] "The program of the Section [of Aboriginal American History] therefore falls naturally into two parts, the one concerning itself with events and social conditions, the other with the ecology of the area in which those events took place and those conditions arose. The ultimate

aim of the research is to paint, in the light of these two categories of information, a true historical picture." (Kidder, 1934, p. 81)

A study of Carnegie publications fails to uncover any account of the "social conditions" mentioned in the above statement. Events remain the only results.

[80] Compare Kidder's "history" of Pecos pueblo (1932a, pp. 1-4) with Thompson's "surveys."

[81] "The investigations have added to our understanding of the intellectual achievements of the Maya in mathematics and astronomy, have served to point out strategic areas for intensive excavation and, most important of all, have aided in establishing upon the sure foundation of a dated chronology, the sequence of the principal categories of Maya remains. But proper utilization of these data, in other words their interpretation in terms of history, can be made only in the light of accurate information as to the biological nature of the population concerned and as to the environment in which they lived. These factors form respectively the raw material of and the setting for the course of historical events, and without understanding of them it is impossible to reach valid historical conclusions." (Kidder, 1930b, p. 145)

"Most recently, the Institution has sponsored a survey of the entire range of Maya history, a study supplemented by research upon the varied environmental factors which throughout the centuries have influenced the career of the Maya and their Spanish conquerors. This investigation throws light upon events in the pre-Columbian New World. It has even wider bearings upon general anthropological theory." (Kidder, 1940b, p. 262)

[82] "Their work upon the glyphs . . . . has served to define the main currents of Maya history and to place in their relative order the principal groups of cities." (Kidder, 1930a, p. 101)

". . . . ceramic documents, so precious for the reconstruction of Maya history." (Kidder, 1935b, p. 123)

The implications that "Maya history" means "Maya chronology" are very apparent in these statements; it certainly cannot mean "historiography" in the sense of a full cultural context.

[83] See also: Kidder, 1933, pp. 82-83; 1940a, p. 535.

[84] "Southwestern archaeology has long occupied a prominent place in North American anthropological researches." (Roberts, 1935, p. 507)

"Of greatest interest to the anthropologist, the student of man, are the people who live here now . . . . those people who were found here by the Conquistadores . . . . and those people whose customs and industries are known least of all because of their great age and the lack of written accounts concerning them." (Haury, 1936a, p. 15)

[85] The practice of quantifying and identifying the source material of rare objects and the types having few examples is found throughout his reports, e.g., 1929b, Shell Ornaments, p. 142; 1930, Pipes, p. 153; 1932, Bone Fleshing-tools, p. 137; 1940, Bone Rings, p. 116.

[86] A similar case is that of the cupboard at the Village of the Great Kivas (1932, p. 31); "several bone and stone implements" were found in it, but Roberts says nothing as to their nature. He merely makes a comparison to a corner doorway at Chaco and suggests that such cupboards must have been derived from such features.

[87] An indication of what he did intend may be had from the following quotations: "The bulk of the pottery described in the following pages came from pit house and jacal sites. Only a small collection was obtained from the pueblo. The latter is sufficient, however, to show the distinct difference between the two groups." (1931, p. 119)

"It [the building of dooryard terraces] does not seem to have been peculiar to any one group or horizon and has no period or cultural significance." (1932, p. 41)

[88] "In several cases these [superimposed graves] had statigraphic significance from the standpoint of the sequence of types of artifacts and the information thus obtained checked with that from the tests made in the mounds and from the pillars in the house pits." (1940, p. 135)

[89] For other examples, *see:* Webb and Funkhouser, 1929a, pp. 706ff.; Webb, 1938, pp. 72-74; Webb, 1941, pp. 253ff. For detailed sequences of events, *see:* Webb and Elliott, 1942, pp. 488-491; Webb, 1943a, pp. 515-518.

[90] In the Pickwick Basin report (Webb and De Jarnette, 1942) we have the following: Reference to waterfowl, which are migratory and therefore seasonal and whose presence in certain young or adult forms might indicate season (p. 308); references to turtles and ground hogs which hibernate (pp. 146, 308); references to deer and other animals which, if found in a young or immature state, would indicate season (pp. 146, 308); references to floods, low and high water periods, which might be correlated with known seasonal fluctuations of the river (pp. 101, 353, 380); reference to embryonic mollusks (p. 369); references which postulate discontinuous occupation to account for reversals of usual stratigraphy (p. 310) and relative scarcity of certain food mollusks (p. 380); reference which states the intermittent character of the occupation without going into the above lines of possibly supporting evidence (p. 383).

The following series of quotations presents a problem with regard to an apparent absence of physical stratigraphy in the Wheeler Basin sites coupled with several unrelated ceramic traditions. The postulation of a seasonal and exclusive occupation of these sites by varying and alternating groups of people might be found to fit other data and give a lead for further study. The condition of the published evidence, however, prevents pursuing this hypothesis. "There was little data presented which suggested the possibility of stratigraphy at the sites. . . ." (Griffin, 1939, p. 127)

"As the pottery was examined it became more and more evident that there were a number of distinct ceramic traditions belonging to several culturally unrelated horizons. It is recognized that a laboratory student is in no position to arbitrarily assign cultural levels to sites which seem to yield little data showing that such levels were present. For example, if the women who made the shell-tempered pottery at Site Lu° 86 lived there at the same time as those who made the sand and fiber tempered pottery one would expect to find some evidence of that cultural contact in the sherds. There is no such evidence." (*Ibid*, p. 128)

"These four wares [from Wheeler Basin] are distinct and do not show cultural intermixture. Their distribution, cultural associations, and chronological positions are not the same." (*Ibid.*, p. 165)

[91] "In the light of the many recent excavations and from intensive laboratory analysis of the artifact material, it has become increasingly evident to most archaeologists that a generic trait list of the type used in this report for comparison with other sites is hardly adequate for an accurate synthesis of the aboriginal group under study. For a comprehensive report on archaeological findings it seems that the minutiae, which might appear to be insignificant and boring, after all, should necessarily be considered. This is equally true for even the beginnings of a reconstruction of the habits, customs, daily life, and possible appearance of the peoples responsible for the remains. Hence, it is hoped that the *descriptive trait list* that follows will prove of more assistance to other workers than a more generalized list." (Webb and Funkhouser, 1940, p. 225, italics mine)

"While considerable additional evidence on skeletal remains was secured, so few artifact [*sic*] were obtained that a listing of traits is of *no special significance.*

"The traits occurring at this site will be integrated in the final Adena trait list to be prepared on Adena in Kentucky" (Webb, 1943b, p. 604, italics mine). And this is in the face of a statement that "Adena potsherds and other broken artifact [*sic*] show that the debris of a thin and perhaps small village midden was scraped up and used to build this mound. . . ." (p. 604)

[92] "Since archaeology is a historical discipline which aims to reconstruct the past. . . ." (1943, p. 11)

"A set of arbitrary terms is offered [by the "McKern" classification] which implies a certain connection between archaeological units and provides an essential organization of the data to be utilized in the eventual reconstruction of the life and historic development of the peoples who inhabited the area." (1943, pp. 336-337)

"The primary historical method to be employed in a reconstruction of the past life of an ethnological unit is that of archaeology." (1944b, p. 359)

[93] In his *Additional Hopewell Material from Illinois* (1941), for example, he has listed the zoological identifications of shells but has failed to indicate their sources, whether local or foreign, from what coast or waterway (p. 185-186); perforated animal teeth are noted but no identifications are made, the rubric of "perforated teeth" seeming to satisfy Griffin's needs (pp. 186, 206). In describing a figurine, he says: "A loin cloth, similar to that on one of the Turner figurines, is the only piece of covering on the body" (p. 210); which Turner figurine, what sort of a loin cloth seems not to interest him.

No analysis is made of Barker's extensive zoological materials from sites along the Illinois River. (Griffin and others, 1941)

"Bone beads were always present in the graves containing artifacts, and they were common in the village site. Some have incised lines forming various patterns" (1943, p. 43). Nothing is mentioned as to the nature of these designs, so that no correlation, if any actually exists, can be worked out between design, grave type, other grave goods, sex of interment, location in site, etc.

In one of his publications (1937c, p. 54) Griffin says: "I tried to separate things which I thought would be significant. For example, the use of bone awls is a trait which could be broken up into subdivisions such as turkey metatarsal awls. Then I also included notched turkey metatarsal awls because at all five sites a certain percentage of awls made from that bone were notched. These became determinants of equal value for the Fort Ancient culture, but in a larger cultural division we may find them relatively unimportant." That these notched awls might have had an association which would indicate their cultural significance, or which might make their value for comparative purposes even greater, seems not to have concerned Griffin. Apparently he has not himself analyzed their provenience and association to arrive at conclusions, either positive or negative, upon this point. It is enough for him that notched awls can be compared with notched awls. In his "exhaustive and comprehensive" work on the Fort Ancient Aspect, he continues to regard notched awls as purely comparative features and evidently has made no attempt to look for the possible cultural significance of this specialized artifact.

[94] "Though it is true that both the Iroquois and the Fort Ancient people utilized many bone tools having shapes in common, there also are distinct differences in the shapes, so that if the bone-implement assemblage from sites of the two cultures were laid side by side it would be possible to distinguish between them. For example, one of the common tools of the Fort Ancient Aspect is the bone beamer, or drawshave, which is decidely rare in Iroquoian sites. . . . . On the other hand, bone harpoons are representative of Iroquoian sites, particularly those in the eastern division, whereas they are very rare at Fort Ancient sites, appearing only at

Madisonville, where they are not the same as the Iroquoian type" (1943, pp. 231-232). How can the significance of this difference be understood, or even compared, without investigating whether the environment might have had a limiting effect upon harpoons in the country of the Fort Ancient sites, or whether as a whole the Iroquois remains point to a stronger fishing complex, or whether other evidence indicates a strong wood-working complex in Fort Ancient sites, etc., etc. Merely to compare one artifact type with another on a descriptive level is to lose or obscure much of the evidence.

[95] "Comparison between components and cultural divisions should be made on the basis of the total traits as represented in the respective lists of the components and divisions, and it actually matters little how these traits are arranged." (1943, p. 335)

[96] Ritchie has also noted this when he said: "What, for instance, is the 'hair-spreader,' often referred to as a characteristic of the Fort Ancient Aspect, but nowhere, so far as I can tell, either described or illustrated?" (1945b, p. 400)

[97] "Such a method of cultural comparison [trait lists and percentages of trait concurrence between sites] will enable American archaeology to divorce itself from subjective general statements such as 'high and low cultures,' and substitute an objective, detailed, trait for trait comparison." (1935, p. 5)

"This analysis [discussion of traits on his trait lists and their comparables in other classificatory units] represents what might be called the more objective statement of the characteristics of the cultural content of the Baum Focus and its interrelationships with other groups." (1943, p. 69)

". . . . and after having prepared this report in what I choose to term an objective manner. . . ." (1943, p. 303)

"A trait list offers a recounting in a fairly objective form of the material remains of the inhabitants of the site excavated." (1943, p. 340)

[98] For example, in Griffin's paper, *An Analysis of the Fort Ancient Culture* (1935), he designates two types of plain bone beads, one type short and the other long. However, neither bone tubes nor bone or antler pendants are subdivided; their dimensions are neither recorded nor classified. Since there are no reasons given for this differential treatment, Griffin can hardly claim that the method is objective. Somehow judgments have been made, and, what is more, they have been made without giving the bases upon which they rest. Griffin, however, does give some explanation: "In selecting the traits [for the trait lists] a good deal of the reliability of the traits an individual selects depends upon his archaeological experience. From the literature and after visiting the Ohio State Museum, I tried to separate things which I thought would be significant" (1937c, p. 54). This is an explanation, but it hardly indicates the objectivity claimed for the trait lists.

"When foci are combined into the more generalized unit called an aspect a personal [Griffin evidently shies away from using the word *subjective*] conception of the important features is introduced and individual elements are selected and recombined in a pattern which, in a sense, never actually existed." (1943, p. 205)

[99] "The time and effort expended in trying to determine the elements held in common throughout the Woodland pattern (which is a valuable abstraction but not an historical entity). . . ." (1945b, p. 407)

[100] *An Analysis of the Fort Ancient Culture* (1935). "The one serious difficulty encountered in attempting to identify the Fort Ancient culture with the. . . . In other words, cultural forces influenced the Fort Ancient peoples from all directions, so in seeking to identify them, I should look for a people, tribe or tribes, who were in a sense marginal to both the southern and northern areas" (1937b, p. 276). Here he is looking for a tribe, or tribes, which possessed a pattern of culture that "never actually existed."

"It is the purpose of this paper to present some of these data in the belief that it will aid in the understanding of the possible place of the Adena culture in Ohio Valley prehistory." (1942, p. 345)

The phrase "Fort Ancient culture" is used in many places in *The Fort Ancient Aspect* (1943), e.g., pp. 5, 193, 195, 197.

[101] In *The Archaeological Remains of the Chiwere Sioux* (1937a), he makes the effort to correlate a taxonomic unit, the Oneota Aspect, with a group of tribes linguistically connected, the Chiwere Sioux. He finds a "high probability of correlation."

In *An Interpretation of Siouan Archaeology in the Piedmont of North Carolina and Virginia* (1945a), he uses the term "Fort Ancient culture" several times in his attempt to indicate the cultural position of remains attributed to the eastern Siouan tribes relative to such "prehistoric cultures." (p. 329)

[102] "The close cultural connection between the Baum site and the Gartner site was recognized by Mills and other students of Ohio archaeology and is graphically presented in Tables VII-XIV, listing the non-pottery traits. The two sites together have a total of 123 different traits of which they have ninety-eight, almost 80 percent, in common." (1943, p. 65)

[103] "Our inability to connect the prehistoric with the historic is a stumbling block to a sound reconstruction of aboriginal culture history in the State." (Griffin and others, 1941, p. 49)

[104] "There are at least two valid approaches to a clearer understanding of the prehistory of the area under discussion. The first is a classification of cultures on the basis of their determinant traits. . . . The second approach is to determine the ethnological relationship of the archaeological cultures." (1937c, p. 48)

"Included in this monograph is a series of chapters in which the place of the Fort Ancient Aspect in its cultural setting is discussed. In the chapter entitled 'Speculations' are set forth several interpretations concerning cultural affiliations. . . . Another chapter gives consideration to the possible historic connection between the Fort Ancient Aspect and known linguistic or tribal groups. Other chapters are devoted to comparisons with other cultural units and areas and include a short statement upon the probable chronological position of the Fort Ancient Aspect." (1943, p. 6)

The series of chapters on the "cultural setting" I take to be the chapters describing the various sites or components, the summaries of which are purely comparative and do not synthesize any of the cultural data into a context. Thus it is seen that the stated result of the volume is entirely comparative with an eye to the cultural and chronological position and the ethnologic connections. The chapter on "The Geographical Background" is a somewhat gratuitous inclusion which is not made use of in the succeeding pages.

CHAPTER 4

[105] Abel, 1930; Bain, 1937, 1942; Benedict, 1931; Bernard, 1925, 1930; Bidney, 1942, 1944; Bierstedt, 1938; Blumenthal, 1936, 1937a, 1937b, 1938a, 1938b, 1940; Boas, 1932; Bowdery, 1941; Case, 1927; Choukas, 1936; Denness, 1942; Dollard, 1939; Ellwood, 1944; Ford, 1939, 1942; Frank, 1940, 1943; Gillin, 1939, 1944; Goldenweiser, 1929; Harlan, 1944; Hart and Pantzer, 1925; Kluckhohn, 1941; Kluckhohn and Kelly, 1944; Linton, 1945a; Lynd, 1939, pp. 19ff.; Malinowski, 1936, 1939, 1941; Marett, no date; Merton, 1936a; Miller and Dollard, 1941, esp. p. 5; Monachesi, 1937; Murdock, 1932, 1940; MacIver, 1931; Ogburn, 1937; Roheim, 1943; Sapir, 1924, 1927; Sorokin, 1943; Stern, 1929; Sutherland and Woodward, 1940, pp. 15-21; Warden, 1936, pp. 12-13, 25, 32-34, 62, 101; White, L., 1940; Wissler, 1913, 1916; Woodward, 1936.

CHAPTER 5

[106] The following is an introductory bibliography to the subject of typology and classification based upon the works which have influenced my own treatment of this topic:

Allport, 1939; Becker, H., 1940; Bennett, J. W., 1943c; Black and Weer, 1936; Brew, 1946, pp. 32-66; Byers, 1941; Chamberlain, 1897; Cole and Deuel, 1937, pp. 207-223; Colton, 1939, pp. 5-22, 1943a; Creighton, 1913, pp. 81ff.; Croizat, 1941; Cutter, 1939; Davenport and Blankinship, 1898; Deuel, 1935; Driver and Kroeber, 1932; Fairbanks, 1938, 1941; Finkelstein, 1937; Gorodzov, 1933; Guthe, 1936; Henderson, 1935, p. 109; Hsu, n.d.; Johnson, 1937; Kluckhohn and Reiter, eds., 1939, pp. 151-162; Kluver, 1925; Krieger, 1940, 1944; Kroeber, 1940a; Lundberg, 1940; McKern, 1933, 1937, 1938, 1939, 1940, 1942, 1943, 1944; McKern, Deuel, Guthe, 1933; Mead, 1939; Osgood, 1942, pp. 22-25; Roberts, 1937; Rouse, 1939, 1944; Steward, 1941, 1942, 1944; Tallgren, 1937; Vaihinger, 1925.

[107] I wish to express my thanks to Dr. A. Wetmore, Secretary of the Smithsonian Institution and then Director of the United States National Museum, and to Mr. Frank M. Setzler, Head Curator of Anthropology of the latter Museum, for permission to use the unpublished findings of the Museum's 1940-1941 Coahuila Expedition, of which I was Director. Although final analysis may possibly modify the figures presented here, it is not expected that the relationships pertinent to this discussion will be changed.

[108] The same vewpoint is expressed when he suggests "a trial of the method developed by Kroeber and Driver for handling ethnographic data. Applied to archaeology, it would be sounder statistical procedure and would yield more reliable results" (1941, p. 367). He then refers to Kroeber's article, "Statistical Classification" (1940a).

[109] Webster's New International Dictionary (1937) gives the following definitions: *Affinal:* "Related by marriage; from the same source." *Correlative:* "Having, indicating, or involving, a reciprocal relation; of the nature of correlates; reciprocally or mutually related; conjoint. . . ." *Legatary:* "Of, pertaining to, or being, a legacy." A legacy is defined in its second meaning as "Something coming from an ancestor or predecessor. . . ."

CHAPTER 6

[110] "Nothing pertaining to the intangible aspects of life can be rescued with the help of the spade. Thus we may learn about skeletal types, about implements and utensils used, about the steps in their manufacture; but no information is forthcoming to tell us about languages, customs, beliefs." (Boas, 1938, p. 2)

"An archaeologist may recover the material but not the substance of aboriginal artifacts. The exact meaning of any particular object for the living group or individual is forever lost, and the real significance or lack of importance of any object in an ethnological sense has disappeared by the time it becomes a part of an archaeologist's catalogue of finds." (Griffin, 1943, p. 340)

"Archaeology, or course, is limited not only to consideration of the material aspects of culture, but also to those of its manifestations which have produced imperishable remains." (Kidder and Thompson, 1938, p. 495)

"Prehistory reveals only material phenomena, and only part of them. . . . In short, it determines accurately certain phases of technology and nothing else." (Lowie, 1937, p. 22)

"This insufficiency of prehistory for establishing the intellectual culture must be all the more emphasized. . . ." (Schmidt, 1939, p. 299)

". . . . since archaeological remains illustrate only the arts and crafts, the material culture of a people. . . ." (Speck, 1935, p. 7)

[111] "In other words, in 1937, Colton set up a new type on the basis of *one* sherd. Further-more, he did this one year after Haury had published a usable description of Mogollon Red-on-Brown. Now in 1941, he withdraws the type, although he has already clogged the literature with his description, which later turns out *not* to be a new type, and asks us to accept eleven more new types instead!" (Rinaldo and Martin, 1941, p. 656)

[112] The site referred to here is CM 79 at Piedras de Lumbre in central Coahuila, Mexico.

[113] I wish to thank Professor Donald Scott, Director of the Peabody Museum of Harvard University, for permission to examine and use the material in the Palmer Collection. The burial bundle in the National Museum is from Coyote Cave (CM 88 in the general Coahuila survey); it apparently is one of "2 or more mummies left with Galindo and sent to the U.S.N.M. by Ed. Palmer," U.S.N.M. accession 9462, cat. 45581. I wish to thank Dr. Wetmore and Mr. Setzler for permitting me to examine and use this material.

[114] These specimens are from the Emerson Collection at the Peabody Museum of Harvard University. I wish to thank Professor Scott for permission to examine and use this material. The sites, as they have been redesignated in the general Coahuila survey, are: CM 92 (Cave B1), CM 93 (Cave B2), CM 95 (Cave B4), CM 96 (Spring Cave), CM 97 (Cave 1), CM 98 (Cave 2).

[114a] At the Annual Meeting of the American Anthropological Association held at Albuquerque, December 28-31, 1947, Dr. Colton presented a paper containing many of the ideas included in this example. His conclusions were arrived at independently and completely unbeknown to me.

[115] *See:* Guernsey, 1931, p. 112; Roberts, 1929, p. 14; 1932, p. 16; Setzler, 1935, pp. 109-110; Smith, V. J., 1931, p. 69; 1932; 1933, pp. 63ff.; Zingg, 1939, 1940.

[116] Another and equally influential reason for conducting this particular investigation was to provide a large amount of quantitative data with which to try the applicability for archeology of the statistical maneuver known as the Poisson sampling test (Simpson and Roe, 1939, pp. 78-83). This experiment has not yet been carried out, so that conclusions are not yet available.

[117] I am indebted to Harald A. Rehder, Assistant Curator, Division of Molluscs, Department of Biology, U. S. National Museum, for identification of the shells.

[118] In many months of tramping the mountains and deserts of Coahuila, I have seen only one living specimen of *Humboldtiana*. The location was in a relatively well-watered and well-vegetated, and therefore most exceptional, canyon directly opposite the canyon of Frightful Cave. None has been found in the latter area or in any other, although search has been made.

[119] There is a very small, scrubby piñon tree within some 500 meters of Frightful Cave, but it is an isolated example and is growing against the cliff face where more moisture collects than elsewhere. The nearest growth of piñon is at the top of the mountain, very much higher and at least three miles away by tortuous foot travel.

[120] I wish to thank Dr. D. D. Brand, Chairman of the Department of Anthropology, University of New Mexico, for permission to use these data which were gathered at the University's Field Session at Chaco Canyon in 1939. Mr. F. M. Setzler was Archeologist in Charge, and I was Assistant Archeologist with immediate supervision of the excavations whose results are described here. This account will have to do only with the details of room construction.

[121] The figures of Table 6 are taken from the following sources: Bryan, 1931; Cosgrove and Cosgrove, 1932; Fewkes, 1915, 1916, 1923, 1924.

BIBLIOGRAPHY

ABEL, T.
   1930   Is a Cultural Sociology Possible? *American Journal of Sociology*, Vol. XXXV, pp. 739-752.

ADAIR, JAMES
   1775   *History of the American Indians*. S. C. Williams, ed., Johnson City, Tennessee, 1930.

AGASSIZ, LOUIS
   1840   *Etudes sur les Glaciers*. Neuchatel.

ALLPORT, F. H.
   1939   Rule and Custom as Individual Variations of Behavior Distributed upon a Continuum of Conformity. *American Journal of Sociology*, Vol. XLIV, pp. 897-921.

AMERICAN ANTIQUARIAN SOCIETY
   1820   Archaeologia Americana. *Transactions and Collections*, Vol. I.

AMERICAN HISTORICAL ASSOCIATION
   1945   Guide to the American Historical Review. *Annual Report of 1944*, Vol. I, Pt. 1.

AMSDEN, CHARLES
   1930   What is Clockwise? *American Anthropologist*, n.s., Vol. XXXII, pp. 579-580.

ANDREWS, E. W.
   1943   The Archaeology of Southwestern Campeche. *Contributions to American Anthropology and History*, Vol. VIII, pp. 1-100. Carnegie Institution of Washington.

ANONYMOUS
   1718–1747   *Vetvsta Monvmenta: quae ad rerum brittanicarum memoriam conservandam antiqvariorum Londini svmptu svo edenda cvravit*. London.

ANONYMOUS
   1800   *A Copy of the Royal Charter and Statutes of the Society of Antiquaries of London; and of Orders and Regulations Established by the Council of the Society*. London.

ANONYMOUS
   1899   Obituary notice of D. G. Brinton. *American Anthropologist*, n.s., Vol. I, p. 764.

ARCHAEOLOGICAL INSTITUTE OF AMERICA
   1880   *First Annual Report of the Executive Committee*.
   1881–1890   *Papers*, American Series, Vols. I-V.
   1882–1890   *Papers*, Classical Series, Vols. I-III.
   1885   *Journal of American Archaeology and of the History of the Fine Arts*, Vol. I.

ARNOLD, THOMAS
   1842   *Lectures on Modern History*. Oxford.

ATWATER, CALEB

    1820 Description of the Antiquities Discovered in the State of Ohio and Other Western States. *Transactions and Collections,* Vol. I. American Antiquarian Society.

BAIN, READ

    1937 Technology and State Government. *American Sociological Review,* Vol. II, pp. 860-874.

    1942 A Definition of Culture. *Sociology and Social Research,* Vol. XXVII, pp. 87-94.

BARNES, H. E.

    1924 Some Contributions of Anthropology to History. *Journal of Social Forces,* Vol. II, pp. 362-373.

    1925 *The New History and the Social Studies.* New York.

    1936 History—Its Rise and Development. *Encyclopedia Americana,* Vol. XIV, pp. 205-264.

BARTON, B. S.

    1797 *New Views of the Origin of the Tribes and Nations of America.* Philadelphia.

BEALS, R. L., G. W. BRAINERD, and W. SMITH

    1945 *Archaeological Studies in Northeast Arizona.* University of California Press, Berkeley.

BEARD, C. A.

    1934 Written History as an Act of Faith. *American Historical Review,* Vol. XXXIX, pp. 219-229.

    1935 That Noble Dream. *Ibid.,* Vol. XLI, pp. 74-87.

BEARD, C. A., and A. VAGTS

    1937 Currents of Thought in Historiography. *Ibid.,* Vol. XLII, pp. 460-483.

BECKER, CARL

    1932 Everyman His Own Historian. *Ibid.,* Vol. XXXVII, pp. 221-236.

    1938 What is Historiography? *Ibid.,* Vol. XLIV, pp. 20-28.

BECKER, HOWARD

    1940 Constructive Typology in the Social Sciences. *American Sociological Review,* Vol. V, pp. 40-55.

BECKWITH, E. G.

    1855 Report of Explorations for a Route for the Pacific Railway on the Line of the 41st Parallel. *Survey for Railroad from the Missouri to the Pacific,* Vol. II. Washington.

BEERS, H. A.

    1901 *A History of English Romanticism in the Nineteenth Century.* New York.

BELTZ, R.

    1927 Nordischer Kreis. In: *Reallexikon der Vorgeschichte,* Max Ebert, ed., Vol. IX. Berlin.

BENEDICT, RUTH

    1931 The Science of Custom. In: *The Making of Man,* V. F. Calverton, ed. New York.

    1934 *Patterns of Culture.* New York.

BENNETT, J. W.

1943a A History of the Mississippi Cultures. *The Wisconsin Archeologist,* n.s. Vol. XXIV, pp. 33-42.

1943b Recent Developments in the Functional Interpretation of Archaeological Data. *American Antiquity,* Vol. IX, pp. 208-219.

1943c Some Comments on Colton's "Principle of Analogous Types." *American Anthropologist,* n.s. Vol. XLV, pp. 637-641.

1944a The Interaction of Culture and Environment in the Smaller Societies. *Ibid.,* Vol. XLVI, pp. 461-478.

1944b Middle American Influences on Cultures of the Southeastern United States. *Acta Americana,* Vol. II, pp. 25-50.

BENNETT, W. C.

1945 Interpretations of Andean Archeology. *Transactions,* Ser. II, Vol. VII, pp. 95-99. New York Academy of Sciences.

BERNARD, L. L.

1925 A Classification of Environments. *American Journal of Sociology,* Vol. XXXI, pp. 318-332.

1930 Culture and Environment. *Journal of Social Forces,* Vol. VIII, pp. 327-334.

BERNHEIM, ERNST

1903 *Lehrbuch der Historischen Methode und der Geschichtsphilosophie,* 3rd and 4th eds. Leipzig.

BERR, HENRI

1911 *La Synthèse en Histoire, Essai Critique et Théorique.* Paris.

BERR, HENRI, and L. FEBVRE

1937 History. *Encyclopedia of the Social Sciences,* Vol. VI, pp. 357-368.

BIDNEY, DAVID

1942 On the Philosophy of Culture in the Social Sciences. *Journal of Philosophy,* Vol. XXXIX, pp. 449-457.

1944 On the Concept of Culture and Some Cultural Fallacies. *American Anthropologist,* n.s., Vol. XLVI, pp. 30-44.

BIERSTEDT, ROBERT

1938 The Meaning of Culture. *Philosophy of Science,* Vol. V, pp. 204-216.

BLACK, G. A., and P. WEER

1936 A Proposed Terminology for Shape Classification of Artifacts. *American Antiquity,* Vol. I, pp. 280-294.

BLOM, FRANS

1935 Maya Calculation and Construction. *The Military Engineer,* January-February, pp. 1-6.

BLUMENTHAL, ALBERT

1936 The Nature of Culture. *American Sociological Review,* Vol. I, pp. 875-893.

1937a *The Best Definition of Culture.* Marietta College Press, Marietta, Ohio.

1937b *Culture Consists of Ideas. Ibid.*

1938a *The Importance of the Most Useful Definition of the Term "Culture." Ibid.*

1938b *The Relations between Culture, Human Social Interaction, Personality and History. Ibid.*

1940 A New Definition of Culture. *American Anthropologist*, n.s., Vol. XLII, pp. 571-586.

BOAS, FRANZ

1896 The Limitations of the Comparative Method of Anthropology. In: *Race, Language, and Culture*, pp. 270-280. New York, 1940.

1904 The History of Anthropology. *Science*, Vol. XX, pp. 513-524.

1932 The Aims of Anthropological Research. *Ibid.*, Vol. LXXVI, pp. 605-613.

1934 Introduction. In: *Patterns of Culture*, by Ruth Benedict, pp. xi-xiii. New York.

1936 History and Science in Anthropology: a Reply. *American Anthropologist*, Vol. XXXVIII, pp. 137-141.

1938 Introduction. In: *General Anthropology*, Franz Boas, ed. New York.

BORLASE, WILLIAM

1764 *Antiquities, historical and monumental, of the County of Cornwall*, 2nd ed. London.

BOUCHER DE PERTHES, J.

1847–1857 *Antiquités Celtiques et Antédiluviennes*, 2 vols. Paris.

1863–1866 *Sous Dix Rois, Souvenirs de 1791 à 1860*, 7 vols. Paris.

1908 Inauguration de la Statue de Boucher de Perthes. *Bulletins* No. 3 and No. 4, Societé d'Emulation d'Abbeville.

BOULE, MARCELLIN

1921 *Les Hommes Fossiles*. Paris.

BOWDERY, G. J.

1941 Conventions and Norms. *Philosophy of Science*, Vol. VIII, pp. 493-505.

BOYD, J. P.

1934 State and Local Historical Societies in the United States. *American Historical Review*, Vol. XL, pp. 10-37.

BOYS, W.

1792 *Collection for an History of Sandwich in Kent*. Canterbury.

BRADFORD, A. W.

1843 *American Antiquities, and Researches into the Origin and History of the Red Race*. New York.

BRAINERD, G. W.

1940 Study of Yucatan Pottery. *Yearbook*, No. 39, pp. 270-274. Carnegie Institution of Washington.

BRAND, D. D.

1937 The Status of Anthropology in the Western United States. *The New Mexico Anthropologist*, Vol. II, pp. 4-16.

BREW, J. O.

1946 Archaeology of Alkali Ridge, Southeastern Utah. *Papers*, Vol. XXI. Peabody Museum of American Archaeology and Ethnology.

BRINTON, CRANE

1938 *The Anatomy of Revolution*. New York.

BRINTON, D. G.

1866a The Mound-builders of the Mississippi Valley. *The Historical Magazine*, Vol. X, pp. 33-37.

1866b The Shawnees and Their Migrations. *Ibid.*, Vol. X, pp. 1-4.

1892 The Nomenclature and Teaching of Anthropology. *American Anthropologist*, o.s., Vol. V, pp. 263-266.

1895 The Aims of Anthropology. *Science*, n.s., Vol. II, pp. 241-252.

1896a The Aims of Anthropology. *Proceedings*, Vol. XLIV, pp. 1-17. American Association for the Advancement of Science.

1896b *An Ethnologist's View of History.* Philadelphia.

BRITTON, JOHN

1836 *Cathedral Antiquities, historical and descriptive.* London.

BROWN, L. G.

1944 Anthropology and Sociology. *Journal of Social Forces*, Vol. XXIII, pp. 153-155.

BRYAN, B.

1931 Excavation of the Galaz Ruin. *Masterkey*, Vol. IV, pp. 179-189; Vols. VI and VII, pp. 221-226.

BUCKLE, H. T.

1876 *History of Civilization in England*, 2 vols., ed., 1920. New York.

BURCKHARDT, JACOB

1860 *The Civilization of the Renaissance in Italy.* Trans. by S. G. C. Middlemore, 2 vols., 1878. London.

BUREAU OF AMERICAN ETHNOLOGY

1907 Handbook of American Indians. *Bulletin* 30, 2 vols. Washington.

BURTON, H.

1938 A Survey of Japanese Historiography. *American Historical Review*, Vol. XLIII, pp. 489-499.

BURY, J. B.

1903 The Science of History. In: *Selected Essays*, H. Temperley, ed., 1930. Cambridge.

1906 The Place of Modern History in the Perspective of Knowledge. *Ibid.*

1909 Darwinism and History. *Ibid.*

BUTLER, MARY

1931 Dress and Decoration of the Maya Old Empire. *The Museum Journal*, Vol. XXII, pp. 155-183. University of Pennsylvania.

BYERS, D. S.

1941 The Taxonomic Approach Redefined. *Bulletin*, Vol. II, pp. 21-25. Massachusetts Archaeological Society.

CAIRD, JOHN

1899 *University Addresses.* Glasgow.

CAMBRIDGE ANCIENT HISTORY

1923-1939 Preface to Volume I. Cambridge.

CAMBRIDGE UNIVERSITY

1937 *The Students Handbook to the University and Colleges of Cambridge.* Cambridge.

CARTAILHAC, EMILE

1877 *L'Age de Pierre dans les Souvenirs et Superstitions Populaires.* Paris.

CASE, C. M.
  1927 Culture as a Distinctive Human Trait. *American Journal of Sociology,* Vol. XXXII, pp. 906-920.

CHAMBERLAIN, A. F.
  1907 Thomas Jefferson's Ethnological Opinions and Activities. *American Anthropologist,* n.s., Vol. IX, pp. 499-509.

CHAMBERLAIN, L. J., and E. A. HOEBEL
  1942 Anthropology Offerings in American Undergraduate Colleges. *Ibid.,* Vol. XLIV, pp. 527-530.

CHAMBERLIN, T. C.
  1897 Multiple Working Hypotheses. *Journal of Geology,* Vol. V, pp. 837-848.

CHENEY, E. P.
  1924 Law in History. *American Historical Review,* Vol. XXIX, pp. 231-248.

CHILDE, V. G.
  1937 A Prehistorian's Interpretation of Diffusion. In: *Independence, Convergence, and Borrowing in Institutions, Thought, and Art,* pp. 3-21. Harvard University Press, Cambridge.
  1939 *The Dawn of European Civilization,* 2nd ed. New York.

CHOUKAS, M.
  1936 The Concept of Cultural Lag Re-examined. *American Sociological Review,* Vol. I, pp. 752-760.

CLARK, GRAHAME
  1939 *Archaeology and Society.* London.
  1940 *Prehistoric Egland.* London.

CLARK, KENNETH
  1928 *The Gothic Revival.* London.

COCHET, ABBÉ
  1855 *La Normandie Souterraine.* Paris.

COHEN, M. R.
  1931 *Reason and Nature.* New York.

COHEN, M. R., and ERNEST NAGEL
  1934 *An Introduction to Logic and Scientific Method.* New York.

COLE, F. C., and T. DEUEL
  1937 *Rediscovering Illinois.* University of Chicago Press.

COLLIER, D., and G. I. QUIMBY, JR.
  1945 Review of *The Fort Ancient Aspect,* by J. B. Griffin. *American Anthropologist,* n.s., Vol. XLVII, pp. 142-146.

COLLINGWOOD, R. G., A. E. TAYLOR, and F. C. S. SCHILLER
  1922 Are History and Science Different Kinds of Knowledge? *Mind,* Vol. XXXI, pp. 442-466.

COLTON, H. S.
  1939 Prehistoric Culture Units and Their Relationships in Northern Arizona. *Bulletin* 17, Museum of Northern Arizona.
  1942 Archaeology and the Reconstruction of History. *American Antiquity,* Vol. VIII, pp. 33-40.

1943a The Principle of Analogous Pottery Types. *American Anthropologist,* n.s., Vol. XLV, pp. 316-320.

1943b Reconstruction of Anasazi History. *Proceedings,* Vol. LXXXVI, pp. 264-269. American Philosophical Society.

COLTON, H. S., and L. L. HARGRAVE

1937 Handbook of Northern Arizona Pottery Wares. *Bulletin* 11, Museum of Northern Arizona.

COLUMBIA UNIVERSITY

1940 *Bulletin of Information,* 40th Series, Nos. 26 and 34.

COSGROVE, H. S., and C. B. COSGROVE

1932 The Swarts Ruin, a Typical Mimbres Site in Southwestern New Mexico. *Papers,* Vol. XV. Peabody Museum of American Archaeology and Ethnology.

COULBORN, RUSHTON

1941 An Historian's Consolation in Philosophy. *Southern Review,* Vol. VII, pp. 40ff.

1944 The Meaning of History. *Ethics,* Vol. LV, pp. 46-63.

COULBORN, R., and W. E. B. DUBOIS

1942 Mr. Sorokin's Systems. *Journal of Modern History,* Vol. XIV, pp. 500-521.

CRAMER, G. F.

1938 Determination of a Mayan Unit of Linear Measurement. *American Mathematical Monthly,* Vol. XLV, pp. 344-347.

CRAWFORD, O. G. S.

1932 The Dialectical Process in the History of Science. *The Sociological Review,* April-June, pp. 165-173.

CREIGHTON, J. E.

1913 *An Introductory Logic.* New York.

CRESSMAN, L. S.

1942 *Archaeological Researches in the Northern Great Basin.* Publication No. 538, Carnegie Institution of Washington.

CRESSON, F. M.

1938 Maya and Mexican Sweat Houses. *American Anthropologist,* n.s., Vol. XL, pp. 88-104.

CROCE, B.

1921 *Theory and History of Historiography.* Trans. by Douglas Ainslie. London.

1933 Letter to C. A. Beard and the American Historical Association. *American Historical Review,* Vol. XXXIX, pp. 229-231.

CROIZAT, LEON

1941 A Further Comment on Stability in Nomenclature. *Science,* n.s., Vol. XCIII, pp. 109-110.

CURWEN, E. C.

1937 *The Archaeology of Sussex.* London.

CUST, LIONEL, and SIDNEY COLVIN

1898 *History of the Society of Dilettanti.* New York.

CUTTER, G. F.

1939 Northeastern Classification. *American Antiquity,* Vol. IV, p. 352.

DAVENPORT, C. B., and J. W. BLANKINSHIP

   1898   A Precise Criterion of Species. *Science,* n.s., Vol. VII, pp. 685-695.

DAVIS, A., B. B. GARDNER, and M. R. GARDNER

   1941   *Deep South: A social anthropological study of caste and class.* University of Chicago Press.

DELAFIELD, JOHN, JR.

   1839   *An Inquiry into the Origins of the Antiquities of America.* New York.

DELLENBAUGH, F. S.

   1918   A Memorial to J. W. Powell. *American Anthropologist,* n.s., Vol. XX, pp. 432ff.

DENNESS, W. R.

   1942   Conceptions of Civilization: Descriptive and Normative. In: *Civilization,* Publications in Philosophy, Vol. XXIII, pp. 161-190. University of California.

DEUEL, THORNE

   1935   Basic Cultures of the Mississippi Valley. *American Anthropologist,* n.s., Vol. XXXVII, pp. 429-446.

DIESERUD, J.

   1908   *Science of Anthropology, its scope and content.* Chicago.

DOLLARD, JOHN

   1939   Culture, Society, Impulse, and Socialization. *American Journal of Sociology,* Vol. XLV, pp. 50-63.

DOUGLAS, JAMES

   1793   *Nenia Britannica: or, a Sepulchral History of Great Britain from the Earliest Period to its General Conversion to Christianity.* London.

DOW, E. W.

   1899   Features of the New History; apropos of Lamprecht's Deutsche Geschichte. *Report,* Vol. III, pp. 431-448. American Historical Association.

DRAKE, S. G.

   1832   *Biography and History of the Indians of North America.* Boston.

DRIBERG, J. H.

   1932   *At Home with the Savage.* New York.

DRIVER, H. E., and A. L. KROEBER

   1932   Quantitative Expression of Cultural Relationships. *Publications in American Archaeology and Ethnology,* Vol. XXXI, pp. 211-256. University of California.

DROYSON, J. G.

   1882   *Grundriss der Historik.* Leipzig.

DUGDALE, WILLIAM

   1655-1673   *Monasticon Anglicanum.* London.

   1656   *Antiquities of Warwickshire.* London.

ECCARD(US)

   1750   *De Origine Germanorum eorumque vetustissimis coloniis migrationibus ac rebus gestis libri duo.* Goetingae.

EGGLESTON, EDWARD

   1900   The New History. *Report,* Vol. I, pp. 35-48. American Historical Association.

ELLWOOD, C. A.
    1944   Culture and Human Society. *Journal of Social Forces,* Vol. XXIII, pp. 6-15.
EMBREE, J. F.
    1944   Community Analysis—an example of anthropology in government. *American Anthropologist,* n.s., Vol. XLVI, pp. 277-291.
EMORY, W. H.
    1848   Notes on a Military Reconnaissance, from Fort Leavenworth, in Missouri, to San Diego, in California including parts of the Arkansas, Del Norte, and Gila Rivers. Made in 1846-1847. *Senate Executive Documents,* 31st Congress, 1st Session. Washington.
ENCYCLOPEDIA BRITANNICA
    ed. 1911   New York.
ENCYCLOPEDIA OF THE SOCIAL SCIENCES
    1930-1936   War and Reorientation. Vol. I, pp. 189-228.
EVANS, JOHN
    1897a   *The Ancient Stone Implements, Weapons, and Ornaments of Great Britain.* 2nd ed. London.
    1897b   Presidential Address of the British Association for the Advancement of Science. *Science,* n.s., Vol. VI, pp. 269-283.
FAIRBANKS, C. H.
    1938   *Classification Problems of Southeastern Archaeology in Relation to Work Done in the Tennessee Valley.* (Mimeographed.)
    1941   Classification in the Southeast. *News Letter,* Vol. II, pp. 10-13. Southeastern Archaeological Conference.
    1942   The Taxonomic Position of Stalling's Island. *American Antiquity,* Vol. VII, pp. 223-231.
FAIRCHILD, H. N.
    1928   *The Noble Savage; a study in romantic naturalism.* Columbia University Press.
FELLOWS, G. E.
    1896   The Relation of Anthropology to the Study of History. *American Journal of Sociology,* Vol. I, pp. 41-49.
FEWKES, J. W.
    1914   Archaeology of the Lower Mimbres Valley, New Mexico. *Miscellaneous Collections,* Vol. LXIII, pp. 1-53. Smithsonian Institution, Washington.
    1916   Prehistoric Remains in New Mexico. *Ibid.,* Vol. LXV, pp. 62-72.
    1916   Animal Figures on Prehistoric Pottery from Mimbres Valley, New Mexico. *American Anthropologist,* n.s., Vol. XVIII, pp. 535-545.
    1923   Designs on Prehistoric Pottery from the Mimbres Valley, New Mexico. *Miscellaneous Collections,* Vol. LXXIV, pp. 1-47. Smithsonian Institution.
    1924   Additional Designs on Prehistoric Mimbres Pottery. *Ibid.,* Vol. LXXVI, pp. 1-46.
FINKELSTEIN, J. J.
    1937   A Suggested Projectile-Point Classification. *American Antiquity,* Vol. II, pp. 197-203.

FLINT, ROBERT

    1893   *Historical Philosophy in France and French Belgium and Switzerland.* London.

FORD, C. S.

    1939   Society, Culture, and the Human Organism. *Journal of General Psychology,* Vol. XX, pp. 135-179.

    1942   Culture and Human Behavior. *Scientific Monthly,* Vol. LV, pp. 546-557.

FORDE, C. D.

    1939   Human Geography, History and Sociology. *The Scottish Geographical Magazine,* Vol. LV, pp. 217-235.

FOWKE, GERARD

    1902   *Archaeological History of Ohio.* Columbus.

FOWLER, H. N., and J. R. WHEELER

    1909   *A Handbook of Greek Archaeology.* New York.

FRANK, L. K.

    1940   Science and Culture. *Scientific Monthly,* Vol. L, pp. 491-497.

    1943   Man's Multitudinous Environment. *Ibid.,* Vol. LVI, pp. 344-357.

FRAZER, J. G.

    1898   *Pausanias's Description of Greece,* 6 Vols. London.

FREEMAN, E. A.

    1886   *The Methods of Historical Study.* London.

FUNKHOUSER, W. D., and W. S. WEBB

    1929   The So-called "Ash Caves" in Lee County, Kentucky. *Reports in Archaeology and Anthropology,* Vol. I. No. 2. University of Kentucky.

    1937   The Chilton Site in Henry County, Kentucky. *Ibid.,* Vol. III, No. 5.

GANN, T., and J. E. THOMPSON

    1931   *The History of the Maya.* New York.

GIDDINGS, F. H.

    1922   *Studies in the Theory of Human Society.* New York.

GIFFORD, E. W., and W. E. SCHENCK

    1926   Archaeology of the Southern San Joaquin Valley, California. *Publications in American Archaeology and Ethnology.* Vol. XXIII, pp. 1-122. University of California.

GILLIN, JOHN

    1939   Some Unfinished Business in Cultural Anthropology. *Ohio Archaeological and Historical Quarterly,* Vol. XLVIII, pp. 44-52.

    1944   Cultural Adjustment. *American Anthropologist,* n.s., Vol. XLVI, pp. 429-447.

GLADWIN, H. S., E. W. HAURY, E. B. SAYLES, and N. GLADWIN

    1937   Excavations at Snaketown. *Medallion Papers,* Vol. XXV. Globe, Ariz.

GLOTZ, GUSTAVE

    1925   *The Aegean Civilization.* London.

GOGUET, A. Y.

    1758   *Les Origines des Lois, des Arts et des Sciences, et de leurs Progres chez les Anciens Peuples.* 3 vols. Paris.

GOLDENWEISER, A. A.

  1918   History, Psychology and Culture. *Journal of Philosophy, Psychology, and the Scientific Method*, Vol. XV, pp. 561-571; 589-607.

  1933a   Cultural Anthropology. In: *History, Psychology, and Culture*, pp. 121-164. New York.

  1933b   *History, Psychology, and Culture*. New York.

GOLDSMITH, W. M.

  1945   Trepanation and the "Catlin Mark." *American Antiquity*, Vol. X, pp. 348-352.

GOOCH, G. P.

  1913   *History and Historians in the Nineteenth Century*. New York.

GORODZOV, V. A.

  1933   The Typological Method in Archaeology. *American Anthropologist*, n.s., Vol. XXXV, pp. 95-102.

GRIFFIN, J. B.

  1935   An Analysis of the Fort Ancient Culture. *Notes from the Ceramic Repository of the Eastern United States*, Vol. I. University of Michigan.

  1937a   The Archaeological Remains of the Chiwere Sioux. *American Antiquity*, Vol. II, pp. 180-181.

  1937b   The Chronological Position and Ethnological Relationships of the Fort Ancient Aspect. *American Antiquity*, Vol. II, pp. 273-276.

  1937c   A Classificatory System as a Working Base for the Study of North American Archaeology. *Indianapolis Archaeological Conference*, pp. 48-50. National Research Council, Division of Anthropology and Psychology, Committee on State Archaeological Surveys.

  1938   The Ceramic Remains from Norris Basin, Tennessee. In: "An Archaeological Survey of the Norris Basin in Eastern Tennessee," by W. S. Webb. *Bulletin* 118, pp. 253-358. Bureau of American Ethnology, Washington.

  1939   Report of the Ceramics of Wheeler Basin. In: "An Archaeological Survey of Wheeler Basin on the Tennessee River in Northern Alabama," by W. S. Webb. *Bulletin* 122, pp. 127-165. Bureau of American Ethnology.

  1941   Additional Hopewell Material from Illinois. *Prehistoric Research Series*, Vol. II, pp. 165-223. Indianapolis.

  1942   Adena Pottery. *American Antiquity*, Vol. VII, pp. 344-358.

  1943   *The Fort Ancient Aspect, its cultural and chronological position in Mississippi Valley Archaeology*. University of Michigan Press, Ann Arbor.

  1944a   The DeLuna Expedition and the "Buzzard Cult" in the Southeast. *Journal*, Vol. XXXIV, pp. 299-303. Washington Academy of Sciences.

  1944b   The Iroquois in American Prehistory. *Papers*, Vol. XXIX, pp. 357-374. Michigan Academy of Science, Arts and Letters.

  1945a   An Interpretation of Siouan Archaeology in the Piedmont of North Carolina and Virginia. *American Antiquity*, Vol. X, pp. 321-330.

  1945b   Review of *The Pre-Iroquoian Occupation of New York State*, by W. A. Ritchie. *American Antiquity*, Vol. X, pp. 401-407.

GRIFFIN, J. B., and C. W. ANGELL
    1935 An Experimental Study of the Technique of Indian Pottery Making.
    Papers, Vol. XX, pp. 1-6. Michigan Academy of Science, Arts and Letters.
GRIFFIN, J. B., and G. NEUMANN
    1942 Burial Terminology and Description. *Notebook*, Vol. II, pp. 70-79. Society
    for American Archaeology.
GRIFFIN, J. B., and others
    1941 Contributions to the Archaeology of the Illinois River Valley. *Transactions*,
    n.s., Vol. XXXII. American Philosophical Society.
GROSE, FRANCIS
    1773-1787 *The Antiquities of England and Wales.* London.
GUERNSEY, S. J.
    1931 Explorations in Northeastern Arizona. *Papers*, Vol. XII, No. 1. Peabody
    Museum of American Archaeology and Ethnology.
GUERNSEY, S. J., and A. V. KIDDER
    1921 Basket-Maker Caves of Northeastern Arizona. *Ibid.*, Vol. VIII, No. 2.
GUTHE, C. E.
    1936 Review of "Basic Cultures of the Mississippi Valley," by Thorne Deuel.
    American Antiquity, Vol. I, pp. 249-250.
    1942 Foreword to *The Fort Ancient Aspect*, by J. B. Griffin. University of
    Michigan Press, Ann Arbor.
HADDON, A. C.
    1934 *History of Anthropology.* London.
HALL, H. R.
    1915 *Aegean Archaeology.* London.
HALLOWELL, A. I.
    1935 *Handbook of Psychological Leads.* (Mimeographed.)
HAMY, E. T.
    1906 Materiaux pour servir à l'Histoire de l'Archeologie Prehistorique. *Revue
    Archeologique*, Vol. VII, pp. 239-259.
HARLAN, H. H.
    1944 The Culture of Infants. *Journal of Social Forces*, Vol. XXII, pp. 311-314.
HARRISON, W. H.
    1838 *A Discourse on the Aborigines of the Valley of the Ohio.* Cincinnati.
HART, H., and A. PANTZER
    1925 Have Subhuman Animals Culture? *American Journal of Sociology*, Vol.
    XXX, pp. 703ff.
HARVARD UNIVERSITY
    1941 *Catalogue.* Cambridge.
HAURY, E. W.
    1934 The Canyon Creek Ruin and The Cliff Dwellings of the Sierra Ancha.
    Medallion Papers, Vol. XIV. Globe, Ariz.
    1936a A Glimpse of the Prehistoric Southwest. *Indians at Work*, Vol. IV,
    pp. 15-22.

1936b   The Mogollon Culture of Southwestern New Mexico. *Medallion Papers*, Vol. XX. Globe, Ariz.

1936c   Some Southwestern Pottery Types, Series IV. *Ibid.*, Vol. XIX.

1940   Excavations in the Forestdale Valley, East-central Arizona. *Bulletin*, Vol. XI, No. 4. University of Arizona.

HAVEN, S. F.

1855   Archaeology of the United States. *Contributions to Knowledge*, Vol. VIII. Smithsonian Institution, Washington.

HAWKES, C. F. C.

1940   *The Prehistoric Foundations of Europe to the Mycenean Age.* London.

HAYDEN, F. V.

1867-1883   United States Geological and Geographical Survey of the Territories. *Annual Reports*, Vols. I-XII. United States Geological Survey.

HAYWOOD, JOHN

1823   *The Natural and Aboriginal History of Tennessee, up to the first settlement therein by the white people.* Nashville.

HEARNE, THOMAS (ed.)

1720   *A Collection of Curious Discourses, written by eminent antiquaries upon several heads in English antiquities.* London.

HEARNSHAW, F. J. C.

1931   The Science of History. In: *An Outline of Modern Knowledge*, W. Rose, ed., pp. 773-812. London.

HEIERLI, JAKOB

1901   *Urgeschichte der Schweiz.* Bern.

HENDERSON, L. J.

1935   *Pareto's General Sociology.* Harvard University Press, Cambridge, Mass.

HENSHAW, H. W.

1905   Popular Fallacies Respecting the Indians. *American Anthropologist*, n.s., Vol. VII, pp. 104-113.

HILL, W. W.

1939   Stability in Culture and Pattern. *Ibid.*, Vol. XLI, pp. 258-260.

HOARE, R. C.

1812-1821   *The Ancient History of Wiltshire.* London.

HOBBS, W. H.

1934   J. W. Powell. *Scientific Monthly*, Vol. XXXIX, pp. 519-529.

HOLMES, W. H.

1907   Archeology. In: "Handbook of American Indians." *Bulletin* 30, Bureau of American Ethnology, Washington.

1919   Handbook of Aboriginal American Antiquities. *Bulletin* 60, Bureau of American Ethnology.

HONIGSHEIM, PAUL

1942   The Philosophical Background of European Anthropology. *American Anthropologist*, n.s., Vol. XLIV, pp. 376-387.

HOUGH, WALTER

1898   Otis T. Mason. *American Anthropologist*, o.s., Vol. X, pp. 661-667.

234 BIBLIOGRAPHY

HSU, F. L-K.
    n.d. *The Meaning of "Typical" in Sociology.* National Yunan University, **Kunming.**
HUGHES, J. T.
    1848 *Doniphan's Expedition: containing an account of the conquest of New Mexico.* Cincinnati.
HUIZINGA, JOHAN
    1936 A Definition of the Concept of History. In: *Philosophy and History; Essays Presented to Ernst Cassirer.* Ed. by Raymond Klibansky and H. J. Paton. Trans. by D. R. Cousin. The Claredon Press, Oxford.
HULME, E. M.
    1942 *History and Its Neighbors.* Oxford University Press.
HUNT, WILLIAM
    1884 *Early Britain—Norman Britain.* London.
HUXLEY, T. H.
    1871 Mr. Darwin's Critics. *The Contemporary Review,* Vol. XVIII, pp. 443-476.
JAMESON, J. F.
    1891 *The History of Historical Writing in America.* Boston.
JEFFERSON, THOMAS
    1788 *Notes on the State of Virginia.* Philadelphia.
JEWITT, L.
    1877 *Half-hours among some English Antiquities.* London.
JOHNSON, FREDERICK
    1937 Problems Surrounding the Classification of Certain Culture Complexes in New England. *American Antiquity,* Vol. III, pp. 161-165.
    1944 Review of *The Pre-Iroquoian Occupations of New York State,* by W. A. Ritchie. *American Anthropologist,* n.s., Vol. XLVI, pp. 530-535.
JUDD, N. M.
    1940 Progress in the Southwest. In: "Essays in Historical Anthropology." *Miscellaneous Collections,* Vol. C, pp. 417-444. Smithsonian Institution, Washington.
KENDRICK, T. D.
    1927 *The Druids, a study in Keltic prehistory.* London.
KIDDER, A. V.
    1915 Pottery of the Pajarito Plateau and of Some Adjacent Regions in New Mexico. *Memoirs,* Vol. II, pp. 407-462. American Anthropological Association.
    1924 An Introduction to the Study of Southwestern Archaeology. *Papers,* No. 1, Southwestern Expedition. New Haven.
    1926 *The Mimbres Excavations, season of 1926.* (Typewritten.)
    1930a *Year Book,* No. 29. Carnegie Institution of Washington.
    1930b An Archeological Research and Its Ramifications. *Scientific Monthly,* Vol. XXXI, pp. 145-150.
    1930c Conference at Chichen Itza. *Science,* Vol. LXXI, pp. 391-392.
    1931a The Future of Man in the Light of the Past: the viewpoint of an archeologist. *Scientific Monthly,* Vol. XXII, pp. 289-293.

1931b *Year Book*, No. 30. Carnegie Institution of Washington.

1932a The Artifacts of Pecos. Southwestern Expedition, *Papers*, No. 6. New Haven.

1932b *Year Book*, No. 31. Carnegie Institution of Washington.

1933 *Ibid.*, No. 32.

1934 *Ibid.*, No. 33.

1935a Notes on the Ruins of San Agustin Acasaguastlan, Guatemala. *Contributions to American Archaeology*, Vol. III, pp. 105-120. Carnegie Institution of Washington.

1935b *Year Book*, No. 34. Carnegie Institution of Washington.

1936a The Archaeology of Peripheral Regions. *Southwestern Lore*, Vol. II, pp. 46-48.

1936b Introduction, and Discussion. In: "The Pottery of Pecos," Vol. II, by A. V. Kidder and A. O. Shepard. *Papers*, No. 7, Southwestern Expedition. New Haven.

1936c Speculations on New World Prehistory. In: *Essays in Anthropology, presented to A. L. Kroeber*, pp. 143-151. University of California Press.

1937a The Development of Maya Research. *Proceedings*, Pan-American Institute of Geography and History, 2nd General Assembly. Washington.

1937b Foreword. In: "Excavations at Snaketown, II," by H. S. Gladwin. *Medallion Papers*, No. 26. Globe, Ariz.

1937c A Program for Maya Research. *Hispanic American Historical Review*, Vol. XVII, pp. 160-169.

1939 Carnegie Institution of Washington, *Year Book*, No. 38.

1940a Looking Backward. *Proceedings*, Vol. LXXXIII, pp. 527-537. American Philosophical Society.

1940b *Year Book*, No. 39. Carnegie Institution of Washington.

1942 Foreword. In: "Rio Grande Glaze Paint Ware," by A. O. Shepard. *Contributions to American Anthropology and History*, Vol. VII, pp. i-iv. Carnegie Institution of Washington.

1945a Excavations at Kaminaljuyu, Guatemala. *American Antiquity*, Vol. XI, pp. 65-75.

1945b George Clapp Vaillant. *American Anthropologist*, n.s., Vol. XLVII, pp. 589-602.

KIDDER, A. V., and S. J. GUERNSEY

1919 Archaeological Explorations in Northeastern Arizona. *Bulletin* 65, Bureau of American Ethnology. Washington.

1922 Notes on the Artifacts and on Foods. In: "A Basket-Maker Cave in Kane County, Utah," by J. L. Nusbaum. *Indian Notes and Monographs*. Museum of the American Indian, Heye Foundation.

KIDDER, A. V., and A. O. SHEPARD

1944 Stucco Decorations of Early Guatemala Pottery. *Notes on Middle American Archaeology and Ethnology*, Vol. II, pp. 23-30. Carnegie Institution of Washington.

KIDDER, A. V., and J. E. THOMPSON

1938   The Correlation of Maya and Christian Chronologies. *Cooperation in Research*, pp. 493-510. Carnegie Institution of Washington.

KLUCKHOHN, CLYDE

1939   On Certain Recent Applications of Association Coefficients to Ethnological Data. *American Anthropologist*, n.s., Vol. XLI, pp. 345-377.

1940   The Conceptual Structure in Middle American Studies. In: *The Maya and Their Neighbors*. New York.

1941   Patterning as Exemplified in Navaho Culture. In: *Language, Culture, and Personality*, L. Spier, A. I. Hallowell, and S. S. Newman, eds., pp. 109-130. Menasha.

1943   Covert Culture and Administration Problems. *American Anthropologist*, n.s., Vol. XLV, pp. 213-227.

KLUCKHOHN, C., and W. H. KELLY

1944   *The Concept of Culture* (Mimeographed). Abridged version in: *The Science of Man in the World Crisis*, R. Linton, ed. Columbia University Press, New York.

KLUCKHOHN, C., and P. REITER (eds.)

1939   Preliminary Report of the 1937 Excavations, Bc50-51, Chaco Canyon, New Mexico. *Bulletin* 345, Anthropological Series, Vol. III, No. 2. University of New Mexico.

KLÜVER, H.

1925   The Problem of Type. *Journal of Philosophy*, Vol. XXII, pp. 225-234.

KOHN, A., and C. MEHLIS

1879   *Materialien zur Vorgeschichte des Menschen im Ostlichen Europa.* Jena.

KRAUS, MICHAEL

1937   *A History of American History.* New York.

KRIEGER, ALEX

1940   "The Basic Needs of American Archaeology, a Commentary." *American Anthropologist*, n.s., Vol. XLII, pp. 543-546.

1944   The Typological Concept. *American Antiquity*, Vol. IX, pp. 271-288.

KROEBER, A. L.

1915   Frederick Ward Putnam. *American Anthropologist*, n.s., Vol. XVII, pp. 712-718.

1923   *Anthropology.* New York.

1935a   History and Science in Anthropology. *American Anthropologist*, n.s., Vol. XXXV, pp. 539-569.

1935   (ed.) Walapai Ethnography. *Memoirs*, No. 42. American Anthropological Association.

1936   So-Called Social Science. *Journal of Social Philosophy*, Vol. I, pp. 317-340.

1937   Archaeology. In: *Encyclopedia of the Social Sciences*, Vol. II, pp. 163-167.

1940a   Statistical Classification. *American Antiquity*, Vol. VI, pp. 29-44.

1940b   Stimulus Diffusion. *American Anthropologist*, n.s., Vol. XLII, pp. 1-20.

1943   Review of *A Study of History*, by A. J. Toynbee. *Ibid.*, Vol. XLV, pp. 294-299.

1944   *Configurations of Culture Growth*. University of California Press, Berkeley.

1946   History and Evolution. *Southwestern Journal of Anthropology*, Vol. II, pp. 1-15.

KUBLER, GEORGE

1943   The Cycle of Life and Death in Metropolitan Aztec Sculpture. *Gazette des Beaux-Arts*, Ser. vi, xxiii, pp. 257-268.

LABARRE, WESTON

1938   The Peyote Cult. *Publications in Anthropology*, No. 19. Yale University.

LAFITAU, J. F.

1724   *Moeurs des Sauvages Ameriquains, comparées aux moeurs des primiers temps*. 2 vols. Paris.

LANGLOIS, C. V., and C. SEIGNOBOS

1898   *Introduction to the Study of History*. Trans. by G. G. Berry, 4th imp. 1932. London.

LAPHAM, J. C.

1853   The Antiquities of Wisconsin. *Contributions to Knowledge*, Vol. VII. Smithsonian Institution, Washington.

LEEDS, E. T.

1936   *Early Anglo-Saxon Art and Archaeology*. Oxford.

LEIGHTON, A. H.

1945   *The Governing of Men*. Princeton University Press.

LESSER, A.

1935   Functionalism in Social Anthropology. *American Anthropologist*, n.s., Vol. XXXVII, pp. 386-393.

1939   Research Procedure and Laws of Culture. *Philosophy of Science*, Vol. VI, pp. 345-355.

LEWIS, T. M. N.

1943   Late Horizons in the Southeast. In: "Recent Advances in American Archaeology." *Proceedings*, Vol. LXXXVI, pp. 304-312. American Philosophical Society.

LEWIS, T. M. N., and M. KNEBERG

1946   *Hiwassee Island*. University of Tennessee Press, Knoxville.

LINTON, RALPH

1936a   Errors in Anthropology. In: *The Story of Human Error*, by J. Jastrow, pp. 292-321. New York.

1936b   *The Study of Man*. New York.

1938   Culture, Society and the Individual. *Journal of Abnormal and Social Psychology*, Vol. XXXIII, pp. 425-436.

1945a   *The Cultural Background of Personality*. New York.

1945b   *The Science of Man in the World Crisis*. R. Linton, ed. Columbia University Press, New York.

1945c   The Scope and Aims of Anthropology. In: *The Science of Man in the World Crisis*. R. Linton, ed. New York.

1945d   Foreword to *The Psychological Frontiers of Society*, by Abram Kardiner, pp. v-xiii. Columbia University Press.

LOUD, L. L., and M. R. HARRINGTON
    1929 Lovelock Cave. *Publications in American Archaeology and Ethnology*, Vol.
          XXV, No. 1. University of California.
LOWELL, J. R.
    1870 *Among My Books.* Elmwood Edition, 1904. Cambridge.
LOWIE, R. L.
    1917 *Culture and Ethnology.* New York.
    1936a Cultural Anthropology: a science. *American Journal of Sociology*, Vol.
           XLII, pp. 301-320.
    1936b Professional Appreciation. In: *Essays in Anthropology presented to A. L.
           Kroeber*, pp. xix-xxiii. University of California Press, Berkeley.
    1937 *The History of Ethnological Theory.* New York.
LUNDBERG, G. A.
    1940 Some Problems of Group Classification and Measurement. *American
          Sociological Review*, Vol. V, pp. 351-360.
LYELL, CHARLES
    1830-1833 *Principles of Geology.* 3 vols. London.
    1863 *The Geological Evidence of the Antiquity of Man, with remarks on
          theories of the origin of species by variation.* Philadelphia.
LYND, R. S.
    1939 *Knowledge for What?* Princeton University Press.
LYND, R. S., and H. M. LYND
    1929 *Middletown.* New York.
    1937 *Middletown in Transition.* New York.
MacCURDY, G. G.
    1899 Extent of Instruction in Anthropology in Europe and the United States.
          Science, n.s., Vol. X, pp. 910-917.
    1902 Teaching of Anthropology in the United States. *Ibid.*, Vol. XV, pp. 211-216.
    1924 *Human Origins.* New York.
MacIVER, R. M.
    1931 Is Sociology a Natural Science? *Publications*, Vol. XXV, pp. 25-35. Ameri-
          can Sociological Society.
MAJEWSKI, E. DE
    1908 *La Science de la Civilisation.* Paris.
MALINOWSKI, B.
    1931 Culture. In: *Encyclopedia of the Social Sciences*, Vol. IV, pp. 620-645.
    1934 Introduction. In: *Law and Order in Polynesia*, by H. I. Hogbin. New York.
    1936 Culture as a Determinant of Behavior. *Scientific Monthly*, Vol. XLIII,
          pp. 440-449.
    1939 Review of six essays on culture by Albert Blumenthal (see above).
          American Sociological Review, Vol. IV, pp. 588-592.
    1941 Man's Culture and Man's Behavior. *Sigma Xi Quarterly*, Vol. XXIX, Nos. 3
          and 4, pp. 182-196.
    1944 *A Scientific Theory of Culture and Other Essays.* University of North
          Carolina Press, Chapel Hill,

MANDELBAUM, MAURICE
  1938   *The Problem of Historical Knowledge.* New York.
MARETT, R. R.
  n.d.   The Beginnings of Morals and Culture: an introduction to social anthro-
         pology. In: *An Outline of Modern Knowledge,* W. Rose, ed. London.
  1934   The Growth and Tendency of Anthropological and Ethnological Studies.
         Compte-rendu, Vol. I, pp. 39-53. Congres International des Sciences Anthro-
         pologiques et Ethnologiques. London.
MARTIN, A. VON
  1932   *Sociology of the Renaissance.* Trans. by W. L. Leutkens, ed., 1944. London.
MARTIN, P. S.
  1938   Archaeological Work in the Ackmen-Lowry Area, Southwestern Colorado,
         1937. *Anthropological Series,* XXIII, No. 2. Field Museum of Natural
         History, Chicago.
  1939   Modified Basket Maker Sites, Ackmen-Lowry Area, Southwestern Colo-
         rado, 1938. *Ibid.,* No. 3.
MASON, O. T.
  1883   The Scope and Value of Anthropological Studies. *Proceedings,* Vol. XXXII,
         pp. 367-383. American Association for the Advancement of Science.
MCCULLOH, J. H., JR.
  1829   *Researches, Philosophical and Antiquarian, concerning the Aboriginal
         History of America.* Baltimore.
MCGREGOR, J. C.
  1941   *Southwestern Archaeology.* New York.
MCILWAIN, C. H.
  1937   The Historian's Part in a Changing World. *American Historical Review,*
         Vol. XLII, pp. 207-224.
MCKERN, W. C.
  1933   Local Types and the Regional Distribution of Pottery Bearing Cultures.
         Transactions, Vol. XXV, pp. 84-86. Illinois State Academy of Science.
  1937   Certain Culture Classification Problems in Middle Western Archaeology.
         The Indianapolis Archaeological Conference, pp. 70-82. National Research
         Council, Division of Anthropology and Psychology, Committee on State
         Archaeological Surveys. Washington.
  1938   Review of *Rediscovering Illinois,* by Cole and Deuel. *American Antiquity,*
         Vol. III, pp. 368-374.
  1939   The Midwestern Taxonomic Method as an Aid to Archaeological Culture
         Study. *American Antiquity,* Vol. IV, pp. 301-313.
  1940   Application of the Midwestern Taxonomic Method. *Bulletin,* Vol. III,
         pp. 18-21. Archaeological Society of Delaware.
  1942   Taxonomy and the Direct Historical Approach. *American Antiquity,* Vol.
         VIII, pp. 170-172.
  1943   Regarding Midwestern Archaeological Taxonomy. *American Anthropolo-
         gist,* n.s., Vol. XLV, pp. 313-315.
  1944   An Inaccurate Description of Midwestern Taxonomy. *American Antiquity,*
         Vol. IX, pp. 445-446.

MCKERN, W. C., T. DEUEL, and C. E. GUTHE

 1933 (No title) On Midwestern Taxonomic Method. National Research Council. (Mimeographed.)

MEAD, A. D.

 1939 The Species Complex in Biology and Education. *Science,* Vol. XC, pp. 241-246.

MEAD, MARGARET

 1928 *Coming of Age in Samoa.* (Included in: *From the South Seas,* 1939.) New York.

 1930 *Growing Up in New Guinea.* (Included in *Ibid.*)

MEADOWS, PAUL

 1944 The Scientific Use of Historical Data. *Philosophy of Science,* Vol. XI, pp. 53-58.

MENGHIN, O.

 1918 Die archäologische Kartographie am nördlichen Balkan. *Antropos,* Vol. XIII, pp. 1069-1081.

MERA, H. P.

 1935 Ceramic Clues to the Prehistory of North Central New Mexico. *Bulletin* No. 8, Laboratory of Anthropology, Technical Series.

MERTON, R. K.

 1936a Civilization and Culture. *Sociology and Social Research,* Vol. XXI, pp. 103-113.

 1936b Review of "Primitivism and Related Ideas in Antiquity," by A. O. Lovejoy and George Boas. *American Sociological Review,* Vol. I, pp. 156-157.

MICHAELIS, A.

 1908 *A Century of Archaeological Discoveries.* London.

MILLER, HUGH

 1939 *History and Science.* University of California Press, Berkeley.

MILLER, N. E., and J. DOLLARD

 1941 *Social Learning and Imitation.* Yale University Press, New Haven.

MITRA, P.

 1933 *A History of American Anthropology.* Calcutta University Press.

MONACHESI, E. D.

 1937 Sociology and Culture. In: *Man and Society,* E. P. Schmidt, ed., pp. 1-54. New York.

MONTESQUIEU, C. L. DE S.

 1748 *L'Esprit des Lois.* Paris.

MORGAN, L. H.

 1848 Report to the Regents of the University upon the Articles Furnished the Indian Collection. *3rd Annual Report,* 1850. Regents of the University. Albany.

 1851 *League of the Ho-De-No-Sau-Nee or Iroquois.* Rochester.

 1871 Systems of Consanguinity and Affinity of the Human Family. *Contributions to Knowledge,* No. 17. Smithsonian Institution, Washington.

MORLEY, S. G.

1943 Archaeological Investigations of the Carnegie Institution of Washington in the Maya Area of Middle America, during the Past Twenty-eight Years. *Proceedings*, Vol. LXXXVI, pp. 205-219. American Philosophical Society.

MORRIS, E. H.

1939 *Archaeological Studies in the La Plata District.* Publication No. 519, Carnegie Institution of Washington.

MORRIS, E. H., and R. F. BURGH

1941 *Anasazi Basketry. Ibid.,* No. 533.

MORRIS, E. H., J. CHARLOT, and A. A. MORRIS

1931 *The Temple of the Warriors. Ibid.,* No. 406.

MULLER, S.

1897 *Nordische Altertumskunde.* Strassburg.

MUNRO, ROBERT

1894 On the Relation between the Erect Posture and the Physical and Intellectual Development of Man. *Report,* pp. 885-895. British Association for the Advancement of Science.

MURDOCK, G. P.

1932 The Science of Culture. *American Anthropologist,* n.s., Vol. XXXIV, pp. 200-215.

1940 The Cross-cultural Survey. *American Sociological Review,* Vol. V, pp. 361-370.

1945 The Common Denominator of Cultures. In: *The Science of Man in the World Crisis,* R. Linton, ed., pp. 123-142. New York.

MURDOCK, G. P., *et al*

1945 Outline of Cultural Materials. *Yale Anthropological Studies,* Vol. II.

MYRES, J. L.

1916 The Influence of Anthropology on the Course of Political Science. *Publications in History,* Vol. IV, pp. 1-78. University of California.

1930 *Who Were the Greeks?* Berkeley.

NATIONAL RESEARCH COUNCIL

1940 A. V. Kidder. *International Directory of Anthropologists,* Section I, Western Hemisphere, p. 78. Washington.

NELSON, N. C.

1914 Pueblo Ruins of the Galisteo Basin, New Mexico. *Anthropological Papers,* Vol. XV, pp. 1-124. American Museum of Natural History.

1937 Prehistoric Archaeology, Past, Present, and Future. *Science,* n.s., Vol. LXXXV, pp. 81-89.

NESBITT, P. H.

1931 The Ancient Mimbreños. *Publications in Anthropology,* Bulletin No. 4. Logan Museum, Beloit, Wis.

NEVILLE, R. C.

1852 *Saxon Obsequies.* London.

NEVINS, ALLAN

1938 *The Gateway to History.* Boston.

NUSBAUM, J. L.
   1922   A Basket Maker Cave in Kane County, Utah. *Indian Notes and Mono-graphs.* Museum of the American Indian, Heye Foundation.

OGBURN, W. F.
   1937   Culture and Sociology. *Journal of Social Forces,* Vol. XVI, pp. 161-169.

OLMSTEAD, A. T.
   1927   Anthropology and History. In: *The Social Sciences,* W. F. Ogburn, ed., pp. 37-49. Boston and New York.

OPLER, M. E.
   1935   A Note on the Cultural Affiliations of Northern Mexican Nomads. *American Anthropologist,* n.s., Vol. XXXVII, pp. 702-706.

OSBORN, H. F.
   1929   *From the Greeks to Darwin,* 2nd ed. New York.

OSGOOD, CORNELIUS
   1942   The Ciboney Culture of Cayo Redondo, Cuba. *Publications in Anthro-pology,* No. 25. Yale University.
   1943   Excavations at Tocorón, Venezuela. *Ibid.,* No. 29.

OXFORD UNIVERSITY
   1935   *Handbook to the University of Oxford.* Oxford.

PARETO, V.
   1935   *Mind and Society.* New York.

PARKER, A. C.
   1922   The Archaeological History of New York. *Bulletins* 235 and 236. New York State Museum, Albany.

PARSONS, TALCOTT
   1937   *The Structure of Social Action.* New York.
   1938   The Role of Theory in Social Work. *American Sociological Review,* Vol. III, pp. 13-20.

PEET, S. D.
   1879   A Comparison between the Archaeology of Europe and America. *The American Antiquarian,* Vol. I, pp. 211-224.

PENNIMAN, T. K.
   1935   *A Hundred Years of Anthropology.* London.

PEPPER, G. H.
   1902   The Ancient Basket Makers of Southeastern Utah. *Journal,* Vol. II, No. 4, American Museum of Natural History.

PHILLIPS, PHILIP
   1942   Review of "An Archaeological Survey of Pickwick Basin in the Adjacent Portions of the States of Alabama, Mississippi and Tennessee," by W. S. Webb and D. L. DeJarnette. *American Antiquity,* Vol. VIII, pp. 197-201.

PIGGOTT, STUART
   1937   Prehistory and the Romantic Movement. *Antiquity,* Vol. XI, pp. 31-38.

PIGORINI, L.
   1874   *Materiaux pour l'historie de la paleoethnologie italienne.* Parma.

PILSBRY, H. A.
1939 *Land Mollusca of North America.* Philadelphia.

PIRENNE, HENRI
1923 De l'influence allemande sur le mouvement historique contemporaine. *Scientia,* Vol. XXXIV, pp. 174ff.
1931 What are Historians Trying to Do? In: *Methods in Social Science,* S. A. Rice, ed., pp. 435-445. University of Chicago Press.

PITT-RIVERS, A. H. LANE-FOX
1869 Examination of the Hill Forts of Sussex with an Account of Excavations at Cissbury and Highdown. *Archaeologia,* Vol. XLII, pp. 27-52.
1887-1898 *Excavations in Cranborne Chase, near Rushmore, on the Border of Dorset and Wilts.* London.

POLLOCK, H. E. D.
1936a The Casa Redonda at Chichen Itza, Yucatan. *Contributions to American Archaeology,* Vol. III, pp. 129-154. Carnegie Institution of Washington.
1936b *Round Structures of Aboriginal Middle America.* Publication No. 471, Carnegie Institution of Washington.

POWDERMAKER, H.
1939 *After Freedom: a cultural study of the Deep South.* New York.
1945 Review of "The Origin and Function of Culture," by G. Roheim. *American Anthropologist,* Vol. XLVII, pp. 308-312.

POWELL, J. W.
1875a The Ancient Province of Tusayan. *Scribner's Monthly,* Vol. XI, pp. 193-213.
1875b *Exploration of the Colorado River of the West and Its Tributaries.* Washington.
1877-1893 (ed.) Contributions to North American Ethnology. *Geographical and Geological Survey of the Rocky Mountain Region.* 7 vols. Washington.
1879 On Limitations to the Use of Some Anthropologic Data. *1st Annual Report,* pp. 73-86. Bureau of American Ethnology, Washington.

PRESTWICH, MRS.
1899 *Life and Letters of Joseph Prestwich.* London.

PRIEST, JOSIAH
1835 *American Antiquities and Discoveries in the West,* 5th ed. Albany.

PRINCETON UNIVERSITY
1941 *The University Catalogue.* Princeton.

PROTHERO, G. W.
1909 Historical Societies in Great Britain. *Annual Report,* pp. 237ff. American Historical Association.

PRUDDEN, T. M.
1897 An Elder Brother to the Cliff Dwellers. *Harper's Monthly Magazine,* Vol. XCV, June-November.

PUGIN, A. C. and E. J. WILLSON
1850 *Examples of Gothic Architecture.* London.

RAFINESQUE, C. S.
1824   Ancient Annals of Kentucky; or, Introduction to the History and Antiqui-
        ties of the State of Kentucky. In: *The History of Kentucky*, by H. Marshall,
        Vol. I. Frankfort.

RANDALL, J. H., JR.
1940   *The Making of the Modern Mind*. Oxford.

REDFIELD, ROBERT
1937a   Introduction to *Social Anthropology of North American Tribes*, Fred
        Eggan, ed., pp. vii-xii. University of Chicago Press.
1937b   The Second Epilogue to Maya History. *The Hispanic American Historical
        Review*, Vol. XVII, pp. 170-181.
1940   The Folk Society and Culture. *American Journal of Sociology*, Vol. XLV, pp.
        731-742.

REICHARD, GLADYS
1936   *Navaho Shepherd and Weaver*. New York.

REINACH, S. M.
1898   Esquisse d'une historie de l'archeologie gauloise. *Revue Celtique*, Vol. XIX,
        pp. 101-117, 292-307.

REITER, PAUL
1938   Review of "Handbook of Northern Arizona Pottery Wares," by H. S. Col-
        ton and L. L. Hargrave. *American Anthropologist*, n.s., Vol. XL, pp. 480-491.

RHODES, J. F.
1909   *Historical Essays*. New York.

RICKERT, H.
1896-1902   *Die Grenzen der Naturwissenschaftlichen Begriffsbildung*, 5th ed.,
            1929. Tübingen.
1898   *Kulturwissenschaft und Naturwissenschaft*, 4th and 5th eds., 1921.
        Tübingen.

RICKETSON, O. G., JR., and E. B. RICKETSON
1937   *Uaxactun, Guatemala*. Publication No. 477, Carnegie Institution of Wash-
        ington.

RINALDO, JOHN, and P. S. MARTIN
1941   Review of "Winona and Ridge Ruin, Part I," by J. C. McGregor. *Ameri-
        can Anthropologist*, n.s., Vol. XLIII, pp. 654-656.

RITCHIE, W. A.
1930   Early Huron-Neutral Sand Knoll Sites in Western New York. *Researches
        and Transactions*, Vol. VII, pp. 62-78. New York State Archaeological Asso-
        ciation, L. H. Morgan Chapter.
1932   The Lamoka Site. *Ibid.*, pp. 79-134.
1934   An Algonkin-Iroquois Site on Castle Creek, Broome County, New York.
        Research Records, Vol. II. Rochester Municipal Museum.
1936a   New Evidence Relating to the Archaic Occupation of New York. *Re-
        searches and Transactions*, Vol. VIII, pp. 1-23. New York State Archaeological
        Association, L. H. Morgan Chapter.

1936b   A Prehistoric Fortified Village Site at Canandaigua, Ontario County, New York. *Research Records*, Vol. III. Rochester Museum of Arts and Sciences.

1940a   New York State Prehistory Room. *Museum Service*, Vol. XIII, pp. 100-101. Rochester.

1940   Two Prehistoric Village Sites at Brewerton, New York. *Research Records*, Vol. V. Rochester Museum of Arts and Sciences.

1944   The Pre-Iroquoian Occupations of New York State. *Memoir* I, Rochester Museum of Arts and Sciences.

1945a   An Early Site in Cayuga County, New York. *Researches and Transactions*, Vol. X, New York State Archaeological Association, L. H. Morgan Chapter.

1945b   Review of *The Fort Ancient Aspect*, by J. B. Griffin. *American Antiquity*, Vol. X, pp. 398-401.

RIVERS, W. H. R.

1920   "History and Ethnology." *History*, July.

ROBERTS, F. H. H., JR.

1929a   Recent Archeological Developments in the Vicinity of El Paso, Texas. *Miscellaneous Collections*, Vol. LXXXI, No. 7. Smithsonian Institution.

1929b   Shabik'eshchee Village, a Late Basket Maker Site in the Chaco Canyon, New Mexico. *Bulletin* 92, Bureau of American Ethnology.

1930   Early Pueblo Ruins in the Piedra District, Southwestern Colorado. *Bulletin* 96, *Idem*.

1931   The Ruins at Kiatuthlana, Eastern Arizona. *Bulletin* 100, *Idem*.

1932   The Village of the Great Kivas on the Zuni Reservation, New Mexico. *Bulletin* 111, *Idem*.

1935   A Survey of Southwestern Archaeology. *Annual Report*, pp. 507-533. Smithsonian Institution.

1937   (No title). *The Indianapolis Archaeological Conference*, pp. 35-38. National Research Council, Division of Anthropology and Psychology, Committee on State Archaeological Surveys, Washington.

1939   Archeological Remains in the Whitewater District, Eastern Arizona, Part I. *Bulletin* 121, Bureau of American Ethnology.

1940   Archeological Remains in the Whitewater District, Eastern Arizona, Part II. *Ibid.*, *Bulletin* 126.

ROBERTS, H. B.

1931   Problems in the Study of Maya Ceramics. *Year Book*, No. 30, pp. 114-116. Carnegie Institution of Washington.

ROBINSON, J. H.

1911   The New History. *Proceedings*, Vol. L, pp. 179-190. American Philosophical Society.

1912   *The New History*. New York.

1930   The Newer Ways of Historians. *American Historical Review*, Vol. XXXV, pp. 245-255.

RÓHEIM, GÉZA

1943   The Origin and Function of Culture. *Nervous and Mental Disease Monographs*, No. 69. New York.

ROTH, W. E.

    1924   An Introductory Study of the Arts, Crafts, and Customs of the Guiana Indians. *38th Annual Report*, 1916-1917. Bureau of American Ethnology.

ROUSE, B. I.

    1939   Prehistory in Haiti, a Study in Method. *Publications in Anthropology*, No. 21. Yale University.

    1944   On the Typological Method. *American Antiquity*, Vol. X, pp. 202-204.

ROUSSEAU, J. J.

    1750   *Discours sur les sciences et les arts*. Dijon.

    1762   *Le contrat social*. Amsterdam.

ROYAL ANTHROPOLOGICAL INSTITUTE OF GREAT BRITAIN AND IRELAND

    1929   *Notes and Queries on Anthropology*, 5th ed. London.

ROYS, L.

    1934   The Engineering Knowledge of the Maya. *Contributions to American Archaeology*, Vol. II, pp. 29-105. Carnegie Institution of Washington.

RUPPERT, K.

    1943   The Mercado, Chichen Itza, Yucatan. *Contributions to American Anthropology and History*, Vol. VIII, pp. 223-260. Carnegie Institution of Washington.

SABINE, G. H.

    1906   Hume's Contribution to the Historical Method. *Philosophical Review*, Vol. XV, pp. 17-38.

SALVEMINI, GAETANO

    1939   *Historian and Scientist*. Cambridge.

SAPIR, EDWARD

    1924   Culture, Genuine and Spurious. *American Journal of Sociology*, Vol. XXIX, pp. 401-417.

    1927   The Unconscious Patterning of Behavior in Society. In: *The Unconscious: a symposium*, E. S. Dummer, ed., pp. 114-142. New York.

    1938   Why Cultural Anthropology Needs the Psychiatrist. *Psychiatry*, Vol. I, pp. 7-12.

SCHENCK, W. E.

    1926   The Emeryville Shellmound. *Publications in American Archaeology and Ethnology*, Vol. XXIII, pp. 147-282. University of California.

SCHENCK, W. E., and E. J. DAWSON

    1929   Archaeology of the Northern San Joaquin Valley. *Ibid.*, Vol. XXV, pp. 289-413.

SCHILLER, F. C. S.

    1934   *Must Philosophers Disagree?* London.

SCHLESINGER, A. M.

    1925   *New Viewpoints in American History*. New York.

    1937   What Social History Is. *Harvard Educational Review*, Vol. VII, pp. 57-65.

SCHLIEMANN, H.

    1878   *Mycenae: a narrative of researches and discoveries in Mycenae and Tiryns*. New York.

1880 *Ilios: the city and country of the Trojans.* London.

1885 *Tiryns: the prehistoric palace of the kings of Tiryns.* New York.

SCHMIDT, WILLIAM

1939 *The Culture Historical Method of Ethnology.* Trans. by S. A. Sieber. New York.

SCHOOLCRAFT, H. R.

1853-1856 *Information Respecting the History, Condition and Prospects of the Indian Tribes of the United States.* Philadelphia.

SCHORR, P.

1935 The Genesis of Prehistoric Research. *Isis,* Vol. XXIII, pp. 425-443. Bruges.

SCHOULER, JAMES

1896 *Historical Briefs.* New York.

SETZLER, F. M.

1935 A Prehistoric Cave Culture in Southwestern Texas. *American Anthropologist,* n.s., Vol. XXXVII, pp. 104-110.

1942 Archeological Accomplishments during the Past Decade in the United States. *Journal,* Vol. XXXII, pp. 253-259. Washington Academy of Sciences.

SETZLER, F. M., and J. D. JENNINGS

1941 Peachtree Mound and Village Site, Cherokee County, North Carolina. *Bulletin* 131, Bureau of American Ethnology.

SHEPARD, A. O.

1936 The Technology of Pecos Pottery. In: "The Pottery of Pecos, Vol. II," by A. V. Kidder and A. O. Shepard. *Papers,* No. 7, pp. 389-587. Southwestern Expedition.

1939 Technology of La Plata Pottery. In: *Archaeological Studies in the La Plata District,* by E. H. Morris. Publication No. 519, Carnegie Institution of Washington.

1942 Rio Grande Glaze Paint Ware. *Contributions to American Anthropology and History,* Vol. VII, pp. 129-262. Carnegie Institution of Washington.

SHOTWELL, J. T.

1922 *An Introduction to the History of History.* New York.

1929 History. In: *Encyclopaedia Britannica,* 14th ed., Vol. XI, pp. 594-598.

ŠIMEK, EMANUEL

1914 Grundzüge der Vorgeschichte Böhmens. *Wiener Prähistorische Zeitschrift,* Vol. I, pp. 22-38, 88-136.

SIMKOVITCH, V. G.

1929-1936 Approaches to History. *Political Science Quarterly,* Vol. XLIV, pp. 481ff.; Vol. XLV, pp. 481ff.; Vol. XLVII, pp. 410ff.; Vol. XLVIII, pp. 23ff.; Vol. XLIX, pp. 44ff.; Vol. LI, pp. 117ff.

SIMPSON, G. G., and A. ROE

1939 *Quantitative Zoology.* New York.

SIMPSON, J. H.

1852 *Journal of a Military Reconnaissance, from Santa Fe, New Mexico, to the Navaho Country.* Philadelphia.

SMITH, A. L.

    1932   Two Recent Ceramic Finds at Uaxactun. *Contributions to American Archaeology*, Vol. II, pp. 3-25. Carnegie Institution of Washington.

    1937   Structure A-XVIII, Uaxactun. *Ibid.*, Vol. IV, pp. 1-27.

SMITH, A. L., and A. V. KIDDER

    1943   Explorations in the Motagua Valley, Guatemala. *Contributions to American Anthropology and History*, Vol. VIII, pp. 101-182. Carnegie Institution of Washington.

SMITH, H. I.

    1899   The Ethnological Arrangement of Archaeological Material. *Report for 1898,* Sheffield Meeting. Museum Association of the United Kingdom.

SMITH, R. E.

    1937   A Study of Structure A-I Complex at Uaxactun, Peten, Guatemala. *Contributions to American Archaeology*, Vol. III, pp. 189-231. Carnegie Institution of Washington.

SMITH, V. J.

    1931   Archeological Notes of the Big Bend Region. *Bulletin* 3, pp. 60-69. Texas Archeological and Paleontological Society.

    1932   The Relation of the Southwestern Basket Maker to the Dry Shelter Culture of the Big Bend. *Ibid.*, 4, pp. 55-62.

    1933   Sandals of the Big Bend Culture with Additional Notes Concerning Basket Maker Evidence. *Ibid.*, 5, pp. 57-65.

SMITH, WILLIAM

    1815   *A Geological Map of England and Wales, with Part of Scotland.* London.

SOROKIN, PETRIM

    1937   *Social and Cultural Dynamics.* New York.

    1943   *Sociocultural Causality, Space, Time.* Duke University Press, Durham.

SPECK, F. G.

    1935   Speaking of the Delawares. *The Pennsylvania Archaeologist*, Vol. IV, No. 4. Milton.

SPIER, LESLIE

    1917   An Outline for a Chronology of Zuni Ruins. *Anthropological Papers*, Vol. XVIII, pp. 207-332. American Museum of Natural History.

    1918   Notes on Some Little Colorado Ruins. *Ibid.*, pp. 333-362.

    1919   Ruins in the White Mountains. *Ibid.*, pp. 363-387.

    1921   The Sun Dance of the Plains Indians. *Ibid.*, Vol. XVI, pp. 459-527.

    1929   Problems Arising from the Cultural Position of the Havasupai. *American Anthropologist*, n.s., Vol. XXXI, pp. 213-222.

SQUIER, E. G.

    1849   Aboriginal Monuments of the State of New York. *Contributions to Knowledge*, Vol. II. Smithsonian Institution.

SQUIER, E. G., and E. H. DAVIS

    1848   Ancient Monuments of the Mississippi Valley. *Ibid.*, Vol. I.

STAFFORD, C. E.
1941 *Paracas Embroideries, a Study of Repeated Patterns.* New York.
STEEFEL, L. D.
1937 History. In: *Man and Society*, E. P. Schmidt, ed., pp. 305-322. New York.
STEMMERMANN, P. H.
1934 *Die Anfänge der 'Deutschen Vorgeschichtsforschung.* Leipzig.
STERN, B. J.
1929 Concerning the Distinction between the Social and the Cultural. *Journal of Social Forces*, Vol. VIII, pp. 264-273.
STEWARD, J. H.
1941 Review of "Prehistoric Culture Units and Their Relationships in Northern Arizona," by H. S. Colton. *American Antiquity*, Vol. VI, pp. 366-367.
1942 The Direct Historical Approach to Archaeology. *Ibid.*, Vol. VII, pp. 337-344.
1944 *Re* Archaeological Tools and Jobs. *Ibid.*, Vol. X, pp. 99-100.
STEWARD, J. H., and F. M. SETZLER
1938 Function and Configuration in Archaeology. *Ibid.*, Vol. IV, pp. 4-10.
STOCKÝ, A.
1924 Le développement de la science préhistorique tchèque. *Anthropologie*, Vol. II, Supplement, pp. 45-56. Praha.
STRONG, W. D.
1935 An Introduction to Nebraska Archeology. *Miscellaneous Collections*, Vol. XCIII, No. 10. Smithsonian Institution.
1936 Anthropological, Theory and Archaeological Fact. In: *Essays in Anthropology presented to A. L. Kroeber.* University of California Press, Berkeley.
STRONG, W. D., W. E. SCHENCK, and J. H. STEWARD
1930 Archaeology of the Dalles-Deschutes Region. *Publications in American Archaeology and Ethnology*, Vol. XXIX, pp. 1-154. University of California.
STUBBS, WILLIAM
1886 *Seventeen Lectures on the Study of Medieval and Modern History and Kindred Subjects.* Oxford.
SUMMERS, MONTAGUE
1941 *A Gothic Bibliography.* London.
SUTHERLAND, R. L., and J. L. WOODWARD
1940 *Introductory Sociology*, 2nd ed. Chicago.
SYMONDS, J. A.
1908 *Renaissance Italy.* New York.
TALLGREN, A. M.
1922 Zur Archäologie Eestis I. *Acta et Commentationes*, Vol. III, No. 6; Vol. VIII, No. 1. University of Dorpat.
1937 The Method of Prehistoric Archaeology. *Antiquity*, Vol. XI, pp. 152-161.
TANNER, THOMAS
1744 *Notitia Monastica, or an account of all the abbies, priories and houses of friars, heretofore in England and Wales; and also of all the colleges and hospitals founded before A.D. 1540.* London.

TAYLOR, W. W.

    1943   Review of "A Reconstruction of Uto-Aztekan History" and "Report on the Archaeology of Southern Chihuahua," by R. R. Zingg. *American Antiquity,* Vol. VIII, pp. 307-310.

TEGGART, F. J.

    1916   Prolegomena to History; the Relation of History to Literature, Philosophy, and Science. *Publications in History,* Vol. IV, No. 3. University of California.

    1918   *The Processes of History.* Yale University Press, New Haven.

    1919   Anthropology and History. *Journal of Philosophy, Psychology, and Scientific Method,* Vol. XVI, pp. 691-696.

    1925   *The Theory of History.* Yale University Press, New Haven.

THOMAS, W. I., and F. ZNANIECKI

    1918-1920   *The Polish Peasant in Europe and America.* 5 vols. University of Chicago Press.

THOMPSON, A. H.

    1935   *Bede, His Life, Times, and Writings.* Oxford.

THOMPSON, J. E.

    1927   The Civilization of the Mayas. *Anthropological Leaflets,* No. 25. Field Museum of Natural History, Chicago.

    1934a   Maya Chronology: the Fifteen Tun Glyph. *Contributions to American Archaeology,* Vol. II, pp. 243-254. Carnegie Institution of Washington.

    1934b   The Sky Bearers, Colors, and Directions in Maya and Mexican Religion. *Ibid.,* pp. 209-242.

    1939a   *Excavations at San José, British Honduras.* Publication No. 506, Carnegie Institution of Washington.

    1939b   The Moon Goddess in Middle America: with Notes on Related Deities. *Contributions to American Anthropology and History,* Vol. V, pp. 127-173. Carnegie Institution of Washington.

    1942a   Late Ceramic Horizons at Benque Viejo, British Honduras. *Ibid.,* Vol. VII, pp. 1-36.

    1942b   Maya Arithmetic. *Ibid.,* pp. 37-62.

    1942c   Representations of Tezcatlipoca at Chichen Itza. *Notes on Middle American Archaeology and Ethnology,* Vol. I, pp. 48-50. Carnegie Institution of Washington.

    1943   Representation of Tlalchitonatiuh at Chichen Itza, Yucatan, and at Baúl, Escuintla. *Ibid.,* pp. 117-121.

    1944   The Fish as a Maya Symbol for Counting and Further Discussion of Directional Glyphs. *Theoretical Approaches to Problems,* No. 2. Carnegie Institution of Washington.

    1946   Some Uses of Tobacco among the Maya. *Notes on Middle American Archaeology and Ethnology,* Vol. III, No. 61. Carnegie Institution of Washington.

TOYNBEE, A. J.

    1934-1939   *A Study of History.* 6 vols. London.

TRIK, A. S.
    1939 Temple XXII at Copan. *Contributions to American Anthropology and History,* Vol. V, pp. 87-106. Carnegie Institution of Washington.

TSCHOPIK, HARRY
    1937 *Textiles Motifs from Uloa Valley Pottery,* Ms. Peabody Museum of Harvard.

UEBERWEG, FRIEDRICH
    1872-1874 *History of Philosophy.* Trans. by G. S. Morris. New York.

UNDSET, INGWALD
    1887 Le préhistorique Scandinave, ses origines et son developpement. *Revue d'Anthropologie,* 3ᵉ serie, Vol. II, pp. 313-332.

UNIVERSITÉ DE PARIS
    1939 *Livret de l'Etudiant, 1939-1940.*

UNIVERSITY OF CALIFORNIA
    1940 *General Catalogue.* Berkeley.

UNIVERSITY OF CHICAGO
    1940 *The College and the Divisions.*

UNIVERSITY OF EDINBURGH
    1939 *Edinburgh University Catalogue, 1939-1940.*

UNIVERSITY OF LIVERPOOL
    1938 *Calendar, 1938-1939.*

UNIVERSITY OF LONDON
    1939 *The Calendar.*

UNIVERSITY OF PENNSYLVANIA
    1940 *The College: Announcement.* Philadelphia.

UNIVERSITY OF WISCONSIN
    1940 General Announcement, 1940-1941. *Bulletin,* Madison.

VAIHINGER, HANS
    1925 *The Philosophy of "As-If."* Trans. by C. K. Ogden. New York.

VAILLANT, G. C.
    1930 Excavations at Zacatenco. *Anthropological Papers,* Vol. XXXII, No. 1. American Museum of Natural History.
    1941 *Aztecs of Mexico; Origin, Rise and Fall of the Aztec Nation.* Garden City.

VAN LOON, W. H.
    1937 *The Arts.* New York.

WALLIS, W. D.
    1917 The Influence of Anthropology upon History. *Scientific Monthly,* Vol. V, pp. 433-438.
    1937 Social Anthropology. In: *Man and Society,* E. P. Schmidt, ed., pp. 92-143. New York.

WARDEN, C. J.
    1936 *The Emergence of Human Culture.* New York.

WARE, C. F. (ed.)
    1940 *The Cultural Approach to History.* Columbia University Press, New York.

WARING, A. J., and P. HOLDER
    1945   A Prehistoric Ceremonial Complex in the Southeastern United States.
    American Anthropologist, n.s., Vol. XLVII, pp. 1-34.
WARNER, W. L., and P. S. LUNT
    1941   *The Social Life of a Modern Community.* Yale University Press, New Haven.
WAUCHOPE, ROBERT
    1934   House Mounds of Uaxactun, Guatemala. *Contributions to American Archae-
    ology,* Vol. II, pp. 107-171. Carnegie Institution of Washington.
    1938   *Modern Maya Houses.* Publication No. 502, Carnegie Institution of Wash-
    ington.
WEBB, W. S.
    1938   An Archaeological Survey of the Norris Basin in Eastern Tennessee. *Bulletin*
    118, Bureau of American Ethnology.
    1939   An Archaeological Survey of Wheeler Basin on the Tennessee River in
    Northern Alabama. *Bulletin* 122, *Idem.*
    1941   The Morgan Stone Mound, Site 15, Bath County, Kentucky. *Reports in
    Anthropology and Archaeology,* Vol. V, No. 3. University of Kentucky.
    1942   The C. and O. Mounds at Paintsville, Sites Jo2 and Jo9, Johnson County,
    Kentucky. *Ibid.,* No. 4.
    1943a   The Crigler Mounds, Sites Be 20 and Be 27, and The Hartman Mound,
    Site Be 32, Boone County, Kentucky. *Ibid.,* No. 6.
    1943b   The Riley Mound, Site Be 15, and the Landing Mound, Site Be 17, Boone
    County, Kentucky, with additional notes on the Mt. Horeb Site, Fa 1, and
    Sites Fa 14 and Fa 15, Fayette County. *Ibid.,* No. 7.
WEBB, W. S., and D. L. DE JARNETTE
    1942   An Archeological Survey of Pickwick Basin in the Adjacent Portions of
    the States of Alabama, Mississippi, and Tennessee. *Bulletin* 129, Bureau of
    American Ethnology.
WEBB, W. S., and J. B. ELLIOTT
    1942   The Robbins Mounds Sites Be 3 and Be 14, Boone County, Kentucky.
    Reports in Anthropology and Archaeology, Vol. V, No. 5. University of Ken-
    tucky.
WEBB, W. S., and W. D. FUNKHOUSER
    1928   *Ancient Life in Kentucky.* Kentucky Geological Survey, Frankfort.
    1929a   The So-Called "Hominy-holes" of Kentucky. *American Anthropologist,*
    n.s., Vol. XXXI, pp. 701-709.
    1929b   The Williams Site in Christian County, Kentucky. *Reports in Archaeology
    and Anthropology,* Vol. I, No. 1. University of Kentucky.
    1931   The Tolu Site in Crittenden County, Kentucky. *Ibid.,* No. 5.
    1940   Ricketts Site Revisited, Site 3, Montgomery County, Kentucky. *Reports
    in Anthropology and Archaeology,* Vol. III, No. 6.
WEBB, W. S., and W. G. HAAG
    1939   The Chiggerville Site, Site 1, Ohio County, Kentucky. *Reports in Anthro-
    pology,* Vo. IV, No. 1.
    1940   Cypress Creek Villages, Sites 11 and 12, McLean County, Kentucky. *Ibid.,*
    No. 2.

WEBB, W. S., and C. E. SNOW

    1945   The Adena People. *Reports in Anthropology and Archaeology*, Vol. VI.

WEBSTER'S NEW INTERNATIONAL DICTIONARY

    2nd ed., 1937   Springfield, Mass.

WEDEL, W. R.

    1941a   Archeological Investigations at Buena Vista Lake, Kern County, California. *Bulletin* 130, Bureau of American Ethnology.

    1941b   Environment and Native Subsistence Economies in the Central Great Plains. *Miscellaneous Collections*, Vol. 101, No. 3. Smithsonian Institution.

    1943   Archeological Investigations in Platte and Clay Counties, Missouri. *Bulletin* 183, United States National Museum.

WEST, J.

    1945   *Plainville, U.S.A.* Columbia University Press, New York.

WHEELER, G. M.

    1875-1889   *Report upon United States Geographical Surveys West of the One Hundredth Meridian, in Charge of First Lieutenant Geo. M. Wheeler . . . under the Direction of the Chief of Engineers, U.S. Army.* 7 Vols. Washington.

WHIPPLE, A. W.

    1856   Report of Explorations for a Railway Route, near the Thirty-fifth Parallel of North Latitude from the Mississippi River to the Pacific Ocean . . . 1853-1854. Vol. III of the Pacific Survey Reports, *Senate Executive Documents*, No. 78, 33rd Congress, 2nd Session. Washington.

WHITE, A. D.

    1896   *A History of the Warfare of Science with Theology in Christendom.* London.

WHITE, LESLIE

    1940   The Symbol: the Origin and Basis of Human Behavior. *Philosophy of Science*, Vol. VII, pp. 451-463.

    1943   Energy and the Evolution of Culture. *American Anthropologist*, n.s., Vol. XLV, pp. 335-356.

    1945a   "Diffusion vs Evolution": an Anti-evolutionist Fallacy. *Ibid.*, Vol. XLVII, pp. 339-356.

    1945b   History, Evolutionism, and Functionalism: Three Types of Interpretation of Culture. *Southwestern Journal of Anthropology*, Vol. I, pp. 221-248.

WHITEHEAD, A. N.

    1927   *Science and the Modern World.* New York.

WHO'S WHO IN AMERICA

    1944-1945   A. V. Kidder. Vol. XXIII, p. 1149. Chicago.

WILSON, DANIEL

    1863   *Prehistoric Annals of Scotland.* 2nd ed. London.

WILSON, THOMAS

    1899   The Beginnings of the Science of Prehistoric Anthropology. *Proceedings*, pp. 309-353. American Association for the Advancement of Science.

WINCKLEMANN, J. J.
  1763-1768   Geschichte der Kunst des Altertums. In: *Sämtliche Werke,* Vols. III-
      VI. Donauöschingen, 1825.

WISSLER, CLARK
  1913   The North American Indians of the Plains. *The Popular Science Monthly,*
      Vol. LXXXII, pp. 436-444.
  1915   Riding Gear of the North American Indians. *Anthropological Papers,* Vol.
      XVII, pp. 1-38. American Museum of Natural History.
  1916   Psychological and Historical Interpretations for Culture. *Science,* n.s., Vol.
      XLIII, pp. 193-201.
  1923   *Man and Culture.* New York.
  1938   *The American Indian.* 3rd ed. New York.
  1942   The American Indian and the American Philosophical Society. *Proceedings,*
      Vol. LXXXVI, pp. 189-204. American Philosophical Society.

WOODWARD, J. W.
  1936   A New Classification of Culture. *American Sociological Review,* Vol. I,
      pp. 89-102.

WRIGHT, THOMAS
  1885   *The Celt, the Roman, and the Saxon.* 4th ed. London.

WYLIE, WILLIAM
  1852   *Fairford Graves.* Oxford.

WYMAN, L. C., and C. KLUCKHOHN
  1938   Navaho Classification of Their Song Ceremonials. *Memoirs,* No. 50, Ameri-
      can Anthropological Association.

YALE UNIVERSITY
  1939   General Catalogue Number. *Bulletin.* New Haven.

ZILSEL, E.
  1941   Physics and the Problem of Historico-sociological Laws. *Philosophy of
      Science,* Vol. VIII, pp. 567-579.

ZIMMERMAN, C. C.
  1938 · *The Changing Community.* New York.

ZINGG, R. R.
  1939   A Reconstruction of Uto-Aztekan History. *Contributions to Ethnography,*
      Vol. II. University of Denver.
  1940   Report on Archaeology of Southern Chihuahua. *Contribution I,* University
      of Denver, Center of Latin American Studies.

ZNANIECKI, F.
  1934   *The Method of Sociology.* New York.

INDEX

Adams, J.: commended by J. W. Bennett, 89
Affinities, 93, 111–12, 115, 116, 120
Agassiz, Louis, 16
Age of Enlightenment, 12
American Anthropologist, 24
Americanist archeologists, 44, 45, 92, 93
—archeology: scope of analysis, 4, 23; condition, 4, 43–92; theoretical framework, 6, 9; genesis, 19; antiquarian research, 20–21; early Americanists, 20–21; development, 21; research under anthropology, 21; subject matter, 23; disagreement in aims, 23–25; sub-discipline cultural anthropology, 23–24, 91–92; objectives historical, 24; questions about, 24–25; weaknesses in structure, 25; critical examination proposed, 43; criterion for judging, 43; reports criticized, 43; selected works analyzed and criticized, 45–88; major role of ceramic studies, 52; selected works commended, 88–91; time-space limits, 90; dichotomy within conceptual structure, 91; unhealthy state, 92; typological classifications, 122–40; groups, 143; need for method of reference for specific finds, 194–95; subsidized technical research needed, 199. *See also* Archeology
Andrews, E. W.: Maya work, 52
Anthropologist(s), 4, 21, 25, 26, 28, 35–42 *passim,* 93, 107, 141
Anthropology, 4, 21, 24, 26, 27, 28, 30–45 *passim,* 59, 66, 69, 73, 92, 93, 96, 122, 141, 143, 191, 200
Antiquarianism, 9–15, 17, 21–22, 200
Antiquarianist, 33
Archeological apprenticeship, 196–98
—classification, 85, 113, 141. *See also* Archeological typology; Classification; Cultural classification; Typological classification; Typology

—cultural context, 112–13, 169
—data, 94, 111–13, 115, 131, 138, 152, 153, 157, 165, 171, 179, 183, 189, 191, 200
—ethnography, 168
—ethnology, 166
—materials, 5, 41, 95, 103, 110, 111, 128, 129, 139, 141, 142, 143, 154–61 *passim,* 188, 190, 193–94
—method, 148–49, 155
—problems, 5, 152, 153, 154. *See also* Problem
—report: procedures using conjunctive approach outlined, 150–96; summarized, 200
—research: theoretical should relate to actual, 3; conceptual scheme for, prompted study, 3; practical procedures for, 4, 5, 150–200; chronological development of, 9–22; considered historiography, 41; chronology's role, 60–61; interpretation and inference needed, 68–69, 71, 72, 112, 113, 120, 122, 123, 145, 155–56, 191; Comparative approach for, criticized, 93; dependence on specialists, 198–99
—stratigraphy, 14, 180
—studies, 83, 84, 115, 121–22, 123, 137, 138
—taxonomists, 129–30, 132, 140
—taxonomy, 145, 148
—techniques, 155, 196–97
—theory, 143
—typology, 85, 113–22
Archeologist(s): must focus on objectives, 5–6; theoretical framework, 6; separation within ranks, 22; as technician, 41, 153, 196–97; gathering of cultural materials of utmost importance, 42; criteria for selecting Americanists, 43; primary data breakdown, 96; limited to material results of behavior, 111; interested in cultural context, 120; empirical categories important, 120–21; "objectivity" and

255